Music

of the

Baroque

Music
of the
Baroque

DAVID SCHULENBERG

New York • Oxford
OXFORD UNIVERSITY PRESS
2001

Oxford University Press

Oxford   New York
Athens   Auckland   Bangkok   Bogotá   Buenos Aires   Calcutta
Cape Town   Chennai   Dar es Salaam   Delhi   Florence   Hong Kong   Istanbul
Karachi   Kuala Lumpur   Madrid   Melbourne   Mexico City   Mumbai
Nairobi   Paris   São Paulo   Shanghai   Singapore   Taipei   Tokyo   Toronto   Warsaw

and associated companies in
Berlin   Ibadan

Copyright © 2001 by Oxford University Press, Inc.

Published by Oxford University Press, Inc.
198 Madison Avenue, New York, New York 10016
http://www.oup-usa.org

Oxford is a registered trademark of Oxford University Press

Library of Congress Cataloging-in-Publication Data

Schulenberg, David
    Music of the Baroque / David Schulenberg.
        p. cm.
    Includes bibliographical references and index.
    ISBN 0-19-512232-1 (alk. paper)
    1. Music—17th century—History and criticism. 2. Music—18th century—History and
criticism. I. Title.
ML193 .S38 2001
780'.9'032—dc21   00-036679

Printing (last digit): 9 8 7 6 5 4 3 2

Printed in the United States of America
on acid-free paper

To Mary

CONTENTS

Preface

This is a study of European music history from the seventeenth through the mid-eighteenth centuries, the period that music historians call the Baroque. It is intended primarily as a textbook for historical surveys typically offered to upper-division music majors, and for graduate courses in music history and literature. It is accompanied by an anthology of musical scores, most of which are discussed in depth within the present text; items in the anthology (*Music of the Baroque: An Anthology of Scores*) are referred to by number ("anthology, Selection 1").

The Baroque is the period of such composers as Monteverdi, Schütz, Lully, Handel, and Bach. This was a time that saw the invention of opera and oratorio and the emergence of such instrumental genres as the sonata, suite, and concerto, which composers continue to write to the present day. During this period, the typical performing ensemble shifted from the vocal and instrumental consorts of the late Renaissance to ensembles corresponding in many ways to those of the present-day concert, choral, and operatic traditions. Instruments such as the piano, violin, oboe, and transverse flute emerged or began to acquire their modern forms, and performing techniques and practices drew significantly closer to those of today, although still remaining distinctly different. Throughout the period, public concerts in the modern sense were rare; more typical occasions for performance were church services and private concerts in the homes of the wealthy. In the course of the Baroque, however, public performances of opera and oratorio became increasingly common, and the beginnings of the modern concert tradition appeared in certain cities. By the end of the Baroque, moreover, a middle class growing in numbers and economic power was becoming an important patron of music, both as audience members and as amateur performers of an expanding repertory of printed music.

Any survey such as the present one must face the difficult question of how to approach the complex historical problems and the enormous musical repertory of the period. Since the mid-twentieth century, musicians, musicologists, and listeners have applied considerable scrutiny to Baroque music from a variety of viewpoints, and a textbook must balance current perspectives with older ones, recognizing that tried and true approaches from the past may not always be relevant to today's students—nor will every current musicological fashion or discovery retain its excitement tomorrow. There is no agreement as to how Baroque music should be taught—whether in a course devoted to the topic or

in one covering a larger period, whether through a small number of closely studied works or a more wide-ranging survey of the repertory. Different instructors
will naturally have their favorite composers, works, and special topics within
the general category of "Baroque," and the needs and degree of preparation of
one group of students will differ from those of another. The very term *Baroque*
is open to question; many music historians have misgivings about attaching a
simple label to a wide swatch of music history.

The idea of Baroque music is nevertheless convenient for understanding a
period that encompasses a number of unifying features and continuous traditions. This book focuses on several of those traditions: the unbroken stream of
dramatic and quasi-dramatic vocal music represented by opera and cantata, the
equally powerful strand of sacred vocal music that includes the cantatas and oratorios of Bach and Handel, and the distinctive traditions of music for instrumental ensemble and for solo keyboard. In order to treat each of these traditions in a coherent manner, the book focuses on one at a time. This has the
advantage of demonstrating the continuity of various musical traditions, and it
encourages students to understand the development of a concept such as musical rhetoric from the earliest examples of monody through such late Baroque
masterpieces as the Bach cantatas. Of course, this approach has the disadvantage of not being strictly chronological, and the music of certain composers (notably Bach and Handel) must be treated in several different chapters of the book.
But no survey of the period can entirely avoid such difficulties, and the present
work uses cross-references between chapters to minimize the possibility of confusion.

This book originated as a course packet for undergraduate music history
courses and has been written with today's students in mind. Increasingly, graduate students as well as undergraduates enter music programs possessing a relatively limited knowledge of the European "classical" repertory, particularly that
dating from the period covered by this book. Such students often come with
backgrounds in jazz and popular music or other types of valuable musical experience. Thus they are not necessarily any less prepared than others for the
study of European music history, and they will potentially derive no less benefit from it. But it is no longer possible in a book of this sort to presume previous knowledge of European history or music. The reader of this book is assumed to have had some experience with score reading and the rudiments of
tonal analysis, such as the identification of keys and chord functions. But the
book requires no special knowledge beyond this, and virtually all musical terms
are defined on first use. A possible disadvantage, that this reduces the sophistication of many introductory discussions, is compensated for by the heightened
focus on the analysis of individual works in the latter parts of most chapters.

By the same token, the expectation of scholars for thorough documentation
and discussion of the music's broader cultural context—including controversial
historical and critical issues—has had to be balanced against the requirement
to convey essential information about the music itself to students who are not
(at least, not yet) musicologists, while keeping the book within manageable proportions. Modern critical musicology has emphasized the inseparability of music history from the general history of human culture. This textbook recognizes

the importance of situating music within its broader cultural context while retaining its focus on music, experienced and enjoyed in our own time and our own ways. Thus another distinguishing feature of this book is its balanced presentation of more strictly historical material—composers' biographies, the social and economic context of music, changes in musical forms, styles, and modes of performance—alongside the examination of individual musical compositions. Many students at some point in their theoretical or practical training devote intense study to a few Baroque compositions, but these are often limited to a few inventions, fugues, or four-part chorale settings of J. S. Bach. This book offers in-depth analysis of at least one example of each of the major genres studied, giving the reader the opportunity to understand some of the distinctive features of the individual works and composers covered.

The decision to focus attention on individual compositions has made it necessary to be selective in choosing the repertories that are covered in depth. Virtually all of the works selected for close study belong to what can be called the central European tradition, which during this period is essentially that of Italy, followed by France and with a substantial German strand woven in during the latter half. Some English music is considered, but, regrettably, many other works and musical traditions could be mentioned only in passing. It is worth reiterating that this volume is not intended to be a comprehensive history of Baroque music—something that, if it could be written today, would have limited practicality as an introduction to the subject. Rather, this volume acquaints the reader with several central traditions while providing a background and suggesting models for the study of other repertories. The selection of works or repertories for inclusion here is not intended as a value judgment. On the other hand, the approach taken here allows the reader to appreciate the distinctive musical personalities of certain composers whose works have, for various reasons, been highly valued and exerted widespread influence over the last few centuries. The book does not merely focus on "canonical" works and composers, however. It also covers in depth some relatively unfamiliar figures, such as Barbara Strozzi, Marc-Antoine Charpentier, Elizabeth-Claude Jacquet de La Guerre, and C. P. E. Bach.

The mention of this last name raises a difficult issue: Where does one draw the boundaries of the Baroque? At issue is not some theoretical definition of the style or period but a practical matter of pedagogy. The present book opens with a prologue that introduces some of the most important composers and genres of the late Renaissance. Understanding this material will help many students in grasping the transition to the Baroque. In courses that begin with the Baroque, this section will serve as a helpful review of earlier material. Other courses will find it useful in reinforcing students' grasp of terms and other material that continue to be important in the study of later music. The book ends with an epilogue that covers repertory that is generally viewed as transitional between the Baroque and the Classical: opera seria and instrumental music of the *galant* style, which are sometimes lost in the cracks between the two more thoroughly investigated periods.

One additional feature of this book worth noting is its attention to historical performance practice. Although the concept of historical authenticity in performance has become for some a controversial issue, it is no longer possible to survey the music of the past without considering how it was originally performed and how it is being performed today. Thus the book raises issues of performance practice for most works, and the repertory selected for detailed discussion includes music that is available in recent, reasonably stylish recorded performances. The accompanying anthology includes a selection of about forty works, some in new editions, others in reprints; each score is accompanied by a commentary that explains important points of the notation and its interpretation.

I have been fortunate in having had the opportunity to teach this material numerous times at various institutions. I am grateful to the students whom I have had the privilege of teaching, many of whom provided me with valuable feedback about early versions of this text and the accompanying anthology. John Walter Hill, Christopher Hogwood, Igor Kipnis, David Kopp, John Koster, Marcellene and Walter Mayhall, Drew Minter, and Howard Schott furnished advice and materials at a crucial time, and André P. Larson, director of America's Shrine to Music Museum at the University of South Dakota, and members of his staff generously made available illustrations of instruments and other material from the museum collection. Several readers of the manuscript, including Stephen A. Crist, Lois Rosow, and Jeanne Swack, provided very valuable suggestions, and Larry Hamberlin was the expert copyeditor. The staff of Oxford University Press, including Maribeth Payne, Jon Wiener, Justin Collins, John Bauco, and especially Maureen Buja, has been consistently encouraging and helpful. Above all, I thank my wife, Mary Oleskiewicz, for her constant support and love—not to mention sage advice and innumerable hints and suggestions based on her vast practical and scholarly knowledge of Baroque music.

A Note on Pitch References

Citations of exact pitches (as opposed to pitch classes) use the Helmholtz system, according to which middle C is designated as c', the note below it is b, and the note above it is d'. An octave higher these notes are $b'-c''-d''$, an octave below B–c–d, and so forth.

Music

of the

Baroque

CHAPTER 1

INTRODUCTION

Music History, 1600–1750: Some Basic Ideas

This book explores the music of the Baroque, the predominant culture of western Europe from the early seventeenth century through the mid-eighteenth century. Music historians think of this music as following that of the **Renaissance** and leading to that of the **Classical** period.

Musicologists of the early twentieth century borrowed the terms *Renaissance* and *Baroque* from art historians, who in turn took them from literary and cultural history. The noun *Renaissance* originally referred to the rediscovery of ancient Greek and Roman literature by fifteenth-century scholars, whereas the word *Baroque* is an adjective referring to what were thought to be the ostentatious and elaborately ornamented forms of art, architecture, and literature favored in the seventeenth and early eighteenth centuries.[1] Art historians (like most historians in general) consider the Renaissance to extend from around 1400 to the mid-sixteenth century, and for them the Baroque coincides roughly with the seventeenth century. In music, however, we tend to apply both terms to slightly later periods: roughly 1450 to 1600 for the Renaissance, 1600 to 1750 for the Baroque. Music historians rarely speak of a revival of ancient Greek or Roman music during the Renaissance, for none was then known to survive. Likewise, few today regard Baroque music as unduly ostentatious or overly decorated.

Nevertheless, use of these terms is so engrained that we can hardly avoid employing them. Indeed, a word such as *Baroque* refers not only to a time period but to the musical style that was customary during that period. Yet the use of a particular musical style rarely coincides in a precise way with a particular historical era. Innovative composers such as Giovanni Gabrieli and Claudio Monteverdi were writing in what we recognize as Baroque musical styles well before the beginning of the seventeenth century. At the end of the Baroque period—that is, around 1750—composers such as Johann Sebastian Bach were still looking back to the sixteenth century and employing elements of Renais-

---

[1] Outside the study of music, the word *baroque* has the implication of gaudy or overdecorated.

sance style in certain works. Yet Bach's personal style and the types of music that he composed are enormously different from those of Gabrieli and Monteverdi. Thus it would be a mistake to think of music from 1600 to 1750 as constituting a single Baroque style that is entirely distinct from that of the Renaissance; there is great diversity within both periods.

For this reason it will be important to identify individual musical compositions not simply as "Baroque" but as belonging to individual countries and more specific periods—for instance, "German music of the early eighteenth century." In doing so we recognize an important distinction between Baroque music and that of the preceding period. During the Renaissance, musical style was relatively uniform throughout western Europe. In 1550 a musician could travel—as many did—from Italy in the south to England or Germany in the north, only to find more or less the same types of music being performed in roughly the same way. But by 1700 there were considerable differences in the musical styles and practices of these countries.

As the preceding discussion suggests, we will be concerned particularly with musical **style**. Style can be thought of as a set of practices that define a given musical tradition; it can also be viewed as a set of common musical patterns that help a listener make sense out of a large number of works. Style can be defined broadly or narrowly: we can speak of the style of Baroque music in general as well as the style of early seventeenth-century opera. Style, moreover, can be defined either in terms of musical composition or in relation to musical performance; in speaking of a historical performance style we often use the expression *performance practice*. A particularly useful idea in considering musical style is **genre**. A genre is a category of musical compositions written for a particular purpose and employing a particular type of scoring, form, verbal text (if any), and performance practices. For example, the genre of the cantata in the Baroque consists of works for solo voices and instruments, usually in several sections or movements and with a poetic text. Originally the texts of cantatas were lyrical in nature and the works were performed by small ensembles, most often for the enjoyment of individual music lovers in private homes, but later Baroque cantatas may have dramatic or even sacred texts and were performed during services or public concerts in churches and other public spaces.

Our history of music will be to a considerable degree a history of genres. Thus it will be important to bear in mind the defining features of each category (genre) of music that we study: cantatas, sonatas, concertos, and so on. But composers and performers do not create "categories"; they create individual works or performances of music, each with a particular character and containing some unique or innovative feature. It will therefore be equally important to recognize the distinctive aspects of each individual work that we study. In studying a cantata by Bach, one might begin by identifying those features of the scoring, text, and form that define it as a cantata. But to appreciate what makes this one cantata special—what makes it worth studying—it is necessary to analyze the music, observing what makes the composition an individual work of genius. Analysis also helps identify any special demands the work imposes on the performer and what interpretive decisions one must make in performing it.

As we examine individual works, we shall find that general labels of style and genre do not always fit each piece equally well. For example, there are works by Monteverdi that can be described as either madrigals or cantatas; there are instrumental works by Telemann that were called both concertos and sonatas. We shall also find that certain labels apply to very different types of music; the word *concerto*, for example, originally described a type of music for voices and instruments and only later came to refer strictly to orchestral compositions.

To help reduce the potential for confusion, in this book the first discussion or definition of an important term is signaled by the use of **boldface** type. A few terms, such as *concerto*, are introduced more than once, as different uses of the same word come up. A number of important concepts are discussed in depth in boxes outside the main text; other boxes contain additional useful information, such as plot summaries for operatic works and biographical information about composers. Texts and translations of most of the vocal works are included in the accompanying anthology (*Music of the Baroque: An Anthology of Scores*).

HISTORICAL BACKGROUND: WESTERN EUROPE 1600–1750

The period we are studying saw important social, economic, and political developments throughout Europe. Nevertheless, certain things remained constant. The great western states of France, England, and Spain retained their identities as relatively unified kingdoms, as did the Austrian empire, which included not only modern Austria but large portions of the surrounding region, including parts of northern Italy, Hungary, and southern Germany. Elsewhere, particularly in what is now Germany, western Europe remained a patchwork of small states ruled by variously titled dukes, counts, princes, and others.

Despite their diverse political structures, life in these states had certain things in common. The great majority of the population consisted of the lower classes, composed mainly of poor rural peasants. They grew the food and provided the labor that made everything else possible. Their lot remained hard and primitive throughout our period, and it actually got worse in parts of Germany, Spain, and Italy.

Considerably better off were the middle classes, composed especially of merchants and tradespeople in the cities. On the whole, their numbers had grown in size, wealth, and political power during the earlier part of the Renaissance (roughly 1400–1550). Particularly in Italy and Germany, independent city-states such as Venice and Hamburg, which were governed by councils of wealthy businessmen or minor aristocrats as opposed to kings or individual nobles, achieved political and cultural importance that sometimes surpassed that of the major kingdoms. But for various reasons, the power and economic condition of the cities (and of most rural areas) declined during the seventeenth century. Instead, the latter saw a centralization of power in the ruling dynasties of the great states, leading to what is referred to as royal absolutism; this was true above all in France and, to a varying degree, most other European countries.

The growth of royal absolutism coincided, particularly in Germany and Italy, with a relative decline in the fortunes of the middle classes. At the same time

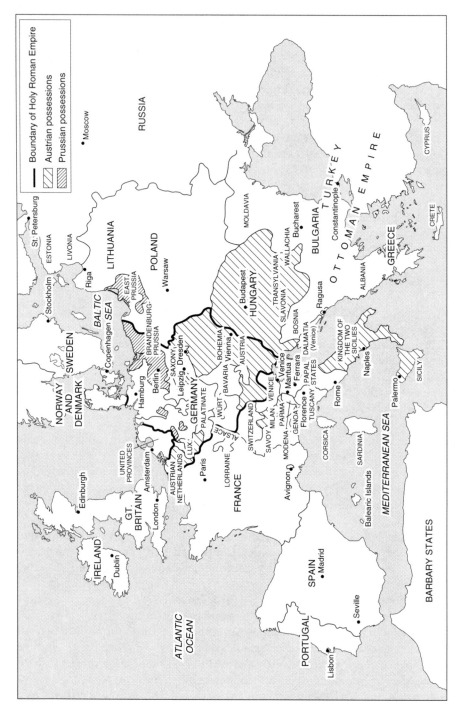

Figure 1.1 Europe in 1721. (LUX = Luxemburg; WÜRT = Württemberg)

there was spectacular growth in the major **courts,** that is, the administrative and cultural institutions centered around the rulers of the various monarchies. Each court was now—for the first time—permanently located in a capital city, and thus during the Baroque such municipalities as Paris, Vienna, and London became the chief centers of artistic production. Of the great independent city-states that had survived beyond the Renaissance, by 1700 only Venice, Hamburg, and a few others retained some importance. Even the Roman Catholic Church, which had been the single strongest western European institution for the thousand years preceding, was eclipsed by the great kingdoms, although the pope, with his capital in Rome, remained a local monarch, the absolute ruler of a region in central Italy.

Many rulers were important patrons of the arts. But the typical activity of rulers was warfare; hardly a year of true peace went by. Although the pretexts for warfare varied from one conflict to another, most of the fighting during the seventeenth century was due to rivalries between France, Spain, and Austria for control of Italy and parts of northern Europe (including Germany, Poland, and the Netherlands). The greatest conflagration occurred early in our period: the Thirty Years' War (1618–48), which involved most of the states of western Europe. Further conflicts of a relatively limited nature continued into the eighteenth century. Among these was a series of wars involving France, England, and the Netherlands in the second half of the seventeenth century, as well as the War of the Spanish Succession (1700–1713), which actually took place mainly in Italy, Germany, and Poland. There were also major internal conflicts, notably the civil wars in England and France in the 1640s and 1650s, respectively. Each of these conflicts wrought vast devastation; in particular, the Thirty Years' War, which was fought mainly in Germany, left that region depopulated and economically deprived until well into the eighteenth century—with severe consequences for the composition and performance of music, among other things.

Conflicts such as these were, ultimately, the products of underlying social and economic forces that are still incompletely understood. One major factor, however, was the Protestant Reformation: the long historical process by which various states and peoples had broken the religious, cultural, and political ties that had linked them with Roman Catholicism since the Middle Ages. Associated above all with the German theologian Martin Luther (1483–1546), the Reformation had led to the establishment of separate Protestant churches in the countries of northern Europe. After a period of intense doctrinal debate and warfare during the sixteenth century, the situation had stabilized to one in which Spain, France, Austria, southern Germany, and Italy remained mainly Roman Catholic; northern Germany and Scandinavia were mostly Lutheran; the Netherlands and parts of Germany and Switzerland were Calvinist (Reformed); and England had its own Protestant denomination known as the Anglican (or Episcopal) church.

Under the terms of the Peace of Westphalia, which ended the Thirty Years' War in 1648, each ruler had the right to impose his or her faith on those who lived under his or her rule. Thus the Lutheran elector or duke of Saxony ruled over Lutheran subjects, whereas the inhabitants of Austria, northern Italy, and

Figure 1.2 A Baroque cityscape: *View of Dresden with the Frauenkirche at Left*, 1747, oil on canvas by Bernardo Bellotto (Italian, 1720–80). North Carolina Museum of Art, Raleigh, Purchased with funds from the State of North Carolina (52.9.145). Dresden, capital of Saxony, appears as seen from across the river Elbe; at the far left is the Frauenkirche (Church of Our Lady), where Johann Sebastian Bach's son Wilhelm Friedemann was organist in the 1740s. The figures at the center foreground facing the viewer may have been members of the royal chapel choir, which performed in the Hofkirche (Court Church) seen at the center. Bach, Handel, and numerous other musicians visited this musical center, where Heinrich Schütz had worked in the seventeenth century.

Bohemia (now in the Czech Republic) were Roman Catholics like the emperor who reigned over them. But religious conditions could change as the result of wars and political developments; thus in 1697 the ruler of Saxony, Augustus II, converted to Catholicism as a prerequisite to his accepting the crown of Poland. Roman Catholic churches were immediately established in the Saxon capital of Dresden, although the vast majority of the population—including J. S. Bach and other important composers—remained Lutheran. The ruler's conversion was nevertheless important for music history, since the Saxon court, which had previously been a patron of distinctively Lutheran religious music—notably that of Heinrich Schütz—now commissioned numerous Roman Catholic works. It was typical of the time, however, that even Lutherans, Bach among them, continued to provide music for the Saxon court. No one seems to have questioned the ability of musicians to perform and compose in a suitable manner, regardless of their religion; personal belief was considered irrelevant to one's ability to serve a patron.

MUSIC IN EUROPEAN HISTORY, 1600–1750

Music was, presumably, cultivated wherever there were people. But the music whose scores have survived for us to study—music of the type we now refer to as "art" music—was associated almost exclusively with perhaps the top 2 or 3 percent of the population: the royalty and aristocracy and the wealthiest and best-educated members of the middle classes. As in previous periods, much of this music was written for the church—not the local parish churches of the peasants and lower middle classes, but churches associated with the upper classes:

the private chapels of the rulers, as well as the cathedrals and central churches of the great cities. In Roman Catholic regions, certain monasteries and convents also played an important role as patrons and producers of music. But several developments led to a somewhat wider dissemination of art music than in earlier times and its increasing use for secular purposes.

First, during this period the church's power and wealth relative to those of the state diminished; moreover, its very identity had been and continued to be profoundly altered by the Protestant Reformation. Second, the continuing development of music printing, which had begun in 1501, meant that art music no longer had to be copied by hand by and for a narrow group of specially trained professionals (mostly churchmen). Instead, trained amateurs could begin to participate in serious music making outside the church, and sacred music too could achieve wider distribution. Nevertheless, printed music remained expensive until the end of the Baroque; manuscripts continued to be the chief means of preservation and dissemination of music through the mid-eighteenth century.

A third factor was the centralization of wealth and power in the major courts and the largest cities. This led to the development of new genres of music that involved new types of ensembles, new instruments, and new combinations of music with poetry, dance, and other art forms. The most spectacular development of this sort was opera, whose emergence around 1600 marks the beginning of the Baroque. The tremendous expense of opera meant that productions could be undertaken on a regular basis only in the great musical centers, often under royal or aristocratic patronage. But many lesser rulers followed the lead of the great monarchs by investing considerable sums of money in their musical and theatrical establishments, which might consist of small-scale but first-rate vocal and instrumental ensembles. Moreover, a number of cities—notably Venice, Hamburg, and London—saw the founding of public opera theaters that were intended, at least in principle, to be self-sustaining commercial ventures. Nevertheless, most professional musicians aspired to a position in the court of an important ruler or, at least, in one of the principal churches of a major city.

Particularly in Lutheran Germany, the Protestant Reformation had led to the development of new genres of church music. Moreover, the Roman Catholic response to Protestantism, known as the Counter-Reformation, continued to influence musical style in Italy and other Catholic countries well into the seventeenth century. But secular patronage became equally decisive for musical innovation during the Baroque, and the presence of a sophisticated musical establishment came to be seen as a symbol of a ruler's wealth and benificence. During the late sixteenth and early seventeenth centuries, the greatest musical centers were the aristocratically ruled cities of northern Italy. These were joined—indeed, surpassed—by France during the reign of Louis XIV in the later seventeenth century. Thus Paris became a major center, as did other capital cities, including Vienna, London, Dresden, and Berlin. In addition, Venice, despite its diminishing political importance, remained a musical center of the first rank throughout the Baroque; so too was Rome, at least until around 1700.

Patterns in the development of Baroque musical genres and in the careers of individual musicians were directly influenced by the rise of these new centers.

Whereas musicians and musical forms during the Middle Ages had often originated in northwestern Europe and migrated south- and eastward, by the end of the Renaissance the trend had been reversed. Throughout the seventeenth and eighteenth centuries, Italian artists and styles traveled north to Germany, France, and England; French music and musicians became equally influential in Germany and England by the end of the seventeenth century.

Meanwhile, Spain and Portugal, which steadily declined in wealth and power from the 1550s onward, retained a distinctive musical culture but one that had little influence elsewhere in Europe, although it was exported to their colonies in the New World. England, although relatively poor and small in population until the eighteenth century, also retained a distinctive musical style that was, moreover, continually reinvigorated by Italian and French influences. Thus a flowering of music under the reign of Elizabeth I (1558–1603) was echoed in that of the Restoration period (1660–88) one hundred years later. Central and northern Germany, like Spain and southern Italy, was something of a provincial backwater through much of the seventeenth century. But even at the height of the Thirty Years' War, Germany was home to a composer of supreme genius, Heinrich Schütz, who was able to adapt the style of early Baroque Italian vocal music to the needs of his native language. Eighteenth-century Germany also produced a series of important figures, notably Handel, Telemann, and Bach and his sons, whose works combined what had become the very different French and Italian styles into a distinctive late Baroque German synthesis.

The Place of Music and Musicians in Society

With few exceptions, Baroque musicians belonged to the middle classes; moreover, like many other members of the middle classes they worked chiefly for the ruling classes. Thus Lully in Paris was head of the musical establishment of King Louis XIV; Monteverdi was choirmaster (*maestro di capella*) at the Basilica of St. Mark's, the personal church of the ruling *doge* (duke) of Venice; Bach in Leipzig was the city's director of church music, overseeing performances for the entire population but composing new music chiefly for the two churches whose congregations included the wealthiest citizens. Just as most middle-class printers, bakers, and other artisans handed their skills and occupations on to their descendents, most musicians' families continued their professional activity in music from one generation to the next. Only the wealthy could afford to study music for its own sake, and although a few noble amateurs (such as the Marcello brothers of Venice) produced music of distinction, the importance of the upper classes for music history in this period was chiefly that of patrons: buyers of music and employers of musicians.

Most music was still produced on demand for a particular occasion or purpose: an aristocratic wedding celebration, a religious service on a given day of the church year. This does not mean, however, that music once composed was forgotten; most works were written in the expectation that they would circulate, either in manuscript or in printed form, once the occasion for which they were written was over. Nevertheless, to understand fully most compositions of

Figure 1.3 Banquet following the swearing of allegiance to Emperor Charles VI as archduke of Austria, 8 November 1705, engraving from Johann Baptist Mairn von Mairsfeld, *Beschreibung was auf Ableiben weyland Ihrer Keyserl. Majestät* (Vienna, 1712). This is an example of the type of grand ceremonial occasion in which Baroque musicians played an essential role. From the balcony, an ensemble of trumpets and strings, directed by the figure holding a rolled-up sheet of paper, adds splendor to an elaborate formal dinner.

this period it is often necessary to know for what or for whom they were written. For example, Monteverdi's opera *Orfeo* was composed for private performance in a room of a noble palace; its first audience was a society of aristocratic enthusiasts who had a special interest in the culture of ancient Greece. This helps explain the work's mythological plot, its relatively short duration and small cast of major characters, and the lack of what we would consider realistic action. When we turn to sacred music, we find that most works were still, as in the Middle Ages and Renaissance, composed for performance in church as part of a particular service on a particular day. Thus a work for Christmas employs a text and other features that distinguish it from a work for a saint's day or some other occasion.

As we have seen, patrons were generally unconcerned about the religious faith (or lack of it) of their musicians. Handel, a Lutheran, wrote music for the Anglican chapel of the king of England, whereas Bach, also a Lutheran, sent an early version of his B Minor Mass to his sovereign, the Roman Catholic elector of Saxony, who was also the king of Poland.[2] This was possible because musical style was not, in general, dependent on religion. Genres that originated in Roman Catholic Italy, such as the cantata, were enthusiastically adopted by Protestant patrons and musicians. Indeed, throughout the Baroque there were few essential differences between sacred and secular music. The same music could even be used for both purposes; Monteverdi, Schütz, and Bach all followed the common practice of adopting secular music to church use, attaching new sacred words to existing compositions.

Throughout our period, the place of women in society, and therefore in music, was particularly restricted. Although a small number of aristocratic women achieved distinction during the later Middle Ages as rulers, writers, and in one or two cases composers, the status of women in general declined during the Renaissance. Toward the end of the sixteenth century, however, professional women singers began to appear in a few northern Italian courts, and in the 1600s women musicians—as well as dancers and actors—became highly visible in Paris and a number of Italian cities; a few became composers. But in most places laws and customs continued to bar women from participation in church music and from careers as professional musicians. Moreover, some states, notably Rome, often prevented the appearance of women in operas and other theatrical performances. One result was the widespread use of male voices for the higher vocal parts in both sacred and secular music; even in opera and ballet, men often took female roles (the reverse also occurred, but less frequently and only in certain places).

PERFORMANCE PRACTICES

The use of men in what we would consider women's roles is only the most extreme instance of a historical performance practice that today seems strange and unexpected. In every work we study, we must ask ourselves how the composer expected the music to be performed. Baroque musical notation is generally close to that of today—far closer than that of earlier periods. But many things that we expect to be indicated in a musical score, such as the specific voices and instruments for which it is written, as well as dynamic and tempo markings, are often absent. This is partly because composers were often participants in performances of their works, making it unnecessary to indicate everything in writing. In addition, many performance practices were understood by convention rather than fixed in notation.

This remains true today; we do not, for example, expect an orchestral score to tell us precisely how many violins play each part or what bowings they should use, even though decisions about these matters can drastically affect the sound of a work. To some degree these matters are open to the discretion of the conductor or section leader, but beyond a certain point they are governed by con-

---

[2]Bach eventually received in return the honorary title of Saxon court composer.

Figure 1.4 *Family Music-Making*, Pieter de Hooch (Dutch, 1629–83). Oil on canvas, 98.7 × 116.7 cm. © The Cleveland Museum of Art, 2000, Gift of the Hanna Fund, 1951.355. This painting depicts members of a well-off urban family engaged in domestic music making. The seated woman at the center holds a music book in her lap and beats time with her right hand; she is probably singing, accompanied by recorder, cittern, and violin (at left, a bass viola da gamba leans against a table). Note the relaxed position in which the violin is held, resting on the chest rather than squeezed between the neck and shoulder as in present-day practice.

vention; one would not, for example, perform a Beethoven symphony with just two or three first violins. We are so accustomed to the symphonies and other works of the modern concert repertory that we rarely think about the conventions they involve. But in earlier music the conventions are less familiar to us. Thus we have to be careful in interpreting Baroque scores—both the notes themselves and any verbal indications for such things as instrumentation or tempo. For example, the word *soprano* in a Bach choral work may mean not a section comprising several female singers but a single boy or an adult male falsettist. Instrumental parts also require careful consideration; for instance, the word *flute* sometimes means not the modern transverse flute, which is held to the side, but the recorder, a distinct woodwind instrument held vertically. By the eighteenth century, most of the instruments of the modern orchestra existed in some form. But all differed in important ways from their modern counterparts, with respect to playing technique as well as their physical structure and materials.

Figure 1.5 *Concert*, drawing (pencil, ink, and washes on blue paper), French, eighteenth century, attributed to Lancret. America's Shrine to Music Museum, Vermillion, South Dakota, Witten-Rawlins Collection, 1984 (no. G-8). An ensemble of cello, harpsichord, violin, and transverse flute performs before an audience; such a scene might have occurred during one of the many semipublic concerts held in the homes of both the aristocracy and certain better-off musicians in eighteenth-century France and Germany.

Modern concert performers are accustomed to playing or singing exactly the notes that we see on the page. But professional musicians of the Baroque were trained in the improvisation of embellishments and variations, much as modern jazz musicians are. Every good musician understood how to interpret certain signs used as shorthand for ornaments; keyboard players learned in addition how to improvise harmony or counterpoint, sometimes following written clues notated through the symbols of what is known as figured bass. Most musicians also understood conventions that involved the alteration of certain notated rhythms. Conventions varied from time to time and place to place; principles that govern the performance of ornaments such as trills in Bach's music do not necessarily apply in the earlier music of Monteverdi or Lully.

Figure 1.6 A public ball during celebrations of the marriage of the Dauphin to Princess María Teresa of Spain, Paris, 23 February 1745, engraving from *Fêtes publiques donnés par la ville de Paris* . . . (Paris, 1745). A large band provides music for a public dance sponsored by the city of Paris; the dancing is informal, by contrast to that of the royal court or at the opera and ballet.

Hence, in addition to understanding the development of compositional style and the notable elements of individual works, it is important to understand distinctive aspects of the notation and performance practices of each piece. Performance practice includes such considerations as (1) *where* works were performed, (2) *who* performed them, and (3) *how* musical scores were interpreted. Given, say, an oratorio by Handel, we would like to know (1) the sort of hall or theater for which it was written; (2) the size and makeup of the ensemble that Handel's own performances used, including the precise number and type of voices and instruments; and (3) the conventions that governed the interpretation of Handel's score and the vocal and instrumental techniques used—for example, the bowings used by the string players, or the use or nonuse of vibrato by singers as well as instrumentalists.

Usually we know far less about such things than we would like. Scholars often differ with one another about the use of a particular historical performance practice, and so-called authentic performances or recordings may adopt very different approaches to the same work. Nevertheless, specialists in early performance practices have acquired an impressive amount of knowledge and practical experience in the repertories that we will be considering. Music that only a few decades ago seemed dry or impossible to perform has been revealed as exciting and eminently practical. Even familiar works have been presented in a new light. Musicians who are not in a position to acquire old types of instruments or to learn historical techniques can still gain new ideas about performance by studying historical practices. And it goes without saying that, even as specialists in early music continue to refine their ideas about historical performance, the music of major Baroque composers such as Bach and Handel will continue to be performed by "modern" musicians as well.

CHAPTER 2

A SIXTEENTH-CENTURY PROLOGUE
Motet and Madrigal

In order to understand the beginnings of Baroque music, let us first examine some of the music of the preceding period, the Renaissance. We shall consider works of just two genres—motet and madrigal—from the end of the Renaissance, that is, the late sixteenth century. These will give us a good idea of the state of European musical style as the turn of the century—that is, the year 1600—approached. The motet was one of the most important forms of sacred vocal music throughout the Renaissance; the madrigal was its secular counterpart during the later sixteenth century. Both genres continued in use during the Baroque, although in considerably altered forms.

The composers discussed in this chapter remained well known and influential for much of the Baroque period. Indeed, most musicians at the beginning of the seventeenth century were hardly aware of a significant change in musical style. As far as they were concerned, they were simply continuing to compose and perform in the traditions of the previous century.

Renaissance Composers

The chief composers of the early Renaissance—Guillaume Dufay (1400–1474), Gilles Binchois (ca. 1400–1460), and Johannes Ockeghem (ca. 1425–97)—were northerners: natives of the Netherlands or northern France who eventually found employment with some of the great rulers of their time: kings of France, dukes of Burgundy, and the like. Most spent at least a portion of their careers in southern France and Italy, and as far we know they wrote exclusively vocal music. Moreover, all were singers; that, at least, is how they were usually described in contemporary documents, although some obtained titles as church or court officials as well. Josquin des Prez (ca. 1455–1521), the greatest composer of the next generation, still led such a career, but by the mid-sixteenth century things had begun to change. Palestrina and Lassus (discussed below) both worked in the choirs of great rulers, and both continued to write only vocal music.[1] But

---

[1] A number of keyboard works published under Palestrina's name are probably not actually his compositions.

Palestrina was Italian, spending his entire career in his native country: the first of many such composers whom we will meet. Moreover, he began his career as an organist, signaling a trend that would continue through the Baroque, when the majority of important composers would be instrumentalists, particularly keyboard players. Nevertheless, the typical career path of a composer remained constant throughout the fifteenth and sixteenth centuries: early training as a choirboy in the church of one's native city, followed by a series of appointments as singer, organist, or choir director in increasingly prestigious ecclesiastical or court positions.

Vocal Polyphony of the Renaissance

The music of the composers mentioned above is for vocal ensembles in which each voice has an independent melodic line. Such music is referred to as **vocal polyphony**; it is for three, four, or more vocal parts, each equal to the others in importance and similar in rhythm and melodic content. Frequently, each part was sung by a single person, not by a section in a large chorus as is often heard in modern performances of this repertory. Instruments sometimes replaced or doubled one or more of the voices, but in principle this music remained purely vocal, the complete verbal text appearing beneath the notes in each part. Adult male voices were the rule, although boys might have sung the top lines of some works, women as well in secular music.[2] We will be particularly interested in two aspects of late Renaissance polyphony: its use of *imitative counterpoint* and its increasing emphasis on *musical rhetoric*. Both features continued to be of great importance throughout the Baroque.

Musical Rhetoric

Perhaps the most important single element in vocal music of the late Renaissance and the Baroque is the composer's approach to the setting of texts. By the end of the sixteenth century, writers on music had articulated the principle of **musical rhetoric**. By itself, the word *rhetoric* refers to the effective presentation of ideas through the spoken or written word. Rhetoric in this sense has been a fundamental element of European education since ancient times, and Renaissance and Baroque writers, emulating those of ancient Greece and Rome, used numerous special devices or *figures* of rhetoric, such as metaphors and similes, to render their arguments more compelling or their poems more beautiful.[3] When Joachim Burmeister and other late Renaissance and Baroque theorists began to apply similar ideas to vocal music, they were in effect considering a musical composition as a *reading* of its text. That is, just as a speaker or writer uses particular verbal techniques to articulate the form, meaning, and expressive content of a piece of writing or an oration, a composer uses musical devices to articulate the structure and content of the text that he is setting to music. This

---

[2]Women probably participated in performances of sacred polyphony in some convents and in Protestant countries, but public performances of any kind by women were extremely limited.

[3]We still use the expression "figures of speech" to refer to metaphors, rhetorical questions, and other verbal devices that ultimately derive from ancient rhetoric.

principle remained paramount in vocal compositions through the Baroque. For that reason, in examining vocal music we shall be especially concerned with how the composer "reads" the text, that is, uses musical means to reflect both the form of the text and its content. Understanding the musical rhetoric of vocal works will be a continuing concern throughout this book.

Texture

One of the many musical tools employed in the service of musical rhetoric was the manipulation of musical **texture**. Musicians speak of texture in various ways; in vocal polyphony we can understand texture as a particular relationship between the individual parts. It will be useful for us to distinguish three types of texture: homophonic, antiphonal, and contrapuntal. Imitative counterpoint is a variety of contrapuntal texture that received particular attention from sixteenth-century composers, whose works are studied to this day for their refined use of this type of writing. Each of these textures will be considered as we examine individual motets and madrigals in detail.

Sacred Polyphony of the Renaissance

By the mid-sixteenth century, the motet and the cyclic mass had been for some hundred years the chief forms of sacred polyphony. Both terms, *motet* and *cyclic mass*, are modern expressions that cover several types of music that were originally regarded as distinct. We now use the word **motet** to refer to almost any sacred polyphonic vocal work of the Renaissance, except for masses and a few other special categories.[4] The motets that concern us here were composed chiefly for performance as part of the liturgy of the Roman Catholic church—that is, as music to be heard at some point during a worship service.

The **mass** is, in this context, the principal worship service of the Roman Catholic Church; its elements include the **proper**, a set of readings and ritual actions that vary from day to day, and the **ordinary**, another set that in principle remains the same throughout the year. Since the fifteenth century, five sections of the ordinary of the mass have customarily been set to music; these are the Kyrie, Gloria, Credo, Sanctus, and Agnus Dei, each named after its opening word or words. In an actual religious service, most of these sections are separated from one another by elements of the proper; nevertheless, composers frequently set them as a group, creating a **cyclic mass**. In most cyclic masses of the Renaissance, the five movements are unified by their common use of preexisting musical material: either a popular or sacred melody (such as a Gregorian chant), or a motet or some other polyphonic work.[5]

---

[4]The word *motet* is also used for certain types of medieval work, both sacred and secular, as well as for nineteenth-century sacred vocal music composed in imitation of the Renaissance motet.

[5]The terms *paraphrase* and *parody* are used to describe the techniques by which preexisting material is incorporated into a mass or other work. Thus a cyclic mass based on portions of a preexisting melody is a paraphrase mass; one that incorporates portions of a complete polyphonic work such as a madrigal is a parody mass. Sixteenth-century musicians described such techniques as *imitation*, a term preferred by some scholars today.

Baroque composers continued to write motets and masses, often in styles close to those of the late sixteenth century. One of J. S. Bach's last works, the B Minor Mass, completed in about 1749, contains several movements that reflect his study of and admiration for the music of Palestrina, composed some two centuries earlier.

THE LATE RENAISSANCE MOTET: GIOVANNI PIERLUIGI DA PALESTRINA AND ROLANDE DE LASSUS

Palestrina

Giovanni Pierluigi da Palestrina (1525/6–94) was probably the most influential composer of Roman Catholic church music during the late Renaissance. Named after his birthplace, the Roman suburb of Palestrina, he achieved recognition as a composer at an early age and spent much of his career in the service of high church officials at Rome, including several popes. The greatest part of his extant output consists of about one hundred cyclic masses and several hundred motets and related sacred works. Particularly famous is the *Pope Marcellus* Mass, named after a pope who served for just three weeks in 1555. During his brief papacy, Marcellus is supposed to have encouraged his musicians, including Palestrina, to write in a style that made the words readily comprehensible to listeners. Whether true or not, the story reflects the tendency of the Counter-Reformation—the Roman Catholic response to the Protestant movement— to favor sacred music that renders the words of the text in a clear and distinct manner.

Most of the texts that Palestrina set to music are in Latin, the official language of the Roman Catholic Church throughout the period that we are studying. The language of the ancient Roman Empire, Latin was still understood and indeed used in everyday speech by the Roman aristocrats and churchmen for whom Palestrina worked. Hence the texts that he set to music would have been familiar to his chief patrons. Indeed, through the Baroque most vocal music was used to set texts whose language would have been meaningful to its intended audience.

Palestrina's Music

Palestrina's music is for vocal ensembles of from three to twelve voices. Four-, five-, and six-part writing predominates. Following the practice of the time, works sometimes remained in manuscript for many years prior to their publication. Because few of Palestrina's own manuscripts survive, in most cases we know only the dates of publication, not of composition. The masses were his best-known works; about half of them were based on preexisting music, including twenty-four of Palestrina's own compositions.[6] Palestrina is famous

---

[6] An example of such a work is the *Missa Dum complerentur*, based on the motet *Dum complerentur*, which is discussed below.

above all for his perfection of compositional devices that had been pioneered by earlier Renaissance composers. He is especially known for his mastery of imitative counterpoint, and musicians to this day study his works as examples of the polished use of this difficult compositional technique.

The Motet *Dum complerentur*

This work (anthology, Selection 1) was first published in 1569, two years after the *Pope Marcellus* Mass, at a time when Palestrina was recognized as one of Europe's leading musicians. Its Latin text is based on the account in the New Testament of Pentecost, originally a Jewish festival. Christians believe that at the observation of this holiday fifty days after Jesus's resurrection, the Holy Spirit was manifested to the disciples (the followers of Christ) in the form of a great wind. This the text describes in lines 3–4. As with all sacred works of art, it is important to understand the original religious significance of this composition, regardless of one's own faith or convictions. Only by considering the sacred text in relation to Palestrina's music can one fully appreciate the craft and expressive values that the composer has instilled in it.[7]

The Text of the Motet

In considering a vocal composition of this period we might begin by examining the text—both its *form* and its *content*. In form, this text falls into two parts, each comprising four lines (see the text and translation accompanying the musical score in the anthology). The last line of each part is the same; this is indicated by the three dots (*ellipsis*) after the opening words of line 8. In addition, lines 2, 3, and 4 each end with the word *alleluja*—an expression of joy—as does line 8. As a first principle of musical rhetoric, we may expect the music to contain some reflection of these formal aspects of the text.

A second point concerns the content of the text—both its meaning and its emotional implications. For example, we might well expect the music to reflect the joyful character of the text, which is indicated by the repeated *allelujas*. But we cannot assume that a sixteenth-century composer would have expressed joy through the same musical means as would a later composer. Indeed, this music may not sound especially joyful to us—particularly if it is not sung with the lively tempo that was probably the composer's intention. We shall find that composers of the later Renaissance and the Baroque tended to focus much more closely on individual words in the text than did later composers. Thus, instead of expressing the abstract idea or emotional effect of "joy," this motet focuses on individual words and brief phrases of the text—some of which indeed represent ideas relevant to joy—highlighting each in some distinctive way. To un-

---

[7]Line 6 of the motet's text is not found in the New Testament; it is instead a potentially anti-Semitic addition to the biblical text. Its presence shows that even in a musical work one must confront the prejudices characteristic of the time and place in which it was composed.

derstand how the music reflects the words, one must be on the lookout for distinctive musical settings of small fragments of the text.

The Music of Palestrina's Motet: Texture

In turning to any vocal composition, we shall be interested not only in the musical style and structure but also in their relationship to the words. As in any piece of music, however, our initial impression of the motet arises from what we actually hear. At the outset, three relatively high voices or vocal parts sing together (see score, mm. 1–3). They present line 1 of the text, at first all moving in the same rhythm, forming chords in which we attend mainly to the line sung by the top part or **cantus** (soprano). In other words, the cantus sings a melody that is accompanied by the **altus** (alto) and **tenore** (tenor). Such a texture can be described as **homophonic,** a word derived from a Greek expression literally meaning "same sound," although it is applied in various ways to music.

In measure 3 the tenor begins to move independently of the two upper voices, and in the next two measures all three have their own distinctive rhythms and melodic contours. This is a type of **contrapuntal** texture typical of much vocal polyphony; the three voices move in **counterpoint,** from words referring to distinct musical lines that move against ("counter to") one another.

At measure 6 the cantus and altus drop out, and we now hear a group of four low voices, again presenting line 1 of the text. We can, then, speak of an alternation between two contrasting groups; such an alternation is an example of **antiphony** (from Greek words meaning "against" and "voice"). This is a third basic type of texture. Note, however, that while we can speak of measures 1–11 as being **antiphonal,** within each of the work's two phrases we can also speak of separate homophonic and contrapuntal passages.

Thus far we have not heard any obvious instances of the **imitative counterpoint** for which Palestrina is famous. Such a texture first occurs with the upbeat to measure 18, when the cantus and altus together introduce the word *alleluja.* One measure later, the **quintus** (second tenor) enters with the same melodic idea, overlapping with the lines of the two upper voices, which continue.[8] Gradually, the remaining voices enter, and in measure 23 the cantus enters for a second time with the same melodic idea. The latter now begins on the second beat of the measure, so that the first note is written as a dotted quarter, not a quarter tied to an eighth; it is important not to overlook such renotated entries.

The brief melodic idea that is treated in imitation is termed a **subject;** each entry of this subject (save for the first) joins an existing group of voices, taking part in an increasingly complex web of counterpoint. The subject itself takes various shapes. Some entries exactly imitate the cantus's first entry, through the downbeat of measure 19. In others only the rhythm or the general melodic con-

---

[8]The word *quintus* is Latin for "fifth"; this voice, together with the *sextus* or "sixth" voice (second alto), was viewed as an addition to the four basic parts of cantus, altus, tenor, and *bassus* (bass).

tour is recognizable. Later composers took a similarly flexible approach to imitation; only rarely was the latter expected to be exact.[9]

Text and Music in Palestrina's Motet

Palestrina's use of imitative counterpoint has long been admired as a finely developed aspect of compositional craft. But to the composer and his listeners, it was chiefly a means toward the effective presentation of the text—that is, an element of musical rhetoric. Palestrina's music reflects not only the form of the text but also its grammar and accentuation; in a few instances it clearly responds to its meaning as well. Each of these aspects of musical rhetoric is carried out through the use of specific compositional devices.

One such device is musical form. **Form** includes such elements as the division of the music into sections and the recurrence or repetition of individual sections. The form of this motet directly reflects that of its text. As we have seen, the text falls into two sections, each ending with the same words (line 4 = line 8). The music, like that of many sixteenth-century motets, is similarly in two sections; these correspond to those of the text. Moreover, the two identical lines of the text receive essentially identical musical settings (compare mm. 53–84 of part 1 with mm. 34–66 of part 2). This repetition of text and music is somewhat unusual for the period; most sixteenth-century motets are **through-composed**: each section employs new music, without any substantial repetitions or restatements of previously heard material.[10]

In addition to considering form at the large scale, we can speak of form at smaller levels, that is, within each of the two sections of the motet. Even at the local level, the musical form reflects that of the text. For instance, lines 1 and 2 of the text each present complete ideas in the original Latin; that is, each is a self-contained clause. The same is true of the music for these two lines, which falls into two distinct sections of different types. Line 1, as we have seen, is set antiphonally—sung once by the upper voices, once by the lower ones. Line 2 is then sung by all six voices together (mm. 12–17). The entry of line 2 is also marked by a change of texture: the antiphony of line 1 is replaced by six-part homophony. The change of texture thus articulates the beginning of a new segment of the musical form. Subsequently, the shift to imitative texture in measure 18 articulates the beginning of another segment.

Another element of musical rhetoric arises through musical **declamation**: the music reflects the rhythm and accentuation of the words as these would occur in spoken language. We tend to think of accentuation as a matter of volume or dynamics: an accented note or word is one that is sung more loudly than another. But this motet, like most of the music we shall study, contains no

---

[9]A piece, or a section of a piece, constructed through exact imitation is called a **canon**.

[10]The repeated final line of poetry and music could be considered an example of a refrain, an idea from popular song employed in various Renaissance and Baroque genres; for an example from early opera, see the anthology, Selection 6b (the lines beginning "Ahi, caso acerbo," from Monteverdi's *Orfeo*).

written dynamics or accent marks. Nor did performers necessarily stress the first note of each measure; indeed, the notation of the piece as originally printed lacked barlines altogether.[11]

Musical declamation in Renaissance and Baroque music is a product of the rhythms and melodic contours used to set particular words. For example, most of the words in lines 1–2 receive a **syllabic** setting, a single note falling on each syllable. Syllables that would be accented in spoken Latin often receive longer note values, as does the first syllable of *erant* ("were") in measure 12.[12] Other accented syllables fall on relatively high notes or are preceded by leaps. Thus, on the accented third syllable of *complerentur* (m. 3), the cantus and altus each ascend by a step, while the tenor descends by a fifth (a leap). An accented syllable can be further highlighted by a **melisma**: a series of notes sung to the same syllable. This occurs first on the word *dies* ("day") in measures 3–4, and again on *dicentes* ("saying") in measures 15–17. Longer melismas occur later on *alleluja*, further emphasizing that word.

Our analysis of the musical form suggests that Palestrina must have considered the text grammatically before setting it to music, observing where each verbal clause begins and ends. The musical form that he then produced reflects his analysis of the text. He must also have considered the accentuation and relative importance of individual words; his musical declamation reflects this. Until the mid-sixteenth century, form and declamation were the principal elements of musical rhetoric, and they remain so in Palestrina's music. But Palestrina was also concerned with the meaning of his texts, as is evident from the textural design of the first section of the motet. The text here describes a gathering of different people. This seems to be represented, first, by the use of antiphony for line 1. The two antiphonal groups of voices then join together in homophony at the word *omnes* ("all") in measure 13. A similar change of texture marks the beginning of line 3: the words *et subito* ("and suddenly") are marked by a sudden shift back to antiphonal homophony (m. 32). The focus on individual words is typical of much of the vocal music of the sixteenth through eighteenth centuries. But later composers went far beyond Palestrina in their attention to the meanings of specific words in the texts they set to music.

Cadences

We have seen how the sections of the motet are subdivided by changes in scoring (number of voices), texture, and treatment of the text. Generally, each subdivision ends with a **cadence**, which in its most general sense can be defined as a form of musical punctuation that marks the end of a distinct segment. In Renaissance polyphony the definition of *cadence* is more specific: most cadences

---

[11]Most sixteenth-century vocal polyphony was published in separate part-books, one for each voice. When scores were produced, barlines were sometimes employed in an irregular manner, but only in the course of the Baroque did the modern system of regular barlines become the rule.

[12]Some editions of the music indicate accented syllables by placing accent marks over the relevant vowels in the text.

involve the motion of two voices from an imperfect to a perfect consonance at the end of a phrase. The octave is a perfect consonance, as are fifths and fourths; thirds and sixths are imperfect consonances (all other intervals are dissonances).[13]

Thus, in Example 2.1 the cantus and altus come to rest on an octave (c'/c''); this is preceded by a major sixth (d'/b').[14] In terms of Renaissance theory, this is all that is needed to recognize a cadence; what the other voices (not shown) are doing is irrelevant. (For more on Renaissance cadences, see Box 2.1.) The Renaissance view reflects the contrapuntal character of sacred polyphony. A glance at the full score at the point in question (m. 26) reveals that, as the cantus and altus conclude their phrase, the sextus is in the middle of one and the quintus is just entering. This reflects the independence of the parts typical of sixteenth-century polyphony. Only at the most important cadences, such as the end of the first *alleluja* section (m. 31), do all six voices come to rest at the same time.

Example 2.1 Palestrina, *Dum complerentur*, mm. 24–26 (cantus and altus only; lower four voices omitted)

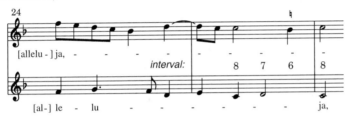

Modality

Today this motet may sound to us as being in F major. We might even analyze it as if it were a tonal composition, using Roman numerals to represent the harmonic functions of individual sonorities. But sixteenth-century musicians would have described the pitch structure of the music in another way, using the principles of **modality. A mode** can be thought of as a set of melodic principles that governs a particular tune or, in vocal polyphony, the individual vocal parts. In Palestrina's music the mode determines the ranges of the individual voices as well as the predominant notes and melodic intervals that they employ. Modality differs substantially from the **tonality** of eighteenth- and nineteenth-century music, which is primarily harmonic in nature: a system involving the qualities of chords and their relationships.

---

[13]Fourths count as perfect consonances only when they do not involve the lowest sounding voice. Thus, on the downbeat of m. 11 the fourth between sextus and tenor (d'/g') is a consonance, but the one between bass and quintus (g/c') is a dissonance.

[14]The natural on the note b' is an editorial addition to the original notation and therefore is placed above the notehead. Renaissance composers often omitted necessary accidentals (especially naturals and sharps), expecting performers to add them based on their knowledge of style; such altered notes are often referred to today as **musica ficta.**

Box 2.1

Cadences in Sixteenth-Century Music

In Renaissance polyphony, cadences are understood as being formed through the motion of pairs of voices from an imperfect consonance (third or sixth) to a perfect consonance (unison, fifth, or octave). Example B2.1a shows several such cadences.

Example B2.1a Cadences (two voices)

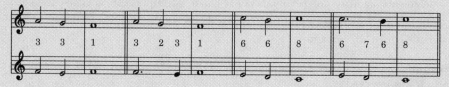

Each simple cadence can be ornamented by introducing a **suspension**. For instance, in the second cadence in Example a, the note f′ is lengthened by a dot. This creates a **dissonance**, the major second f′/g′. The dissonance then **resolves** to an imperfect consonance, the minor third e′/g′. The latter in turn completes the cadence by moving to a unison, f′/f′. This progression constitutes the most common sort of cadence in both sixteenth-century music and that of the Baroque.

Any two voices in a polyphonic composition can form a cadence. Usually, the voice pair that forms a cadence is accompanied by at least one other voice. Typically this is a lower voice, such as the bass line given in Example B2.1b. Such a bass is likely to leap by a fourth or a fifth at the cadence, as shown in the first three cadences of the example. Each of these cadences would be considered a full (or perfect) cadence in tonal music.

Example B2.1b Cadences (third voice added)

Not every cadence follows these patterns. In measures 5–6 of Palestrina's motet, the cantus and altus come to rest on a major third (f′/a′); the same is true of sextus and quintus in measure 11 (c′/e′). These major thirds are imperfect consonances; strictly speaking, then, one might not identify these resting points as cadences. But in both cases there is another pair of voices that *does* form a perfect consonance at the end of the phrase: altus and tenor in measure 6, quintus and bass in measure 11.

Modality originated as a theory of chant. Only in the mid-sixteenth century did certain composers, including Palestrina, begin to apply the theory of modality to polyphony in a consistent way. Paradoxically, they did so at a time when other composers, such as Lassus, were consciously writing music that could *not* be described as modal. Nevertheless, Palestrina's motet is a clear-cut example of what is known as the fifth or Lydian mode. This is evident from the melodic characteristics of the individual voices, especially the tenor (see Box 2.2).

Modern concepts of tonality were developed gradually by music theorists of the seventeenth and eighteenth centuries, but through much of that period the older principles of modality remained in use as well. Indeed, most Baroque compositions continue to show both modal and tonal characteristics in varying proportions. The exact relationship between modality and tonality remains a point of contention among scholars. We can think of modality and tonality as two different systems, each useful for analyzing different aspects of a given composition. Whereas modality is helpful in describing the individual vocal parts of Palestrina's music, we shall use the more familiar language of tonality to analyze most of the later music that we shall encounter.

Lassus

Rolande de Lassus (1530/2–94), also known as Orlando di Lasso, was, with Palestrina, one of the two most renowned and influential composers of the sixteenth century. Although almost exact contemporaries, the two led very different careers and wrote different types of music. Whereas Palestrina worked all his life in and around Rome, Lassus was born in northern France and held a series of positions in France and Italy before becoming a singer and eventually music director for the duke of Bavaria, at Munich, in southern Germany. In addition to writing sixty masses and hundreds of motets, he also wrote substantial numbers of secular works: Italian madrigals, French chansons, and German part-songs or lieder. The linguistic and stylistic diversity of his output reflects his international career, reminiscent of that of earlier northern composers such as Josquin des Prez. It must also reflect to some degree his cosmopolitan and gregarious nature, seemingly quite different from Palestrina's. We have some evidence about Lassus's personality from his surviving letters to the Bavarian dukes, from which we learn that he had a lively wit. He was not above taking roles in staged comedies, in which he must have acted as well as sung.

Lassus's Music

The great extent and diversity of Lassus's output makes generalizing about it difficult. He was capable of the most refined contrapuntal writing in the style now associated with Palestrina, whose madrigal *Io son ferito* he made the basis of one of his own cyclic masses (Palestrina never returned the favor). On the other hand, some of his secular works adopt a simple, direct style in keeping with their humorous and sometimes bawdy texts.

His contemporaries and followers noted Lassus's particular concern for musical rhetoric. Indeed, the vivid musical rhetoric of some of his works, particu-

BOX 2.2

Modes in Sixteenth-Century Music

A **mode** can be thought of as a way of describing the melodic behavior of a chant or of any one part (voice) in a polyphonic composition. When we say that a melody is in a mode, we imply that it forms cadences to certain notes and that it emphasizes certain melodic intervals.

A **key** (or **tonality**) is a way of describing the harmony and form of a polyphonic or homophonic composition. When we say that a piece is in a key, or that it is tonal, we imply that it forms cadences to certain chords and that it uses certain recurring chord progressions.

- Most but not all Gregorian chant is modal.
- Most medieval polyphony is neither clearly modal nor clearly tonal.
- Renaissance polyphony usually shows some aspects of both tonality and modality.
- Baroque, Classical, and Romantic works are usually tonal.

THE MODES IN CHANT

Western theories of modality originated in relation to Gregorian chant, a type of medieval sacred song used in the Roman Catholic liturgy and consisting of unaccompanied melodies for a solo voice or for several voices singing in unison. The mode of a chant melody is determined from (a) its last note or **final,** (b) its range, and (c) its principal melodic intervals and cadence points. Most chant melodies move within the range of an octave. If the highest note lies an octave above the final—that is, if the melody moves largely *above* the final—the mode is said to be **authentic.** If the highest note lies a fifth above the final—that is, if the melody tends to move on both sides of the final—then the mode is **plagal.**

Medieval chant theory recognized eight modes: four authentic and four plagal, using the finals d, e, f, and g. It is possible to think of each mode as a diatonic scale, as shown below. Each mode can be referred to by either a number or a Greek name. In each case, the final is shown in italics.

1. Dorian:	d	e	f	g	a	b	c′	d′
2. Hypodorian:	A	B	c	d	e	f	g	a
3. Phrygian:	e	f	g	a	b	c′	d′	e′
4. Hypophrygian:	B	c	d	e	f	g	a	b
5. Lydian:	f	g	a	b	c′	d′	e′	f′
6. Hypolydian:	c	d	e	f	g	a	b	c′
7. Mixolydian:	g	a	b	c′	d′	e′	f′	g′
8. Hypomixolydian:	d	e	f	g	a	b	c′	d′

The final is only one of several notes on which phrases are likely to end; other such *cadence points* may be the third or fifth above the final. In addition, a chant in a given mode will tend to repeat or outline certain melodic intervals. For example, a chant in mode 5 will frequently leap between f and c′ or trace melodic lines rising or falling between those two notes.

THE MODES IN RENAISSANCE POLYPHONY

During the sixteenth century, Palestrina and his contemporaries often wrote motets and other polyphonic works that represent specific modes. In such works, each voice follows the melodic principles outlined above for Gregorian chant and thus possesses its own mode. The mode of the composition as a whole is considered to be that of the tenor.

Thus, in the first part of Palestrina's motet *Dum complerentur*, the tenor ends on the note f and has the range f–g′. Another frequently occurring cadence point in this voice is c′ (as at the end of part 2). The tenor, and therefore the entire motet, can be assigned to mode 5. The work is notated with what we would call a key signature of one flat, but this is not considered to affect the mode of the composition, so long as the final is f. (In other cases, however, a signature indicates a *transposed* mode; for example, a work with a signature of one flat whose tenor ends on g might be in the Dorian mode transposed from d to g.)

The cantus (soprano) and quintus (tenor 2) are also in mode 5. The quintus moves in the same range as the tenor, and the cantus lies an octave higher. The altus and sextus (alto 2) are in the plagal version of this mode, that is, mode 6. They move a fifth above the tenor but have the same final. The bassus moves in the same mode as altus and sextus, an octave below them.

In addition to the eight modes of chant, some Renaissance theorists recognized four more modes. These correspond to the modern major and natural minor modes, but they were referred to by Greek names:

9. Aeolian:	*a*	b	c′	d′	e′	f′	g′	a′
10. Hypoaeolian:	e	f	g	*a*	b	c′	d′	e′
11. Ionian:	*c′*	d′	e′	f′	g′	a′	b′	c″
12. Hypoionian:	g	a	b	*c′*	d′	e′	f′	g′

Not every Renaissance work can be assigned to a mode. Lassus's *Timor et tremor* is not clearly modal or tonal, although portions of it might be considered one or the other. Baroque composers sometimes retained the traditional modal labels in their titles, but such music can often be described as well in terms of common practice tonality.

larly his motets, had as great an influence on later musicians as did Palestrina's counterpoint. Apart from the greater variety of his output, Lassus is distinct from Palestrina in the more individual character of his melodic and rhythmic ideas, which seem more frequently to reflect the meaning as well as the rhythm of the words. Hence Lassus's music tends to give the impression of being more rhetorical than Palestrina's, especially in the more declamatory nature of many of this settings. In general, homophonic textures are better suited to effective declamation of a text than are contrapuntal ones, and thus homophonic textures are probably more frequent in Lassus's music. But complex imitative counter-

Figure 2.1 Orlando di Lassus, *Patrocinium musices: Missae aliquot quinque vocum* (Munich: Adam Berg, 1589), title page. BY PERMISSION OF THE BRITISH LIBRARY. This elaborate title page is typical of late-Renaissance printed collections of vocal polyphony. In the borders around the title are the heraldic arms of the pope, emperor, and other European rulers; those of Lassus's patron, the Duke of Bavaria, are at the center, immediately above a picture probably meant to depict the musicians of his chapel. They are performing from the part books lying open on the table; the seated player at the keyboard instrument (a virginal) is possibly intended to be Lassus, while the two boys just behind the table are probably singers. Other instruments include flute, cornettos, trombones, lute, and viols. Although this suggests that Lasso's sacred music might be performed by some such mixed vocal and instrumental ensemble, pictures on title pages and elsewhere do not always depict realistic scenes or actual practices.

point is by no means rare, particularly in his sacred works. Early in his career he wrote a few stylistically radical works that anticipate certain extreme music-rhetorical devices used by Gesualdo and other composers at the end of the century. There are hints of this tendency in the work considered below, but in general Lassus avoided the types of exaggerated musical expression that came into fashion toward the close of the sixteenth century.

The Motet *Timor et tremor*

This motet (anthology, Selection 2) is a famous example of Lassus's heightened concern with musical rhetoric. First published in 1564, early in Lassus's Munich period, it was presumably composed for performance in the Bavarian court chapel. Like all sixteenth-century motets, it is ostensibly for voices only, but it is likely that some of the six vocal parts were sometimes doubled or replaced by instruments. A painting in an illuminated manuscript by the Bavarian court painter Hans Mielich shows Lassus seated at a harpsichord, surrounded by players of recorders, violas da gamba, sackbuts (trombones), and other instruments. A similar picture graces the title page of a 1589 collection of Lassus's masses (Fig. 2.1).[15] Although an ensemble of this sort would not have performed in

Figure 2.2 Octave virginal by Onofrio Guarracino, Naples, 1694. America's Shrine to Music Museum, Vermillion, South Dakota. Purchase funds gift of Margaret Ann and Hubert H. Everist, Sioux City, Iowa, 1997 (no. 6041). This small virginal, sounding an octave above written pitch, is an example of the type of keyboard instrument shown in Figure 2.1. Photograph by Simon Spicer.

[15]For a reproduction of the Mielich picture, see James Haar, "Orlande de Lassus," in Gustave Reese et al., *The New Grove High Renaissance Masters* (New York: Norton, 1984), 183; further discussion in George Kubler, *Studies in Ancient American and European Art* (New Haven: Yale University Press, 1985), 184–8.

every piece, such music making must have made an impression on the Venetian composer Giovanni Gabrieli, who worked at Munich during the 1570s and later wrote an equally original setting of the text of *Timor et tremor*, also in six voices.

The text is a compilation of fragments from the Book of Psalms; like the text of Palestrina's motet, it is divided into two parts (see anthology). It constitutes a prayer for protection and comfort; the final line *non confundar* implies something like: "do not confuse [or distress] me by failing me in my hour of need." Each half of the text falls into two distinct sentences, the second of which directly addresses the deity as "Lord" (*Domine*). This grammatical structure is emphasized in Lassus's setting, which closely reflects the form and speech rhythms of the text. Both the grammatical divisions and the accentuation of individual syllables are marked musically in ways described earlier for Palestrina. Lassus also finds vivid ways of responding musically to the specific content of text phrases and individual words.

At the very beginning, the six voices repeat the three opening words in a predominantly homophonic texture. This already suggests a highly rhetorical approach to the text; the first three words do not even form a complete clause, comprising just two nouns joined by the conjunction *et* ("and"). By repeating the three words as a unit, the music suggests that they are of special significance, the main subject of the entire work. Musical highlighting of an opening textual phrase would remain an important device in the Baroque, although the exact musical means by which the emphasis is accomplished would be quite different.

Cross Relations and Chromaticism

Lassus's music not only articulates the words of the text distinctly; it also represents their meaning. A vivid example of this occurs at the beginning of the motet, where the alto is heard alone, then is joined by the other voices. Together, the six voices form a C-major chord that lasts through the first half of measure 3. At that point, however, where the five lower voices sing the word *tremor*, the sonority changes to an A-major chord. Lassus and his contemporaries would not have described the passage in such a manner; instead, they might have pointed to the **cross relation** that occurs in measure 3: the note C in the first half of the measure (alto and bass) is followed immediately by C♯ in the second half (sextus). Cross relations are similar to the *chromaticism* encountered later in the piece (see below); both devices involve the juxtaposition of "natural" notes against notes altered by accidentals. In a cross relation, the juxtaposition involves two (or more) different voices; in extreme cases the two forms of the note may even be sounded simultaneously.[16]

---

[16]For an example of a simultaneous cross relation, see J. S. Bach, Cantata 127 (anthology, Selection 19), third movement, m. 2, where the oboe sounds a♮' against the second recorder's a♭".

Text Painting

Cross relations are unusual in sixteenth-century music, within whose largely diatonic structure they sound strange and abnormal. In addition, they negate the sense of mode, for no modal scale contains both natural and sharp versions of the same note. Hence, cross relations were considered appropriate to words describing abnormal or negative feelings or ideas—including our word *tremor* ("trembling"). Lassus's use of a cross relation at this point is therefore an example of **text painting** or **word painting**: the use of music to represent the meaning of an individual word or phrase in the sung text. Lest there should be any doubt that Lassus intended to draw an association between the extreme emotion of the text and the cross relation in the music, the latter is repeated in measure 6. There the note B♭ on the downbeat (cantus and sextus) is juxtaposed with B♮, again on the word *tremor* (alto).

Virtually any musical device can serve the purposes of word or text painting when used in an appropriate context. In the Palestrina motet, the entrance of all the voices on the word *omnes* ("all") was another example. The present motet contains many further examples. Text painting is a part of musical rhetoric, and as such it is an important aspect of music composed throughout the late Renaissance and Baroque.

Musical Rhetoric in Lassus's Motet

The arresting opening of this motet sets the tone for the whole work; it tells us that this is to be a highly rhetorical composition paying close attention to each significant word in the text. Indeed, the music proceeds as a series of short phrases, each employing one or more devices of musical rhetoric to reflect specific words or expressions in the text (for a list of such devices, see Box 2.3). In considering the use of musical rhetoric within any piece, it is important not to be misled by chance details. For example, the tenor has a rising melisma on the word *tremor* in measure 7. But the brief melisma should not be understood as a rhetorically significant underlining of the word; it occurs only once, hidden within one of the inner voices. This melisma seems to serve mainly a rhythmic function, helping to propel the music forward to the cadence that the tenor forms with the sextus on the following downbeat.

On the other hand, the motet closes with a passage containing numerous repetitions in all six voices of the two words *non confundar* ("do not confound me"; see part 2 of the motet, mm. 28–43). The many repetitions of these words constitute a rhetorical device, a way of emphasizing this phrase of the text; so too does the uniformly syllabic setting of the words. But the most vivid aspect of the musical rhetoric here is the text's musical painting, which takes two forms. First, there are two instances of **chromaticism**: the successive use of natural and altered forms of a note within a single voice. Thus at measure 30 the cantus moves from g' to g♯'; the sextus imitates this in the following measure, moving from d' to d♯'. Like the cross relations at the beginning of the work, chromaticism sounds strange in the context of sixteenth-century style and thus

---

Box 2.3

Devices of Musical Rhetoric

Devices that articulate form
   Cadences marking the ends of sections and subsections
   Changes of texture or scoring at the beginnings of sections
   Rests that separate words or larger units of the text

Devices for declamation of the text
   High or long notes on accented syllables
   Short notes on unaccented syllables
   Leaps before accented syllables
   Melismas on accented syllables
   Homophonic texture to emphasize words or expressions
   Repetition of words or expressions

Devices that reflect the meaning of words (text painting)
   Chromaticism
   Upward or downward motion
   Small as opposed to large note values (lively versus sustained motion)
   Melismas on such words as "sing," "fly"
   Unusual rhythms or melodic intervals

---

was appropriate for a word that means something like "confuse" or "confound." Beginning at measure 33, a different device represents the same word: for seven measures the cantus sings against the beat; almost every note is syncopated or tied over the barline. The text here is actually a prayer *against* confusion. It is typical of Renaissance and Baroque musical rhetoric, however, that the music reflects the single vivid word *confundar*, not the broader meaning of the phrase as a whole.[17]

THE MADRIGAL: DON CARLO GESUALDO AND CLAUDIO MONTEVERDI

Composers of Palestrina's and Lassus's generation knew many types of secular as well as sacred polyphony. The texts of most secular works used vernacular languges—Italian, French, German, and so forth—and different musical styles were associated with each of these languages. Hence Lassus, who wrote French chansons and German lieder as well as Italian madrigals, employed a distinct customary style for each. Nevertheless, as the century progressed, composers of secular music tended to adopt the rhetorical and contrapuntal artifice of sacred

---

[17]One might argue, on the other hand, that the unusual musical devices in this section of the motet represent unusual emotional urgency rather than a response to the single word *confundar*.

music. This was particularly true in the **madrigal**, a polyphonic setting of any of various types of Italian poetic text, usually short and lyrical.

Today the word *madrigal* is sometimes used indiscriminately for all sorts of Renaissance polyphony. But it is best applied only to the original Italian genre and its imitations in other countries, especially England. Madrigals are thought to have been usually intended for performance with a single voice on each part; as in sacred polyphony, instruments might substitute for one or more voices. The madrigal continued as an important genre well into the seventeenth century, but its musical characteristics by then were greatly changed. What remained constant, however, was the use of poetry that revealed a high level of diction and craft—that is, not folk poetry (or pseudo-folk poetry) as in more popular genres such as the *villanesca*, and not a strophic song such as the *canzonetta*, in which successive stanzas or verses are sung to the same music.[18] The musical settings of madrigals are accordingly elevated in style, taking particular care for musical rhetoric. For this reason madrigals are **through-composed**: music within a madrigal is rarely repeated, and the same music is almost never used for different words.

The madrigal, like other types of sixteenth-century song, originally played an important role in amateur and domestic music making. During the middle decades of the sixteenth century it was fashionable to sing polyphonic songs as a form of after-dinner entertainment, and in Italy and elsewhere educated members of the upper classes were expected to be able to sing such music at sight during social gatherings. The enjoyment of these songs lay as much in the words as in the music; as in the motet, a major attraction of the polyphonic madrigal lay in the graceful melding of music and text. Among the composers of such madrigals were Jacopo Arcadelt (ca. 1505–68) and Cipriano da Rore (1516–65), northern (Netherlandish) musicians whose popular four-part madrigals composed in the 1530s and 1540s continued to be reprinted and performed into the early seventeenth century.

In the course of the sixteenth century, however, the musical rhetoric of the madrigal, at first relatively restrained, became increasingly intense. In addition, the vocal requirements of the music became more demanding: the ranges of the individual parts widened, and composers increasingly wrote out melodic embellishments that had previously been heard only as improvised additions to the written parts.[19] As a result, the madrigal gradually moved out of the sphere of amateur music making and into that of the professional. By the end of the sixteenth century the most important of these works were being performed not by cultivated amateurs but by professional specialists attached to the courts of the aristocracy. Four composers—all but one Italian, and all working in Italy—are particularly noted for madrigals of this type: Luca Marenzio (1553–99), Giaches de Wert (1535–96), Gesualdo, and Monteverdi. We shall examine examples composed by the last two.

---

[18]For more on strophic songs, see the discussion of the early aria on p. 67.

[19]The addition of unwritten ornaments and embellishments was an important part of Renaissance and Baroque performance practice; some examples of the practice are discussed in later chapters.

Gesualdo

Don Carlo Gesualdo, Prince of Venosa (ca. 1560–1613), was technically an amateur, that is, a music lover rather than a professional musician. Such was the only socially acceptable role for a musically accomplished Renaissance nobleman such as Gesualdo, who nevertheless composed some of the most astonishing works ever written. A wealthy landowner in southern Italy, he spent much of his time at the northern Italian court of Ferrara, a center of musical innovation and experimentation during the late sixteenth century. He gained notoriety for murdering his first wife in a particularly gruesome manner after discovering her in bed with a lover (who was also murdered). Apart from this, his reputation rests on the last two of his six published books of five-voice madrigals, in which he extended the expressive devices of sixteenth-century music to the most extreme point ever reached.

Gesualdo's *Beltà poi, che t'assenti*

This work (anthology, Selection 3) is from Gesualdo's Sixth Book of Five-Part Madrigals, published in 1611 but probably composed significantly earlier. Unlike earlier madrigal poems, its anonymous text is of scant literary quality but, as in many of Gesualdo's madrigals, comprises a few brief phrases capable of conveying the extreme emotional effects that the composer evidently sought to express in his music.

The most immediately striking feature of this music is its chromaticism, expressed at the very beginning by a progression that we would describe as moving from a G-minor chord to an E-major chord.[20] As in Lassus's *Timor et tremor*, the chromaticism discourages hearing the passage in any particular mode or key; coming at the outset of the work, it establishes the madrigal's sharply painful tone. Surprisingly, the chromaticism falls on the word *beltà* (beauty), which would normally receive a more diatonic, less disturbing setting. The use of chromaticism here suggests that this "beauty" is not what it (or she) seems; indeed, this work is perhaps a contemplation of the deceptiveness of superficial beauty, even as it creates beautiful effects out of what were conventionally regarded as ugly or unnatural sounds.

Despite his radicalism, Gesualdo follows earlier madrigal composers—and Palestrina and Lassus in their motets—in setting the text in a predominantly through-composed fashion. Only the final section, presenting the last two lines of the text, is repeated, reflecting the fact that those two lines present a single thought that serves as a conclusion to the poem as a whole.[21] Despite the strangeness of much of the music, we can recognize many of the same music-rhetorical devices employed by Palestrina and Lassus. For example, line 1 and the first half of line 2 (mm. 1–4) are set homophonically; the second half of line

---

[20]Gesualdo and his contemporaries probably would have described this passage in the language of modality, speaking of a shift between the Dorian mode—transposed so that its final is G— and the Phrygian mode with raised third degree (G♯).

[21]Similar repetitions occur in earlier madrigals and in contemporary chansons.

2 (mm. 5–11) is thus set off by its use of imitation. The subject used for the latter, however, is highly chromatic, doubtless representing the word *tormenti* ("torments"). Subsequent passages continue to alternate between homophony and imitative counterpoint; the beginning of the final section is marked by the sudden outbreak of simple diatonic homophony at measure 20.

One might nevertheless conclude that the overall effects are of musical fragmentation and extreme rhetorical gestures used for their own sake. To many modern listeners it seems as if the recurring chromaticism on such words as *tormenti* and *dolore* (sadness) has become an end in itself, employed not for the purpose of real expression but simply to create a series of bizarre musical effects. There is, however, little evidence of such a reaction among Gesualdo's original audiences. His music continued to be studied and imitated well into the seventeenth century.

Monteverdi

Already by the 1590s a composer who would eventually occupy a central position in European music history was making a name for himself in the northern Italian city of Mantua. We shall meet Claudio Monteverdi (1567–1643) again when we turn to the developments that are considered to mark the beginning of the Baroque in music.

Monteverdi published his first music—a collection of motets for three voices—at the age of fifteen. By 1592 he was working as a player of stringed instruments for the duke of Mantua, eventually becoming the latter's music director (*maestro di capella*). Monteverdi published nine books of madrigals in all; Books 6–9 represent the Baroque version of the genre and depart substantially from the sixteenth-century tradition. Already in Books 4 and 5 Monteverdi established himself as something of a radical, like Gesualdo, but one with a greater interest in integrating each madrigal into a fully coherent composition. Moreover, instead of using brief texts compiled from fashionable if expressive clichés, Monteverdi retained a genuine interest in and appreciation for good poetry. When a printed attack published in 1600 accused Monteverdi of arbitrarily abandoning the principles of proper composition, he was able to reply convincingly that he did so the better to express the content of his poetic texts.

Monteverdi's *Luci serene*

Monteverdi's Fourth Book of Madrigals was published in 1603, but it is clear that by then some of the works had been in existence for at least three years, perhaps for as many as six or seven. *Luci serene* (anthology, Selection 4), the eighth madrigal in the volume, might have been composed in response to Gesualdo's Fourth Book of Madrigals, which opens with a setting of the same text.[22]

---

[22]It was common for various madrigal composers to set the same text, vying with one another to produce the most effective setting. The text set by both Gesualdo and Monteverdi is attributed to Ridolfo Arlotti, a Ferrarese poet.

The poem is relatively short and concludes with a witty twist or conceit, like other madrigal texts set by Gesualdo and by Monteverdi in his Fourth Book. Although the words refer to elemental emotions of pain and pleasure, by this date those ideas had become clichés in madrigal poetry. Many such texts may have been understood ironically or appreciated as clever variations on familiar themes. In any case, they served well as the basis for expressive or ingenious musical settings; Monteverdi's setting gives this brief text a monumentality that its poet could hardly have expected.

In some respects, much of what Monteverdi does here is familiar from earlier sixteenth-century vocal polyphony. Each poetic line or other unit of the text is distinguished by particular textures and melodic ideas, and the more vivid images of the poem receive the expected text painting. Especially notable among the latter are the noun *foco* ("fire") and the verb *strugge* ("melt, be consumed") in lines 8 and 9. These are represented through a lively twisting or turning figure (tenor, m. 42) and a syncopated rhythm (tenor, m. 44), respectively. Even the first word of the text is "painted": on the word *luci,* here a poetic word for "eyes," singers would have seen in their parts two semibreves, equivalant to whole notes; these were understood as symbols for two eyes, a convention established by earlier madrigal composers.

Yet Monteverdi's musical rhetoric goes deeper than conventional text painting. He separates the first word of the poem—the eyes of the beloved, which the poet addresses in lines 1–3—from the rest of the music. This is accomplished through the homophonic chordal setting of the word *luci* on long notes followed by a rest—a device reminiscent of Gesualdo's setting of *beltà,* though without the latter's chromaticism. Instead of mechanically following the division of the poem into lines, Monteverdi follows its sense and grammatical structure. Thus the end of line 2 combines with the beginning of line 3 in a single musical phrase (mm. 13–16). This phrase is sung homophonically, in chords whose lively rhythm approaches that of actual speech more closely than the declamatory passages of earlier works.[23]

Form

Monteverdi's sensitive attention to the text extends beyond individual words and phrases to the poem's overall structure, for which he finds a unique musical reflection. The poem falls into three stanzas, each comprising three lines; Monteverdi accordingly divides his setting into three sections. The first two sections have much the same music, whereas the last section is repeated with alterations, producing the musical form AA'BB'. The reuse of the A music is contrary to the through-composed writing characteristic of the sixteenth-century madrigal and is very unusual in Monteverdi's output. But it reflects the fact that lines 4–6 of the poem are a variation of lines 1–3, with parallel grammar, syntax, and meaning. Virtually the same music can be employed for both,

---

[23]Monteverdi's use of this device is often traced to the influence of Wert, who as *maestro di capella* at Mantua from 1565 onward was Monteverdi's superior there during the 1590s.

although Monteverdi transposes the repetition upward. Thus the first word of line 4, *dolci* ("sweet"), is sung to an E-major chord in measures 20–21, a whole step above the opening D-major harmony.

This transposition reflects an important discovery made by composers of the late sixteenth century: that a passage could be restated within a composition at a different pitch level. We take this procedure for granted, thanks to its common use in music of the eighteenth and nineteenth centuries. But transposed repetition is rare in works written before 1600, except in very short passages. The procedure that Monteverdi used here to reflect a particular aspect of the poem would become a fundamental compositional element by the eighteenth century.

The Artusi–Monteverdi Controversy

In 1600 the Bolognese music theorist Giovanni Maria Artusi published an attack on Monteverdi's style, focusing on the as yet unpublished madrigals of the composer's Fourth and Fifth Books. Artusi's pamphlet seems to have been a response to an earlier publication defending Monteverdi. Additional exchanges followed, the most famous installment of which was a reply to Artusi written by Monteverdi's brother Cesare. Cesare, who was a composer himself, clearly reflected his brother's own views.[24]

Essentially, Artusi objected to certain departures that Monteverdi had made from the type of counterpoint found in the works of earlier composers. Monteverdi defended his innovations as justified by the need to express the meaning and emotional content of the text. He applied the term *prima pratica* ("first practice") to the older tradition, describing his own method as the *seconda pratica* ("second practice"), although he argued that Rore, Marenzio, and others had already used it before him.[25]

Neither writer's argument was entirely sound. Artusi simply refused to accept practices that lacked the stamp of tradition—a tradition that he, in effect, defined arbitrarily as that which followed certain rules of counterpoint. Monteverdi claimed that his music was merely a "servant" of the text, as if his departures from tradition were dictated to him by the poetry. But this failed to explain the musical rationale for his innovations; if he was justified in using irregular dissonances to express "pain" mentioned in a text, why did he use one particular dissonance and not another? Indeed, why did he not simply abandon consonant sonorities altogether in such passages and write what we would call atonal music? In fact, neither side in the controversy was able or willing to see that all musical expression is governed by conventions, and that the conventions were undergoing a transition at just this time.

---

[24]Artusi's first attack and Cesare Monteverdi's reply are translated in Oliver Strunk, *Source Readings in Music History*, ed. Leo Treitler (New York: Norton, 1998), 526–34.

[25]Nowadays Monteverdi's expression *prima pratica* refers to the strict compositional technique characteristic of the vocal polyphony by Palestrina and later imitators, whereas *seconda pratica* is used for the harmonically more adventurous music of Monteverdi and his followers.

Dissonance Treatment in the "Second Practice"

Even in *Luci serene*, most of the dissonance treatment is conventional; that is, most dissonances are prepared and resolved by the same voice moving by step. Thus, in the cadence in measures 9–10, the quinto (second soprano) has a suspension: a prepared dissonance against the canto (first soprano) that is resolved by the motion of the note f′ downward to e′ (Ex. 2.2). (To review sixteenth-century cadential practice, see Box 2.1.)

Elsewhere in the same passage, however, Monteverdi repeatedly contradicts the *prima pratica*. On the downbeat of measure 9 the canto is holding the note c″, which forms a seventh with the quinto (d′) and a ninth with the bass (B♭). These dissonances are properly prepared—no cause for objection on that account. But instead of resolving these dissonances conventionally, the canto drops down by a fifth to f′; we never hear the expected b♭′ in the upper voice. Similarly, on the downbeat of measure 11 the canto's d″, which forms a dissonance against the bass's e, resolves upward instead of falling downward. Monteverdi presumably would have justified both procedures as part of the impassioned statement of the word *voi* ("you!").

Example 2.2 Monteverdi, *Luci serene*, mm. 8–10

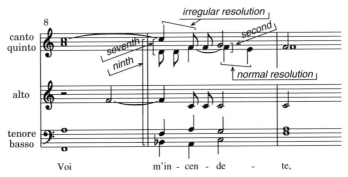

improperly resolved dissonances.

Even worse, from Artusi's point of view, is the situation in measure 53 (Ex. 2.3). The canto, whose e″ forms dissonances with the quinto and tenore, resolves the dissonances improperly by leaping downward to b′. But the latter note is still dissonant, forming a tritone (augmented fourth) with the quinto's f′ and a ninth with the alto's a. We might imagine Monteverdi's defending this passage as expressive of the canto's word *more* ("dies").

dissonance to a tritone!

Monteverdi was right in his claim that he had not invented such things. They also occur in Gesualdo's music and that of other contemporaries. Moreover, many irregular dissonances probably arose in earlier music when performers improvised embellishments. If so, then Monteverdi's *seconda pratica* might have differed from the first practice above all in that its unconventional dissonances were actually notated on the page for all to see. Despite Artusi, Baroque composers continued to commit flagrant violations of the rules of sixteenth-century counterpoint, particularly to express violent emotions or abnormal states of mind. Nevertheless, the old rules of counterpoint followed by Palestrina and

Example 2.3 Monteverdi, *Luci serene*, mm. 52–55

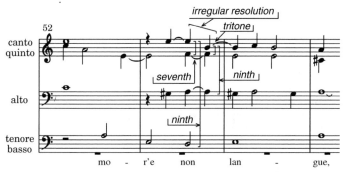

Lassus remained the basis of Baroque composition. Even Monteverdi wrote a number of old-fashioned pieces in the *prima pratica*. In the course of the seventeenth century, although dissonances were treated more freely than in sixteenth-century music, the ostentatious use of irregular dissonance treatment characteristic of Monteverdi's "second practice" became a rarity; composers had more significant innovations to think about.

CHAPTER 3

TRANSITIONS AROUND 1600

Since the early twentieth century, it has been customary for music historians to see significant changes in European musical style as having taken place around 1600. Generally these changes are described as the transition from Renaissance to Baroque style. Innovations in the works of Gesualdo and Monteverdi, as well as in music by composers whose works we have yet to explore, coincided with significant changes in performance practice as well. By the 1620s or 1630s the genres, styles, performing practices, and even the social place of music in western European culture were substantially different from those of fifty years earlier.

Yet it is all too easy to focus on a single round-number year, such as 1600, and suppose that it marked a turning point in music history. In fact, the madrigal had been undergoing crucial developments during the previous decades, and it continued to develop for another forty years; thus the years right around 1600 may not have been especially crucial for the madrigal when viewed within the complete history of the genre. The same is probably true of other genres, such as the motet. Moreover, musicians in many places continued to write and perform after 1600 just as they had done previously. If, for example, a musical revolution ever took place in musically conservative England, it did not occur until the 1660s or later, when the restoration of the monarchy (following the civil wars of midcentury) led to the influx of large numbers of more up-to-date musicians from France and Italy.

This reminds us that the transition from Renaissance to Baroque at first took place chiefly within a limited area. It initially involved a relatively small number of experimental or avant-garde musicians in a few northern Italian cities whose rulers or upper classes were unusually open to new types of musical composition and performance. For that reason, as we begin our consideration of musical developments in the seventeenth century, we shall be particularly concerned with the manner in which musical practices associated with one city or region may have spread elsewhere. In particular, we shall see that certain unusual or experimental practices of Ferrara, Mantua, and Florence were carried only gradually to Venice and Rome, and from there to France, Germany, and eventually England. On the way, moreover, these musical practices changed, so that what was characteristic of early Baroque music in one location might not so in another.

SOME GENERAL DEVELOPMENTS

Although generalities can be misleading, it is possible to list a few distinctions between Renaissance and Baroque music in most genres and repertories.

Distinct National Styles

First, whereas music of the sixteenth century was, at least in certain genres, relatively homogeneous from one western European country to the next, in the seventeenth century we find striking national differences, particularly between France and Italy.

New, More Sharply Distinct Genres of Composition

Even within local traditions, the stylistic distinctions between genres grew sharper. For example, there emerged various types of secular song for solo voice and instrumental accompaniment, each involving new styles of composition and performance; among these were the distinct varieties of recitative and of aria that became basic elements in the new vocal genres of cantata and opera. New types of sacred vocal work, such as the oratorio, also employed the new types of solo vocal writing. At the same time, new categories of instrumental music, such as the sonata and the concerto, emerged as well. Certain older genres, including madrigal, motet, and mass, as well as various types of instrumental music, continued in use after 1600, but in each case the music employs new compositional and performing techniques.

Use of Instruments

As we saw in Chapter 2, most sixteenth-century vocal music consisted in principle of polyphony for unaccompanied voices. Even in instrumental music—which sixteenth-century composers wrote in substantial quantities—the parts were often for unspecified instruments, each part playable on any instrument whose range encompassed that of the part.[1] Beginning in the seventeenth century, however, composers normally wrote specifically designated instrumental parts, and even vocal works usually contain a substantial instrumental component. Moreover, composers developed idiomatic styles of composition suited to each of the commonly used instruments, especially the violin and the various keyboard and plucked string instruments.

Ornamentation and Improvisation

In addition, composers increasingly wrote out various types of melodic decoration that previously had been left for performers to improvise. As we shall see,

---

[1]An exception exists in the case of music for solo keyboard and plucked string instruments (such as the lute).

Baroque melodies frequently incorporate standard melodic figures that had arisen as improvised additions to existing music. Sixteenth-century performers had routinely added such embellishments to their parts; during the Baroque, particularly in France, it became customary for composers to specify ornamentation with great precision, using special signs for ornaments. In short, musical elements such as instrumentation and embellishment that had once been parts of performance practice now became basic elements of composition as well. Improvisation nevertheless remained important, perhaps even more so than previously. It was, for example, an essential element in the realization of the basso continuo (see below)—and the presence of the basso continuo in most Baroque ensemble works is another important distinction between sixteenth-century music and later.

Tonality

The new approaches to composition and improvisation incorporated a freer use of dissonance—what Monteverdi had described as the "second practice" in his reply to the critic Artusi. But the unprepared dissonances and other previously unacceptable types of voice leading employed by many seventeenth-century composers were only the most striking of the many ongoing changes in compositional technique. At a more fundamental level, music was undergoing a shift from modality to tonality. Both systems remain at work in seventeenth-century music, as they had been in the sixteenth. But by 1700 such tonal practices as modulation and the establishment of contrasting key areas, which we take for granted in later music, had become firmly established, while the modes had for practical purposes been reduced to two, the major and the minor.

New Performing Practices

Some changes, such as the professionalization of performance and the introduction of the basso continuo, had begun to take effect in certain places well before 1600; the process continued afterward. Whereas the church had been virtually the sole locale for public performance before 1600, public theaters for opera and other types of musical works began to appear in the seventeenth century. Attendance was still restricted to the relatively small percentage of the general population who could afford it, but the audience for serious music did broaden to some degree, contributing to a proliferation of new genres, each with its own performance traditions. The latter included the invention of new types of instruments and new vocal and instrumental performing techniques.

Many of the new techniques were conditioned by the increasing emphasis on solo virtuosity. The range (or compass) of pitches used in both vocal and instrumental music grew wider, and many special techniques that had formerly been confined to improvised use by virtuosos became standard practice. For the first time, dynamics were indicated notationally as well, leading to greater appreciation and cultivation of such effects as sudden contrasts of *forte* and *piano* or gradual crescendos and diminuendos.

None of these changes necessarily constitutes evolutionary "improvements" toward what are now the more familiar performing practices of nineteenth- and twentieth-century music. Standards of performance in both the Renaissance and the Baroque were as high as in any period, but musicians were judged on somewhat different aspects of performance. For example, Baroque musicians in general were probably less concerned with the production of high volumes of sound than is now the case. This is because only a limited number of performance locales, such as the largest of the public opera houses of Venice, approached the size of modern concert halls. The majority of works were composed for relatively small ensembles performing in fairly close quarters. Under such conditions, the continuous, unbroken legato favored today was less prized than the clear, controlled articulation of rapid embellishments and ornamentation.

To be sure, performance traditions varied depending on time, place, and the particular genre of music being performed. Today one can find books devoted to supposed "rules" of Baroque performance, but in fact it is impossible to devise universal solutions to the questions of interpretation that arise in the many different types of music practiced during the seventeenth and eighteenth centuries. In particular, the French style of composition that emerged in the course of the seventeenth century was accompanied by performing practices very different from earlier ones in Italy. Even in Italy, early Baroque practice differed substantially from that of one hundred years later.

The Retention of Older Styles

Although most musicians (and their patrons) accepted the innovations described above, to the end of the eighteenth century many also continued to compose and perform works whose conservative style was based on that of the late sixteenth century. The selection of which style to use—older or newer—was only partly a matter of personal choice. Particular genres, especially sacred choral music and certain types of contrapuntal keyboard piece, tended to be associated with older compositional styles. The latter came to be known as the *stile antico* ("former style") as opposed to the *stile moderno* ("current style"). Most works in the *stile antico* are not, however, in a pure "Renaissance" style. They include such "Baroque" elements as a basso continuo part, and in performance they would have included current types of scoring and ornamentation; even had there been interest in older, historically authentic performance practices, little was known about them.

INSTRUMENTS

Although the music discussed in the next few chapters is primarily vocal, the role played in it by instruments is so vital that some discussion of the latter will be helpful. Instruments today are heavily standardized; an orchestra in Germany or Japan will employ instruments virtually identical to those found in an American orchestra and perhaps produced by the same manufacturer, and players will use essentially the same techniques. Things were very different in the

Baroque, when most instruments were built by hand by individual craftsmen who followed specific local customs. Consequently, although most Baroque instruments correspond roughly to those of today, there are important differences not only between Baroque instruments and modern ones but also between, say, a French violin and bow of about 1675 and Italian ones of the same period. Only by reconstructing the instruments of a particular time and place and learning to play them in period style can musicians begin to have a good idea of how a particular piece sounded. The discipline known as **performance practice** includes the reconstruction of both early instruments and their performance techniques, as well as the rediscovery of early vocal techniques. Thanks to careful work in performance practice by musicians and scholars, much is now known about the sound and, therefore, the expressive qualities of Baroque music, although much also remains uncertain.

Baroque instruments include winds, strings, and keyboards; at present we will be concerned chiefly with strings and keyboards, as these were the chief instrumental components of vocal music throughout the period (more detailed information about these and other instruments can be found in Chapters 10 and 12). Strings include both bowed and plucked instruments, and baroque bowed strings are divided into two groups: the viol and the violin families. The Baroque viol, more precisely referred to as the **viola da gamba** (often shortened to "gamba"), has six or seven strings, and its fingerboard is fretted like that of a guitar. It was built in several sizes corresponding in range to soprano, alto or tenor, and bass voices. All sizes, even the soprano—known as the treble viol—are held vertically on or between the knees; the expression *da gamba* means "of the leg." The instrument's rich but gentle tone made it particularly suited to domestic music making, and during the sixteenth century it was popular among wealthy amateurs, especially when played as part of a **consort** of three to six instruments of different sizes. In the course of the Baroque, consort use of the viol diminished, but the bass viol remained important both as a solo instrument and in accompanying others.

The Baroque **violin** family includes instruments corresponding to the modern violin, viola, and cello, all of which were already in widespread use by 1600. These were sometimes distinguished from the gamba family by the name *viola da braccio*, referring to the fact that the the higher members of the family were played on the arm (*braccio*). The Baroque instruments differ from their modern equivalents in the use of gut strings and shorter bows, and the neck is set at a smaller angle from the body of the instrument (see Fig. 12.1). These differences result in a somewhat lower level of physical tension and a somewhat quieter sound than with the modern instrument; on the other hand, they encourage a highly articulate type of playing, and the sound is still brighter and more piercing than that of the viols. These characteristics led to the frequent use of violin consorts for dance music during the sixteenth century; the modern orchestra developed from such groups over the course of the seventeenth and eighteenth centuries.

Plucked strings include the guitar and harp, both of which were much used during the later Renaissance and Baroque, albeit in forms considerably different from the modern instruments. More widespread than either was the **lute**,

Figure 3.1 Tenor viol by Gregor Karp, Königsberg, East Prussia (now Kaliningrad, Russia), 1693. Ex-coll.: Canon Francis W. Galpin, Harlow, England. America's Shrine to Music Museum, Vermillion, South Dakota, Arne B. and Jeanne F. Larson Fund, 1989 (no. 4573). Various forms of viol (or viola da gamba), a bowed stringed instrument held on the knees or legs, were used throughout the Renaissance and Baroque. Note the six strings, rounded shoulders, C-holes, frets, and fanciful scroll on this beautifully decorated example, probably made for a music-loving aristocrat (possibly Christian Ludwig, Margrave of Brandenburg, to whom Bach dedicated his Brandenburg Concertos). Photograph by Simon Spicer.

which resembles the guitar in basic form but has a more rounded body; its strings are of gut and are plucked with the fingertips. By the mid-sixteenth century the lute had become the instrument most favored by amateur musicians, with a large and varied repertory. During the Baroque it became more the domain of professionals and, like the gamba, came to be restricted to special soloistic and accompanying roles. The Baroque lute exists in a variety of sizes and shapes going by several different names; particularly important for the accompaniment of solo song was the **chitarrone,** a large lute with extra bass strings. The latter were in addition to the six basic **courses**—usually, pairs of strings tuned to the same pitch—found on all Baroque lutes. Unlike the bowed strings, which are primarily melodic instruments used in ensembles, the lute and other plucked strings are chordal, capable of producing full harmony. Hence, the lute possesses a substantial repertory of solo music. Most types of lute are quiet, making them also suitable for the sensitive accompaniment of the solo voice; they were also employed in ensembles alongside bowed strings and keyboards.

The chief keyboard instruments of the Renaissance and early Baroque were the **organ, harpsichord,** and **clavichord.** All share the use of a keyboard connected mechanically to some type of sound-producing device; the differences lie in how the sound is produced. On the organ, **pipes** act, in effect, as an ensem-

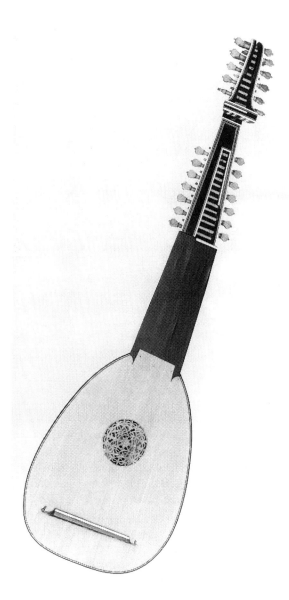

Figure 3.2 Archlute by Pieter Railich for Matteo Sellas, Venice, 1630. Ex coll.: Lord Astor. America's Shrine to Music Museum, Vermillion, South Dakota, Witten-Rawlins Collection, 1984 (no. 3383). The archlute is a type of lute related to the chitarrone; note the extended neck and the second set of tuning pegs, used for extra-long bass strings that made this instrument appropriate for playing basso continuo parts as well as solo pieces. Missing from this example are the adjustable gut frets that would be tied across the fingerboard as on the guitar, lute, and viola da gamba. Photograph by Simon Spicer.

Figure 3.3 Lira da braccio by Francesco Linarol, Venice, 1563. America's Shrine to Music Museum, Vermillion, South Dakota, Rawlins Fund, 1988 (no. 4203). An example of an instrument that fell from use after the early Baroque; the lira is held on the arm or shoulder and played with a bow. One of its uses was probably to accompany the improvised singing of poetry, a sixteenth-century practice that was a forerunner of recitative. Note the two drone strings to the left of the fingerboard and the heart-shaped peg box (in place of a scroll). Photograph by Simon Spicer.

ble of woodwind instruments; the various types of pipe include flutes and reeds producing distinct types of sonority, which the player can select through the use of **stops**, usually knobs or levers at the side of the keyboard. Organs of the period range from elaborate church instruments to small, movable chamber organs used in private homes; the larger the instrument, the greater its potential volume and number of distinct sounds or stops. The harpsichord is a stringed keyboard instrument; each key moves a **plectrum** that plucks a metal string, making this a sort of mechanical lute. On the clavichord, the strings are activated by small metal rods, called **tangents**, which are attached to the keys. Renaissance and Baroque harpsichords exist in various sizes and shapes, but all share a relatively bright, lively sound, as compared to the clavichord, which is extremely quiet. Thus the harpsichord was used in both solo and ensemble playing, whereas the clavichord was limited mainly to private practicing.

Keyboards, like plucked strings, are chordal instruments, and like the lute they not only possess a large solo repertory but were used widely in ensembles (see Fig. 2.1). Despite the great differences between the various keyboard instruments, composers generally avoided specifying the instrument for which keyboard music was written, assuming that it would be played on whichever one was available. Most Baroque keyboard parts can therefore be played on either harpsichord or organ. Today we tend to associate the organ with sacred music, but this was not necessarily the case during the Baroque, and both harpsichord and organ were used in sacred as well as secular music.

MONODY

The Baroque interest in music for solo voice, mentioned above, produced some of the most important innovations of the period around 1600. Already in the sixteenth century, performances of madrigals and other works by a single voice with instrumental accompaniment had given increased prominence to virtuoso soloists, despite the theoretical equality of the four, five, or six voices of a polyphonic madrigal or motet. Recognizing this, by the 1590s some composers were experimenting with music written from the outset as a solo vocal line with a relatively simple instrumental accompaniment. Such music is often described today as **monody,** from Greek words meaning "one song." Although any work for soloist with accompaniment might be considered monody, the term is usually confined to the new forms of solo vocal music introduced around 1600.

The Greek term is appropriate, for many writers around 1600 believed that in turning to monody musicians were recreating musical forms that had been employed in the staged tragedies of ancient Athens: such works as Euripides' *Alcestis*, first performed in 438 B.C.E. It was believed that these works were sung in their entirety and that their music contributed significantly to the extraordinary emotional effect that these dramas were reported to have had on their original audiences. Unfortunately, only tiny fragments of the actual music of ancient Greek drama are known to survive, including that for two of Euripides' plays. These fragments were unknown to sixteenth-century writers, who in any case had no idea of how to read one or two other fragments of ancient Greek music that may have been available to them.

Ancient writings about Greek music nevertheless survived, and these were an inspiration particularly to a group known as the Florentine Camerata. The Camerata, unlike many other learned societies or academies of the day, was never organized as a formal body and had only a brief existence. But several of its members went on to play influential roles in the musical innovations of the next few decades. Meeting during the 1570s and 1580s at the home of Count Giovanni Bardi in Florence, the Camerata included the poet Ottavio Rinuccini

(1562–1621) and the composers Giulio Caccini (1551–1618) and Jacopo Peri (1561–1621), who by the turn of the century would be collaborating on the first examples of what we now refer to as opera. The central figure appears to have been Vincenzo Galilei (d. 1591), a lutenist and composer whose *Dialogo della musica antiqua, et della moderna* (Dialogue on the music of antiquity and of today, 1681) expressed many of the group's theoretical ideas about music.[2] Members of the Camerata enthusiastically embraced monody as a form of musical antiquarianism and, no doubt, because it made possible a particularly clear presentation of the sung poetic text. It was, besides, a natural extension of existing musical practices, and it proved to be of great use in opera, which, not surprisingly, frequently drew its subject matter from ancient history and mythology, especially as recounted by such ancient Roman authors as Virgil and Ovid. The new monodic music actually had nothing to do with the ancient Greeks. But such figures as the mythological musician Orpheus and the god Apollo—the divine patron of the arts and leader of the Muses—would appear frequently in the texts and plots of vocal works of the seventeenth and eighteenth centuries.

Luzzaschi

The earliest monodic works clearly show their continuity with the tradition of vocal polyphony. At Ferrara, where many of Gesualdo's madrigals were probably heard for the first time, the court organist Luzzasco Luzzaschi (ca. 1545–1607) wrote madrigals with highly embellished parts for one, two, and three sopranos. The remaining parts of these polyphonic works are quite simple and intended for performance at the keyboard. Although not published until 1601, these madrigals are thought to have been composed several decades earlier for the so-called Three Ladies of Ferrara, who had been engaged by the duke of Ferrara for the specific purpose of singing virtuoso madrigals of this type in his palace.[3] Among the earliest known professional female musicians, through their skill and fame they helped trigger a fashion for similar music elsewhere. By the seventeenth century the virtuoso soprano voice had become central to the European tradition; for the first time, too, a number of women singers achieved prominence as composers.[4]

---

[2]Galilei is well known to historians of science as the father of the astronomer Galileo Galilei.

[3]Duke Alfonso (or more precisely, his wife, Duchess Margherita) employed various women singers at different times; at its height in the 1580s the group, known in Italian as the *concerto delle donne* (consort of ladies), actually comprised four women: Livia d'Arco (d. 1611), Anna Guarini (d. 1598), Tarquinia Molza (1542–1617), and Laura Peverara (d. 1601).

[4]Important women composers of the late sixteenth century include Madalena Casulana (ca. 1544–1583) and Vittoria Aleotti (ca. 1573–after 1620), who both published books of polyphonic madrigals, and Raffaella Aleotti (ca. 1570–after 1646), who published a book of motets. (It is uncertain whether the names Vittoria and Raffaella Aleotti refer to sisters or were different names for the same person.) Among the many women composers of the Baroque were Francesca Caccini, Barbara Strozzi, and Elizabeth Jacquet de La Guerre, discussed in the main text.

Example 3.1 Luzzaschi, *O Primavera*, mm. 1–8

1 O Primavera, gioventù dell'anno,   O Spring, season of youth,
2 Bella madre de fiori,   Beautiful mother of flowers,
3 D'erbe novelle e di novelli amori,   Of fresh plants, and of new loves,

Luzzaschi was nevertheless a relatively conservative composer. Example 3.1 shows the opening of his madrigal *O Primavera* for soprano and harpsichord. It is a setting of a passage from Giambattista Guarini's famous and widely performed play *Il pastor fido* (The faithful shepherd, completed 1585), which became the basis of a number of operas during the Baroque. Luzzaschi's madrigal characteristically avoids the chromaticism of Gesualdo and other younger contemporaries; rather, it achieves most of its effect through sensitive declamation and the judicious use of written-out embellishment. For example, at the very outset the poem's opening address to spring—"O Primavera"—is repeated, the second time at a higher pitch. Both times a long note falls on "O" and the highest note is reserved for the accented syllable of *primavera*. Written-out embellishment begins in measure 4, where the note c♯" is decorated by a **trill**: a rapid alternation between c♯" and the next higher note. The trill concludes with a

turn: a downward motion to b' that results in a circling or turning motion around c♯". The trill with closing turn, which decorates the cadence to the note d" on the following downbeat, was one of several formulas used to ornament cadences throughout the late Renaissance and Baroque.

More extensive embellishment occurs in measure 7, where the voice sings a rapid scale that ascends through more than an octave, then decorates a cadence to g" with the same trill with turn heard in measure 4. It is no accident that measures 4–5 and 7–8 both mark the ends of lines of the poem; moreover, the embellishments occur on accented syllables of important words. Luzzaschi's use of embellishment is therefore not arbitrary or capricious, but rather a form of musical rhetoric, reinforcing the structure of the poem. We shall find similar use of written-out embellishment in monodic works by Luzzaschi's younger contemporaries. But unlike many of their works, Luzzaschi's madrigals retain the fundamentally polyphonic texture of the midcentury polyphonic madrigal. This texture is evident in the four-part keyboard accompaniment of the present work; the vocal part is an embellished version of the top line of the harpsichord part. It is possible that the harpsichord's unembellished part writing reflects Luzzaschi's first draft of the work, which might have been a conventional polyphonic setting for four voices in a style reminiscent of the early madrigals of Luzzaschi's teacher Cipriano da Rore (1516–65).

The Florentine *Intermedi* of 1589

Luzzaschi's transformation of a simple polyphonic texture through soloistic embellishment recurs in portions of a famous work of 1589, the *intermedi* for Girolamo Baragagli's play *La pellegrina* (The pilgrim). The latter, a comedy, was performed as part of the festivities celebrating a marriage that united the powerful ruler of Florence with one of the great French noble families.[5] An important political event, the wedding was attended by hundreds of invited guests; following custom, it was accompanied by lavish musical and dramatic productions, including *La pellegrina*. The play itself was less substantial than the six musical interludes or ***intermedi*** that took place between its acts. Independent of the plot of the play, each *intermedio* consisted of a staged scene based on ancient mythology, with dances, solo songs, and choruses in up to thirty parts. Many of the leading composers of the day, including Caccini and Peri, took part, as did famous performers such as the soprano Vittoria Archilei (1550–1620s or later).

Among the numerous musical numbers was one, described as a madrigal, that was sung as a monody to the accompaniment of a chitarrone. *Godi turba mortal* occurs in the sixth and last *intermedio* (Ex. 3.2). Here, earthly mortals rejoice in the harmony that Jupiter, king of the gods, has established among them. As in many Renaissance and Baroque stage works, the scene could be readily interpreted as a positive reflection on the local ruler (the duke of Florence). The short poem was by Rinuccini; the music is by Emilio de' Cavalieri (ca.

Figure 3.4 The sixth and final *intermedio* from *La pellegrina*, engraving by Epifano d'Alfano after Bernardo Buontalenti, from Raffaello Gualtarotti, *Descrizione del regale apparato* (Florence, 1589). This is an idealized depiction of the work's actual performance as part of the Medici wedding festivities of 1589. In this scene, musicians representing Jupiter's gift of harmony and rhythm to earthly mortals descended from the clouds, a spectacular effect achieved through ingenious stage machinery.

1550–1602). Rinuccini had been a member of the Florentine Camerata; in 1600 Cavalieri would write a work now considered the earliest oratorio.[6]

Like Luzzaschi's *O Primavera*, the present composition consists of an embellished vocal part accompanied by four unspecified instrumental parts, the highest of which again comprises a simple unembellished version of the vocal line. More than in Luzzaschi's music, however, the embellishment includes a number of figures whose rhythmic diversity reflects Baroque than Renaissance ideals of melodic decoration. For example, the rising dotted figure at the opening (g″–a″–b♭″) is an upward slide of the type that Caccini called an *intonazione* (see below). In measures 2 and 6, the eighth-note motion is sharpened by dotted rhythms in both long-short and short-long patterns. Perhaps most surprising of all is the eighth rest in measure 13, which cuts off what seems to be the beginning of a written-out trill (e♭″–f″). The interruption of such a standard ornament is highly unusual. The dramatic gesture is apparently a bit of text painting on the word *acqueta* (cease)—although the same word is immediately repeated and sung to a climactic melisma (mm. 15–17).

---

[6]*Rappresentatione di anima et di corpo* (The drama of the soul and the body). On Baroque oratorio, see Chapters 7 and 9.

Example 3.2 Cavalieri, *Godi turba mortal*, from Intermedio VI for *La pellegrina* (complete). Text by Ottavio Rinuccini.

1 Godi, turba mortal felice e lieta,   Rejoice, fortunate and happy
                                          mortal gathering,
2 Godi di tanto dono,   Rejoice in this gift,
3 E col canto e col suon   And with singing and playing
4 I faticosi tuoi travagli acqueta.   Break off your difficult labors.

Caccini

A more decisive break with the past can be seen in the music of Giulio Caccini. Together with Jacopo Peri (1561–1633), Caccini is usually credited with
composing the first operas. *Dafne*, composed by the two in collaboration, was
performed in 1598, and each wrote a setting of *Euridice* in 1600.[7] The librettos of all three works were by Rinuccini, and each of the two musicians had
participated in the Florentine *intermedi* of 1589 as both composer and singer.

In many respects the operas of Caccini and Peri, composed for princely gatherings at Florence, had more in common with the old *intermedio* than with later
opera. But Caccini was insistent in declaring himself the inventor of a new type
of music, and in 1601 he published a collection of monodic songs that he called
Le nuove musiche (literally, The new musics). Indeed, both composers were now
writing music that originated as monody for voice and accompaniment, not as
a polyphonic madrigal that was then embellished in virtuoso style. Moreover,
both composers employed distinct types of monody that we now recognize as
recitative and aria, respectively. These two types of monody became the basis
of seventeenth-century solo song.

Le nuove musiche

Giulio Caccini's collection of 1601, like most publications of the period, was
probably the product of many years' work. Hence the music in it may not have
been entirely new at the time of publication, and by 1601 many singers may
have been performing and composing similar music. During the next few
decades large numbers of comparable publications appeared; among the many

---

[7] Only fragments survive of the music for *Dafne*. Peri appears to have been the chief composer.

composers to take up the style was Caccini's daughter Francesca (1587–after 1640), who published her own collection of solo songs in 1618.

Caccini's collection is distinguished by its introduction to the reader, in which the composer offers a theoretical justification for the new style and explains certain aspects of his manner of singing.[8] Referring to the ancient Greek philosopher Plato, Caccini claimed that monodies were uniquely suited to meeting the requirement that vocal music should set forth its text in a clear and effective manner; this had been a doctrine enunciated within the Florentine Camerata. Caccini criticized other singers' use of improvised embellishments, which sometimes obscured the words. Yet he also described various types of ornament that he used in his own singing to intensify the effects of certain words.

Some of these ornaments are written out in Caccini's music. Others were to be added by the singer at appropriate moments. A number of Caccini's written-out decorations are identical to ones used by Luzzaschi and Cavalieri. Among these are the trill with closing turn and the upward slide, which we have already seen in Examples 3.1 and 3.2; Caccini's names for these were *groppo* and *intonazione*, respectively, terms that continued to be used throughout the seventeenth century. Unwritten devices mentioned by Caccini include various types of dynamic swell (*esclamazione*), used for expressive purposes on sustained notes, and the *trillo*, which despite its name is not a trill but a rapidly repeated note or perhaps an intense type of vibrato, sung most often on the penultimate note of a cadence. Although rarely indicated in notation, these devices must have been in wide use by singers after 1600, if not before.

Caccini's preface was only the first of many important Baroque writings on vocal performance practice. Others include the *Remarques curieuses sur l'art de bien chanter* (Paris, 1668) by Bénigne de Bacilly, a French musician of the mid-seventeenth century, and Pier Francesco Tosi's *Opinioni de' cantori antichi, e moderni* (Bologna, 1723), an influential work that was translated into English and German.[9] Each such treatise applies to a particular style and repertory; there never was any one type of "Baroque" vocal technique or method of interpretation. Bacilly is relevant chiefly to French vocal music of the mid-seventeenth century, whereas Tosi's focus is eighteenth-century Italian opera.

Sfogava con le stelle

Caccini's *Le nuove musiche* contains two types of solo songs: arias and madrigals. The arias are **strophic**: songs in which the same music is repeated for each stanza, or strophe, of the text. Such arias played an important role in early opera (see Chapter 4) and, although used with diminishing frequency in opera from the later seventeenth century, continued to be composed as independent songs.

---

[8]Translations of Caccini's introduction can be found in Oliver Strunk, *Source Readings in Music History*, ed. Leo Treitler (New York: Norton, 1998), 608–617 (selections, trans. Margaret Murata) and in H. Wiley Hitchcock's modern edition of *Le nuove musiche* (Madison, Wis.: A-R, 1970).
[9]Both works are available in modern editions; see the bibliography. Particularly useful is Julianne Baird's translation of the German version of Tosi's treatise by Johann Friedrich Agricola, a student of Bach.

The madrigals are through-composed settings of free poetry; in this they resemble earlier polyphonic madrigals, but as monodies they naturally differ in many other respects.

One of the madrigals, *Sfogava con le stelle* (anthology, Selection 5), is to a text by Rinuccini.[10] The vocal style is typical of Caccini's solo songs, which, although notated in treble clef, might have been composed originally for his own performance (he was a virtuoso bass singer). The music is written on just two staves; the lower staff takes the form of a figured bass (further discussion below). Caccini avoids both the imitative counterpoint and the exaggerated chromaticism found in many polyphonic madrigals of the same period. The vocal part is predominantly syllabic, with an irregular melodic line and declamatory rhythm meant to reflect closely the speaking voice. High or long notes are used to accentuate important syllables—notably the exclamation "o" in measure 6. We have already seen this device in Luzzaschi's *O Primavera*, which is probably a somewhat earlier work. But elsewhere Caccini often aims at a more "speaking" approach to declamation, setting whole series of syllables to simple repeated notes. Such writing would be extremely important throughout the Baroque.

In such passages (mm. 1, 12, etc.), the music can be described as **recitative**: an imitation of direct speech for solo voice and accompaniment, characterized by declamatory rhythm, a relatively simple melodic line, and largely syllabic treatment of the text. The music of recitative may sometimes seem of limited interest in itself, but its purpose is to permit a vivid recitation of the words, and it makes all the more dramatic those moments in which the voice breaks into more florid or expressive singing. This happens twice in the present work, in two long melismas that mark the ends of the first and second halves, respectively (mm. 15 and 26–27). Dramatic contrasts in singing style would be an important resource for Monteverdi, who took up the monodic style a few years later.

The Basso Continuo

The instrumental accompaniment of Caccini's monodies is notated as a **figured bass:** a bass line supplemented by numbers ("figures") and other symbols. Caccini was one of the first to publish music containing a figured bass, but within a few years the latter had become a standard element in music for vocal or instrumental ensemble. The symbols represent upper voices that a player—in this case a lutenist or harpsichordist—would improvise above the bass line. In other words, the figured bass is a shorthand for the harmony provided by the accompanist. The improvisatory addition of this harmony is termed the **realization** of the figured bass.

The instrumental part that uses the figured bass notation is known as the **basso continuo,** which literally means "continuous bass." The term probably

---

[10]A setting of a slightly different version of the poem appears in Monteverdi's Fourth Book of Madrigals, published two years later.

refers to the origin of the basso continuo during the sixteenth century as a form of instrumental accompaniment for vocal polyphony. At first, organists and other accompanists seem to have aimed at doubling all of the voices, and to this end would copy the separately printed parts into a score. But often an acceptable accompaniment could be produced by writing only the bass line and improvising appropriate upper parts; the introduction of figures around 1600 and the subsequent development of conventions for their interpretation made it easier to produce such an accompaniment. Virtually all Baroque ensemble music includes a basso continuo part, but composers did not always provide figures for their bass lines; often accompanists still had to guess at the proper harmony, using their musical intuition and sense of style.

Instruments used for playing the basso continuo included the organ, harpsichord, lute, and harp; composers rarely specified which. Any one of these might have been considered sufficient accompaniment for an intimate chamber work such as a solo madrigal; several instruments might have been employed in a large choral or instrumental work. Today one often hears the bass line itself doubled by cello or another low melody instrument, and indeed this became the regular practice in the eighteenth century. In earlier music, however, if the composer desired to have the bass line doubled by a melodic instrument, a separate part was generally provided for it.

The use of a basso continuo part simplified the composer's task by freeing him or her from the necessity of writing out the complete polyphonic texture. It also had the advantage of allowing accompanists to follow the soloist closely without being concerned with the niceties of counterpoint in a fixed number of voices. A lutenist or harpsichordist could, for example, strike a many-voiced chord under a particularly emphatic note in the vocal part (as in m. 6 on "o"), then reduce the accompaniment to just a note or two when the voice grew soft. Each instrument, moreover, could employ its own idiomatic means of varying or embellishing the underlying harmony. Thus players of lute and harpsichord could break or **arpeggiate** certain chords, playing the notes one at a time instead of striking them all at once. A swift arpeggiation might produce the effect of an accent, a slower one that of a gentle crescendo—the choice of effect being determined by the soloist's manner of singing at any given moment.

The disadvantage of this practice was, of course, that the performer had to understand the symbols used in notating the figured bass and the conventions for realizing them. These, however, are explained in a number of treatises from the seventeenth and eighteenth centuries.[11] Modern players have used these treatises, as well as knowledge of the instruments, to reconstruct Baroque traditions of continuo playing. By the eighteenth century, not only lute and keyboard players but all serious musicians were expected to understand figured bass realization, which had become the basis of the teaching of harmony. Indeed, well into the nineteenth century composers such as Beethoven and Brahms learned figured bass and occasionally used it in their compositional sketches. Figured

---

[11]See especially the works by Arnold, North, and Williams in the bibliography, which summarize much matter from the historical treatises.

basses continued to be used in certain types of score, especially recitative and sacred choral music, into the 1820s.

Modern editions often include written-out realizations of the figured bass. These are the work of the editor and thus reflect the editor's understanding of Baroque practice; many realizations, especially those found in older editions, depart from what are now understood to be the original conventions. Today, a practiced continuo player can improvise a part idiomatic to the instrument on which the part is being realized—harpsichord, organ, lute, harp, guitar, or occasionally even a bowed string instrument capable of playing multiple stops, such as the viola da gamba. Such an improvisation is likely to include rapidly arpeggiated chords and other devices that cannot be easily notated—which is why composers left the realization of such parts to the performer in the first place.

Continuo playing and the use of basso continuo parts revolutionized musical practice and composition in the early seventeenth century. For this reason, the Baroque used to be termed the "thoroughbass era" by some music historians, using an old word for figured bass. As we shall see, the basso continuo is an essential element in the larger forms of early Baroque music, to which we will turn in Chapter 4.

MONTEVERDI AND EARLY BAROQUE MUSICAL DRAMA

Opera, oratorio, and ballet were the three most important types of Baroque musical drama. Each emerged around 1600; opera and ballet developed from the sixteenth-century *intermedio* and remained closely linked throughout the following two centuries. Both differed in important respects from their later counterparts; in particular, ballets generally included singing as well as dancing and thus closely resembled operas, into which they were often incorporated. The next few chapters trace the history of Baroque operatic and balletic writing, as well as the closely related form of the cantata. Oratorio, a form of unstaged sacred musical drama, will be taken up in Chapters 7 and 9.

CLAUDIO MONTEVERDI

By 1610 Claudio Monteverdi was clearly the central figure in the new musical practices that were considered in Chapter 3. Although he seems to have had few pupils as such, his works were studied and imitated throughout the seventeenth century. We have already examined one of his polyphonic madrigals in the context of the late sixteenth century (see Chapter 2); now we shall consider his output after 1600.

Born in the northern Italian city of Cremona in 1567, by 1592 Monteverdi was working at the nearby court of Mantua (see Box 4.1).[1] He remained there, with one or two interruptions, until 1612; a year later he became *maestro di cappella* (director of church music) at St. Mark's Basilica in Venice, an appointment he held until his death in 1643. St. Mark's was the official church of the ruler of Venice, at the time the leading cultural center of Italy and arguably of all Europe; hence, in attaining his position Monteverdi had reached the pinnacle of success as a musician.

Monteverdi's initial appointment at Mantua had been as a string player, and many of his later compositions include idiomatic instrumental interludes and

---

[1]Cremona is best known today as the home of the great violin maker Antonio Stradivari (1644–1737). Both Cremona and Mantua were early centers of violin making and playing.

Box 4.1

Claudio Monteverdi (1567–1643)

1567. Born at Cremona in central northern Italy (about one hundred miles west of Venice); studies with Marc'Antonio Ingegneri, *maestro di cappella* at Cremona cathedral and composer of madrigals.

1582–84. Publishes books of motets, sacred madrigals, and canzonettas (polyphonic strophic songs).

1587. Publishes his First Book of Madrigals.

1590–92. Publishes two more madrigal books; enters service of duke of Mantua (between Cremona and Venice). Some works influenced by Giaches de Wert, *maestro di cappella* (d. 1596). Travels in Austria, Hungary, and Flanders (Spanish Netherlands) with the duke.

1601–5. Becomes *maestro di cappella* at Mantua (1601). Publishes Fourth and Fifth Books of Madrigals, both criticized by Artusi; Book 5 contains his first reply.

1607. First version of *Orfeo* performed at Mantua (lost); revised version published in 1609. Many further Mantuan theatrical compositions, mostly lost.

1608. *Arianna* performed at Mantua; lost except for Arianna's lament (published 1623).

1610. Marian Vespers published.

1613. Becomes *maestro di cappella* at St. Mark's, Venice; numerous performances of sacred music, but continues to compose operatic works and ballets, some lost.

1614, 1619. Sixth and Seventh Books of Madrigals published.

1630–31. Plague at Venice; reduction in musical activities followed by a large-scale Mass of Thanksgiving.

1632, 1638, 1640. *Scherzi musicali*, Book Eight of Madrigals, and *Selve morale* published.

1643. First performance of *L'incoronazione di Poppea*; Monteverdi's death in Venice.

1650, 1651. Ninth Book of Madrigals and *Messa et psalmi* (sacred works) published.

---

dances that reflect his string-playing experience. Yet not a single purely instrumental composition by Monteverdi survives. Like his sixteenth-century predecessors, he apparently directed his energies solely to the production of vocal music, albeit vocal music of a constantly changing nature. As with Haydn, Stravinsky, and other composers active during what we regard as transitional periods in music history, Monteverdi's works cover an enormous variety of genres and styles. Thus it is difficult to find common stylistic elements among all his many compositions. Almost invariably, however, his works show sensitiv-

Figure 4.1 Claudio Monteverdi, engraved portrait on the title page of Giovanni Battista Marinoni, *Fiori poetici* (Venice, 1644), a memorial collection of poetry issued shortly after the composer's death. The depiction of numerous instruments, some real, some fanciful, is symbolic of Monteverdi's occupation as a musician and is not intended to represent an actual performing ensemble.

ity to both the form and the content of their texts. Not only did Monteverdi use all of the traditional means of musical rhetoric, but he was also constantly inventing new devices to render each composition an imaginative and dramatic presentation of its words.

Monteverdi's Works

Monteverdi's surviving compositions from Mantua include his first five books of polyphonic madrigals, published from 1587 to 1605. These madrigals, with the exception of several in Book 5, use the traditional all-vocal scoring.[2] Already in Books 4 and 5, however, Monteverdi was employing those innovations of the *seconda pratica* that had aroused the ire of Artusi. Moreover, the last six madrigals of Book 5 include basso continuo parts, and one contains two interludes for strings, signaling Monteverdi's expansion of the madrigal to a mixed

[2]In later editions of Books 4 and 5, Monteverdi added optional continuo parts for all the madrigals.

vocal-instrumental genre. By 1607 Monteverdi had also adopted the monodic style of Peri and Caccini, employing it through much of his opera *Orfeo*, which is recognized as the first great example of such a work.

At Mantua Monteverdi also composed sacred music. Some of it is in the conservative polyphonic idiom that Monteverdi called the first practice, essentially equivalent to what was later termed the *stile antico*. At the same time, however, he was writing motets for solo voice and continuo in the new monodic style. His best-known sacred works from this period are those published in 1610 as part of a large-scale collection of music for vespers (the evening office service) dedicated to the Virgin Mary.[3]

Monteverdi arrived in Venice as *maestro di cappella* shortly after the death of Giovanni Gabrieli (see Chapter 7). Although the latter had held a different position (organist), Monteverdi effectively succeeded him as the principal musician in the leading European musical center. As music director at the city's most important church, Monteverdi was involved in a busy schedule of sacred performances, to which he contributed his own music. The latter included both small monodic works and large polychoral works resembling those of Gabrieli. But probably his most important creative activity remained in the area of secular music, particularly music for the theater.

Monteverdi's Venetian theatrical works included ballets and operas, some written for commissions from aristocratic patrons outside Venice (including Mantua). Unfortunately, much of this output is lost, although a number of ballets and related works were published in his later books of madrigals, and the two operas that Monteverdi composed near the end of his career survive: *Il ritorno d'Ulisse in patria* (Ulysses' homecoming, 1640) and *L'incoronazione di Poppea* (The coronation of Poppea, 1643).[4] Unlike his first operas, commissioned for princely celebrations, these were written for the public opera houses that had begun to open in Venice in the late 1630s. The public nature of Monteverdi's late operas helps explain their considerable differences in style and scoring from the earlier *Orfeo*. An additional factor must also be the evolution of Monteverdi's style, which unfortunately cannot be traced in detail because of the apparent loss of much of his previous Venetian output and the difficulty of dating that which does remain.

During his late years Monteverdi also published several large collections containing mainly earlier works. It is primarily through these publications that we can follow the development of his dramatic style. Among these collections is the Eighth Book of Madrigals (1638), which was actually an anthology of diverse compositions, including several short stage works. Another is the *Selva morale* (literally, "Spiritual forest") of 1640, a collection of sacred works, some

---

[3] Often described today as the "Vespers of 1610," this monumental work actually includes a mass in addition to settings of many of the traditional psalms and other texts for vespers; it has been published in several modern editions and numerous recordings.

[4] It appears that the aging Monteverdi either failed to complete *Poppea* or intentionally left portions of its score, especially the final scene (with its famous concluding duet), to one or two other composers whose identity remains controversial.

of them parodies of earlier secular compositions. Two more large anthologies followed after his death.

CLAUDIO MONTEVERDI'S *ORFEO*

Monteverdi's opera *Orfeo* (Orpheus; anthology, Selection 6) is rightly regarded as one of the pivotal works in music history. In it the leading composer of the time turned to what was then regarded as the most exciting recent innovation in European music. First performed at Mantua in 1607, during the composer's lifetime it was actually overshadowed in fame by his opera of the following year, *Arianna*. Of the latter, unfortunately, only one portion, the famous Lament of Arianna, survives.[5] Both the subject matter and the music of *Orfeo* reveal the exalted intentions of the composer and the poet Alessandro Striggio.[6] In ancient Greek mythology, Orpheus was the greatest of musicians, challenging the gods with his ability to sing and play. For Renaissance and Baroque artists he was a symbol of the power of music, and he continued to be a favorite subject of opera throughout the Baroque and beyond.[7] Box 4.2 contains an outline of the work, including a synopsis of the action and a list of the major roles.

Early Opera

Then as now, **opera** is recognized as a distinct genre for two reasons: (1) the entire text or **libretto** is sung, and (2) the plot is acted out onstage by the singers, who represent specific characters. In addition, *Orfeo* has the following features typical of most Baroque operatic works: (a) the music includes a variety of types and genres; (b) the text and plot are drawn from Classical antiquity or ancient history, involve noble and divine figures, and ostensibly point a moral lesson; and (c) the action incorporates a variety of special scenic effects, including the appearance of supernatural beings who descend from heaven or otherwise come into view of the audience by means of elaborate mechanical devices—for instance, airborne chariots suspended from the ceiling by complex systems of ropes and pulleys (see Fig. 3.4). These mechanical contrivances sometimes required designs by the leading engineers of the day. Thanks to such special effects, some Baroque operas were as much visual spectacles as musical events. In addition, they employed virtuoso singers who became the most highly paid musicians of the day. Baroque operas also tended to require lavish sums

---

[5] Arianna's lament, a monody in recitative style for soprano and continuo, was so famous that Monteverdi eventually published it as a separate work (Venice, 1623); by then he had also published his own arrangement of it for five voices and continuo in his Sixth Book of Madrigals (Venice, 1614).

[6] Striggio, son of a sixteenth-century madrigal composer, was a friend and frequent correspondent of Monteverdi's, and a member of the Accademia degli Invaghiti that commissioned *Orfeo*.

[7] Later musical settings of the Orpheus myth were written by the seventeenth-century composers Luigi Rossi and Charpentier (on the latter, see Chapter 7) and, in the eighteenth century, by Christoph Willibald Gluck.

Box 4.2

Monteverdi: *Orfeo*

Full title: *L'Orfeo: Favola in musica* (Orpheus: A tale in music).
Libretto by Alessandro Striggio, after various models, notably *Euridice*
by Ottavio Rinuccini and ultimately the *Metamorphoses* of the ancient
Roman poet Ovid.
First performed in Mantua, 1607, with the support of the Accademia
degli Invaghiti ("Academy of Charmed Ones," a sort of private social and
intellectual club of noblemen). The music for this first version is lost;
what survives is the revised version (with happy ending) published in
1609 and reprinted in a new edition in 1615.
The work consists of a prologue and five acts performed without a break.
The anthology's Selection 6 comprises portions of Act 2.

Characters

Orfeo (tenor), the mythical singer and symbol of musicians—by far the
    most prominent part

Euridice (soprano), a wood nymph (dryad) whom Orfeo is to marry

Sylvia, referred to in the score as Messenger (soprano), one of Euridice's
    companions, who witnesses her death and narrates it to Orfeo

Music (soprano), a personification of music who sings the prologue

Hope (soprano), another personification who leads Orfeo up to the
    entrance to the underworld

Charon (bass), a supernatural being who ferries dead souls across the River
    Styx to the underworld

Pluto (bass), god and ruler of the underworld

Proserpine (soprano), queen of the underworld

Apollo (tenor), god of the arts, medicine, and prophecy, who appears at
    the end of the opera to take Orfeo up into heaven

A chorus of nymphs and shepherds, several of whom sing substantial solos

SYNOPSIS

Following a brief instrumental introduction, a prologue sung by Music sets the
scene: the fields of Thrace in what is now northern Greece. Thracian nymphs and
shepherds celebrate Orfeo's impending marriage to Euridice in Act 1. In Act 2
Orfeo, having briefly departed, rejoins the celebration, initiating a series of arias.
These are interrupted by the news that Euridice has died of a snakebite. After several moments of shock and indecision, Orfeo vows to bring her back from the
dead, and the chorus laments her death.

In Act 3 Orfeo enters the underworld (home of the dead) after charming Charon with his music and passing over the river Styx. Pluto's wife, Proserpine, persuades him to grant Orfeo's wish in Act 4—if Orfeo can pass a test of self-resolve. But Orfeo fails; as he leads Euridice away from the dead, he cannot help looking at her and thereby loses her. In the original Act 5, Orfeo then returned to Thrace and was killed by worshipers of the god Bacchus, as in the ancient myth. In the surviving version of the opera, Apollo consoles Orfeo by taking him up into heaven.

for costumes, lighting, and the machinery required to transport figures on- and offstage.

The earliest operas were commissioned and produced for specific occasions, such as royal weddings, just as were the *intermedi*. This was true of Monteverdi's *Orfeo*, produced at Mantua in 1607, and it remained so through much of the Baroque in a number of other cities. For example, at Rome during the 1620s a number of popes and members of their families became regular patrons of court opera, as it is known; not surprisingly, the operas performed there employed sacred as well as secular subjects. For instance, in 1632 Cardinal Francesco Barberini, nephew of Pope Urban VIII, oversaw the production of the opera *Il Sant'Alessio* (Saint Alexis) by the Roman composer Stefano Landi (ca. 1590–ca. 1655).

The first commercial opera theater opened in Venice in 1637, and within a few years several different opera theaters were competing there with one another. The leading composers included Monteverdi and his student Francesco Cavalli, who continued to write operas for Venetian performance into the 1670s. Yet the expense of opera was such that elsewhere it remained for a long time confined largely to specially commissioned performances at wealthy courts; commercial theaters like those of Venice opened at Hamburg, London, and other cities only in the later seventeenth and eighteenth centuries. Nevertheless, by midcentury opera had been brought to other countries by means of royal commissions for special works by Italian composers: Cavalli and Luigi Rossi (1598–1653) in Paris, Marc' Antonio Cesti (1623–69) in Vienna. Italian opera—that is, opera with Italian-language text—predominated even outside Italy. But certain cities, notably Paris and Hamburg, saw the establishment of their own distinctive traditions of opera in the local languages.

In many respects, *Orfeo* differs from later operas in its proximity to the tradition of Renaissance theatrical works such as the *intermedio*. It was not composed for public performance but was specially commissioned by the Accademia degli Invaghiti, a learned assembly of Mantuan aristocrats, probably under the sponsorship of Prince Francesco Gonzaga of Mantua. Hence its first performance was not in a public theater but simply in a room specially prepared for the occasion. The room, to be sure, was presumably a large one in a noble palace. But the two or three productions of *Orfeo* that are believed to have taken place in seventeenth-century Mantua were unique events, with musicians and dancers as well as costume and set designers specially engaged for each occasion. With

more nationalism.

the rise of permanent opera companies during the 1630s and 1640s, the nature of Italian opera was considerably altered. The expensive choruses—which included dancers as well as singers—were dispensed with; so too was the large, elaborate group of accompanying instruments employed in *Orfeo* and some other early operas. Outside Venice, the tradition of aristocratically sponsored opera continued, notably at Paris. There the operas of Lully (discussed in Chapter 5) constituted in some respects a more direct continuation of the tradition begun by *Orfeo* than did later Italian opera.

Orfeo

Orfeo's publication in score in 1609 was a rarity, a mark of both its commissioned nature and the importance attached to it. Although full scores of a few other early operas also appeared in print, until the nineteenth century only portions of most operas were published, if they appeared in print at all.[8] Consequently, most surviving Baroque operas remain in manuscript to this day; moreover, they present particularly difficult problems of performance practice, making modern productions rare and difficult to achieve. As in the case of earlier published theatrical works (such as the 1589 *intermedi*), the printed score of *Orfeo* may have been intended more as a record of a special, memorable event than as a template for repeat performances. Fortunately for us, this means that the score specifies details about the original production that were not usually included in musical manuscripts or prints of the time. It shows that the first performances of *Orfeo* involved an unusually large instrumental ensemble, with varied scoring for different sections. Such information has been invaluable in modern reconstructions of early Baroque opera, even if *Orfeo* was probably a somewhat atypical example.

Although comprising five acts, the work is shorter than later operas—it contains less than two hours of music—and it was presumably performed without a break. As in later Baroque operas, the curtain, if any, would have risen at the beginning of the work and stayed up throughout. Thus scene changes would have taken place in full view of the audience, as at the end of Act 2, when the scene shifts from the plains of Greece to the shores of the underworld. Such transformations were accomplished through cleverly devised stage machinery; the resulting visual effects were among the great attractions of early opera. The accompanying instrumental music lent a magical aura to such devices.

The brevity of *Orfeo* meant that only a few characters—chiefly Orfeo himself—could be fully drawn. Moreover, the action had to be delineated through bold strokes of music and poetry. For example, the main event in Act 2 is the

---

[8]Exceptionally, full scores were issued later in the seventeenth century for operas by Lully and a number of other French composers (see Chapter 5); more typical of later opera was the publication of favorite arias and instrumental numbers, as was the case for many eighteenth-century examples by such composers as Handel (see Chapter 8). On the other hand, throughout the Baroque, complete librettos were customarily printed so that listeners could follow the text in performance or study it at their leisure, as remains true of opera today.

arrival of the messenger, who brings news of Euridice's death at the center of the act.[9] This event marks a turning point not only in the action but also in the music, which changes in emotional character, instrumentation, and style. The nature of this change becomes clear if we consider the different types of music heard in the course of the opera.

Aria

In *Orfeo* we can distinguish four types of music: (1) aria, (2) recitative, (3) chorus, and (4) instrumental passages (see Box 4.3). Act 2 begins as a series of arias, as the shepherds of Thrace celebrate the impending marriage of Orfeo and Euridice. In the late sixteenth and early seventeenth centuries, the word **aria** carried quite different connotations from its later usage. At first it referred primarily to strophic dance-songs; Caccini's *Nuove musiche* had included a number of examples. Although such songs are prominent in Act 2 of *Orfeo,* on the whole they form a relatively minor component of the work, which, like most early operas, consists primarily of recitative. Only in the course of the seventeenth century did the aria become the main component of Italian opera, and in the process it changed drastically in nature. Eventually it lost its original strophic form and became a vehicle for virtuoso display by the chief singers. The one common element of arias throughout the Baroque is that their texts are generally short—often just four lines to a strophe—and these follow simple but regular rhyme schemes (such as ABAB) as well as equally regular metrical schemes (e.g., lines of eight syllables). In this they contrast with the surrounding recitative, whose poetry tends to fall into irregular combinations of seven- and eleven-syllable lines, usually without any regular rhyme scheme. The most common purpose of an aria is to permit a character to express an emotional response to the dialogue or events that have unfolded during the preceding recitative.

Not all Baroque arias are for soloists; aria texts might be set as duos, trios, even choruses. Act 2 of *Orfeo* opens with an instrumental *sinfonia* followed by a series of five variously scored arias, presented without a break in celebration of Orfeo's arrival on the scene and his impending marriage. The first aria, whose text consists of a single stanza, is for Orfeo himself ("Ecco pur," anthology, Selection 6a). It is followed by an aria comprising two stanzas for one of the shepherds (anthology, Selection 6b). The three succeeding arias include stanzas sung by a pair of shepherds and by the entire assembly of nymphs and shepherds, singing as a chorus in five parts.

Each of the strophic arias has its own **ritornello,** an instrumental passage that is played before each stanza. Monteverdi assigns a different instrumental ensemble to each ritornello; the vocal soloists, however, are accompanied by continuo alone, a pattern typical of early opera. The arias in this scene were probably accompanied by or alternated with dancing; unfortunately,

---

[9]The messenger scene, used to avoid the depiction of death onstage, was a convention borrowed from ancient Greek tragedy.

Box 4.3

Types of Music in Italian Baroque Opera

VOCAL (FOR VOICES AND INSTRUMENTS)

Recitative

Music composed in imitation of speech, used chiefly for dialogue, narration, and action. Its *text* usually lacks regular rhyme or metrical schemes; in Italian works, recitative texts usually comprise lines alternating irregularly between seven and eleven syllables in length. Its *music* is relatively simple but irregular, avoiding recurring patterns, melismas, or sustained notes; usually syllabic in style, the music of recitative is based on speech and incorporates numerous repeated notes and other elements suggesting recitation. Words of the text are rarely repeated.

Simple recitative (*recitativo semplice*). The usual type of recitative in Baroque works, scored for solo voice and basso continuo. The term is usually applied only in music from around 1650 and later, when the type of recitative used for dialogue and action becomes notably simpler in style than the occasional, more ornate varieties described below.

Accompanied recitative (*recitativo accompagnato*). Recitative accompanied not only by basso continuo but by other instruments, most often strings; usually the musical style is somewhat more elaborate than in simple recitative. It is used for speeches of special importance.

Arioso. Literally, "in aria style"; most often used for a passage within a recitative in which the musical style broadens to approach that of an aria, for instance, through the use of melismas or sustained notes. Arioso is often used to underline individual words or longer parts of the text that are of special importance.

Aria

Song or songlike music, most often used in opera after 1650 to provide the climax of a scene, in which one character expresses an emotional reaction to the preceding events or dialogue and then (usually) exits; in early opera used more freely, in rapid alternation with recitative. An aria *text* is relatively short, with regular rhyme and metrical schemes (lines typically of four, six, or eight syllables), often two or more strophes or stanzas. Its *music* is relatively elaborate, with songlike melody often incorporating melismas and sustained notes, and rhythm often based on that of a dance. Especially after 1650 the music often calls for substantial virtuosity and may include independent instrumental parts for various instruments; each line of text is likely to be repeated several times, and the aria may have a complex formal design.

Strophic aria. An aria whose text comprises two or more stanzas having the same poetic structure, each sung to the same or similar music. (If the music of successive strophes is a variation of that of the first strophe, one speaks of strophic variation form). Strophic arias occur frequently in early opera but grow increasingly rare after 1650.

Ternary (da capo) aria. An aria whose text comprises two stanzas, often expressing contrasting ideas or emotions; the first stanza, with its music, is repeated after the second has been sung. The da capo aria became by far the most common type of aria in Italian opera of the later Baroque; ranging enormously in length, expressive effect, and degree of technical virtuosity, in opera after 1700 or so da capo arias make up the great majority of the music.

Chorus

Any music sung by the ensemble of four or more vocal parts that usually participated in early opera (and in later French Baroque opera). The music may range from brief interjections to extended settings in madrigal style or in aria form. Choruses are relatively rare in Italian opera after 1650; occasionally the solo singers join together to form a choir (especially at the end of an opera).

INSTRUMENTAL

Overture

An independent instrumental composition used to open a dramatic work. The term is most appropriate for the relatively lengthy overtures of eighteenth-century Italian operas, which can be substantial works in several movements and as such were precursors of the Classical symphony. The relatively brief opening instrumental music of early opera is more often termed a *sinfonia* or, in Monteverdi's *Orfeo*, a *toccata*.

Ritornello

Originally, an instrumental passage that alternates with the vocal (texted) sections of an aria. Musically separate from the arias' vocal passages and even optional in some early Baroque examples, after 1650 or so the ritornello is increasingly integrated with the vocal passages and may be repeated several times (in whole or in part) within the body of an aria. In the eighteenth century the term is also applied to passages in concertos and other instrumental music scored for the full ensemble and alternating with solo passages.

Sinfonia

General term for instrumental music in Italian Baroque opera, most appropriately used for transitional music played during scene changes but sometimes applied to overtures and even ritornellos.

little is known about the types of dance or choreography employed in opera of this date.

The vocal writing of all five arias is primarily syllabic, and each employs the same propulsive rhythmic patterns found in its ritornello. Hence, unlike later opera arias, these are more suitable for dancing than as vehicles for virtuoso vocal display. Each aria falls into a few short phrases, one for each line of text; Orfeo's opening aria closes by repeating its first line of text and music, producing a ternary form that we can symbolize through the letters ABA. This aria is therefore a very simple example of a type that, in expanded form, would come to dominate later opera. Although this form is of minor significance in Monteverdi's music, by the early eighteenth century arias in ternary form had replaced recitative as the main element in Italian opera.[10]

Elsewhere in *Orfeo* are two strophic arias of a different type: the prologue, which consists of an aria for the personification of Music, and Orfeo's aria "Possente spirto" in Act 3. Much longer than the simple dance-arias of Act 2, these are composed in a declamatory style that resembles recitative more than dance music. Instead of repeating exactly the same music for each strophe, successive stanzas are set as variations of the first one—hence the expression *strophic variation* often applied today to this form. An example of such an aria in Monteverdi's *Combattimento* is considered later in this chapter.[11]

Recitative

The series of arias at the beginning of Act 2 is rounded off by a short speech, still in aria style, by one of the shepherds ("Mira, deh mira Orfeo," mm. 151–64). With the ensuing arrival of the messenger, who announces the death of Euridice, the entire character of the act changes. Although the text setting remains syllabic, the regular dance rhythms and strophic designs of the arias are abandoned in favor of recitative. Monteverdi's recitative displays extraordinary originality, characterizing each role by a particular type of recitative. Thus the messenger sings in relatively sustained notes, reflecting her sadness, whereas the shepherd's brief responses to her (e.g., m. 171) are composed of quick, irregular rising and falling lines, suggesting his emotional distress. Orfeo's music is more complex, ranging from the very brief, simple phrases in which he expresses his initial shock at Euridice's death (mm. 190–92, 197–98, 200) to the elaborate lament that begins at measure 243.

Monteverdi's recitative makes much use of what he called the second practice. For example, the messenger's opening speech includes an **unprepared dissonance** in measure 165: the voice sings g♯' against bass A, neither part having prepared the dissonance by suspending or repeating its note from the

---

[10]But whereas Orfeo's entire aria comprises a single four-line poetic stanza, later ternary-form arias usually set two strophes of at least four lines each, repeating the first one at the end. Ternary-form arias of this type are often designated *da capo* arias (see Chapter 6).

[11]See also the cantata by Barbara Strozzi discussed in Chapter 6.

previous beat.[12] The unprepared dissonance is a clear response to the word *acerbo* ("bitter") sung here. The same passage contains an unresolved dissonance—the ninth d/e″ between bass line and voice—on the phrase *ciel avaro* ("cruel heaven," m. 169, second beat). Also typical of Monteverdi's recitative are the syncopated rhythms (mm. 166, 168), which seem to reflect the messenger's breathlessless in expressing her feelings. These syncopations create additional irregular passing dissonances.[13] Notable as well in this speech are the choppy rhythms and the unusual melodic leaps, including a downward seventh on the interjection *Ahi* ("Ah," mm. 164–65)', all further indicative of the messenger's emotional trauma.

A long scene composed primarily of recitative might have seemed formless. But Monteverdi (in collaboration with his librettist Striggio) included here a **refrain**: a recurring passage of text and music, which in this case helps unify the scene. The messenger's opening speech is echoed later by the shepherd and, at the end of the scene, by the chorus (mm. 265–80). The idea, suggested by the choral refrains of ancient Greek tragedy, recurs frequently in seventeenth-century opera.

To some degree, each scene is also unified by a coherent tonal structure that is articulated by shifts in key, that is, modulations. In the language of Monteverdi's time, one would have spoken of shifts between modes, rather than modulations between keys. Indeed, the modern idea of major and minor tonalities is misleading if these are understood here as being exactly equivalent to the "key areas" of a movement from a Beethoven symphony, for example. Nevertheless, we can use modern terminology to describe some of the apparent elements of Monteverdi's plan. The first part of Act 2 opens in G minor and concludes with Orfeo's second aria ("Vi ricorda i boschi ombrosi") in G major. The shepherd's speech that follows ("Mira, deh mira," mm. 151–64) is in C major; thus the entry of the messenger (m. 164) in A minor constitutes a tonal contrast to what has come before it. The contrast is heightened by the first harmony of the messenger's first speech: what we would call a first-inversion chord of A major. The bass of this chord is C♯—a note reached by chromatic motion from the preceding C♮. Later in the scene, when the messenger informs Orfeo of Euridice's death, the harmony passes directly from E major (m. 196) to G minor (m. 197), again with chromatic motion in the bass. Sudden chromatic progressions of this type had been made famous by Gesualdo, whose madrigals use them so frequently that they perhaps lose some of their power. Monteverdi wisely reserves them for the most extreme emotional moments in the opera.

Despite the above description of certain passages as being in G minor, those passages are notated under one flat instead of the modern G-minor key signature of two flats. This may reflect the early Baroque view of such music as be-

---

[12]The type of unprepared dissonance found here, in which the voice moves by step to a consonant note, is also termed an **appoggiatura**.

[13]See, e.g., the major ninth A/b′ between bass and voice in m. 166 and the fourth B/e″ at the end of m. 168. The fourth A/d″ at the beginning of m. 166 is, however, a normal dissonance prepared and resolved by the bass line.

ing in the first or Dorian mode, transposed from D to G. But this so-called Dorian notation remained common through the end of the Baroque; Bach still used it in an organ work now referred to, somewhat misleadingly, as the "Dorian" Prelude and Fugue. In such works, the key signature is not a good indicator of whether the music possesses any significant modal character; the modern conventions associating keys with particular signatures were still in the process of being established. For this reason, to determine the key of a Baroque work one must always analyze its tonal structure rather than rely on the "key" signature.

Chorus

The use of the chorus in early opera reflects that in ancient Greek drama. There the chorus always represents a specific body of characters—groups of citizens, soldiers, and so forth—that participate in and comment on the action, remaining onstage throughout. For the Greeks, the word *chorus* originally referred to an ensemble that danced as well as sang. In opera these functions were usually divided between different groups of performers, although all singers would have had some training in dance, which was considered essential not only to proper stage movement but to polite social behavior.

In Act 2 choral singing is confined to one strophe of the fourth aria ("Dunque fà degno Orfeo") and three repetitions of the messenger's lament (at m. 265 and twice again at the end of the act). These three choral restatements of the lament are thus polyphonic arrangements of recitative—odd by later standards of vocal scoring, but common at the beginning of the early seventeenth century.[14] Some of Monteverdi's polyphonic madrigals of a few years earlier had likewise included declamatory passages close to recitative. Indeed, the chorus that concludes our selection is, in effect, a short madrigal, reverting in its second portion (mm. 271–80) to the style of sixteenth-century vocal polyphony.

Instrumental Passages

Ritornellos form the bulk of the purely instrumental music in *Orfeo*. Most of the remaining instrumental passages, including the one that precedes Orfeo's aria at the opening of Act 2, are referred to as *sinfonias*. The term is the equivalent of the later word *symphony*, but in Baroque vocal works it can refer to any purely instrumental passage. Such music served to introduce scenes or even whole works—as in the overture—and to accompany stage action or changes of scene.[15]

The style and scoring of sinfonias usually reflect the character of the music and action that follows. In *Orfeo* the sinfonia for Orfeo's first aria is in the same

---

[14]Compare Monteverdi's polyphonic arrangement of the lament from his next opera, *Arianna* (see note 5). Some of Caccini's solo madrigals underwent similar arrangements by other composers.

[15]*Orfeo* opens not with a sinfonia but with a *toccata*, a word usually reserved for keyboard music but here applied to a fanfare for a five-part ensemble of trumpets doubled by the other instruments.

key and uses the same dance rhythm as the aria itself. It sets the tone not only for Orfeo's aria but for the series of dancelike arias that follows. At the end of Act 2 a solemn sinfonia for seven-part brass ensemble and continuo accompanies the shift to the underworld scenes of Act 3.

The instrumentation of *Orfeo* was unusual for the time in its diversity. Despite his exclusive focus as a composer of vocal music, as a string player Monteverdi must have known these and other instruments and their capabilities intimately. The score of *Orfeo* calls for exotic instruments such as *violini piccioli alla francese*—apparently, small violins of a type then associated with French music—and *flautini*, probably small recorders (end-blown flutes). Both are used in the ritornellos of Act 2. Also notable is Monteverdi's use of the term *viola da braccio* to specify the regular members of the violin family, which furnish the ritornellos for Orfeo's second dance-aria in Act 2. The *viola da braccio* group included the **bass violin,** similar to today's cello but somewhat larger and tuned a step lower.

Despite the variety of instrumental colors employed in the sinfonias and ritornellos, the instrumentation of the continuo part is indicated only in a few special passages. Among these is the messenger scene, where a small organ was added to the continuo accompaniment for the messenger's speeches, imparting to them a solemn or perhaps otherworldly character. The organ contrasts sharply with the harpsichord and bass violin that accompanied the shepherd (m. 171). Most of the recitative, however, may have been accompanied by nothing more than a single chitarrone, the large lute that was the usual accompaniment for Italian song in the early seventeenth century.

THE *COMBATTIMENTO DI TANCREDI E CLORINDA*

Despite his turn to opera, after *Orfeo* Monteverdi continued for at least a while to compose madrigals and even motets and mass movements in a relatively conservative style. By the time of his Eighth Book of Madrigals (1638), however, the old polyphonic madrigal, with its homogeneous all-vocal scoring, had been replaced by various types of setting for anywhere from one to a dozen or more parts. The latter invariably included a continuo part—hence the expression *continuo madrigal* sometimes used for these works. Frequently there were independent instrumental parts as well. Sometimes the latter merely furnished ritornellos for strophic arias, as in Act 2 of *Orfeo*, but increasingly they performed along with the voices, accompanying them or in some cases participating as equal partners.

In addition, some of Monteverdi's late madrigals are divided into distinct sections, and some contain dialogue and action, constituting operatic or ballet scenes. Monteverdi was not the first to write what might be called dramatic madrigals. Before the end of the sixteenth century, several composers, notably Orazio Vecchi (1550–1605), had composed **madrigal comedies**—dramatic works that employ dialogue and narration within the traditional, purely vocal scoring of sixteenth-century polyphony. The best-known such work is Vecchi's *L'Amfiparnasso* (Modena, 1594). Monteverdi's Book 8 includes two famous works that combine sung narrative with staged action; one of these, the *Lamento della ninfa* (Lament of the nymph), is a continuo madrigal in which a solo soprano sings in dialogue with three male voices, whereas the *Combattimento di Tancredi e Clorinda* (The combat of Tancredi and Clorinda) includes a string ensemble in addition to its three solo voices and continuo. Monteverdi signaled the special nature of both works by attaching to each a short preface that gives details of their original quasi-theatrical productions.[16]

The *Combattimento*

Monteverdi explains that this work (anthology, Selection 7), for three voices, strings, and continuo, had been staged in 1624 in the palace of a noble Venetian patron. On that occasion the roles of the two characters—the knight Tancredi (tenor) and his opponent Clorinda (soprano)—had been not only sung but also choreographed in a sort of pantomime. In fact, their vocal parts, although essential to the drama, are minimal; most of the singing is given to a second tenor, the *testo* or narrator. Hence the work, although not exactly a ballet in the modern sense, shared with the latter the element of choreographed action accompanied by music. It is important not only as one of Monteverdi's few surviving stage works from the middle part of his Venetian years, but also for its apparently unprecedented integration of instrumental music into a vocal setting. It is, moreover, a remarkably expressive setting of one of the great poems of the period, vividly dramatizing several of the poem's most memorable scenes. The string parts are for four *viole da braccio*—probably two violins, viola, and cello or bass violin—joined, as Monteverdi's preface explains, by a double-bass viola da gamba or violone (*contrabasso da gamba*) and harpsichord as continuo instruments. Similar ensembles became routine in later Italian opera; with the addition of extra players on each part, they became the string section that is the core of the modern orchestra.

The poet, Torquato Tasso (1544–95), was one of the leading Italian writers of the late Renaissance. A number of his shorter texts had been frequently set to music as polyphonic madrigals during the late sixteenth century by such composers as Gesualdo and Monteverdi himself, who extracted the text of the *Combattimento* from Tasso's epic poem *Gerusalemme liberata* (Jerusalem liberated, 1575). This was a romanticized poetic account of the First Crusade (1095–99), during which Jerusalem and other parts of the Holy Land were seized from their Arab Muslim rulers by western Roman Catholic nobles. In the scenes set by Monteverdi, one of the western knights, Tancredi, is in pursuit of Clorinda, a Muslim warrior. Unbeknownst to Tancredi, Clorinda is a woman in disguise; moreover, he has previously fallen in love with her. At the beginning of Monteverdi's work, Tancredi is chasing her on horseback. He confronts her, thinking she is a man, and after he has dismounted from his horse—for it would be

---

[16]Monteverdi's preface to the *Combattimento* is translated by Stanley Appelbaum in Claudio Monteverdi, *Madrigals: Book VIII (Madrigali Guerrieri et Amorosi)*, ed. Gian Francesco Malipiero (New York: Dover, 1991), xvii.

Figure 4.2 *Tancred Baptizing Clorinda* (c. 1586–1600), oil on canvas by Domenico Robusti (ca. 1560–1635), known as Tintoretto. Museum of Fine Arts, Houston; The Samuel H. Kress Collection (no. 61.77). In this painting Tancredi baptizes the fallen Clorinda with water carried in his helmet from a nearby stream, as described by Tasso in the poem from which Monteverdi drew the text of his *Combattimento di Tancredi e Clorinda*.

dishonorable for him to fight her while only she is on foot—they twice engage in combat. The second encounter is fatal to Clorinda, but as she dies they recognize one another. In that moment, Clorinda accepts Tancredi's love and is converted to Christianity; she asks him to baptize her, which he does with water from a nearby stream. Although the story may seem implausible to us, it was popular in Roman Catholic countries and was a frequent subject for painters of the time, thanks in part to the poem's metaphorical references to the Counter-Reformation.[17] Other episodes from the poem, especially those involving the Crusader hero Rinaldo and the witch Armida, would provide subjects for many later opera librettos.

The *Stile Concitato*

As Monteverdi made clear in his foreword to Book 8, he considered the musical representation of warlike action to be an example of what he termed the **stile concitato** ("agitated style"). This was accomplished musically through the use of such instrumental techniques as *tremolo*—on bowed string instruments, the rapid repetition of one note—and *pizzicato* (plucked as opposed to bowed notes). It was apparently unprecedented for a composer to specify the use of these devices, although one can imagine musicians introducing them extemporaneously in the accompaniments to earlier dramatic works, as Monteverdi himself might have done in his early years as a string player at Mantua. As in the madrigals of Books 4 and 5, Monteverdi justified his departure from conventional writing by citing ancient authors (chiefly Plato). But more fundamental than the use of these particular instrumental effects was the fact that the instruments now depict elements of both the action and the characters' changing emotional states. This went beyond their use in *Orfeo*, where the instrumental music played a secondary role, for the most part merely introducing each strophe of the arias and setting the scene.

The Musical Setting

The structure of this lengthy work—over twenty minutes long—is based on that of the poem, which falls into stanzas of eight lines each. Monteverdi selected sixteen of the poem's nearly two thousand stanzas for musical setting. As in shorter vocal works, however, he sometimes ignored the superficial structure of the poem—its division into lines and stanzas—in order to articulate its underlying division into sentences and larger units. In other words, the music organizes and *dramatizes* the text, as shown in Table 4.1.

Most of the text consists of narration. Much of it is sung as recitative accompanied only by continuo, sometimes in a very plain style, as at the beginning. Nevertheless, this recitative often has the same expressive character that

---

[17]See, for example, Figure 4.2; further discussion as cat. no. 5 in *A Gift to America: Masterpieces of European Painting from the Samuel H. Kress Collection*, ed. Chiyo Ishikawa et al. (New York: Abrams, 1994), 81.

TABLE 4.1
Monteverdi: Il combattimento

Stanza	Measure Numbers	Characters Singing[a]	Instrumentation[b]	Chief Key(s)	Event(s)
1a	1–9			d	introduction
1b–2	10–72	C, T	+ str.	D → G	T finds and challenges C
3	73–132			g	invocation of Night (aria with ritornelli)
4–6	133–219		+ str.	G	first combat
7–10	220–98	C, T		g → a → G, d → D	rest and taunts
11	299–316		+ str.	G	second combat
12–13	317–64			e → d	C falls wounded
14–16	365–445	C, T	+ str.	g → d, a → D	C asks for forgiveness and dies

[a] C = Clorinda; T = Tancredi. Narrator is always present.
[b] + str. = with strings. Continuo is always present.

we have seen in *Orfeo*—particularly in stanzas 12 and 13, where Clorinda's fatal wounding takes place. Here, as in *Orfeo*, Monteverdi reserves the use of second-practice devices for climactic moments. One might note the sudden shift to a B major chord at the beginning of the passage (dominant of E minor, m. 317)—the only occurrence of this harmony in the piece—and the subsequent chromatic progressions (especially in mm. 336–37).

Use of the Strings

Clorinda and Tancredi engage in dialogue in only three sections, and except for Clorinda's final speeches these are accompanied only by continuo, like most of the narration. Yet the strings play an indispensable role, first representing the galloping of Tancredi's horse (mm. 18–30), then in the two battle scenes that constitute the chief action of the work. In each passage the strings play motives that, if sung, would be regarded as text painting: short rhythmic figures on repeated notes to signify the horse (mm. 18–30), then swift repeated notes and other figures during the battle scenes (mm. 148–202, 299–316). The narrator sings similar figures; for example, his rapid declamation of stanza 5, much of it to repeated notes, is a vocal expression of Monteverdi's *stile concitato* (mm. 164–81). Also notable in these scenes are the recurring broken triads played by the strings (as in mm. 31–36, echoed at mm. 303–5). These are imitations of trumpet calls, used at the time as signals to relay commands in actual warfare and thus constituting a realistic detail. The voice takes up similar motives when the text refers to the sound of clattering armor (*che d'armi suone*, mm. 35–38), and we shall find similar representations of military brass music throughout the Baroque.

Another notable use of the strings, although brief, occurs with Clorinda's last words. Here Monteverdi's string parts include his original dynamic markings (in m. 366 and on the final chord), perhaps to represent Clorinda's failing breath.[18] Otherwise the strings serve to accompany her voice homophonically, rather than depicting concrete images. They create a sort of halo around Clorinda's words, suggesting the gravity of the situation. In later works, this type of setting is known as **accompanied recitative**. All recitative is normally accompanied by the continuo, but in accompanied recitative strings or other additional instruments are also present.

Arioso

Also notable is the special treatment of stanza 3 (mm. 73–132). Here the poem addresses the personified figure of Night; this rhetorical device permits the poet to insert his comments about the coming battle. Monteverdi turns the stanza into a moment of reflection, thereby making all the more dramatic the outbreak of battle that follows. The setting of this stanza can be termed an **arioso**: lit-

---

[18]Although performers doubtless would have employed changes in dynamic level elsewhere, here Monteverdi specified their use to insure proper performance of a special effect.

erally, a passage in aria style, although the term implies something intermediate between recitative and aria. An arioso passage can be as brief as a single phrase, setting a single word, or it can be a substantial section that presents an entire stanza of poetry, as in the present instance. In either case, arioso is a way of attaching some special significance to the text through the use of a more "singing" style, in contrast to ordinary recitative. Some passages in *Orfeo* can also be described as arioso (e.g., the messenger's refrain or the end of Orfeo's lament, mm. 234–37).

The shift to arioso style for stanza 3 coincides with the introduction of a new formal device: **strophic variation**. Monteverdi treats the eight lines of this stanza as if they comprised two four-line strophes, placing an instrumental ritornello before each one.[19] Thus the setting of lines 5–8 (mm. 114–33) is a variation of lines 1–4 (mm. 88–105). This is particularly easy to see if one compares the bass lines of the two passages. Apart from rhythmic differences and repetitions of a few notes, the bass lines of the two sections are essentially the same, although the vocal part diverges significantly. This was an important technique for composers of early Baroque vocal music, probably deriving from the improvised singing of strophic poetry during the sixteenth century. *Orfeo* includes two examples, and we shall examine another in the music of Barbara Strozzi (Chapter 6).

In his preface to the *Combattimento*, Monteverdi asked the singers to refrain from adding improvised trills and other figuration. But he made an exception for stanza 3; indeed, there exist two versions of its vocal part, one somewhat more embellished than the other (see anthology, Ex. 7.1). This type of setting would disappear by the end of the seventeenth century. By then, singers and composers had discovered other media for virtuoso display.

VENETIAN OPERA

Monteverdi's *Poppea*

Monteverdi's last opera is believed to have been *L'incoronazione di Poppea* (The coronation of Poppea), thought to have been performed at Venice in 1643. The libretto is by Gian Francesco Busenello, who would collaborate with Monteverdi's student Cavalli in later operas. Composed for one of the city's public opera theaters, *Poppea* illustrates the trend of commercial Baroque opera toward smaller performing ensembles: there are few if any choruses, little or no dancing, and an instrumental accompaniment perhaps as small as three- or four-part strings and continuo. Unfortunately, the work survives only in two manuscripts copied after the composer's death, probably in conjunction with productions that took place in other cities (Naples and perhaps Bologna). The two give the work in significantly different forms, each incorporating some music not by Monteverdi. This reflects a common practice throughout the Baroque; when an

---

[19]The printed edition labels each ritornello a *passaggio*; the first of these is preceded by a short introductory sinfonia.

opera was revived, music would be added or deleted to suit the new singers, and instrumental parts might be newly composed or arranged for varying ensembles. Nevertheless, *Poppea* reveals the sure hand of a veteran composer who by this date could readily draw vivid characters and organize a compelling drama, largely through recitative.

Based on ancient Roman history, the work recounts the successful effort of the ambitious Poppea to displace Octavia as wife of the emperor Nero. Nero was a student of Seneca, a philosopher and poet; he nevertheless turned out to be a murderous tyrant, and his decision to have Seneca killed is the turning point of the opera. Even more than Monteverdi's earlier operas, *Poppea* is admired for the musical characterization of the principal figures. For example, in an early scene in which Nero confronts Seneca, the old philosopher sings in calm recitative, using phrases of homogenous length, pacing, and general style (Ex. 4.1). Nero, on the other hand, sings in short, nervous phrases of changing style and meter. He seems to grow irrationally excited or enraged at the words *ma del mondo* (mm. 32–34), repeating them several times in rapid tempo, and he indulges in a sudden, sweeping scale as he refers to his own absolute power (on the word *scettro*, mm. 36–37). The part of Nero is for a soprano; it is an early example of one of the *castrato* parts that would come to dominate male roles in later Italian Baroque opera (see Chapter 8). The contrast between Seneca's low bass and Nero's shrill soprano reinforces the psychological contrast between the two characters.

Example 4.1 Monteverdi, *Poppea*, Act 1, scene 9 (mm. 10–38)

Seneca

1 Signor, nel fondo alla maggior dolcezza
2 Spesso giace nascosto il pentimento.

3 Consigler scellerato è'l sentimento
4 Ch'odia le leggi e la ragion disprezza.

Nerone

5 La legge è per chi serve, e se vogli'io
6 Posso abolir l'antica e indur le nove;

7 È partito l'impero, è'l ciel di Giove,

8 Ma del mondo terren lo scettro è mio.

Seneca

Lord, in the greatest sweetness
Often lurks cause for
repentance.
Sentiment is an evil counselor
That hates law and does not
value reason.

Nero

Laws are for servants, and if I wish
I can abolish old ones and create
new ones.
The government [of the universe] is
divided; that of heaven is Jupiter's,
But rulership of the earth is mine.

Like *Orfeo*, the work includes retrospective allusions to older style, but these
are chiefly limited to a single scene, in which several friends or pupils of Seneca
lament his iminent death in what amounts to a three-voice continuo madrigal
(Ex. 4.2). More typical of later opera is the inclusion of numerous arias for the
major characters, most with ritornellos. These arias, unlike those of later opera,

Example 4.2 Monteverdi, *Poppea*, Act 2, scene 3 (mm. 22–30)

Famigliari
Non morir, Seneca, non morir.

Friends [Seneca's students]
Do not die, Seneca, do not die.

remain closely integrated with the surrounding recitative, and the style can pass rapidly between recitative and aria in the course of a single scene. For example, in a scene in which the lovestruck Poppea is being put to sleep by the nurse Arnalta, Poppea's reprise of a flowing arialike passage (sung once before in the same scene) gradually falls into hesitant recitative (Ex. 4.3).

Seventeenth-Century Italian Opera after Monteverdi

Vocal music at Venice continued to be influenced by Monteverdi after his death in 1643, although by then his student Cavalli had established himself as the city's leading composer. Opera would play a leading role in the city's musical life to the end of the eighteenth century, but other genres of vocal music were also cultivated, including the secular cantata and various types of sacred music.

Example 4.3 Monteverdi, *Poppea*, Act 2, scene 10 (mm. 46–60)

Poppea

1 Amor, ricorro a te.
2 Guida mia speme in porto,
3 Fammi sposa—
4 Par che'l sonno m'aletti,
5 A chiuder gl'occhi alla quiete in grembo?

Poppea

Love, I run back to thee.
Bring my hopes to fruition,
Make me wife [of Nero]—
How does sleep overcome me,
Closing my eyes as I fall silent?

As Italian opera houses were established elsewhere in Europe, many followed the model of the Venetian theaters. In Germany, Spain, England, and elsewhere, opera librettos thus generally remained wholly or in part in Italian, and Italian musicians received high fees to compose and perform them. Even when the music itself was not Italian, Venetian librettos were often reused or adopted for new operas elsewhere. Older works were frequently revived, but usually in new versions, often with substantial alterations that might extend anywhere from the expansion of the instrumentation to the omission or insertion of whole scenes.

The Growth of the Aria

The single most important stylistic development in Italian opera after Monteverdi was the increase in the number of arias and their importance to the

Figure 4.3 The Teatro Grimani a San Giovanni Grisostomo (the Grimani Theater), engraving, from Vincenzo Maria Coronelli, *Venezia festeggiante* (Venice, 1709). This theater, owned by Giovanni Carlo and Vincenzo Grimani, was designed by Tomaso Bezzi and opened in 1678. Larger than earlier Venetian opera houses, it is still small by modern standards, but note the extraordinary depth of its stage, which made possible impressive perspective effects.

drama. In the operas of his younger contemporaries (especially Cavalli), recitative remains the usual style for the most important speeches of the principal characters, as well as for action. Most arias remain short and dancelike, many being sung by minor figures in the drama. But almost every scene now contains at least one aria or arialike passage, and with time the arias grow increasingly varied, serving to reflect the changing emotional states of the major figures.

The dramatic function of these arias is still very different from that in eighteenth-century opera, where each aria tends to be a large virtuoso set piece that serves as the climax of a scene. Instead, in Venetian opera of the mid-seventeenth century each scene typically contains a fluid alternation between recitative and aria, as in *Poppea*. Sometimes single lines of poetry within a recitative may be set in aria style, that is, as arioso; a favorite device is to repeat such a line at several points within a scene as a sort of refrain, as we have seen in Act 2 of *Orfeo*. The most memorable scenes in mid-seventeenth-century Italian opera often remain lengthy monologues sung in recitative by major characters. But other types of substantial solo occur as well: strophic variation arias, such as we have noted in the prologue of *Orfeo* and the invocation to Night in the *Combattimento*, as well as extended laments of the type described below.

Another trend is the growing use of obbligato instrumental parts. Although the continuo remains the sole accompaniment to the voice most of the time, short ritornellos are increasingly common, and the instruments are more and more integrated with the voices, in the type of writing seen in portions of the *Combattimento*. Unfortunately, the loss of the original scores for many works leaves uncertainties about their original instrumentation and performance practices. Performances today, even those that purport to be historically authentic, sometimes employ modern arrangements that reflect later scoring and instrumental practice.

Cavalli

The leading composer of Venetian opera during the mid-seventeenth century was Francesco Cavalli (1602–76). Born at Crema in central northern Italy, he entered the choir of St. Mark's, Venice, in 1616. There he served under Monteverdi, who had arrived four years earlier. Apart from a brief stint (1660–62) in France, he spent his entire career in Venice, where in 1639 he became—like Giovanni Gabrieli—organist at St. Mark's. Despite his employment in an instrumental position, his surviving works are virtually all vocal and are dominated by some thirty-three operas.

Cavalli's *Giasone*

The opera *Giasone*, first performed in 1649, was Cavalli's most famous work. Based on the Greek myth of Jason and the Golden Fleece, its libretto, by the Florentine poet Giacinto Andrea Cicognini, was typical of the period in incorporating numerous secondary characters and subplots, some of them of a comic nature (see Box 4.4). In this it represents a departure from early opera, which maintained a uniformly high-minded point of view, avoiding comic scenes. By the end of the century fashion would turn again, so that Cavalli's operas came to be dismissed as inappropriately mixing the comic with the serious. This was hardly the view of his contemporaries, however.

The most famous scene in *Giasone* is one in which the witch Medea conjures up a demon (anthology, Selection 8a). Similar scenes occur in many later works, notably by the English composer Purcell and the French Rameau. Medea's music opens with a miniature strophic aria, complete with a six-measure ritornello. The remainder of the scene alternates between aria and recitative styles; the final arialike section (*Si, si, si, vincerà*) is preceded by a chorus of spirits.

The Lament

The final scene of *Giasone* includes a long monologue for Isifile (anthology, Selection 8b); primarily a lament, it is also an impassioned expression of her anger at Giasone, and its text contains some extraordinary imagery. Yet Cavalli chooses not to dwell on some of Isifile's more horrendous outbursts, making little musically of her list of exhortations to Giasone in measures 29–36, for example. Instead the music focuses attention on several passages that are set lyrically, in aria style. This approach differs from that of Monteverdi in Orfeo's lament, which had been nothing more than an extended recitative of an especially in-

---

BOX 4.4

Cavalli: *Giasone*

Libretto by Giacinto Andrea Cicognini (1606–ca. 1650).
First performed at the Teatro San Cassiano in Venice, 1649; numerous
revised productions in Italy during the next forty years.

Chief Characters

Giasone [Jason] (alto), Greek hero, leader of the Argonauts
Isifile [Hypsipyle] (soprano), queen of Lemnos, wife of Giasone
Medea (soprano), witch, ruler of Colchis

SYNOPSIS

The work consists of a prologue and three acts. At the beginning of Act 1, Giasone has sailed across the Aegean Sea with his followers the Argonauts to capture
the Golden Fleece. The latter, a magical ram's fleece, is guarded by monsters near
the witch Medea's castle in the Asian city of Colchis. Previously Giasone has spent
a year on the island of Lemnos, where he has married Queen Isifile, but at Colchis
Medea has become his lover. In our first excerpt (scene 14), Medea conjures up a
demon, who gives her a ring that will bring Giasone victory over the monsters.

In Act 2 Giasone wins the Golden Fleece, and at the beginning of Act 3 Medea
and Giasone are living happily together. But when a follower of Giasone makes
an attempt on Medea's life, she is saved by a former lover, whom she now sends
to kill Giasone. Giasone is saved in turn by Isifile. In the final scene, Giasone declares that he still loves Medea. But after hearing Isifile's lament—our second excerpt—he realizes that he in fact loves Isifile. The opera concludes with the two
happily reunited (and Medea returning to her former lover).

---

tense nature. The later Venetian lament is longer and typically incorporates one
or more arialike sections constructed over an **ostinato** bass—that is, a continuo
part consisting of a short phrase, usually four or eight measures in length, which
is repeated many times, serving as the basis for a series of variations in the vocal part.

Isifile's lament includes such an ostinato passage, beginning at the words
"Regina, Egeo, amici" (mm. 71–99). The four-measure ostinato, initially played
alone, returns numerous times in the course of the passage, both in its original
key (G minor) and transposed. Unlike some contemporaneous laments, whose
bass is limited to statements of the ostinato, this one includes free bass writing
as well, but its ostinato character is clear.[20] Equally typical of the seventeenth-

---

[20]Cavalli probably meant this passage to be performed by voice and continuo alone; at least one
recording adds string parts, apparently composed by the conductor.

century lament are the triple meter and minor mode. All of these characteristics can be traced to Monteverdi's famous *Lamento della ninfa* (Lament of the nymph) in his Eighth Book of Madrigals. They are still found in Dido's lament, from Purcell's opera *Dido and Aeneas* (1689), and there even exist instrumental imitations, such as the *Lamento* movement of Bach's *Capriccio on the Departure of a Most Beloved Brother* for keyboard instrument (ca. 1707). So common are laments over descending ostinato bass lines that the latter have been termed emblems of lamentation, although the device also occurs in contexts where it is difficult to find a specific meaning or emotional significance.[21]

After Cavalli, Venetian opera continued to evolve through the end of the Baroque, indeed to the end of the eighteenth century. We shall, however, turn at this point to France, where, over the course of the seventeenth century, a very different type of musical drama emerged. When we return to Italian opera, in Chapter 8, it will be to a new type, the *opera seria*, which emerged at the end of the seventeenth century.

---

[21]For a study of the chromatic version of this device throughout European music history, see Peter Williams, *The Chromatic Fourth* (Oxford: Oxford University Press, 1998). For the view of descending ostinato basses as "emblems," see Ellen Rosand, " The Descending Tetrachord: An Emblem of Lament," *Musical Quarterly* 55 (1979): 346–59.

CHAPTER 5

LULLY AND FRENCH MUSICAL DRAMA

France in the first half of the seventeenth century was torn by conflict, both between the dominant Roman Catholics and the minority Protestants (known as Huguenots), and also between rival noble factions, some supporting an alliance with Italy and the Austrian empire, others opposing it. Although the level of violence did not reach that of the Wars of Religion in the sixteenth century, it did impede the flourishing of the arts until the absolute rule of King Louis XIV was firmly established, in 1661.

Musical developments reflected political ones. The royal court had dominated French musical life since the sixteenth century, and under Louis XIII's queen Anne of Austria (1601–66) and their Italian first minister Cardinal Mazarin (1602–61), Italian music was heavily patronized. Italian operas by Luigi Rossi (*Orfeo*, 1647) and Cavalli (*Serse*, 1660; *Ercole amante*, 1662) were performed in Paris, and Italian-born musicians such as Jean-Baptiste Lully, discussed below, entered the court. But Italian political influence, and the political instability associated with it, ended when Louis XIV came to power. The entire French aristocracy was required to pay homage to him on a regular basis at his palace of Versailles, which became a center for all manner of artistic activity under royal patronage. The royal musical establishment, like the country at large, was placed under a rigorously centralized administration; the latter controlled many aspects of musical production and hence had a substantial impact on the nature of French music during the late seventeenth and early eighteenth centuries. Among those to benefit were French musical institutions such as the Twenty-four Violins of the King (*Vingt-quatre Violons du Roi*), which had been furnishing dance music for the court since the late sixteenth century; under Louis XIV the Twenty-Four Violins became one of Europe's most famous ensembles, imitated at the English royal court and elsewhere.[1] Another important institution was the Royal Academy of Music, founded in 1672, which for more than a century would produce French opera under the indirect control and patronage of the king.

---

[1] The word "violin" (*violon*) here refers to members of the entire violin family, not just the familiar treble instrument; the Twenty-Four Violins was a complete string orchestra.

THE FRENCH STYLE

France had developed a distinctive musical culture by the end of the sixteenth century, characterized in particular by the court air (*air de cour*) and the court ballet (*ballet de cour*). Both genres continued to flourish in the seventeenth century. The ballet, like the Italian *intermedio*, often included elaborate dramatic staging and substantial vocal music and was frequently performed before a large public audience. The *air de cour*—which was hardly confined to the royal court— grew out of the older polyphonic chanson. The seventeenth-century *air de cour* usually consisted of strophic monody with lute accompaniment, although some early examples exist in polyphonic versions as well.[2] Among the leading composers were Pierre Guédron (ca. 1570–ca. 1620), Antoine Boësset (1586–1643), and Etienne Moulinié (ca. 1600–after 1669). Later composers, including Lully, Charpentier, and Couperin, composed similar songs under the headings *airs sérieux* (serious songs) and *airs à boire* (literally, drinking songs, although these were not necessarily very different in style from the serious ones).

A distinctive feature of many *airs de cour* was the absence of a regular meter. This is clear in Example 5.1, an *air de cour* by Guédron that was published in a number of early seventeenth-century anthologies.[3] There is no regular time signature; instead, the meter shifts fluidly between what we would call $\frac{3}{4}$, $\frac{4}{4}$, and $\frac{3}{2}$ time. The text is set syllabically, mainly in quarter and half notes, which correspond to short and long syllables of the French text. Syllables that receive particular stress, such as the opening word *vous* ("you") and *mourez* ("will die") at the beginning of line 3, receive melismatic embellishments, but the overall length of each of these syllables remains that of a half note.

This type of rhythm somewhat resembles that of recitative, yet it does not imitate actual speech. Unlike recitative, the *air de cour* reflects the principles of *vers mesuré* (literally, "measured verse"), a theory developed in the late sixteenth century on the basis of ancient Greek poetry. The latter was (and still is) believed to have been sung in alternating long and short note values, closely reflecting the lengths of the syllables of the text. Although this type of declamation is thought to have reflected the ancient Greek language as actually spoken, its application to modern French was artificial. Nevertheless, the resulting style of declamation had a profound influence on both French vocal music and the spoken French of the Baroque theater. It led to the so-called *musique mesurée* ("measured music") of Claude Le Jeune (ca. 1530–1600): polyphonic chansons whose syllabic settings and irregular meter were direct antecedents of the monodic type of song shown in Example 5.1.[4]

---

[2]Ensemble versions exist for other early examples of monody, including some of the solo madrigals of Caccini and Monteverdi and most of the songs or airs by the English composer John Dowland (1563–1626).

[3]The version in Ex. 5.1 was published in *A Musical Banquet* (London, 1610), edited by Robert Dowland (son of the more famous John Dowland).

[4]Le Jeune's most famous work was *Le printemps* (Spring), a collection of polyphonic chansons published posthumously in 1603.

Example 5.1 Guédron, *Vous que le bonheur rappelle*

1 Vous que le bonheur rappelle
2 À un servage ancien,
3 Mourez aux pieds de la belle
4 Qui vous daigne faire sien.
[six more stanzas follow]

You whom good fortune calls
To an old servitude [i.e., love]
Will die at the feet of the beauty
Who wishes to make you her own.

Although the theory of *vers mesuré* was eventually abandoned, the strict approach to musical declamation typical of the *air de cour* was retained in French vocal writing through the end of the seventeenth century. While Italian composers and performers were turning the aria into a virtuoso showpiece and the main element of Italian opera, the French *air* remained restrained in style—rather similar to recitative, which likewise retained its importance throughout French seventeenth-century opera. Moreover, French composers until the end of the Baroque retained a special interest in rhythmically defined musical forms. Among these was a specifically French form of recitative as well as a large number of dance genres, each characterized by particular types of tempo and rhythm.

The Role of Lully

Paradoxically, the leading role in French music under Louis XIV was taken by the Italian-born Jean-Baptiste Lully (1632–87) (see Box 5.1). He had come to Paris from Florence in 1646 in the retinue of a French aristocrat with royal connections. By 1653 he had entered the young King Louis XIV's service as a composer of music for the court ballets, and by the time the king reached adulthood and began to rule in his own name in 1661, Lully had become the head of the court musicians, a position that gave him control of the vast budget and

> ## Box 5.1
> ### Jean-Baptiste Lully (1632–1687)
>
> **1632.** Born in Florence (northern Italy) as Giovanni Battista Lulli; the nature of his early training is uncertain.
>
> **1646.** In France in the service of Mademoiselle de Montpensier, niece of Roger de Lorraine, a relative of King Louis XIII; serves as dancer and violinist. Reportedly studies composition with several French musicians.
>
> **1652.** Returns to Paris after the exile (for political reasons) of his patroness; enters service of Louis XIV a year later.
>
> **1653.** Dances alongside Louis XIV in *Ballet de la nuit*; appointed composer of instrumental music to the king. Contributes increasing amounts of music to court ballets.
>
> **1661.** Appointed superintendent of court music and royal chamber music composer.
>
> **1664.** Appointed director of the Grande Bande (the Twenty-Four Violins of the King)
>
> **1664–70.** Collaborations with Molière (comic playwright), including *Le bourgeois gentilhomme* (1670).
>
> **1672.** Acquires right to direct the Royal Academy of Music (opera company); collaborates with poet Philippe Quinault in their first opera (*Cadmus et Hermione, tragédie en musique*), performed 1673.
>
> **1681.** Acquires title of royal secretary.
>
> **1687.** Dies at Paris of gangrene developed after injuring himself while conducting. His last opera, *Achille et Polyxène*, completed by his student Pascal Collasse.

personnel of the royal musical establishment. Ten years later he obtained the exclusive right to present operas within the French kingdom, making possible his establishment of the Royal Academy of Music—actually a private enterprise, but under royal protection.[5] Through the Royal Academy, Lully produced operatic works at the rate of usually one each year from 1672 until the end of his life, exercising the same dictatorial control over staging and musical execution that he exercised in his ballets for the royal court. The tradition of French opera under royal protection continued until the Revolution (1791), although apart from Rameau no one composer ever again dominated the field to the degree that Lully did.

---

[5] Lully also obtained a monopoly on the printing of his own music within France. Royally protected monopolies of this type were a standard feature of the seventeenth- and eighteenth-century European economy, granted to makers of weapons, ceramic wares, and other commodities as well as to writers, printers, and musical or theatrical entrepreneurs such as Lully.

By the end of his life, Lully had amassed considerable personal wealth and power—as well as enemies. No other musicians were allowed to challenge his prominence or to perform works that might rival his. Thus Lully effectively brought to an end the career of the composer Robert Cambert (ca. 1627–77), who in 1671 performed the first French opera (*Pomone*, music mostly lost). Charpentier, the one French contemporary whose musical genius might have challenged Lully's, had to content himself with writing mainly sacred music until Lully's death, and even then only one of his operas was performed by the Royal Academy (*Médée*, 1693).

But it was not merely personal power that made Lully so successful and influential. He clearly was a gifted and imaginative musician, and his dance and vocal music exerted an enormous influence over several generations of musicians throughout Europe. Although a distinctive French style existed before him, it was Lully who was credited with establishing *the* French style as it was known in the later seventeenth and eighteenth centuries: a style taken for granted by later French composers, such as Jacquet de La Guerre, Couperin, and Rameau, and imitated by many of the leading composers elsewhere, including Purcell in England and Handel and Bach in Germany. For this reason the French style of the later Baroque was sometimes referred to more specifically as the Lullian style.

Lully's Works

Lully's earliest significant works were probably individual dances and airs composed for court ballets, most of which were, like the Renaissance *intermedio*, collaborative efforts. Lully's participation would not have been limited to music, for as a talented dancer and mime he took many roles, probably providing his own choreography.[6] Among his dancing partners was the teenaged Louis XIV—for members of the royal court took part in the ballets, and the young king was an avid dancer. In this the king followed the tradition of his father, Louis XIII, who had taken an active role in the production of court ballets, even composing the music for one. Louis XIV would be similarly involved in the production of Lully's operas, selecting their subjects and approving their librettos prior to the composition of the music.

By the late 1650s Lully was the sole composer of the most important court ballets. In the 1660s this led to a series of collaborations with the most important writers of the day, notably the comic playwright Jean-Baptiste Molière (1622–73). Among their *comédies-ballets*, as their collaborations are known, was *Le bourgeois gentilhomme* (The village aristocrat, 1670), their last and most popular work. Soon thereafter, however, Lully's attention was taken up by the operas of the Royal Academy, for which he, together with the poet Philippe Quinault (1635–88), invented a distinctively French version of the Italian genre. Together they created eleven operas, or, as they termed them, *tragédies*

---

[6]No written choreographies by Lully are extant, but those of later French dancing masters survive, including a few for music by Lully (see Fig. 5.2).

Figure 5.1 A performance at Versailles of Molière's comedy *Le malade imaginaire*, engraving from André Félibien, *Les divertissemens de Versailles . . .* (Paris, 1676). This performance, given 6 July 1674, is presumably being directed by Lully (standing, beating time with a rolled-up sheet of paper); the King is seated at the center of the audience.

en musique (tragedies in music).[7] We shall be examining their last completed opera, *Armide*.

Dance in French Music

Thanks in part to the prominence of dance at the royal court, dance music was of somewhat greater artistic significance in France than in Italy. Just as French song tended to employ accentual and durational patterns derived from the formal recitation of poetry, dance music tended to follow specific rhythmic patterns that corresponded to the steps of particular dances. For each of the common dances there was thus a specific type of music, defined by tempo, meter, and certain recurring rhythmic patterns.[8] In the course of the seventeenth century, the pavane, galliard, and allemande—the chief French court dances of the late sixteenth century—gave way to the courante, sarabande, minuet, gigue, and other dances, each with its corresponding type of music. The importance of these dances extended far beyond ballets as such, for independent instrumental works, airs, and even sacred music all frequently borrowed the rhythms

---

[7]Lully wrote two further operas in conjunction with other poets, and was working on a third when he died.

[8]Some of the individual dance rhythms are considered in Chapter 10.

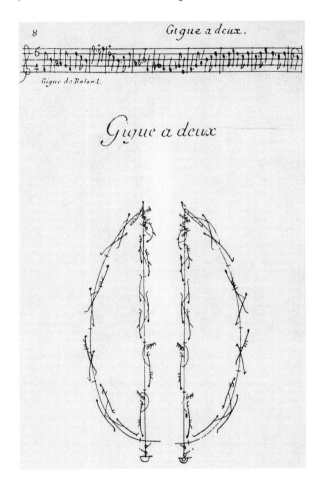

Gigue à deux.

Gigue à deux

Figure 5.2 *Gigue à deux* (jig for a couple), from *Recueil de dances composées par M. Feuillet* (Paris, 1700). An example of Baroque choreography, using a system of notation invented by the author of the treatise from which the illustration is taken. Individual signs indicate the various types of steps, leaps, and other figures performed by the dancers; the geometric design of the diagram as a whole shows the path that each dancer traces across the floor or stage (note the precise symmetry, typical of French theatrical dance). Although the music is from Lully's *tragédie en musique Roland* of 1685, the choreography is not necessarily that used in the work's original staging.

of particular dances. Often, the tempo and expressive character of a work could be inferred from the presence of dance elements in the music; in the absence of verbal expression markings, musicians recognized the dance type of a particular composition—and thus its proper tempo and character—from the rhythm of its opening measures.

The performance of dance music requires rhythmic precision and sureness of tempo from the instrumentalists, to avoid giving the dancer unpleasant surprises. For this reason the Twenty-Four Violins of the King cultivated a style of playing that, under Lully, became famous for its precise coordination, rhythmic sureness, and spirited articulation. Improvised ornamentation was banned, and bowings were dictated by a system that always placed downbows on accented beats. The frequent retaking or lifting of the bow required by this system led to a cleanly articulated, lively sort of melody and rhythm, much more airy than the continuous legato cultivated in nineteenth-century violin technique. Although the French string style did not encourage the solo virtuosity prized by Italian violinists, foreign listeners were amazed by the precision and unanimity of Lully's orchestra. The underlying conventions of performance were apparently unknown in Italy and elsewhere, although similar rules were adopted by string bands founded in Germany and England in imitation of the French one.[9]

Conventions of Tempo and Rhythm

Another set of conventions came to govern tempo and the interpretation of rhythmic notation. Tempo in dance music was largely determined by that of the dance itself. For example, gigues tend to be quick and sarabandes slow, although there were frequent exceptions, particularly in earlier seventeenth-century works, before conventions had hardened into rules. Eventually, too, certain types of rhythm came to be performed differently from what a literal interpretation of the notation might imply.

In Example 5.2, for instance, the rhythm of measure 2 came to be notated in the simpler manner shown between the staves. Yet this later form of notation would have been executed in the same manner as the original. The underlying convention is known today as **overdotting**; the expression **double dotting** is also used, since Lully's original notation is equivalent to a double-dotted quarter note followed by a sixteenth. Both terms are misleading, however, in-

Example 5.2 Lully, *Armide*, Act 3, scene 4, *prélude* for La Haine (Hate) (three inner string parts omitted)

---

[9]Specific rules for string performance in the French style were published by the German composer Georg Muffat; see bibliography under "Instruments and Instrumental Practice."

sofar as they imply a specific interpretation of each dotted note. The dot evidently was understood as being variable in length, its exact meaning depending on the larger musical context.[10] That Lully expected his dotted notation to be interpreted somewhat freely is suggested by measures 5–7, whose notation is arithmetically imprecise and cannot be played literally; what Lully may have intended is suggested beneath the staves.

Another convention, known as ***notes inégales*** (unequal notes), led to the lengthening of the first note in certain pairs of small note values. For instance, in Example 5.3 the eighth notes might actually have been performed as shown above and below the staves. The precise degree of inequality used in a given piece would vary, depending on the character of the music. A fairly gentle rhythm, that is, one with only a small degree of inequality, might be appro-

Example 5.3 Lully, *Armide*, Act 2, scene 2, Sidonie's air "Sur des bords séparés"

1 Sur des bords séparés	On shores separated
2 Du séjour des humains,	From the ways of people,
3 Qui peut arracher de vos mains	Who can take from your hands
4 Un ennemy qui vous adore?	An enemy [Renaud] who adores you?
5 Vous enchantez Renaud,	You enchant Renaud;
6 Que craignez-vous encore?	What then do you fear?

---

[10]It is uncertain when this convention became established; certainly its application varied over the course of the seventeenth and eighteenth centuries.

priate in Example 5.3, where the singer is consoling the unhappy Armide. But elsewhere a more vigorous (i.e., more unequal) style might be desirable. Indeed, in the type of instrumental movement known as the French overture, some rhythms written "equally" might have been performed in dotted style—if not during Lully's day, then perhaps later, in the eighteenth century (Ex. 5.4).

Example 5.4 Lully, *Armide*, overture (mm. 1–4; three inner string parts omitted)

Nevertheless, it is important to distinguish overdotting from inequality. The former applied chiefly in the opening sections of overtures and similar types of instrumental music; the latter came to be a nearly universal element in French music, like the "swinging" of notes in jazz. Without inequality, much French Baroque music is lifeless—a point made by a number of French Baroque writers.[11] Hence, proper performance of French Baroque music requires an understanding of its rhythmic conventions, which are described (with varying degrees of clarity) in contemporary treatises and other documents.[12]

Ornaments

Another important set of conventions in French Baroque music involves the use of melodic ornaments. French musicians tended to avoid the free type of melodic embellishment that had been common in the sixteenth century and that continued in use by Italian virtuosos of the Baroque.[13] But French Baroque music, like Italian, also employs numerous stereotyped melodic ornaments: small figures, such as trills, that decorate single notes rather than whole phrases. Instead of being written out, these could be indicated by signs, as we do with the modern *tr* or trill sign. It is useful to refer to this standardized type of melodic decoration, which can be notated through symbols, as **ornamentation,** reserving the word **embellishment** for the more elaborate variety whose patterns can be indicated only by writing out the notes.

---

[11]For example, Michel de Saint-Lambert wrote in his *Principes du clavecin* (Paris, 1702): "[We play some notes unequally] because the inequality gives them more grace" (p. 25).

[12]For useful introductions, see the works by Robert Donington and Mary Cyr listed in the bibliography under "General Works on Performance Practice."

[13]See, for example, the scalar embellishment written out by Luzzaschi in Ex. 3.1 (m. 7), or the alternate, embellished version of the invocation of Night in Monteverdi's *Combattimento* (anthology, Selection 7, mm. 130–32).

The French tradition of ornamentation is most familiar today from keyboard music, since Bach and other eighteenth-century composers outside France adopted many of the French ornament signs in their own keyboard music. Some modern writers have supposed that these ornaments were employed to overcome the inability of a stringed keyboard instrument such as the harpsichord to sustain notes. But the appoggiaturas, trills, mordents, and other ornaments of the French Baroque tradition were fundamental to the technique of all instruments—and of the voice as well, for solo and choral singing was as heavily ornamented as violin, flute, or keyboard music. When marked by the composer, these ornaments constitute an essential element in the shape and expressive content of a melodic line.

The original seventeenth-century prints of Lully's music employed only a single ornament sign—the letter *t*, set above or below the ornamented note, as in Examples 5.2–4. Lully's musicians presumably knew the conventions well enough to understand which particular ornament was required at any given point. Later composers used different signs for different ornaments, but there was never a standard set of ornament signs. To clarify what sign was being used for what ornament, some French composers included tables of ornaments in their publications, beginning in the late seventeenth century. Chapter 11 will examine several ornament tables published in conjunction with eighteenth-century French harpsichord music, which, like other French music of that period, continued to employ many of the conventions established under Lully.

French Opera under Lully

Lullian opera was in many respects a synthesis of earlier French genres, incorporating a style of solo song derived from the *air de cour* alongside dances from the royal court ballet. But like Italian opera it also includes recitative, albeit of a distinctly French variety. As in Monteverdi's *Orfeo* and a number of other early Italian operas, the drama itself is preceded by a prologue addressed to the work's patron: in this case, the king. Most of the dialogue for the principal characters is presented in poetry of a generally serious character; there are few comic scenes in Lully's *tragédies en musique*. This dialogue is set as monody: primarily in recitative, but interspersed with short airs and alternating with ballet scenes or *divertissements*—one in each act—in which dancers as well as the chorus and secondary singing characters often play prominent roles. Occasionally these *divertissements*, like the *intermedi* inserted into older comedies or the ballets that Lully had written for plays by Molière, constitute diversions from the main plot. But more often they present battles, marriage and funeral rites, and other impressive actions essential to the drama, and as such they constituted one of the main attractions of this type of opera.

Present throughout each such work is the chorus, which, as in *Orfeo*, was based on the chorus of ancient Greek drama, serving as both a participant in and commentator on the action. By Lully's day the chorus had disappeared from most Italian opera; thus its presence is, with the ballet, one of the defining features of French Baroque opera. Among the most typical Lullian uses of the chorus, although absent from *Armide*, is its role in scenes of lamentation where, as in *Orfeo*, it may provide a poignant refrain (as in Lully's operas *Alceste* and *Atys*).

Lullian Recitative

[handwritten margin note: different language is from Italian]

The charm and freshness of Lully's dance music was a major achievement and is one of the chief attractions of his works. Equally impressive, however, was his invention of a distinctive type of recitative suitable for the French language, whose accentual patterns are very different from those of Italian. Italian recitative is invariably notated in common time, with rhythm and tempo determined to a considerable degree by the performer. Although writers of the period prescribe freedom in French recitative as well, the precision with which it was notated implies a relatively strict manner of interpretation. In particular, Lully's notation of recitative fluctuates between duple, triple, and quadruple meters, the changing time signatures determining the tempo of each section relative to the previous one, according to certain conventions. Evidently the intended result was recitative that possesses clear rhythm and a definite tempo, although the latter might vary with the sentiment of each line of poetry.[14]

Just as the Lullian air avoided the trend toward virtuosity characteristic of the Italian aria, Lullian recitative never became as "dry" or as purely speechlike as the later Italian type. Lengthy recitation on repeated notes is a rarity, and thus French Baroque recitative retains much of the melodic character of the air; indeed, the two are sometimes almost indistinguishable in style. It is sometimes said that French Baroque vocal music has a more "speaking" style than that of Italy, and indeed, Lully and other French composers explicitly modeled their vocal style on the stylized poetic declamation of the spoken French theater of their time. This in turn was modeled on that of the ancient Greeks—yet another example of the continuing influence of antiquity on Baroque artistic thinking.

Scoring

French opera never adopted the tradition of using high voices for men's roles, as became the norm in Italian Baroque opera, nor were the tenor and bass voices accordingly neglected. Tenor parts retain the prominence they had in Monteverdi's early works, and important male roles are often taken by basses. The female alto voice is unknown, however. Its place in the operatic chorus was taken by the high male voice known as the *haute-contre*, as in French Baroque choral music generally.[15]

---

[14]See anthology, Selection 9b, and the accompanying discussion of performance issues. Although some questions about the conventions of French Baroque recitative remain unresolved, the very free rhythm heard in many modern performances may be contrary to historical practice.

[15]The *haute-contre* was probably not a pure falsetto voice but rather involved considerable blending of full and head voice, at least in the upper part of the range.

The functional division of Lully's works between the main action, presented in recitatives and airs, and the *divertissements* or ballet scenes was reflected in a functional division of the instruments. As in early Italian opera, recitative and air are accompanied mainly by the continuo, which was furnished by the usual small group of instruments: in France, harpsichords, lutes, and bass viola da gamba. Another small group of violins and woodwinds provided ritornellos and sinfonias as well as the instrumental parts that occasionally accompany the solo voices; *Armide* is unusually rich in airs and recitatives with such instrumental parts.

A larger string band essentially identical to the Twenty-Four Violins provided the music for the overture and ballet scenes. Unlike the modern string orchestra (or the Italian string ensemble of the eighteenth century), the French seventeenth-century violin band was usually scored in five parts, following a tradition inherited from sixteenth-century dance music. It was dominated by a single upper part for violin and an equally strong bass line, both of these parts being doubled by numerous players. There was at first no continuo, the harmony being filled out by the three inner parts, which were played on instruments corresponding to the modern viola. Under Lully the string music may have been played from memory, perhaps reflecting another old custom. Lully himself is thought to have composed only the outer voices in most cases, leaving the inner parts to assistants. The dance music played by this ensemble was directed not from the harpsichord, as was customary in Italian orchestras of the later Baroque, but by a conductor who beat time either with a baton or a rolled-up sheet of music paper; evidently this was sometimes intentionally struck against a music desk or other object, creating an audible beat described by contemporary observers that has yet to be imitated in modern reconstructions.

The prevailing string color was modified by woodwinds; the chief instruments were the **recorder**, an end-blown wooden flute, and the Baroque oboe and bassoon. Wind instruments were used chiefly for special effects. Recorders, for example, might be heard in scenes where a character sleeps or has a dream, which would be depicted by a ballet scene. Each woodwind instrument came in multiple sizes, from which an entire consort or instrumental choir could be formed, as in the sixteenth century; the bassoon served as the bass of the oboe choir. All of the woodwinds underwent modifications during Lully's lifetime; it is often claimed that the alterations were undertaken specifically to reflect the needs of his works, and if so, then the modern forms of these instruments owe something to Lully and the seventeenth-century French opera orchestra.

JEAN-BAPTISTE LULLY'S *ARMIDE*

Lully's last completed *tragédie en musique* was composed to a libretto by Quinault and first performed in 1686. It was widely regarded as his greatest work; revivals continued into the 1760s. The story, a popular one derived from Tasso's *Gerusalemme liberata*, was the basis for many other operas before and since, including Handel's *Rinaldo* (1711). It concerns the encounter of the medieval Christian Crusader Renaud (Rinaldo) with the sorceress Armide (Armida), whose

Figure 5.3 *Lully's opera "Armide" performed at the Palais-Royal*, 1747; Gabriel de Saint-Aubin, France (1724–1780). Pen, water color and gouache over pencil. 12-1/4 × 19-3/4 in (31.1 × 50.2 cm). Gift of Elizabeth Paine Cardin, in memory of her father, Robert Treat Paine 2nd, 1970.36. Courtesy, Museum of Fine Arts, Boston. Reproduced with permission. © 1999 Museum of Fine Arts, Boston. All Rights Reserved. This drawing, showing an eighteenth-century revival of Lully's *Armide* in the Grande Salle (Great Hall) of the Royal Palace, appears to depict the *divertissement* in the fifth act.

role is central to Lully's opera. This was unusual, for Armide was not a noble heroine or historic figure but a witch, and, for Lully and his contemporaries in France, a representative of the exotic Middle East rather than the Christian West. She nevertheless becomes a sympathetic figure in Quinault and Lully's treatment (for a plot synopsis, see Box 5.2).

The Overture

The prologue of *Armide* is unusually short, but it opens with the type of overture (anthology, Selection 9a) that had been customary in French theatrical works since the ballets of the 1650s. So closely is this type of overture associated with Lully's operas that it has come to be known as the **French overture.** It was used not only to open operas and other theatrical works but as an independent instrumental genre through the end of the Baroque.

In origin, the French overture is related to certain types of instrumental piece popular at midcentury, including the brief sinfonias used to introduce the operas of Cavalli and other Italian composers as well as French-style compositions that Lully might have heard at court in his native Florence. In his mature works the French overture typically consists of two sections, each repeated. The first, in duple or quadruple time, is pervaded by dotted rhythms (e.g., dotted quar-

Box 5.2

Lully: *Armide*

Libretto by Philippe Quinault (1635–88).
Tragédie en musique, first performed at Paris, 1686.

Chief Characters

Armide (soprano), pagan sorceress
Phénice, Sidonie (sopranos), companions of Armide
Renaud (tenor), Crusader general

SYNOPSIS

As the opera begins, Renaud is the only Crusader general who has not been defeated by the forces of Armide and her uncle Hidraot (bass, pagan king of Damascus, Syria). Armide therefore decides to conquer Renaud through magic and deception. At the end of Act 2 Armide has captured Renaud and intends to kill him, but she stops when she realizes that she is fatally attracted to him. She therefore has her demons carry him off to her enchanted castle.

As Act 3 opens, the theater represents the desert surrounding Armide's palace. She wanders, pondering her situation. Her companions Phénice and Sidonie arrive and remind her that Renaud is in her power, since he loves her. She replies that he loves her only because he has been enchanted, whereas she truly loves him (refrain, "my love is of a different sort"). To strengthen her resolve to kill Renaud, she calls forth the demon Hate and her followers. But after they arrive Armide changes her mind. Hate warns her of dire consequences and abandons her to Love.

As Act 5 opens, Renaud is being held prisoner by Armide in her enchanted palace. Using all her magical powers, she invites him to love in a grand *divertissement* danced and sung by a chorus of happy lovers. Immediately afterward, however, two of Renaud's companions arrive; they have obtained a magic shield that breaks Armide's spell. Renaud is freed and Armide, in despair, destroys her palace and herself—one of the few genuinely tragic endings in Baroque opera.

SELECTIONS DISCUSSED IN THIS CHAPTER

Prologue: Overture.

Act 2, scene 5: Armide standing over the enchanted Renaud: (a) *prélude* (orchestra); (b) Armide: recitative "Enfin il est en ma puissance"; (c) Armide: air "Venez, venez, seconder mes désirs"; (d) entr'acte (orchestra).

Act 3, scene 2: Armide joined by Sidonie and Phénice: (a) recitative; (b) Sidonie: air "Sur des bords"; (c) Armide: "De mes plus doux regards."

——, scene 3: Armide alone, calling on Hate: air with string accompaniment "Venez, Haine implacable!"

————, scene 4: Ballet: Hate and her followers (fellow demons). (a) *prélude*, then accompanied recitative "Je réponds à tes voeux"; (b) *prélude* and air with chorus "Plus on connait l'Amour"; (c) first instrumental air (*entrée*).

Act 5, scene 2: *Passacaille.*

ter and eighth) and is grand and energetic in character. The second section may be in any meter but is usually somewhat faster than the first. It often opens imitatively, in the manner of a fugue, although the counterpoint is usually not very complex. Often there is a return to dotted rhythm and a somewhat slower tempo at the end.

Unlike the overtures of nineteenth-century works, those of Baroque operas rarely have any musical or expressive connection with what follows. Rather, the French overture was, as the French term *ouverture* implies, simply a way of opening a work. In Lully's operas, the overture is not only heard at the beginning of the prologue but is repeated at the end, where it serves as an *entr'acte* or transition to the first act. Later composers, notably Handel, sometimes employed additional overtures at other points in the opera as well, and Lully often used the same dotted rhythm and grand style from the opening section of the overture for ritornellos or brief sinfonias that introduce an important character or point forward to some significant event that is about to happen.

Thus the ballet or *divertissement* in Act 3 of *Armide* opens with an orchestral *prélude* in dotted overture style (Ex. 5.2). Moreover, the first of the two dances in this ballet (the *premier air*) is an *entrée grave*, a dance whose music employs the dotted rhythm of the opening part of an overture.[16] Modern writers have sometimes supposed that French overtures were specifically associated with the French king or with the idea of royalty. This type of overture was indeed recognized as a specifically French genre, but it could have any number of meanings within a given work.

Other Instrumental Music

Together with the overture, the dances of the prologue and the five *divertissements* constituted the majority of the music assigned to the orchestral ensemble in a Lullian opera. Imaginatively choreographed, the dances were among the glories of French Baroque culture, as modern reconstructions have revealed. The basic rhythmic patterns and steps were usually those of the standard court dances. The latter were modified, however, to suit the characters and dramatic situations of each work. Thus in Act 3 of *Armide*, the *entrée* might have been entrusted to a single virtuoso male dancer; he would have represented the leader of the demons whom Armide calls onto the stage. Like the principal

[16]The adjective *grave* ("slow" or "serious") was often omitted from the titles of similar pieces by Lully's imitators in Germany.

characters—singers as well as dancers—he would have worn a fanciful costume that indicated at a glance who he was.[17]

As in the Italian theater, the curtain went up at the outset and remained up throughout a work. Scene changes took place in full view of the audience and were one of the attractions of the opera, thanks to the beauty and ingenuity with which, for example, the "agreeable island" of Act 2 was transformed into the desert of Act 3. To accompany such changes, and also to cover up any noises made by the stage machinery, Lully generally had the orchestra repeat a dance that had been heard during the previous act. An *entr'acte* of this type often reflects the general character of the following scene, like the sinfonias in Monteverdi's *Orfeo*.

Recitative and Air

The most famous vocal music in the opera is that of Armide's monologues, particularly that which concludes Act 2 (excerpts in anthology, Selection 9b). The scene is introduced by an orchestral prelude (in dotted overture style) and concluded by an air. But it consists chiefly of a lengthy recitative for the title character, who expresses her conflicting emotions as she hesitates between killing Renaud and falling in love with him. Reflecting this, her vocal line frequently rises and falls in relatively large leaps and is broken up by numerous rests (see especially mm. 34–42).

Lully's close integration of recitative and air is clear in the second scene of Act 3, where Armide's companions attempt to comfort her. Here the music shifts fluidly between recitatives and short airs; the latter resemble the *air de cour* in their relatively simple melodic lines and regular rhythm. Several employ recognizable dance rhythms. Sidonie's first air (Ex. 5.3) resembles a sarabande, a dance in triple time with a slow to moderate tempo. Armide's air "Plus Renaud m'aimera" (Ex. 5.5) employs the rhythm of the courante, a dance in compound duple time recognizable by its use of **hemiola:** an alternation between duple and triple divisions of the measure. For example, measure 1 is in $\frac{6}{4}$, as notated, with accents on the first and fourth quarter-note beats of the measure. Measure 2, however, is effectively in $\frac{3}{2}$, with accents on beats 1, 3, and 5 (as is clear from the accentuation of the last syllable of the word *serai*).

The *Divertissement* of Hate

By the end of Act 3, scene 2, Armide has decided that she wishes to hate Renaud, not love him. Her attempt to banish love from her heart is represented in an elaborate ballet or *divertissement* in which Hate itself appears onstage, per-

---

[17]Singing characters frequently were doubled by dancers wearing an identical costume, thus permitting the same figure to appear in both song and dance, although not simultaneously. For contemporary illustrations of such costumes, see the facsimile of the engraved second edition (Paris: Ballard, 1713) of Lully's *Armide* (Beziers: Société de Musicologie de Languedoc, [1980]) and the color drawings of Renaud and Armide in Philippe Beaussant, *Lully, ou Le musicien du soleil* (Paris: Gallimard, 1992), plates 14–15.

Example 5.5 Lully, *Armide*, Act 3, scene 2, Armide's air "Plus Renaud m'aimera"

Plus Renaud m'aimera, moins je serai tranquille;	The more Renaud loves me, the less I will be at peace;
J'ai résolu de le hair.	I have resolved to hate him.
Je n'ai tenté jamais rien de si difficile;	I have never attempted anything so difficult;
Je crains que pour forcer mon cœur à m'obéir	I fear that for forcing my heart to obey me
Tout mon art ne soit inutile.	All my magic will be useless.

sonified as a demon and her followers.[18] Armide calls upon Hate to "save" her from Love—also understood here through a personification—in a magnificent air perhaps inspired by conjuring scenes in contemporary Italian opera, such as we saw in Cavalli's *Giasone*. Unusual here, for Lully, is the accompaniment of the solo voice by the full five-part orchestra (Ex. 5.6). The latter plays a vigor-

---

[18]Although Hate and her entourage are female, they are represented onstage by men, in keeping with seventeenth-century conventions of staging. Her followers are identified in the libretto as Furies—supernatural beings taken from ancient Greek mythology—and as personifications of cruelty, vengeance, rage, and "passions [emotions] dependent on Hate."

Example 5.6 Lully, *Armide*, Act 3, scene 3, Armide's air "Venez, Haine implacable," vocal entry

Venez, venez, Haine implacable,   Come, restless Hate,
Sortez du gouffre épouvantable.   Emerge from your dreadful cave.

ous accompaniment fashioned from numerous statements of a lively rhythmic motive (eighth and two sixteenths).

The insistent use of this rhythm might have been a conscious reminiscence of what Monteverdi called the *stile concitato*. The same motive is used in slightly different form in the ballet proper, where Hate sings an air with a similar accompaniment (Ex. 5.7). Hate's followers repeat her air as a chorus of male voices.

The *Passacaille*

The most famous dance in the opera occurs in the *divertissement* in the fifth act. Here Armide, having failed in her effort to hate Renaud, conjures up a grand supernatural ballet intended to seduce him. The scene presents a lush spectacle as singers and dancers representing Armide's supernatural servants and assistants perform in groups varying from a few soloists to the entire ensemble. The music takes the form of a **passacaglia** (in French, *passacaille*); its opening is shown in Example 5.8a.

The passacaglia is usually defined today as a set of variations on a ground bass, that is, an ostinato bass line. In this it is similar to the **chaconne** (Ital-

Example 5.7 Lully, *Armide*, Act 3, scene 4, La Haine's air "Plus on connaît l'Amour," vocal entry

Plus on connaît l'Amour,
Et plus on le déteste,
Détruisons son pouvoir funeste.

The more one knows Love (Cupid),
The more one detests him;
Let us destroy his deathly power.

ian *ciacona*). In fact, both genres were originally dances, not necessarily involving an ostinato bass, and the music of French Baroque chaconnes and *passacailles* is always in triple meter, with a moderate tempo. Phrases generally comprise four measures and frequently begin on the second beat of the measure. Hence upbeats of two quarter notes are common, as at the beginning of Example 5.8b.[19]

Although not all French Baroque chaconnes and *passacailles* employ variation form, use of the latter made these dances particularly suitable for grand ballet scenes, and the examples from Lully's operas are by far the longest and most elaborate of the individual numbers—vocal or instrumental—in these works. In these dances, passages for the full instrumental ensemble often alternate with more thinly scored ones, suggesting corresponding effects in the choreography;

---

[19]The origins of the passacaglia and chaconne and the differences between them are not entirely clear despite long study by music historians. Passacaglias tend to be more serious and in minor keys, whereas the chaconne was originally lighter and more often in the major mode. In the later Baroque, however, the two genres often seem to be musically indistinguishable.

Example 5.8 Lully, *Armide*, Act 5, scene 2, *Passacaille*: (a) mm. 1–12; (b) mm. 24–28; (c) mm. 100–110; (d) mm. 97–101

for example, a couple or a soloist might take center stage at points where smaller musical ensembles are playing. The *passacaille* in *Armide* comprises both a lengthy instrumental portion, which would have been danced, and equally ambitious sections that follow for solo and choral voices.

The ground bass employed for most of the present movement is one that was used frequently in seventeenth-century *passacailles*. It consists of a simple four-note descent, as in the first phrase of Example 5.8a. Lully occasionally substitutes other patterns, as in Example 5.8b, which is played by a trio of two recorders and viola. In another trio passage the ostinato disappears entirely as the music modulates to several other keys—B-flat major, then D minor (Ex. 5.8c). The original ostinato bass line is also varied melodically, as in Example 5.8d, where chromatic intervals are interpolated.

Thanks to the magnificent effect of this type of scene, passacaglias in the Lully style became a favorite component of later opera and ballet. With their hypnotically repeating ostinato basses, they could be extended almost indefinitely, making for some of the longest individual movements in the Baroque repertory. They became popular in other media as well; for example, the French composer Jean-Henri D'Anglebert (1628–91), who played harpsichord at the Royal Academy under Lully, published harpsichord arrangements of several of Lully's *passacailles*, including the one from *Armide*. Among the many foreign composers attracted to the form were the Englishman Henry Purcell and the Germans Biber and Bach; Bach's Cantata 78 opens with a choral passacaglia in G minor whose initial ritornello is remarkably close to several passages in the *passacaille* from *Armide* (which Bach probably knew through harpsichord transcriptions).

Today, the ballet scenes in Lully's operas are sometimes viewed as irrelevant interruptions to the action, the conjuring up of Hate in Act 3 of *Armide* a mere pretext for an amusing ballet scene. Yet these scenes were taken seriously by Lully's audiences, who would have recognized the *divertissement* of Hate as an **allegory**—an extended metaphor in which fundamental human emotions or philosophical ideas are represented symbolically. Similar scenes occur frequently in Baroque painting and in the spoken drama of the time. For Lully and other French Baroque composers, such scenes were ways of representing the evolving emotional states of the chief characters—more important, in this regard, than the brief airs.

In addition, Lully's use of *stile concitato* in several dances here recalls Monteverdi's use of that term in connection with the ancient Greek theater; he had cited Plato's approval of Greek war dances. Stylistically, Lully's music may seem almost as distant from Monteverdi's as the latter had been from that of the ancient Greeks. Yet in their integration of song, recitation, and dance, Lully's musical dramas were as successful as any Baroque work in realizing the recurrent dream of recreating the theater of antiquity.

CHAPTER 6

SECULAR VOCAL MUSIC OF THE LATER SEVENTEENTH CENTURY

From the 1640s onward, opera may have commanded more attention from the musically literate public than any other form of Baroque vocal music. But the rise of opera was paralleled by that of the cantata, the most important form of secular vocal chamber music in the Baroque and the main subject of this chapter. The term **cantata,** which literally means anything that is sung, came to be applied in the early seventeenth century to various types of secular vocal music for solo voice that differed from Caccini's madrigals and strophic airs simply by virtue of their greater length. By the end of the Baroque it was being used for sacred as well as secular works for one or more solo singers and instruments, comprising several distinct movements. Nowadays we often use the word for similar works that include choral movements as well. A number of Monteverdi's late madrigals might be considered cantatas, and we can think of the cantata as the successor to the madrigal as a nontheatrical serious setting of Italian poetry.

Cantatas were among the most popular compositions of the seventeenth and eighteenth centuries, in part because they employed the poetic and musical language of opera but could be performed without the expense and elaborate production required by a large staged work. During the mid-seventeenth century the Roman composer Giacomo Carissimi (1605–74), now best known for his oratorios, and the opera composers Antonio Cesti and Luigi Rossi wrote them literally by the hundred. By the end of the century the form had been taken up in France, England, and Germany, and by the early eighteenth it was being adopted for sacred use.

Barbara Strozzi

Among the most significant composers and performers of cantatas in the mid-seventeenth century was Barbara Strozzi (1619–77), who published nine volumes of arias, madrigals, motets, and cantatas between 1644 and 1664. Little is known about her biography except that she spent her whole life in Venice, where she studied with Cavalli. She was almost certainly the illegitimate daughter of Giulio Strozzi, a poet whose texts were set to music by her as well by Monteverdi and Cavalli.

Giulio Strozzi was the founder of the Accademia degli Unisoni (Academy of the Unisons), a Venetian society of musically inclined writers and nobles similar to that which had commissioned Monteverdi's *Orfeo*. Giulio's association was actually a subgroup of a larger one, the Accademia degli Incogniti (Society of the Disguised Ones), whose members—all men, in keeping with the custom of the day—included the librettists of Monteverdi's two last operas. The sometimes unconventional philosophical and political ideas of these groups evidently encouraged Barbara Strozzi's close association with the Unisoni; unusual for a woman, she participated in their learned debates and probably performed music at their meetings. Her works—all vocal—include numerous settings of texts by her father and other members of the group; reportedly a gifted writer herself, she may have set her own texts as well. Had Strozzi's parents been married, she probably would have married herself and led a more conventional career. Even so, a professional career as an opera composer or church musician was out of the question, and for this reason her works consist almost entirely of virtuoso secular vocal compositions probably written for her own performances before the Unisoni or similar private gatherings.

Strozzi's *Ardo in tacito foco*

Whereas Luigi Rossi, Carissimi, and other contemporaries left most of their works unprinted, Strozzi was a prolific publisher of vocal music. Her known works include seven published collections devoted to her cantatas and other vocal works, mostly for solo soprano accompanied by basso continuo. These range from simple strophic arias to multimovement cantatas lasting up to fifteen minutes or so; there is also a set of continuo madrigals for as many as five voices, as well as a book of sacred monodies or solo motets.

Among Strozzi's larger works are several cantatas in the form of strophic variations, a type of music we have seen previously in the section of Monteverdi's *Combattimento* that contains the narrator's invocation to Night. *Ardo in tacito foco* (anthology, Selection 10) is a self-contained composition in this form, published in 1654 as the opening cantata in Strozzi's third printed collection.[1] Like the narrator's invocation of Night in the Monteverdi work, it falls into a number of distinct stanzas or strophes, each composed as a variation on an essentially unchanging basic design. But Strozzi's is an altogether larger work; each stanza is itself subdivided into distinct sections that range from simple recitative to aria style, and the entire work lasts close to ten minutes. It is, then, a virtuoso showpiece for a solo soprano; like a number of Strozzi's other works of this sort, it is also reminiscent of the tragic monologues found in Venetian opera of the period—including that of Isifile in *Giasone*. But Strozzi's setting, not tied to the demands of a stage drama, proceeds at a more leisurely pace, permitting the music to respond vividly to each line of the poem.

---

[1] Barbara Strozzi, *Cantate ariete à una, due, e tre voci* (Cantatas and little arias for one, two, and three voices, Venice, 1654), op. 3 (on *opus numbers*, see Chapter 7).

The Text

Scenes of lamentation were a common pretext for Baroque cantatas, and this work is no exception. The text, thought to be by Giovanni Francesco Loredano, founder of the Incogniti, is the complaint of a speaker whose lack of confidence—or, perhaps, of candor—prevents him from declaring his love for another. The poetry is typical of that written within the Strozzi circle; the language is intentionally indirect, using numerous metaphors that today seem artificial but at the time were regarded as elegant and expressive. A peculiarity shared with many of Strozzi's compositions is the presence of a lengthy descriptive title; most cantatas and other works by Baroque composers continued to be referred to by their opening words or *incipits*.

As was customary, the poem must be assumed to be the lament of a male lover, even though Strozzi probably performed it herself. Her music therefore represents a dramatic reading of the poem, not an actual dramatic scene, and we are told next to nothing about the lover and his beloved as people—why he loves her, or why he cannot name her. More significant is that the poem provides both vivid pictorial images, such as fire (*foco*) and wind (*vento*), and many emotionally charged words such as *ardore* (ardor or passion), *sospiri* (sighs), and *morte* (death). Each such word gave the composer an opportunity for an imaginative display of musical rhetoric, especially of the word-painting variety. Those words that call up energetic or lively images, such as "wind," also call forth virtuoso vocal technique in the form of rapid passagework or figuration. But the work as a whole is also a display of the *composer's* virtuosity, and Strozzi finds compelling, imaginative ways of representing even such dark, static ideas as "death," at the end of the poem, or the silence that is the main theme of the text. Although the rapid, even violent alternation between sharply contrasting images and emotions might have led to an incoherent, fragmented musical setting, the use of variation form gives each stanza a recurring structure that imparts to the work as a whole a readily comprehensible design.

The Music

Although the vocal part was clearly intended for a virtuoso soprano, Strozzi did not specify what instrument provides the continuo. She is known to have played the lute and might have accompanied herself on that instrument, although harpsichord or even chamber organ are also possibilities.

Strozzi's music articulates each stanza of the poem into three or four distinct sections (see Box 6.1). These are distinguished by their contrasting meter, tempo, and mode or tonality; moreover, the sections in common time are in recitative style—albeit more ornate and closer to arioso than most operatic recitative of the time—whereas the triple-time passages have a more flowing character resembling that of the aria. Similar alternations of tempo and meter characterize contemporaneous Venetian opera, including Monteverdi's *Poppea* and Cavalli's *Giasone*.[2]

---

[2]The triple-time sections in Strozzi's original publication were marked simply by the numeral "3," as shown in Box 6.1; our edition substitutes for this the modern time signatures $\frac{6}{2}$ and $\frac{3}{2}$ and prints the notes in half their original values.

Box 6.1

Strozzi: *Ardo in tacito foco*

Stanza:	1				2				3		
Lines:	1–5	6–8	9–10	11	12–16	17–19	20	21–22	23–28	29–30	31–33
Measure:	1	31	45	52	63	85	99	103	122	154	171
Meter:	C	3	C	3	C	3	C	3	C	C	C
Tempo indication:	—	adagio	—	—	—	presto	—	—	—	—	—
"Key" signature:	—	♭	—	—	—	♭	—	—	—	♭	—
First and last harmonies:	d–d	F–F	d–e	C–d	d–A	d–F	d	d–d	d–d	F–F	D–d
Significant word(s):	foco	proprio*	sospiri		ristoro, pianto	vento, umor, spento	duol		venti, lamenti, asconde	pietra, foco	morte

*In the modern edition erroneously displaced from m. 40 to m. 42.

A notable feature in the design of each stanza is the presence of a section in which a flat appears as a "key" signature; in each stanza this section ends with an F-major chord (e.g., m. 44). We might well say that these sections are *in* F major, which is the relative major of the D-minor tonality that dominates the outer sections. That this is an anachronistic way of describing this music, which Strozzi and her contemporaries still understood in modal terms, is suggested by the absence of the flat signature in the other sections. Yet it would be equally misleading to describe the outer sections simply as being in the Dorian mode (mode 1). The soprano part here goes well beyond the one-octave range of a normal chant melody or of a part in a Renaissance polyphonic work. And the harmony is essentially tonal, although it contains some surprises from our point of view—in particular, the frequent use of G-*major* chords where we might expect G minor instead (e.g., mm. 20, 51). In short, this music is typical of that of the seventeenth century in combining tonal and modal elements.

Each of the three stanzas follows the same basic structural pattern, yet Strozzi crafts the music of each strophe to fit its words exactly. For example, the opening section in each stanza begins with several measures over a sustained d in the continuo (implying a D-minor chord); line 1 in each case ends with a so-called **Phrygian cadence**, the bass descending by half step (from B♭ to A) and concluding with a major chord (on A). In stanza 1 the vocal part depicts the opening word *ardo* ("I burn") with brief rising melismas. Stanza 2, on the other hand, underlines the word *ristoro* ("consolation") with a descending melisma, which is imitated by the bass line (m. 65). In the third stanza, dissonant sus-

Figure 6.1 Barbara Strozzi, opening of *Ardo in tacito foco,* from the first page of music in her *Cantate ariete à una, due, e tre voci,* op. 3 (Venice, 1654). Strozzi was one of the most prolific publishers of cantatas in the seventeenth century, and her publications reveal exceptional care in the preparation and printing of both poetry and music. As in many other examples of seventeenth-century monody, there is no indication of the intended vocal type or instrumentation; these aspects of the music as well as the realization of the unfigured bass are left to the performer. Because the page was printed from moveable type, used throughout the Baroque for most vocal music, the staff lines are broken up into numerous short segments, each printed with a separate piece of metal type. Eighth and sixteenth notes are also printed separately, without beaming.

pensions represent the meaning of the word *aspro* ("bitter," mm. 122–25); there are no melismas here at all. Nevertheless, the underlying similarities in the structure and musical phrasing for all three lines remain evident.

Strozzi similarly adjusts each stanza as a whole to suit its text. Thus the first triple-time section of the first stanza is marked *adagio* (m. 31), whereas the corresponding section of the second stanza is marked *presto* (m. 85). The *adagio* marking must reflect the unhappiness stressed in lines 6–8 of the first stanza; the unhappy lover has "imprisoned" himself.[3] The *presto* of the second stanza, on the other hand, may be a response to the liveliness of the wind and the tears

---

[3]Strozzi places a melisma on the word *proprio* ("own") in mm. 40–42—shown incorrectly in the modern edition as a melisma on *il* ("the"). This emphasizes the fact that the lover's heart is its *own* "prisoner."

mentioned in lines 18–19.[4] Yet line 19 ends in measure 97 with a sudden pause in the vocal part—a dramatic silence elicited by the word *spento* (literally, "exhausted"). Strozzi repeats the idea for emphasis (m. 98). Significantly, triple time is entirely absent from the final stanza, although there is still a passage that begins and ends on F-major chords, in which the "key" signature changes to one flat (mm. 154–70). The absence of the arialike triple-time music from the final stanza prefigures the closing setting of the word *morte* (death), with its chromatic descents in both soprano and continuo (mm. 176–86). The voice's final cadence, incidentally, borrows a device from Monteverdi's *seconda pratica*: the note d′ forms a dissonance that would normally resolve to c♯′, but the dissonance remains unresolved.[5]

ALESSANDRO SCARLATTI AND THE LATER CANTATA

Opera and cantata continued to be the main genres of Italian secular vocal music through the eighteenth century. But the cantata of around 1700 was quite a different type of work from that of the early seventeenth century. Like opera and other vocal forms, it came to be dominated by the aria, which replaced recitative as the main element of Baroque vocal writing. In addition, the rapid alternation between recitative and aria styles that characterized earlier works grew less common. Instead, most cantatas came to consist of distinct movements, and by the eighteenth century a cantata typically consisted of a pair of arias each preceded by a recitative.

Many cantatas continued to be composed for voice and continuo alone, but more ambitious cantata-like works were also written, incorporating obbligato instrumental parts and multiple soloists. These works might bear various designations, such as *serenata* (serenade) and *dramma per musica* (musical drama); the latter term was also used for operas, and some later cantatas actually approach the dimensions of short operas. Indeed, all these genres tended to share the same musical style, employing similar types of recitative and aria. Moreover, by the first decade of the eighteenth century composers in France, Germany, and England were extending these two types of Italian writing to cantatas and related works on texts in their own languages. Some were on sacred subjects, as in two sets of cantatas published by the French composer Elizabeth Jacquet de La Guerre (Paris, 1708 and 1711). In Lutheran Germany a type of sacred cantata became the most common form of church music, written by the hundred by such composers as Georg Philipp Telemann and J. S. Bach.

In Italy thousands of such works must have been composed during the second half of the seventeenth century alone, some for amateur musicians, others

---

[4]The word *umor*, translated here as "the latter," that is, the "tears," is actually an old word referring to any vital fluid, an idea suggested by the long, winding melisma on which the word is sung.

[5]Compare the final cadence of the *Combattimento*. It is impossible to know whether Strozzi was making a direct allusion to Monteverdi's well-known work here; similar cadences are fairly common in the music of Luigi Rossi and other contemporaries.

for professional performance in the homes and palaces of wealthy patrons. Among the most significant composers were Alessandro Stradella (1644–82), Agostino Steffani (1654–1728), and Alessandro Scarlatti (discussed below), all of whom were opera composers as well. The tradition continued into the eighteenth century; the young Handel produced over one hundred cantatas and similar works during an extended visit to Italy (1707–9).

Probably the majority of such works are on texts whose conventional poetry is concerned with love—often unrequited—between Greek nymphs and shepherds. Reflecting developments in Italian opera, the arias are the main element, and by 1700 the *da capo* (ABA) aria was the most common, indeed practically the only, type of aria in use. In general, the arias of these works, whatever their form, are much longer than those of earlier Italian vocal music, and they possess increasingly complex formal structures; obbligato instruments are increasingly common as well, although Handel and other eighteenth-century composers continued to write many cantatas for voice and continuo alone. The recitatives in these works, on the other hand, are usually simpler than in earlier cantatas, containing fewer arioso passages and greater quantities of straightforward recitation.

As is true of the Italian operas of the period, most of this enormous output of music was never published and remains in manuscript to this day. Even the cantatas of a composer as important as Alessandro Scarlatti have been published only very selectively. The enormous productivity of these composers was made possible by changes in style that by the late seventeenth century permitted a gifted composer, upon being handed a poetic text, to set it to music in an appropriate form and style almost instantly, as if improvising. Compositional procedures had become routine, musical forms such as the da capo aria standardized, and the poetry used for these works was so conventional that it rarely required much thought or planning on the composer's part to produce an adequate musical setting. Indeed, many cantatas must have been commissioned, the poetry dashed off, and the music composed, rehearsed, and performed within the space of a few days.

We might suppose that such a situation would lead to texts and music consisting mainly of clichés, and indeed this is true of the works of many lesser composers. Yet, in the hands of such prodigiously talented musicians as Scarlatti and Handel, this highly conventionalized approach to composition produced numerous masterworks full of attractive melodies and original, compelling harmonic surprises and dramatic effects. It is probably no accident that these composers were also talented improvisers; the prevailing approach to composition favored those who could play or write on their feet, as it were.

Alessandro Scarlatti

So many distinguished composers emerged in Italy during the later seventeenth and early eighteenth centuries that it is almost arbitrary to select one to represent the entire period. Certainly one of the most important, however, was Alessandro Scarlatti (1660–1725), whose enormous output includes over six hundred cantatas.

Scarlatti was born in Palermo, Sicily, into a large family that included several musicians; his son Domenico would carry on the tradition (see Chapter 11). In 1672 Scarlatti was sent to Rome, where he presumably received musical training and heard considerable amounts of music, both sacred and secular. The patronage of the popes had naturally been a decisive factor in Roman music since the fifteenth century, and Palestrina, among others, had worked directly under several popes. But Rome's central place in the Roman Catholic world meant that many other powerful and wealthy patrons also resided there. By the late seventeenth century many of these patrons were as interested in secular music as in sacred works. Still, Scarlatti found it advantageous to divide his career between Rome and Naples, and today he is often associated with a group of opera composers active in the latter city, although he produced operas and other works in both places.

Besides cantatas, Scarlatti's music included perhaps one hundred operas (about seventy survive), as well as some thirty-three smaller theatrical works (serenatas) and about thirty-eight oratorios and other large sacred works. He also wrote masses, over one hundred motets, and keyboard music. A virtuoso harpsichordist, he nevertheless excelled in writing readily singable yet effective arias for the high soprano voices—both male and female—that dominated the Italian opera of his day. Like his cantatas, his operas consist almost solely of numerous arias joined by recitative; the arias in a single opera may number over sixty. The arias in the earlier operas are usually accompanied solely by continuo, but in later works they grow somewhat larger and the number of instrumental parts increases. Despite his unparalleled facility as a composer of melodious arias, Scarlatti was also skilled in the old-fashioned contrapuntal style—the *stile antico*, derived from the vocal polyphony of the Renaissance. Although the latter was now confined largely to church music, Scarlatti occasionally departed from convention by incorporating a substantial contrapuntal element into his secular works, as in the following cantata. Because of its length, we shall be concerned chiefly with two of its arias, although comments are also directed below to its opening instrumental movement and its recitatives.

Scarlatti's *Correa nel seno amato*

This cantata (anthology, Selection 11) dates perhaps from the 1690s. Consisting of ten movements (see Box 6.2), it is longer than the typical Italian cantata of the later Baroque, which often consists of just two arias alternating with as many recitatives. In addition, its inclusion of two violin parts marks it as a more ambitious work than most contemporaneous Italian cantatas, the majority of which were still composed for just voice and continuo; it even includes an instrumental introduction or *sinfonia*. Its anonymous text is the familiar shepherd's lament; here Daliso weeps over the nymph Corilla. The text focuses on a series of images from nature, such as the early-morning frost on the grass, which grows within earshot of the murmuring waves of a conveniently nearby stream. As conventional as such images may have been,

Box 6.2

Alessandro Scarlatti: *Correa nel sen amato*

MOVEMENTS

1. Sinfonia. 2 vlns., b.c. Key: B♭

    (a) [Grave]: slow introduction
        [Allegro]: quick imitative section
        [Largo]: slow conclusion
    (b) *Balletto:* dance in binary form

2. Recitative, "Correa nel seno amato." Sop., b.c.

    (a) arioso, "Correa nel seno amato"
    (b) simple recitative, "Rosseggiante nel viso"
    (c) arioso (triple time), "Tergea tutto pietà"
    (d) simple recitative, "Stanche al fine"
    (e) arioso (Largo, imitative texture), "Così con l'aure"

3. Aria, "Ombre opache." Sop., 2 vlns., b.c. Key: B♭

4. Recitative, "Curilla, anima mia, gioia." Sop., b.c.

5. Aria, "Fresche brine." Sop., 2 vlns. (in rit. only), b.c. Key: C minor. *See summary of form below.*

6. Recitative, "Piante insensate." Sop., b.c.

7. Aria, "Idolo amato." Sop., 2 vlns., b.c. Key: D minor

8. Recitative, "Ma voi, occhi dolenti." Sop., b.c.

    (a) simple recitative, "Ma voi, occhi doltenti"
    (b) arioso (imitative texture), "Ch'arda in fiamme di duolo e pianga"

9. Aria, "Onde belle." Sop., 2 vlns., b.c. Key: G minor. *See summary of form below.*

10. Recitative, "Curilla, anima mia, deh vieni." Sop., 2 vlns. (in final section only), b.c.

    (a) simple recitative, "Curilla, anima mia"
    (b) accompanied recitative, "Volea più dir Daliso"

Aria: "Fresche brine"

Da capo form framed by ritornellos.

    mm. 1–10: ritornello. C minor
    mm. 11–25: A section (lines 1–3, with motto opening). C minor
    mm. 27–49: B section (lines 4–6, twice). F minor → E♭ major
    mm. 51–60: A repeated. C minor
    mm. 61–70: ritornello repeated. C minor

Aria: "Onde belle"

Through-composed, with opening and closing ritornellos whose musical material is integrated with the vocal sections.

    mm. 1–8: ritornello. G minor
    mm. 9–17: lines 1–2. G minor → B♭ major
    mm. 18–29: lines 3–4. G minor
    mm. 30–47: line 5.* G minor

*This line of poetry = line 5 of aria no. 3, "Ombre opache."

---

they served the composer well by inspiring imaginative use of the conventions of word painting.

The Opening Sinfonia

The term **sinfonia** always refers to instrumental music, but not necessarily to anything resembling the symphony of the late eighteenth and nineteenth centuries. Any bit of instrumental music within a vocal work could be referred to as a sinfonia. By Scarlatti's day the term was most often attached to an opening instrumental movement—what we would call an overture. In earlier Italian vocal works, including the operas of Cavalli, the introductory sinfonia might consist of no more than a few short phrases. The present sinfonia, however, constitutes a short but self-contained *trio sonata* in three brief movements.

The trio sonata was the most common form of contemporary Italian instrumental chamber music (see Chapter 12). Its most common scoring, two violins and continuo, was frequently used as the instrumental portion of seventeenth-century vocal works as well. In this work, both the sinfonia and each of the five arias use the same instrumentation, as does the concluding accompanied recitative. Scarlatti, strangely enough, appears not to have composed any trio sonatas as such, but this sinfonia might well have been performed as a separate work.

Text

The nine vocal movements of the cantata alternate regularly between recitative and aria—an alternation determined by the poet, not the composer. As far back as *Orfeo*, aria texts had generally been short, their individual lines also tending toward brevity, typically of six or eight syllables. Recitative texts, on the other hand, usually alternate irregularly between lines of seven and eleven syllables. Earlier composers, such as Monteverdi and Strozzi, had frequently ignored the poet's division of the text, setting recitative verse in aria style and vice versa.

This became less frequent in the later Baroque, as the formal designs of both poetry and music grew more conventionalized.

Recitative

The recitative movements in this cantata constitute a narrator's description of Daliso's unhappy situation; they set the scene for the arias, which express Daliso's own emotional outpourings (often expressed through nature imagery). Although composed for a single singer, without dialogue, the cantata thus reflects the structure of contemporary Italian opera, which likewise consisted of alternating recitative and aria.

The recitatives here are nevertheless somewhat longer and more varied in style than in the operas of Scarlatti and later composers. As Box 6.2 shows, several of these recitative movements actually fall into distinct sections in contrasting styles; thus the second movement alternates between arioso and more simple types of recitative, as in somewhat earlier Venetian opera and the cantatas of Strozzi. As in those works, the changes of style are not arbitrary; each corresponds to a new idea or point of view in the text that the composer wished to bring out.

The first section of the opening recitative is largely in arioso style, with melismas on a number of words, such as the initial word *correa* ("hastened"; Ex. 6.1). As usual by this date, such a melisma provides both text painting and rhetorical emphasis. This melismatic arioso section describes the brilliance of the setting sun, but the style changes to a simpler type of recitative as the subject of the text shifts to Venus, the goddess of love, who is symbolized in the text by the rising of the planet that bears her name (Ex. 6.2). Still later, the poem speaks of Love's wiping away Daliso's tears; this line alone is set in arialike style in triple meter (Ex. 6.3). The effect is ironic, since Love here is described as pitiless, yet the musical style is one often associated in older Italian vocal music with more pleasant aspects of love (cf. Ex. 4.3). The movement concludes with another arioso section, marked *largo*, in which the soprano and continuo parts move in imitation (Ex. 6.4).[6] Such writing is very unusual in Italian recitative, where counterpoint of any sort is rare; it distinguishes this line of text from the remainder of the movement, emphasizing that it forms a separate thought and a distinct grammatical unit. Scarlatti uses the same effect at the end of the eighth movement.[7] In the final movement he sets off the closing words in a different manner, through the use of accompanied recitative; that is, the two violins join the continuo in accompanying the voice (Ex. 6.5).

---

[6]The tempo indication *largo* is one of the few such markings in Scarlatti's score, which, as usual at the time, leaves most tempos up to the performer's understanding of style. The word, which literally means "broad" in Italian, probably did not signify as slow a tempo as it does today; its presence here may have been intended simply to point to the presence of a contrapuntal texture and therefore a need to avoid the free rhythm appropriate in the preceding passage in simple recitative.

[7]The close of movement 8 is unusual in that Scarlatti writes out a contrapuntal realization of the basso continuo part, which elsewhere must be improvised in the customary manner.

Example 6.1 Alessandro Scarlatti, *Correa nel seno amato*, no. 2, recitative "Correa nel seno amato," mm. 1–6

Correa nel seno amato
Ver l'occidente fretoloso il sole . . .

As the sun ran hurriedly
Toward his favored western shore . . .

Example 6.2 Alessandro Scarlatti, *Correa nel seno amato*, no. 2, recitative, "Correa nel seno amato," mm. 21–24

Rosseggiante nel viso,
Sorgea tutta ridente
Dal leto pastoral la bianca Dea . . .

Blushing red,
There rose smiling
From her soft bed the white goddess . . .

Example 6.3 Alessandro Scarlatti, *Correa nel seno amato*, no. 2, recitative, "Correa nel seno amato," mm. 56–66

Tergea tutto pietà spietato Amore.

[His tears] were wiped away in pity by pitiless Love.

Example 6.4 Alessandro Scarlatti, *Correa nel seno amato*, no. 2, recitative, "Correa nel seno amato," mm. 72–79

Così con l'aure e'l vento
Sfogava singhiozzando il suo tormento.

In this manner, to the air and wind
He gave vent, sobbing, to his torment.

Example 6.5 Alessandro Scarlatti, *Correa nel seno amato*, concluding accompanied recitative, mm. 1–6

Volea più dir Daliso,
Ma punto d'improvviso
Dall'immenso dolore cadde svenuto.

Daliso wished to say more,
But at the point of doing so,
Out of great sadness he fell mute.

Performance Conventions in Recitative

The sections of movement 2 that are described above as being in simple style represent what had become the usual type of recitative in Italian cantata and opera by the 1690s. This style is referred to as *recitativo semplice*— "simple" recitative, characterized by frequent recitation on short repeated notes, as in Example 6.2.[8] Two issues arise frequently in the performance of this type of recitative. First, vocal phrases often end with what are notated as two repeated notes (see Ex. 6.1, mm. 2, 3; Ex. 6.2, mm. 1, 2, 4). By the eighteenth century, however, it had become customary to sing the first of these notes on a pitch different from the one notated, as shown in Example 6.6, where the passage notated as in Example 6.6a is actually sung as in Example 6.6b. Often, as in Example 6.6b, this turns the first note into a dissonant **appoggiatura**: an unprepared dissonance (ab') that resolves on the following note (g'). Appoggiaturas of various sorts were common ornaments in later seventeenth- and eighteenth-century performance practice, and this convention must have arisen as a form of ornamentation. But whether it would have been employed consistently in this work, from the 1690s, is uncertain.

Example 6.6 Conventional alterations of pitches sung in Alessandro Scarlatti, *Correa nel seno amato*, no. 2, recitative, "Correa nel seno amato," m. 3

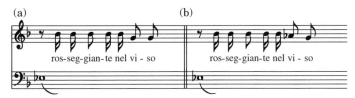

A second convention concerns the notation of the continuo part, which in this work would probably most often have been played by harpsichord and cello together. Although notated in long values, the bass notes of recitative were, by the eighteenth century, frequently performed as short notes—that is, not held out for their full written values. This made for a more lively and more audible presentation, as the singer could present the rapidly declaimed text without having to be heard over the sustained bass line. In Example 6.1 this means that the note B♭ in the bass, together with the B♭-major triad implied as its continuo realization, was actually heard only at the beginning of measure 1. Possibly the note (and chord) would have been repeated on the downbeat of measure 3 or 4. Again, however, it is uncertain when this convention arose. Certainly, however, Scarlatti would have held out the bass notes as written in the final accompanied recitative, where the violins have similar notation (see Ex. 6.5).

---

[8] Today the term *secco* ("dry") recitative is also used for this style, but it is better reserved for the even drier recitative of late eighteenth-century opera.

Arias

Unlike most cantatas composed during the late seventeenth and eighteenth centuries, this one is not yet dominated by arias in da capo form; all but one of the work's four arias are through-composed. The one da capo aria, no. 5, "Fresche brine" (anthology, Selection 11a), also happens to be the shortest and simplest aria in the cantata. As such it is close to the type of aria for which Scarlatti's operas are best known: a relatively brief, lyrical expression of feeling with a singable melody and an uncomplicated instrumental component, the latter often limited to basso continuo.

A **da capo aria** is one whose text falls into two stanzas, which we can designate A and B; in the most common form of such an aria, each stanza is set in a distinct musical section, and both the music and the text of section A are repeated after section B. The text of each stanza usually consists of from two to six lines of poetry, forming a single sentence in each case; thus a da capo aria presents two concise, distinct textual ideas, each having its own distinctive music. Very simple arias of this type already occur in Monteverdi's *Orfeo*, but the fully developed da capo aria emerged only during Scarlatti's lifetime. Its popularity was due in part to the literally thousands of attractive examples that he himself composed.

Our aria is typical of later da capo arias in that it includes an instrumental component (in addition to the basso continuo). But the instruments—that is, the violins—provide only a short ritornello that serves to introduce and then to conclude the vocal portion of the aria. Such would be unusual in the da capo arias of the eighteenth century, where the ritornello is more fully integrated with the vocal portion. In addition, our aria includes only a partial restatement of the opening section, indicated in our score by the words *dal segno* rather than *da capo*. This was by no means uncommon, and the aria can still be regarded as a genuine if brief example of da capo form.

The two stanzas of the text of our aria are of equal length. The first three lines (stanza A) address the drops of frozen dew on the flowers surrounding Daliso; the last three (stanza B) compare them to his tears. In analyzing the musical form of this or any Baroque aria, we are concerned particularly with how its text is laid out relative to the music. In the present case, the A section of the music begins with the ritornello and concludes with a cadence in the tonic (C minor, m. 48). Shortly afterward the voice enters with new text—the B text—in a new key, F minor (m. 53). The B section contains two complete statements of its text, concluding with a cadence in another new key, E♭ (m. 96). The vocal portion of the A section is then repeated verbatim, followed by the ritornello.

With its modulating tonal structure and relatively lengthy musical setting, this is a more extended and far more elaborate design than the brief ABA forms found in *Orfeo*. There the A section was a single phrase of music and poetry—more a simple refrain than a complete section. Here the A section is almost a self-contained composition in itself, yet it is only the first part of the aria (not counting the ritornello). Late Baroque musicians and listeners evidently valued such designs for their own sake, admiring the symmetry and predictable form of the da capo aria as well as the varied, complex music that it could contain. In addition, it became customary for singers to add their own improvised embellishments in such arias, and audiences could enjoy hearing the same music— the repeated A section—decorated in different ways each time a virtuoso sang it. This may, however, have been more true in opera than in the present work, where the simple tunefulness of the one da capo aria would be ruined by virtuoso embellishment.

Apart from its da capo form, this aria is also notable for its use of a device very common in late Baroque arias. The voice, after presenting the first line of the text, rests for two measures, then repeats line 1 (with its music) and continues with the remainder of the A section. The initial vocal entrance (mm. 11–12) is called a **motto,** and an aria of this type is therefore a **motto aria.**[9] The motto is a form of musical rhetoric: by singling out the first line—sometimes just the first word or two—the composer emphasizes it. Typically, line 1 contains a noun that represents the topic of the aria—in this case, *brine* ("frost")—and the motto entrance helps establish this image as the subject of the movement as a whole.

Instrumental Participation in Arias

The cantata's last aria, "Onde belle" (anthology, Selection 11b), is another motto aria: the voice enters in measure 9 and then repeats its entrance two measures later. Unlike "Fresche brine," it is not in da capo form, and in this respect it is somewhat old-fashioned. But its treatment of the violins represents a trend that would continue in the following century.

The aria opens with a ritornello, which unlike that of "Fresche brine," is thoroughly integrated with the vocal portion of the movement. After the ritornello (mm. 1–8), the violins continue to play, accompanying the voice in a four-part contrapuntal texture and rounding off the end of the aria with a short instrumental passage. Brief instrumental passages also punctuate the body of the aria at several points. The longer such passages—those at measures 17, 22, and 45— can be described as ritornellos, even though none literally repeat the opening instrumental section. All nevertheless restate and develop musical material first presented in the opening ritornello.

Particularly important is the theme stated by the second violin in measure 1. This theme can be described as a **ritornello theme,** since it opens the ritornello and is repeated, at least in part, in subsequent ritornellos. In this case, the ritornello theme is also a *subject,* since it is imitated by the first violin (m. 2) and the continuo (m. 3) as each enters.[10] Imitative counterpoint of this type is unusual in the Baroque aria; typical, however, is the voice's repetition of the ritornello theme when it enters (m. 9).

---

[9]Often the German equivalents of these words are used: *Devise* (motto) and *Devisenarie* (motto aria).
[10]The imitative entries of the three instrumental parts follow the same pattern that would be expected in a *fugue,* a type of instrumental movement common in the trio sonata (see Chapters 11 and 12).

The voice's entry reveals that the ritornello theme is more than an abstract musical idea; its first five notes constitute a bit of word painting on *onde* ("waves"), whose first syllable is sung to a short melisma that circles or turns through the interval g'–bb'. This turning motive, as we can call it, not only dominates the ritornellos but continues to be heard in the violin parts after the voice has gone on to other textual ideas. For example, in measures 18–21, as the voice sings the single word *ascoltate* ("hear me!"), the two violins enter in imitation with a version of the ritornello theme (mm. 18–19). The violins then continue with passagework in sixteenth notes that includes several additional statements of the turning motive (mm. 20, 21). Thus a musical depiction of waves accompanies Daliso's anguished prayer that the waves listen to his complaint. Indeed, the "wave" motive permeates the texture of the entire aria, which thus becomes a sort of musical symbol for waves. As we shall see, countless arias from later cantatas and other Baroque vocal compositions use instrumental parts in like manner to help represent the text.

ENGLISH VOCAL MUSIC IN THE LATER SEVENTEENTH CENTURY

At the middle of the seventeenth century in England, civil war and a brief period as a republic (1649–60) had left the country temporarily without a royal court and chapel. Those institutions had been important centers for music under the previous monarchs—Elizabeth I (r. 1558–1603), James I (r. 1603–25), and Charles I (r. 1625–49)—all of whom had been strong patrons of the arts. Music had flourished particularly under Elizabeth and during the first decade of James's reign, during which the leading musician in England was William Byrd (1543–1623). One of the supreme figures of Renaissance music, Byrd wrote not only sacred and secular vocal polyphony but also—unlike Palestrina, Lassus, and other contemporaries on the Continent—music for solo keyboard and for instrumental consort. His output includes numerous songs for voice and instruments; although he largely avoided the madrigal, a number of his younger contemporaries are known for their **English madrigals**—settings of English texts composed in imitation of the polyphonic Italian madrigal of the late sixteenth century—and for strophic songs (called airs) with lute accompaniment. The most famous composer of the latter was John Dowland (1563–1626), a lutenist who also composed many solo works for his own instrument.

War, together with the banning of elaborate sacred and theatrical music by the republican or Commonwealth government, had virtually extinguished this rich musical tradition by midcentury. With the restoration of the monarchy in 1660, however, royal and cathedral musical institutions were reestablished and, in London, commercial theaters were allowed to reopen. Under King Charles II, who had spent much of the preceding period in exile in France, musicians and musical genres were imported from both France and Italy. These mingled with the remnants of the native English tradition, which had been preserved by survivors from pre-Commonwealth days, such as the song composer Henry Lawes (1596–1662; his more prolific composer brother William had died in the Civil War in 1645).

Although no English theater possessed the resources needed to mount full-fledged operas, it became common during the Restoration period (1660–88) for spoken plays to include musical interludes. These ranged from single songs to lavishly staged operatic scenes with dancing and choral singing, somewhat as in the pre-Commonwealth English court masque.[11] In addition, in the Chapel Royal and the cathedrals the distinctively English form of church music called the anthem was again cultivated. The anthem had originated as the Anglican (English Protestant) equivalent of the late sixteenth-century motet. It had retained a conservative contrapuntal style through the earlier seventeenth century, although the voices were generally joined by organ and, in some works, a consort of viols (violas da gamba). After the Restoration, particularly in music written for the monarch's Chapel Royal, instrumental participation was expanded. Violins replaced viols, and composers adopted up-to-date elements of both the French and the Italian styles, including the use of overture-like preludes and virtuoso solo vocal writing.

Henry Purcell

The most significant English composer of the period was Henry Purcell (1659–95), whose lifespan corresponded roughly with the Restoration period—that is, the reigns of Kings Charles II (1660–85) and James II (1685–88)—together with that of Queen Mary II (1689–94), who in theory ruled jointly with her husband, William III (1689–1702). All except William were important patrons of musicians, including Purcell. Born probably at Westminster (in London), Purcell led a career outwardly similar to that of earlier English composers, such as Byrd. As a boy he sang in the newly reconstituted Chapel Royal, and by 1677 he was composing for King Charles II. In 1679 he became organist at Westminster Abbey, the great London church where royal coronations are still held; in that position he succeeded his teacher John Blow (1649–1708), the most talented of his English contemporaries. Purcell continued to enjoy royal patronage for the remainder of his life, composing anthems for the Chapel Royal as well as court odes and royal welcome songs—multimovement vocal works combining instrumental, solo vocal, and choral writing somewhat like the Continental serenata. He also wrote a small but very fine repertory of keyboard music and several sets of extraordinary chamber works for strings (both viol and violin ensembles).

Many of Purcell's works reveal a continuing respect for complex imitative counterpoint, such as Purcell would have found in the music of Byrd and other late Renaissance predecessors. It was in keeping with a certain idiosyncratic conservatism, evident in English music throughout the sixteenth and seventeenth centuries, that this older music was still studied and emulated in Purcell's day. Similarly, Blow, Purcell, and their English contemporaries continued to em-

---

[11]During the first decades of the seventeenth century, the masque had been the English equivalent of the French court ballet (see Chapter 5), which combined dance and singing in a manner reminiscent of the old *intermedio*.

kept blank ✗ 128
dissonances

ploy irregular dissonances and other elements of what Monteverdi called the *seconda pratica*, long after the ostentatious use of such things had ceased to be fashionable elsewhere.

Some of Purcell's most important writing lies in his many songs, most of which were composed for musical scenes in Restoration plays. Many of these songs incorporate recitative and contrasting aria styles, in effect constituting English cantatas. His one short opera, *Dido and Aeneas* (ca. 1689), is similar in style to his other stage music; its best-known music is the lament of Queen Dido, sung to her attendants as she prepares to die. This famous number follows the Venetian lament tradition in its use of a bass ostinato (Ex. 6.7). But characteristic of Purcell, and of English seventeenth-century music in general, are some quirky but highly expressive touches: the asymmetry of the ostinato,

Example 6.7 Purcell, *Dido and Aeneas*, Act 3, scene 2, Dido: "When I am laid in earth," mm. 1–14

When I am laid in earth

May my wrongs create

No trouble in thy breast.

which is five measures in length rather than the more common four; and the combination of chromaticism with descending appoggiaturas, as on the words "laid" and "trouble."

A sort of chamber opera, written for a private performance, *Dido and Aeneas* is in some respects less significant than Purcell's four or five **semi-operas**— plays incorporating substantial musical scenes and produced in London's commercial theaters. Among these works is *King Arthur*, performed in 1691, with a text by the leading English poet of the day, John Dryden. Its musical portions are operatic in length and style; modeled after the *divertissements* of Lullian opera, they combine recitative, solo airs, choral numbers, and dances. Here, as in his other vocal music, Purcell imaginatively adapted elements of both the French and Italian styles of his day for the purpose of setting texts written in English.

From Rosy Bowers

Among the last works of Purcell's short career were a number of musical scenes for Thomas D'Urfey's three-part theatrical adaptation of *Don Quixote*, the famous novel by the Spanish writer Miguel de Cervantes (1547–1616). Purcell's music for one of these scenes, *From Rosy Bowers* (anthology, Selection 12), was published posthumously as "the last song the author set." Like a number of Purcell's other "songs," it is an English cantata, comprising the same alternating recitatives and arias customary in Italian cantatas of the time. Yet it also reflects the stylistic blending that was possible for an English composer. One of the arias is actually a French-style *air*, and the recitatives are longer and closer to arioso than was customary in the *recitativo semplice* of contemporary Italian cantatas.

Although scored only for soprano and basso continuo, this is one of Purcell's most effective stage scenes. It is sung by the female character Altesidora, who has been trying to woo the old knight Don Quixote. To gain his sympathy she sings for him this series of poignant recitatives and arias, each of a distinct type and expressing a different emotion. She ends with a so-called mad song, a common type in the Restoration theater. But Altesidora's madness is all an act; instead of being genuinely troubled or desperate, she is plotting and intriguing. Thus the concluding passage has a triumphant character that seems to look forward to Altesidora's successful accomplishment of her plan.

The opening recitative, in which Altesidora calls on the "god of love" (Cupid), contains many examples of Purcell's vivid musical rhetoric, including frequent chromaticism and sudden outbursts of melismatic arioso. The text of the following air, "Or if more influencing," refers to the arts of Venus and the three Graces, which Altesidora wishes to employ in order to win over Strephon. The poem's image of Greek goddesses dancing on a mountaintop explains why Purcell set it as a *bourrée*, one of the French dances of the period. Like Lully, Purcell frequently used dance types as the basis of vocal numbers (compare Exs. 5.3 and 5.6). The bourrée, like other French dances, is characterized by its use of distinctive meter, rhythm, and form: that is, the duple time signature, the melodic motion in even quarter notes (beginning with a quarter-note upbeat), and the binary form of the air as a whole, whose two halves were probably meant to be repeated.

When Altesidora's dance fails to have its desired effect, she resolves to go mad in the second recitative ("Ah! 'tis in vain"). This recitative is perhaps even more vivid than the first; one instance of word painting was so extreme that an early editor apparently eliminated it from the music. On the word "death" (m. 4), Purcell asked the singer to leap up to the note e♭″ following an e♮′—the rare melodic interval of a diminished octave. The early eighteenth-century edition reproduced in the anthology omits the e♭″.

The work continues with a short air in da capo form, "Or say, ye powers," which Altesidora apparently addresses to the gods of a stream or river into which she threatens to throw herself. The air opens with a short ritornello, played by the basso continuo (mm. 1–8). But this ritornello is not heard again, except for the imitation of the opening motive by the voice (compare mm. 1, 8, and 9). The concluding recitative, "No, I'll straight run mad," begins with a convincing impersonation of madness, followed by a somewhat more regular arioso (starting in m. 5). The last four lines of the poem (mm. 10–20) employ frequent imitation between the two parts—a device that makes more emphatic the word painting on "fly" and "thousand" while bringing the scene to a musically effective ending. It shows, too, that for Purcell, like Alessandro Scarlatti, counterpoint was by no means foreign to the cantata, which to the end of the Baroque continued the tradition of expressive monody invented at the end of the sixteenth century.

CHAPTER 7

SEVENTEENTH-CENTURY SACRED MUSIC

At the beginning of the seventeenth century, while Monteverdi and other Italian composers were transforming the secular genres of the late Renaissance into those of the early Baroque, sacred music was hardly being neglected. The innovations applied to the madrigal, such as the addition of instruments and the frequent substitution of solo voices for vocal polyphony, took place in the motet and mass as well. Yet older traditions were retained as well—more so than in secular music. Composers continued to write polyphonic masses and motets in *stile antico* (the "older style")—a style that remained outwardly close to that of the vocal polyphony of the mid-sixteenth century, save for the addition of a continuo part for the organ. Even Monteverdi published an old-fashioned polyphonic mass in 1610, alongside his famous Marian Vespers. As this publication showed, works in *stile antico* could stand beside up-to-date music in the *stile moderno* within the same printed volume and, presumably, within the same liturgical service.

The Sacred Concerto

Because they were intended to serve the same religious function as older works, the new types of church music continued to use traditional, mostly biblical, texts. Most can still be described as motets or mass movements, although a term frequently used to distinguish motets in the newer style is **concerto.** This word later came to be used for a type of instrumental music involving a soloist and larger ensemble. As applied to seventeenth-century music, it refers to music that includes specific instrumental parts alongside parts for one or more voices. It could be used for secular music—Monteverdi entitled his Seventh Book of Madrigals (Venice, 1619) *Concerto*—but it is most often used for sacred works. The adjective *concertato* is also used to describe such compositions.

Sacred concertos or *concertato* works range from solo motets for a single voice and continuo—that is, sacred monody—to massive polychoral works for a dozen or more vocal and instrumental parts arranged in two or more separate groupings or choirs. The smaller sacred concertos of Monteverdi and other early Baroque composers are close in style to their secular cantatas and continuo madrigals. But their larger *concertato* works are composed on a scale that we have not yet encountered in the works we have considered.

SACRED MUSIC IN VENICE: GIOVANNI GABRIELI

The practice of including instruments in sacred vocal music went back to the beginning of the sixteenth century or earlier, but only around 1600 did composers begin to designate instrumental parts as such in sacred vocal music. The first major composer to do so in a significant number of sacred works was the Venetian Giovanni Gabrieli (ca. 1553/6–1612; see Box 7.1). His uncle Andrea Gabrieli (ca. 1510–86) had been organist at St. Mark's, Venice, and briefly a colleague of Lassus's at Munich in Germany. Giovanni studied with his uncle Andrea and probably with Lassus as well. In 1585 he became second organist at St. Mark's, in effect succeeding his uncle as the city's chief composer of large-scale sacred music.

In addition to composing polyphonic madrigals and organ music and editing a collection of both his own and his uncle's sacred vocal works (1586), Gabrieli produced two immense collections of what he called *sacrae symphoniae*— "sacred symphonies"—which were published in 1597 and 1615.[1] Both volumes consist primarily of polychoral vocal works; those in the second volume are in *concertato* style, that is, with designated instrumental parts alongside those for voices. The first collection also includes a separate series of purely instrumental works, and a second series of such works was published separately in 1615. Hence, Gabrieli, like his English contemporary William Byrd, was one of the few composers active before 1600 who attained supreme stature in instrumental as well as vocal composition.

Because the greater part of his career fell within the sixteenth century, Gabrieli is often considered a composer more of the late Renaissance than of the Baroque. Indeed, unlike Monteverdi, whose career similarly bridged the sixteenth and seventeenth centuries, Gabrieli never took up the more obvious stylistic innovations that we associate with the new Baroque style, such as the wholesale adoption of monody or the unorthodox harmony and dissonance treatment that Monteverdi called the *seconda pratica*. Yet Gabrieli's works proved to be as influential as Monteverdi's on many younger composers, and unlike Monteverdi he was, like his uncle Andrea, a renowned teacher. In fact, Gabrieli trained many of the leading composers of the early Baroque, among them a number of important German musicians who made the difficult trip southward specifically to study with him. For this reason alone it would be important for us to consider Gabrieli's music, although the latter merits consideration in its own right as well.

Gabrieli's influence was great enough that even Monteverdi adopted elements of Gabrieli's style, in a number of sacred works written after Monteverdi came to Venice in 1613. But Gabrieli's influence was felt particularly by a number of northern composers, the greatest of whom, Heinrich Schütz, studied with Gabrieli and closely imitated him in many works (see below). Gabrieli today is famous mainly for the massive sonorities of his large-scale vocal and instrumental works, but his students must also have prized the expressive power of

---

[1] A very short keyboard piece by Gabrieli is given as Ex. 10.2.

Box 7.1

Giovanni Gabrieli (ca. 1553/6–1612)

---

ca. 1553–56. Born at Venice. Studies with his uncle Andrea Gabrieli.

1575–79. Musician for the duke of Munich, working under Lassus.

1584. Appointed second organist at St. Mark's, Venice.

1586. Andrea dies; Giovanni publishes *Concerti* (polyphonic madrigals and motets by both composers) the following year.

1597. Publishes his *Sacrae symphoniae*, Book 1 (polychoral motets, canzoni, and sonatas).

1612. Dies at Venice. His *Sacrae symphoniae*, Book 2, and *Canzoni et sonate* are published posthumously in 1615.

---

his music, including works composed on a smaller scale, such as his Italian madrigals. In general, Gabrieli's vocal works avoid not only the contrapuntal liberties of the second practice but also the vivid word painting and other virtuoso features of late Renaissance and early Baroque vocal music. But they pay careful attention to the declamation of the text, and they frequently employ massive homophonic sonorities to achieve particular expressive effects. Both characteristics can be found in the music of Lassus (see Chapter 2), which remained equally influential on early Baroque composers in Germany; indeed, Gabrieli and his German students can be seen as inheriting Lassus's tradition of expressive yet relatively restrained musical rhetoric.

Polychoral Works

The ambitious scoring of Gabrieli's works reflected the opulence of the Venetian churches for which they were written. Many of these works are **polychoral:** the ensemble is divided into two or more distinct groups, each of which constitutes a separate choir or chorus.[2] A typical work such as the eight-voice *Ego sum qui sum* (published in 1597) is for two four-part groups, each comprising soprano, alto, tenor, and bass (Ex. 7.1). Each phrase of the text is introduced by one of the choirs, then echoed by the second; the two choirs join together to emphasize important words (e.g., *consilium* in mm. 5–6) or to mark the ends of sections. Thus the choral antiphony does more than create an effect of splendor; it is also an element of musical rhetoric, used to articulate the structure of the text.

---

[2]The word *choir* or *chorus* can refer to a body of either voices or instruments. Another term for the use of multiple ensembles within a single work is *cori spezzati* ("separated" or "interrupted" choruses").

Example 7.1 G. Gabrieli, *Ego sum qui sum*, mm. 1–6

Ego sum qui sum, et consilium
meum non est cum impiis.

I am who I am, and my counsel is
not with the impious.

The choirs of a polychoral work do not always comprise equal numbers or types of voices. Some compositions, for example, pit a group of high voices against lower ones. Sometimes the two or more choirs employed in a polychoral work were physically separated, to enhance the "stereo" effect that results from hearing two or more groups performing in different locations within a church or other large structure; balconies and organ or choir lofts were particularly favored for this purpose. But not all polychoral music employed this practice, which often must have led to problems of balance and coordination. It was once believed that polychoral writing was invented specifically to take advantage of the unique architecture of St. Mark's, which includes numerous balconies and other spots where different choirs might have been placed. In fact, by the late sixteenth century polychoral music had become a fairly common feature of vocal works performed in churches throughout Italy and elsewhere, as numerous compositions by Lassus, Palestrina, and other non-Venetian composers demonstrate. What distinguished the Venetian polychoral style was the regular participation of virtuoso instrumentalists as well as a heightened concern for colorful sonority and massive triadic harmony. These features, already evident in the later works of Andrea Gabrieli, are characteristic of most of Giovanni's works and of the polychoral music of his students, notably the German Schütz.

The Scoring of Venetian Polychoral Works

Even in Gabrieli's posthumous 1615 collection of sacred polyphony with instruments, most of the parts are in principle vocal and bear texts. Some works, however, have explicitly labeled instrumental parts, and many others were frequently performed with instruments replacing some of the voices. Thus a work such as that shown in Example 7.1 might have been performed with a soprano singing the top part of one choir and a tenor the third part of the second choir.[3] Instruments would have provided the remaining parts—perhaps recorders or other woodwinds those of the first choir, cornetto and trombones for the second, with an organ providing a basso continuo for each choir.

Such scoring practices, although they came to be widespread in the seventeenth century, reflected local traditions at Venice and particularly at St. Mark's Basilica. Throughout the sixteenth and seventeenth centuries, the musicians of St. Mark's included not only several organists but woodwind and brass specialists. These instrumentalists appear to have been regular participants in performances of sacred music long before composers such as Gabrieli began to write parts specifically for them. Over the years, conventions governing the scoring of such works seem to have been worked out. One basic principle appears to have been that each choir should contain at least one singer, so that the text would be clearly enunciated. Principles governing the instrumentation of such music were eventually published by Schütz and by Michael Praetorius (1571/72–1621), a prolific German composer and author of an important early musical encyclopedia, the *Syntagma musicum* (Treatise on music, 3 vols., 1614–19).[4]

The most important instruments in this music—after the organ, which furnished the basso continuo—were the cornetto and the sackbut. The **sackbut** is the Renaissance trombone, similar to the modern instrument but somewhat mellower in tone; it was employed primarily in alto, tenor, and bass sizes. The **cornetto** (or cornett, *Zink* in German) usually furnished the soprano part or parts. Not to be confused with the modern cornet, a brass instrument resembling the trumpet, Gabrieli's cornetto was rather a sort of woodwind. It has, however, a cup mouthpiece like that used on brass instruments, and its sound blends well with that of the sackbuts. The technique of the cornetto permits both great virtuosity as well as expressive control of articulation and dynamics, and for this reason it was the leading wind instrument in early seventeenth-century Italy, often substituting for the violin in sonatas and other instrumental compositions.

Trumpets, although commonly used in modern performances of Gabrieli's music, were rare participants in *concertato* vocal works, at least at Venice around 1600.

---

[3]At Venice the soprano parts were probably sung by adult male castrati; see Chapter 8.

[4]For Schütz's and Praetorius's views on the instrumentation of their polychoral works, see Anthony F. Carver, *Cori spezzati* (Cambridge: Cambridge University Press, 1988), 1:233–34 and 216–20.

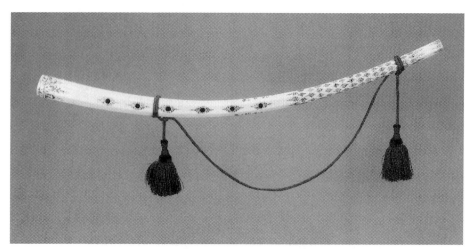

Figure 7.1 Zink, Imperial City of Nürnberg, ca. 1600. Ex coll.: Barons von Rothschild, Vienna. America's Shrine to Music Museum, Vermillion, South Dakota, Joe R. and Joella F. Utley Collection, 1999 (no. 7368). This ornate cornetto, made of ivory, lacks its brass-style mouthpiece. The German city of Nürnberg (Nuremberg) was a center for the production of cornettos and brass instruments. The cornetto was held somewhat like a flute (see Figure 2.1); the tasseled cord on this example is decorative. Photo by Simon Spicer.

Together with the timpani (kettledrums), which were usually played as parts of trumpet ensembles, the trumpet was considered a military and heraldic instrument. To a limited degree, modern trumpets and bugles retain those associations, but now they are largely ceremonial. In an age when military communication required simple visual and aural signals, however, trumpets and drums played practical military roles, conveying commands in battle and regulating the marching of troops. Trumpeters thus served civic and social functions distinct from those of other musicians, and this set them apart in the rigid hierarchy of Renaissance and early Baroque society. Most of their music was apparently memorized or improvised, and written trumpet parts are rare in vocal or instrumental music composed before the second half of the seventeenth century.

Gabrieli's *In ecclesiis*

Today Gabrieli's most famous work is probably the *concertato* motet *In ecclesiis*, published posthumously in the 1615 collection of *symphoniae sacrae* (anthology, Selection 13). A splendid example of the polychoral style, it is scored for three choirs: two vocal choirs, each consisting of soprano, alto, tenor, and bass, and an instrumental choir composed of three cornettos, "violino" (actually a viola), and two trombones. Separate from the three choirs is a continuo part for the organ, whose sustained sound helps bind the work's disparate elements together.[5]

---

[5]Modern performances sometimes add chitarrone or other instruments to this part, but Gabrieli designates it simply *basso per l'organo* (bass for the organ).

The second of the two vocal choirs is designated the **capella,** a term that literally means "chapel" or "chorus" but which came to mean an additional or, in some works, optional vocal chorus. Gabrieli and his contemporaries were well aware that polychoral works were expensive to perform and that not all institutions had the resources to present them as written. Many such works thus include one or two *capella* choruses that add volume and grandeur but are not strictly necessary. The parts for the *capella* tend to be less demanding than those of the principal vocal chorus or choruses. We can think of the latter as being intended for soloists, although in many performances all of the parts, including those of the *capella* choruses, may have been sung by individual performers; **doubling,** in which two or more musicians sing or play the same part, was far from a universal practice and in many places may have occurred only on special occasions, if ever. In the present work, the *capella* enters chiefly to reinforce the first choir, singing only in refrains and in the final section.

Although typical in many ways of polychoral motets from the early seventeenth century, *In ecclesiis* is unusual among Gabrieli's works for several reasons. First, it includes several monodic passages for solo voice and continuo; only in his latest works did Gabrieli employ this type of scoring. Second, Gabrieli rarely specified the instrumental forces as precisely as he did here; perhaps this was because the instrumental choir plays an unusually prominent role in this work, having one section all to itself (mm. 26–34, marked *sinfonia*). Finally, in the climactic final section of the motet (mm. 87–116), Gabrieli employs chromatic voice leading. A rare practice for him, it reflects the direct invocation of the deity (*Deus,* "God!") that occurs at this point in the text.

The text is drawn from various scriptural sources.[6] It includes five statements of the word *alleluia*, used here as a refrain, with essentially the same music each time (see Box 7.2). These refrains divide the work into five sections; each section builds to its climactic statement of the refrain, which thus unifies the composition in a particularly satisfying way.

The impression of a well-integrated composition is deepened by the gradual way in which the scoring is built up. Not until measure 87, at the beginning of the final section, do all fifteen parts sound together. Thus, despite the massive polychoral appearance of the score, most of the work actually has the quality of chamber music. Part 1 is primarily for solo soprano, part 2 for solo bass (both with continuo). The instrumental choir then enters, to be joined by the two remaining soloists (alto and bass) for part 3. This section, incidentally, is composed in eight-voice imitative counterpoint, an impressive feat of polyphonic skill. It contains, moreover, eight successive imitative subjects that increase in rhythmic motion, leading to the lively figures in sixteenth notes in measures 52–55. Part 4 is again chiefly for vocal soloists (soprano and bass, now singing together). In part 5, finally, all voices and instruments perform together in the homophonic chordal writing for which Gabrieli is best known.

---

[6]As in many Latin texts of the Renaissance and earlier periods, the anonymous author of this text appears to have drawn, perhaps from memory, on various biblical texts without exactly quoting any one in particular.

BOX 7.2

Gabrieli: *In ecclesiis*

Published posthumously in *Sacrae symphoniae*, Book 2 (1615)

Section	Lines of Text	Scoring*	Measures
1	1	I: quintus	1–5
	2 (refrain)	+II	6–10
2	3	I: octavus	11–21
	4 (refrain)	+II	22–26
3	— (sinfonia)	III	26–34
	5–6	+I: altus, tenor	35–56
	7 (refrain)	+II	57–61a
4	8–9	I: quintus, octavus	61b–82a
	10 (refrain)	+II	82b–87a
5	11	I, II, III	87b–107a
	12 (refrain)	I, II, III	107b–116

*Roman numerals designate choirs: I = soloists, II = *capella*, III = instruments. All sections include basso continuo, played by the organ.

Gabrieli's Works for Instrumental Ensemble

In addition to a number of organ works, Gabrieli composed an important body of *canzonas* and *sonatas* for instrumental ensemble. The performing forces required range from as few as four to as many as twenty-two players, arranged in one to five choirs. These works are sacred in the sense that they were intended primarily for performance in church: following a Renaissance tradition that continued through the Baroque in Roman Catholic countries, certain portions of the mass and office that were normally sung could be replaced by instrumental music. No doubt Gabrieli's canzonas and sonatas were played in other contexts as well.

Most of the instrumental works published in Gabrieli's 1597 collection declare their connection with sixteenth-century vocal tradition through their use of the title **canzona**. Literally meaning "song," the Italian word was used in the sixteenth century for French polyphonic chansons by such composers as Lassus. Andrea Gabrieli had transcribed a number of such works for solo organ, and like Giovanni he also composed original works for instrumental ensemble in the same style. Giovanni's canzonas no longer have much in common with the original vocal genre, but they do often incorporate a type of repeated-note motive typical of the declamatory style of the sixteenth-century polyphonic vocal chanson (Ex. 7.2). In addition, polychoral canzonas such as that shown in

Example 7.2 employ the antiphonal scoring characteristic of the *concertato* motets that were published alongside them; the individual parts even bear the same Latin names used for voice parts, rather than being designated for specific instruments.

Example 7.2 G. Gabrieli, *Canzon septimi toni* (1597), mm. 1–7

Both the 1597 and 1615 collections include, in addition to canzonas, a number of works designated **sonata**. The term at this date meant little more than music that is played—as opposed to the cantata, which is sung. Gabrieli seems to have reserved the term for pieces that lacked the chansonlike characteristics of his canzonas. The sonatas include massive works in up to twenty-two parts. But one, entitled "Sonata with three violins," includes virtuoso writing of a type that would become typical of the Italian Baroque violin sonata (Ex. 7.3). With its dialoguelike exchanges between the three violins, restrained chromaticism, and written-out embellishment, this work constitutes an instrumental equivalent of the madrigals for three sopranos and continuo published a few years previously by Luzzaschi (see Chapter 3).[7]

---

[7]The three upper parts in Gabrieli's sonata can also be played on other instruments, such as cornettos; the bass line, designated for organ (which provides a continuo realization), can also be joined by an optional fourth string part, most likely for bass viola da gamba.

Example 7.3 G. Gabrieli, *Sonata con tre violini* (1615), mm. 19–28

SACRED MUSIC IN GERMANY: HEINRICH SCHÜTZ

The most significant German composer of the seventeenth century was Heinrich Schütz (1585–1672). In the course of a long career Schütz, like Monteverdi, passed from what we call the style of the late Renaissance to that of the Baroque. Despite his training as an organist, his surviving music consists mostly of sacred vocal compositions. Like Monteverdi, he also wrote a significant number of secular and stage works—including the first German opera—but most of these have been lost. Although he set texts in Italian and Latin, his great accomplishment was to adapt the primarily Italian style of the early Baroque to the rhythms and accents of the German language and to the texts of German writers, notably Luther's translation of the Bible. In the process he created a distinctive personal idiom that was of great influence on several younger generations of northern composers.

Born in Köstritz, a small town in central Germany, Schütz lived during a time when northern Europe was a patchwork of mostly small, independent principalities (see Box 7.3). Those states whose rulers were artistically inclined supported musical establishments of one sort or another. Schütz spent most of his career working for one or another of these rulers, in particular the duke (or elector) of Saxony, who ruled from Dresden, then as now the leading city in southeastern Germany.

For much of his life, however, Schütz was forced to follow an extraordinarily winding career path, quite different from those of his more settled Italian

Box 7.3

Heinrich Schütz (1585–1672)

1585. Born at Köstritz, near Gera in western Saxony (southeastern Germany).

1590. Family moves to Weissenfels, about twenty miles north.

1598. Visiting at the inn owned by Schütz's father, the ruling Landgrave Moritz of Hesse hears Schütz sing; a year later Schütz joins the court of Hesse at Kassel, about one hundred miles to the west.

1608. Enters the University of Marburg, fifty miles southwest of Kassel, and studies law (then a common course of study, not necessarily intended as preparation for a legal career).

1609–12. Studies at Venice with Giovanni Gabrieli; dedicates to the latter his Opus 1, a book of madrigals (1611).

1613–16. Again at Kassel as court musician, but twice called to Dresden (1614, 1615–16).

1617. Kapellmeister (music director) to Elector (Duke) Johann Georg I of Saxony at Dresden; holds that position (with interruptions) the rest of his life.

1619. Publishes *Psalmen Davids* (polychoral psalm settings; revised editions, 1628 and 1661).

1623. Publishes his *Auferstehung Christi* (The Resurrection, oratorio)

1624. Publishes *Cantiones sacrae* (polyphonic motets).

1627. His opera *Dafne* performed at the wedding of Georg II of Hesse (text by Martin Opitz after Rinuccini; music lost).

1628–29. Second visit to Venice; publishes there his *Symphoniae sacrae*, Part 1 (Latin polychoral works).

1631. Saxony enters the Thirty Years' War; economic hardship subsequently leads to diminishment of musical activities at Dresden, causing Schütz to find a series of temporary positions elsewhere.

1634–35. In Denmark; director of music (kapellmeister) to King Christian IV.

1636. Back in Dresden, publishes *Musicalische Exequien* (funeral music) and Part 1 of *Kleine geistliche Konzerte* (small sacred concertos).

1637. Obtains imperial privilege (a form of copyright) for his published works.

1639–41. Publishes Part 2 of *Kleine geistliche Konzerte* (1639); serves as kapellmeister to the duke of Calenberg at Hanover and Hildesheim (in northern Germany).

1641. Back in Dresden; the musical establishment there barely functioning.

1642–44. Second period in Denmark as kapellmeister.

1644–45. Serves the duke of Brunswick at Wolfenbüttel (northern Germany, southeast of Hanover).

1645. Returns to Dresden but begins partial retirement, dividing his time between Dresden and his family home in Weissenfels (about seventy-five miles to the west). Continues to receive commissions from various German rulers.

1647, 1650. Publishes Parts 2 and 3 of his *Symphoniae sacrae* (sacred concertos); also *Geistliche Chormusik* (motets, 1648)

1656. Death of Saxon elector Johann Georg I; Schütz begins full retirement from Dresden, though still providing music and services on occasion.

1660–61. At Wolfenbüttel (where he continued to hold title of kapellmeister); performs his *Historia der Geburth Christi* (Christmas Oratorio, published 1664).

1666. Performs his three Passions (Good Friday music, for unaccompanied voices).

1670–72. Moves to Dresden (1670), composes his *Schwanengesang* ("Swan Song": Psalms 119 and 100 and a Magnificat, in *stile antico*); dies there 1672.

contemporaries. A German musician of Schütz's generation, particularly one born in a relatively provincial place, could obtain a first-rate musical education only by traveling. Schütz made two trips to Venice, first to study with Giovanni Gabrieli, later to hear the music of Monteverdi and others. Unfortunately, the latter part of Schütz's career coincided with the Thirty Years' War (1618–48) and its aftermath. During this period the cities and courts of Germany were repeatedly ravaged by the marauding armies of France, Sweden, and various German princes. The degree of economic devastation varied widely; some places were destroyed, others untouched. But the general suffering and depredation were enormous, and Schütz, like other musicians, was forced to seek employment and commissions from a variety of sources. Hence, although from around 1618 onwards he held the position of kapellmeister—the German equivalent of *maestro di capella* or chapel master—at Dresden, for much of his life he continued to travel, holding temporary positions in Denmark and elsewhere. The distances may seem small by modern standards; even the trip from Dresden to Venice is only about five hundred miles. But at the time such travel involved considerable hardship—slow transport by horse-drawn coach or wagon over bad roads—and it is astonishing that Schütz (and his music) nevertheless traveled widely throughout Germany.

Schütz's Music

Like Monteverdi, Schütz composed so many different types of music over such a long period of transition that it is difficult to characterize his music in general terms. Perhaps the best one can do is to emphasize, as one would for Monteverdi, his continual reverence for the text and his constant search for ways of representing it musically. Schütz, however, was more strongly committed to the *stile antico* than Monteverdi seems to have been. Although he was deeply influenced by Monteverdi's theatrical and second-practice works, the most profound influence throughout his life was certainly that of his teacher Gabrieli. Schütz never abandoned the Gabrieli style, by which is meant here not only the grand Venetian polychoral manner but also the older contrapuntal tradition handed down from Lassus and Andrea Gabrieli. Throughout his career Schütz repeatedly returned to this style in polyphonic motets, sometimes even omitting the continuo parts that had become the norm after 1600.

Figure 7.2 Interior of the Dresden court chapel, after 1662, from the title page of *Geistreiches Gesang-buch* (Dresden, 1676) by Christoph Bernhard, a student of Schütz, possibly intended to show a performance directed by the latter.

Schütz nevertheless composed the bulk of his music in more up-to-date styles. Like other northern musicians who studied with Gabrieli, he began his career by publishing a set of Italian madrigals probably written under Gabrieli's direct supervision (Venice, 1611). A volume of psalms in Gabrieli's polychoral style followed in 1619. He also wrote numerous sacred motets or concertos for one to four solo voices and continuo, particularly during the war years, when most German churches and courts lacked the resources necessary for performing larger works. Many of these compositions employ the expressive devices of monody in the *stile moderno*, including recitative-like declamation and virtuoso vocal writing. Many also include independent instrumental parts, constituting genuine vocal-instrumental chamber music.

The works for smaller ensembles furnished models for younger German composers such as Johann Rosenmüller (ca. 1619–84), Matthias Weckmann (1621–74), and Johann Theile (1646–1724), each of whom knew or studied with Schütz before going on to become significant composers of sacred vocal music. Another student, Christoph Bernhard (1627–92), who succeeded Schütz as kapellmeister at Dresden, preserved the latter's teachings on composition and performance in a number of treatises.[8] Later German composers, including Buxtehude and Bach, if not directly acquainted with Schütz's style, experienced it

---

[8]See bibliography under "Baroque Theoretical Treatises."

indirectly through works by the younger composers just mentioned, who continued Schütz's tradition of sensitive, frequently dramatic settings of German sacred texts.

Numbering Systems and "Works"

Schütz, following a practice that had arisen in Italy during the seventeenth century, attached *opus* numbers to his major publications. The word **opus** is Latin for "work"; its plural is *opera*, not to be confused with the Italian word for a musical drama. The use of the word *opus* by musicians was a sign that they were beginning to recognize their compositions as permanent, substantial works of art comparable to architectural monuments and other concrete visual works. Today we take this for granted, but it was a new concept in the seventeenth century. It probably reflected the beginnings of interest in works and styles of the past—that is, music history. The continuing concern of many composers with the *stile antico* or *prima pratica*, which Monteverdi traced back to Johannes Ockeghem and Josquin des Prez, was one manifestation of this. So too were the posthumous, retrospective publications that were made of the works of a number of composers, including Andrea Gabrieli, Palestrina, and Lassus. Study of the works of older composers, such as Palestrina, would have suggested that music did not necessarily have to fade or disappear with time. Rather, music comprised a permanent body of works, just like the monuments of building, painting, and literature left behind by architects, artists, and writers. The efforts of living composers could result in monuments worthy of standing beside older, established ones, an idea implicit in the choice of the word *opus*.[9]

For seventeenth- and eighteenth-century composers, an *opus* was a large published collection. In most cases the term did not apply to individual compositions, and unpublished works, even major ones such as operas, were rarely given such a designation. Opus numbers were usually applied in chronological order. But because individual works within a collection might have been composed over a long period of time, opus numbers provide at best only a rough guide to the chronology of specific pieces.

For this reason, recent music historians have prepared numbered listings or catalogs of the individual works of major figures. When these catalogs quote the opening themes of the works listed, they can be referred to as **thematic catalogs**. Thematic catalogs sometimes go by the name of the scholar who first drew up the list, as in the case of the Köchel numbers applied to Mozart's works. Schütz's works have been assigned SWV numbers, the letters standing for the German expression *Schütz-Werke-Verzeichnis* ("catalog of Schütz's works"). The Köchel and SWV lists are, at least in principle, chronological, placing early

---

[9]Some modern writings, notably Lydia Goehr, *The Imaginary Museum of Musical Works: An Essay in the Philosophy of Music* (Oxford: Clarendon Press, 1992), argue that the concept of musical "works" dates only from around 1800, but the evidence cited here shows that many Baroque musicians must already have been thinking along similar lines.

works first. Lists for some other composers, including Bach, are not. Therefore one must not assume that a high number represents a late work. At the very least, however, such numbers provide an unambiguous way of referring to individual works. This is particularly useful when, as in the case of Schütz, there may be several settings of the same text all referred to by the same title.

Schütz's *Symphoniae sacrae*

Three of Schütz's published collections bear the title *Symphoniae sacrae* (Sacred symphonies), the same title borne by Giovanni Gabrieli's two great collections. These collections appeared as Opera 6, 10, and 12 in 1629, 1647, and 1650, respectively. Despite the title, many works are for relatively small ensembles, although in some cases these are expandable through the use of optional *capella* choirs. Even in the small-scale works, however, Schütz employs antiphonal textures that refer to polychoral style, and there are frequent passages in contrapuntal texture as well.

The works in the second volume had mostly been composed some years prior to its publication in 1647. The volume consists of vocal solos, duets, and trios with accompaniments for two treble instruments (e.g., violins or cornetti) and continuo. The third volume, published three years later as Opus 12, contains works for larger ensembles. Both reflect the influence of Monteverdi's late monodic works; indeed, one work in the 1647 collection (*Es steh Gott auf*) is a **parody:** a vocal work whose music is largely identical to that of an existing composition, new words being substituted for the original ones. In this case, Schütz fitted the words of Psalm 68 to music from two of Monteverdi's continuo madrigals.[10]

Herr, neige deine Himmel, SWV 361

This work (anthology, Selection 14), from the 1647 volume, is, like most of the compositions in that collection, a setting of a psalm text. It is scored for two bass voices with two violins and continuo. The latter is explicitly for organ, with the bass line doubled by "violone"—here probably meaning bass viola da gamba.

As in other works in Schütz's Opus 10, the style has much in common with the madrigals for one, two, and three voices in Monteverdi's Eighth Book (published in 1638). Thus Schütz takes almost every visual image in the text as a signal for word painting. The word *neige* ("bow down," m. 1) receives a downward melodic line that leaps back up for the following word *Himmel* ("heaven"),

---

[10]Schütz's *Es steh Gott auf*, SWV 356, draws on Monteverdi's *Armato il cor* and *Zefiro torna e di soavi accenti*. Parody had been an important technique for the composition of sixteenth-century masses; Schütz rarely used it, but it was important in the music of J. S. Bach and some other eighteenth-century composers.

and *blitzen* ("lightning," m. 19) elicits the first entry of the violins. Where the text refers to a "new song" (*neues Lied*, mm. 43–44), the music reflects this by shifting to triple meter. This triple meter, incidentally was originally notated in the equivalent of what we would call $\frac{6}{1}$ time, using what look to us like very large note values (six whole notes to the measure). Through a notational convention familiar to musicians of Schütz's time, these would probably have been performed not slowly but in a lively fashion.[11]

In the work of a lesser composer, Schütz's incessant use of text painting might have reduced the music to a disconnected series of musical images. But here each pictorial musical idea becomes a motive that is extensively developed through sequence, imitation, and other means. In many respects this is what one finds in polyphonic madrigals of the later sixteenth century. But the motives now have a stronger rhythmic profile; note, for example, the quick three-note motive used for *lass blitzen*. In addition, the pitch organization is now essentially tonal, defined by cadences in varying keys—that is, genuine modulations in the modern sense.

Thus we would say that the opening phrase begins in D minor but concludes with a cadence in A minor (m. 4), as does the following phrase (m. 9). Cadences in F major (m. 11) and D minor (m. 13) follow. The downbeat of measure 13 actually has a chord of D *major*, as signified by the sharp in the figured bass (this raised third degree today is sometimes called a **Picardy third**). It was common, however, for phrases to end on major chords regardless of their actual mode, and we might best consider the phrase in measures 11–13 as remaining in D *minor*. (Schütz and his contemporaries would have continued to describe these cadences in terms of the old church modes.)

One point of special interest is the writing for the bass voices. One of these almost always is doubled by the basso continuo line. Indeed, when only one voice sings, as at the beginning of the work, the music in effect consists of nothing but a single bass line (plus the improvised continuo realization). This is characteristic of writing for bass voice throughout the early Baroque. Monteverdi and Schütz wrote several works for solo bass in which the entire vocal part is a decorated doubling of the continuo line; the continuo realization must then furnish all of the harmony, that is, the upper voices. Such textures show that particular types of melodic writing are associated with each vocal type in the Baroque. Parts for bass voice thus tend to double the continuo part and to avoid lively passagework. They do not entirely lack the virtuoso coloratura commonly found in soprano and tenor parts of the period; indeed, such writing occurs on the word *fahr* (line 1) in this work. But vocal bass parts also tend to contain greater numbers of leaps than other voices, particularly at cadences. This stems from the tendency of bass lines to leap at cadences by a fourth or a fifth, that is, from the dominant to the tonic—a fact that one might keep in mind when searching for cadences in this and later music, although leaps may occur at other points as well.

---

[11]According to sixteenth-century theory, the triple-time passage would have been performed with three whole notes occupying the same time as one whole note in the previous passage. It is uncertain how strictly this rule was still applied in Schütz's day.

Saul, Saul, was verfolgst du mich?, SWV 415

This work (anthology, Selection 15) was published in 1650 in Schütz's third and last collection of *symphoniae sacrae*. In addition to a six-part choir of vocal soloists, the work calls for two violins as well as two optional *capella* choirs containing four voices each. Underlying the whole is a continuo group comprising organ and "violone," again meaning most likely bass viola da gamba.

Like Gabrieli's *In ecclesiis*, the work makes its greatest impact in its complete polychoral setting. Indeed, despite its brevity this is one of the most powerful compositions of the seventeenth century, justly famous for its vividly dramatic setting of its text. The latter, a single verse from the New Testament book of Acts, depicts the moment when Paul, on the road to Damascus (in Syria) to persecute the Christians there, has a vision. God speaks to him, addressing him by his Hebrew name, Saul; as a result, he is converted to Christianity, eventually becoming the author of the New Testament epistles (letters) attributed to him. The scene was a popular one for late Renaissance and Baroque painters, who frequently gave it a dramatic depiction showing Paul's horse rearing, throwing him to the ground.

Schütz's setting divides the scriptural verse into two halves, which are repeated in the pattern ABABA. The text repetitions are unusual in a seventeenth-century sacred work, and although the music is through-composed, each of the two text segments is associated with recurring motivic ideas. Surely Schütz's most original idea, however, is the extraordinary opening of the work, where Saul's name is repeated by rising pairs of voices, beginning with the lowest notes of the two basses and ascending to the two sopranos, who are echoed by the violins. The *capella* choirs then enter and the entire ensemble repeats the A text together (m. 9), producing a stunning effect.[12]

The two B segments, by contrast, are presented in more conventional style by the solo choir alone: first monodically, by tenor and alto soloists (mm. 13–18), then in imitative texture by all six soloists (mm. 22–34, joined by the violins). In the second B section, two words are singled out for Monteverdian text painting. The word *löcken* ("kick," mm. 24–25) receives an extended melisma.[13] On the downbeat of measure 27 Schütz sets a harsh dissonance—the augmented fifth eb'/b' (tenor and first soprano)—on the word *schwer*, meaning "hard" or "difficult."

The A sections include a number of original dynamic markings: *forte* (m. 9) followed by *mezzopiano* and *pianissimo*. These produce a decrescendo, perhaps representing the dying echo of the words that Saul hears all about him. Gabrieli had been one of the first to use written dynamic indications, in the *Sonata*

---

[12]The opening is in triple meter, originally notated in the same large note values employed in the middle section of *Herr, neige deine Himmel*. When a version of this music returns at m. 16, it is rewritten in duple meter using smaller note values; the actual tempo is only slightly quicker than before, however.

[13]The original Greek text of Acts presents an image of cattle kicking against the prods of their herders; Luther's German translation *wider den Stachel zu löcken* uses a word that can mean either bee stings or thorns, as in the phrase *ein Stachel im Fleisch* (a thorn in the flesh).

pian'e forte (Sonata with piano and forte) of his 1597 collection, an ensemble sonata for eight instruments. Although a common element in performance, dynamics were rarely specified before the mid-eighteenth century except to dictate special or unusual effects, as is the case here.

Modern performances often amplify the work through vocal and instrumental doublings of the two *capella* choirs. Yet even in its full original scoring, it may not have been intended for more than eighteen performers, one on each part. That was already an enormous ensemble for most of the German churches in which the work would have been performed. Thanks to Schütz's remarkable powers of invention, it is all that is necessary for the work to make an overpowering impact. We shall find similar considerations to hold true in later Baroque works as well; bigger does not necessarily mean better.

SEVENTEENTH-CENTURY ORATORIO

In addition to the *concertato* motet and other liturgical forms, seventeenth-century musicians cultivated various types of dramatic or semidramatic sacred music. The Roman operas on sacred themes have already been mentioned; these, however, differed musically hardly at all from operas on the usual mythological or historical subjects. More distinctive was the genre now known as oratorio, which developed in Italy at about the same time as opera and, like opera, eventually traveled to France, Germany, and elsewhere.

An **oratorio** may be defined as a dramatic work on a sacred subject that, like an opera, is fully sung, although it is not normally staged and acted, nor is it normally a part of a church service as such. The origins of the oratorio have been traced to certain quasi-dramatic types of Gregorian chant, such as the presentation of the Passion story on Good Friday. Here the chanting of the New Testament text was divided between one singer who presented the basic narrative and others who sang the words of Jesus and other figures in the story. This tradition, which extended back to the Middle Ages, continued in Baroque Germany and elsewhere. But the immediate source for the quasi-operatic type of music known as oratorio lay in the same innovations of around 1600 that led to opera itself.

Early Oratorio

The word *oratorio* derives from the oratory, a type of structure built in sixteenth-century Italy and later for quasi-liturgical services by various religious communities. Typically holding several hundred people, surviving oratories today are sometimes used as concert halls. This in effect constituted one of their original functions as well: the public presentation of sacred music outside the context of an actual religious service. Such performances, which proliferated at Rome and other Roman Catholic cities during the seventeenth century, were among the predecessors of the modern tradition of public concerts. In Roman Catholic countries they were generally sponsored by religious institutions, and by the end of the seventeenth century comparable traditions had emerged in parts of

Protestant Germany, where they involved performances of oratorios or similar works in existing churches.

Emilio de'Cavalieri is generally credited with writing the first oratorio, the *Rappresentatione di anima e di corpo* (Drama of the soul and the body), at Rome in 1600. He had been one of the musicians involved in the Florentine *intermedi* of 1589, and musically this work is similar to the earliest operas. An allegorical dialogue between body and soul, it consists largely of recitative, interspersed with choruses. Few additional such works were composed, however, and most of the compositions now regarded as oratorios were of a different kind.

Carissimi

The more usual seventeenth-century oratorio is the type of work composed by Giacomo Carissimi (1605–74), who has been mentioned previously as a writer of secular cantatas. Born at Rome, Carissimi spent his entire career there as choir director (*maestro di capella*) at a number of institutions, notably the German College. The latter was one of several religious communities—not colleges in the modern sense—run by the Jesuit order for members of various foreign nationalities. The German College came to be noted especially for its musical performances under Carissimi, as well as for the longtime residence there of the German scholar Athanasius Kircher (1602–80), whose voluminous writings include an encyclopedic treatise on music (*Musurgia universalis*, Rome, 1650) that mentions Carissimi and other contemporary musicians.

It is thanks in part to Kircher that Carissimi, whose cantatas constitute the largest part of his output, is today known chiefly for his oratorios. These works, about two dozen in all, were regarded in his own day as a special type of *concertato* motet; certain related works by other composers bear the title *dialogus* (dialogue), pointing to the works' quasi-dramatic features, in which the speeches of individual characters are assigned to soloists and set monodically, with continuo accompaniment. Most such compositions are short by comparison with later oratorios, since each constituted only a small part of an oratory ritual that included psalm singing and a sermon as well. They range in length from ten to thirty minutes; contemporary accounts describe their performances as among the high points of musical life at Rome in the seventeenth century. The dates of most of Carissimi's oratorios are not known; among their subjects are the Last Judgment and the story of Jonah and the whale.

As in the sacred works of Gabrieli, Monteverdi, and Schütz, the text is divided into sections. Some sections are assigned to soloists, others to the body of singers as a whole. What distinguishes these works from ordinary *concertato* motets is that the Latin texts, which were adapted from the Bible, are narratives containing extensive dialogue. Carissimi's settings assign the speeches of the individual characters to specific soloists, as we might expect in a dramatic work. Yet the soloists also sang as members of the choir in nondialogue sections. Indeed, the "choir" originally used in these works may well have sung one on a part, as was probably true of most seventeenth-century sacred music. Most of Carissimi's oratorios are in five or six parts; each singer would have performed as both a chorus member and as a soloist singing the words of one or more characters.

Carissimi's *Jephte*

The oratorio *Jephte* (anthology, Selection 16) is Carissimi's most famous work, thanks to Kircher's enthusiastic mention of it in his *Musurgia universalis* (which shows that the work had been composed by 1650). The anonymous Latin text is an expansion of a story from the Book of Judges. The ancient Israelite leader Jephtha, preparing to lead his forces into battle, vowed that if he returned victorious he would sacrifice the first being that emerged from his house to greet him. He indeed defeated the Ammonites, enemies of the Israelites, and was greeted on his return by none other than his daughter—whom he accordingly sacrificed to God!

Carissimi's setting is for six voices with continuo. A number of his other oratorios include parts for two violins, but the continuo is the sole instrumental component here. The words of Jephtha and his daughter are assigned to one of the two tenors and one of the three sopranos, respectively. The other voices assist in the narration, which, as in Monteverdi's *Combattimento*, takes up much of the work. But instead of assigning the narration to a single singer, Carissimi distributes it between the four remaining voices (two sopranos, alto, and bass), designating each as *Historicus* (narrator) when singing in this capacity. These parts sometimes sing their narration alone, sometimes in duos and trios. Several times, all six vocal parts join together to form a chorus of Israelites. As in all Roman Baroque religious music (and many operas), the soprano parts would have been sung by male voices, probably castrati.

The musical style is relatively conservative. The monodic passages for the soloists alternate between arioso and aria style and avoid the more extreme effects of the *seconda pratica*. The choruses resemble other Roman motets of the early Baroque in their alternation between homophony and simple imitative counterpoint; in our selection, Carissimi alludes to polychoral style through the use of antiphonal exchanges between the three high and the three low voices, a device already used by Palestrina.[14] Modern performances often double the parts in these choruses, thus allowing the solo parts to stand out more sharply as individual dramatic roles. Yet this may be a misunderstanding of the composition, which can be understood as an expressive and fairly intimate reading of the text—literally, an *oration*—that lacks the fully fleshed-out characters of a true dramatic work.

The most famous music in the work is Jephtha's long lament, which impressed Kircher by its use of relatively remote modulations to express Jephtha's emotional shock. These are already evident at the end of the excerpt given in the anthology, where Jephtha is greeted by his daughter, whom he now must sacrifice. Jephtha's speech "Heu, heu mihi!" contains a few restrained instances of Monteverdi's *seconda pratica*, notably the melodic interval of a diminished

---

[14]Compare the opening of *Dum complerentur* (anthology, Selection 1).

fourth that recurs, refrainlike, in Jephtha's repeated exclamation *heu*. More significant, however, is the sudden shift of tonality that has taken place, wrenching the music from the bright G major of the preceding chorus to the dark A minor that expresses Jephtha's grief—in Kircher's language, a swift change from mode 8 to modes 3 and 4.[15] Jephtha's distress is further represented by the swift changes of tonality within his two lamenting speeches: with his words *decepisti me, et tu pariter* ("you have undone me as well as yourself") we pass from a cadence in G minor to chords of G major and E major. The close juxtaposition of G-minor and E-major harmonies is the same one that Monteverdi had used in the messenger scene of *Orfeo*.

At least a portion of Carissimi's work was known to Handel, who borrowed its closing chorus for his oratorio *Samson* and treated the same story in his last English oratorio (*Jephtha*, 1750).[16] Of greater historical significance, however, was Carissimi's role as one of the leading musicians in Rome through the central decades of the century. Among those who heard his works, and who may also have studied with him, were the German keyboard player and composer Johann Jacob Froberger, whose works we will consider later, and Charpentier, already mentioned as Lully's most important contemporary in France.

Charpentier

Marc-Antoine Charpentier (ca. 1645/50–1704) was the most important French composer of sacred music in the Baroque. His origins are obscure, but he is known to have been at Rome in the 1660s, where he must have studied with Carissimi; among his numerous surviving musical manuscripts are copies of works by Carissimi, including the oratorio *Jephte*. He was clearly influenced by this music, and by the 1680s he was writing similar works in Paris. There he was employed as a musician by the duchess of Guise, a wealthy pro-Italian noble whose relatives earlier in the century had supported the young Lully. This was ironic, for during much Charpentier's career Lully enjoyed a virtual monopoly on the performance of large-scale dramatic music. Other talented musicians, particularly those interested in the theater, were forced to write for relatively modest ensembles.

Charpentier nevertheless produced several successful comedies with Molière, who had previously collaborated with Lully. After Molière's death in 1673, Charpentier continued to write music for the latter's acting troupe, which became the forerunner of the Comédie Française, one of the great French theatrical institutions. A skilled singer (an *haute-contre*), Charpentier also took the lead role in a number of small-scale dramatic musical works composed for the duchess, including the cantata *Orphée descendant aux enfers* (Orpheus's descent to

---

[15]To review the terminology of modal theory, see Box 2.2. The traditional chant-based theory of modes, summarized there, was somewhat modified by Kircher and other Baroque theorists to reflect what we now understand as the developing use of tonality and modulation by Carissimi and other composers.

[16]The borrowed chorus, "Plorate filii Israel" ("Weep, daughters of Israel"), was printed in Kircher's *Musurgia universalis*. On Handel's borrowings, see Chapter 9.

the underworld, 1683). He eventually obtained several positions in the royal musical establishment, including that of director of the Sainte-Chapelle (the royal chapel in Paris) in 1698. His one full-length opera *Médée* (Medea) was produced by the Royal Academy in 1693, six years after Lully's death.

Charpentier's Music

Charpentier is best known for his oratorios and other sacred vocal works, which amount to 439 large and small compositions.[17] He also wrote a smaller number of secular vocal works, including cantatas and *airs*, as well as instrumental pieces, many of them probably for performance as overtures or interludes in larger vocal works. His early sacred music is close to the Roman style of Carissimi, but his theatrical works and his later sacred compositions written at Paris naturally employ elements of the Lullian French style. Frequently, elements of both styles can be identified in individual works.

The Christmas Oratorio *Frigidae noctis umbra*, H. 414

This little oratorio for Christmas (anthology, Selection 17) is one of four such works by Charpentier. In the composer's manuscripts each is designated as a *canticum*, a Latin equivalent of the Italian word *cantata*, which, however, would probably not have been used for a sacred work in the seventeenth century. Charpentier's score names the three sopranos—all women—who participated. From this information it appears that the work was written for Charpentier's patron (the duchess of Guise) during the mid-1680s, perhaps for a private performance on Christmas Day in her great house (*hôtel*) in Paris.

The underlying conception of this work—line-by-line composition, with each phrase of the text reflected by a new musical idea—remains that of a sixteenth-century motet. But the musical style is substantially different, reflecting seventeenth-century developments in both sacred and secular music. It is written for the same six vocal parts as Carissimi's *Jephte*—three sopranos, alto (or *haute-contre*), tenor, and bass—to which Charpentier adds two violins alongside the usual continuo accompaniment. The work falls into several distinct sections, each somewhat more substantial and self-sufficient than those in Carissimi's works (see Box 7.4). Nevertheless, like Carissimi's motets—and like Lullian opera—it was conceived as a single unbroken continuity.

The work opens with a short *praeludium* (prelude) that serves the same function as the brief instrumental *sinfonia* found at the beginnings of some of Carissimi's oratorios and in most Italian operas of the mid-seventeenth century. The two violins and continuo heard in this prelude were also heard frequently in Lullian opera, in the sections for the smaller instrumental ensemble. We have seen this ensemble as well in the sinfonia that opens Scarlatti's cantata *Correa nel seno amato*. The violins also participate in the march near the center of the

---

[17]According to the list drawn up by H. Wiley Hitchcock, after whom Charpentier's works bear "H" numbers; the order is nonchronological.

Box 7.4

Charpentier: Christmas Oratorio *Frigidae noctis umbra*, H. 414

---

1. *Praeludium*. 2 vlns., b.c.

2. *Récit de l'historien* (biblical recitative). 2 sops., b.c.

3. *Angelus* (angel). Sop., 2 vlns., b.c.

4. Chorus. 2 vlns., SSSATB, b.c.

5. *Marche* (march of the shepherds). 2 vlns., b.c.

6. Biblical recitative. Bass voice, b.c.

7. Air with chorus. Strophic design as follows:

   (1) stanza 1: soloist [S1], b.c.
   (2) stanza 2: SSSATB, b.c.
   (3) *ritournelle*: 2 vlns., b.c.
   (4) stanza 3: soloist [S2], b.c.
   (5) *ritournelle*: 2 vlns., b.c.
   (6) stanza 4: soloist [S3], b.c.
   (7) stanza 4 repeated: SSSATB, b.c.
   (8) *ritournelle*: 2 vlns., b.c.

---

work, which represents the shepherds on their way to Bethlehem. This march might reflect Charpentier's reminiscence of a Roman tradition whereby peasants from the neighboring countryside made a pilgrimage into the city in observance of Christmas.[18]

The two narrative sections are assigned to different voices, like the *historicus* passages in Carissimi's oratorios, and the text is treated with the same restraint as the earlier composer would have used. Although most of the narrative text is set as recitative, the angel's appearance before the shepherds is described in a duet in imitative texture (mm. 40–51)—a way of marking the special importance of this text.

The largest portion of the work is taken up by two segments somewhat resembling the *airs* of Lullian opera. The first of these presents the actual words of the angel, sung by the first soprano accompanied by the strings, which thus serve as a symbolic halo—an idea employed in oratorios by Schütz and other Baroque composers as well. As in other French airs, there is a strong dance element, and the flowing groups of three quarter notes suggest the gigue or courante. The second air, which concludes the work, has an elaborate strophic design in which solo voices alternate with the full ensemble and with an instrumental *ritournelle* (ritornello).

---

[18]See the discussion of the pastorale from Corelli's "Christmas" Concerto in Chapter 13.

At the center of the work is a chorus that leads directly into the march. The chorus is in the Roman polyphonic style favored by Carissimi, but it contains unusual refrainlike repetitions of the opening phrase (Ex. 7.4). Also notable in this movement is the use of vocal scoring to produce some slightly arcane text painting: The second text phrase, which refers to the newborn child, is sung by the three sopranos alone (Ex. 7.5). But the third phrase of the text, whose words

Example 7.4 Charpentier, *Frigidae noctis umbra*, H. 414, chorus "Surgamus, festinemus," mm. 1–6 (violins omitted)

Surgamus, festinemus, eamus usque Bethlehem,

Let us arise, hasten, and go to Bethlehem,

Example 7.5 Charpentier, *Frigidae noctis umbra*, H. 414, chorus "Surgamus, festinemus," mm. 158–62 (violins omitted)

Ibi videbimus puerum qui natus est nobis,

There we shall see the child that has been born for us,

Example 7.6 Charpentier, *Frigidae noctis umbra*, H. 414, chorus "Surgamus, festinemus," mm. 172–83 (violins omitted)

Ibi laudabimus et adorabimus
Deum sub forma peccatoris velatum.

There we shall praise and adore
God concealed in the form of a sinner.

forma peccatoris (form of a sinner) refer to the incarnation—the Christian belief in the simultaneous divinity and humanity of Jesus—is reserved for the three lowest voices. This line of the text is combined with a reprise of the opening line, sung by the sopranos (Ex. 7.6).[19] The combination of musical symbolism with clever counterpoint would have been appreciated by Charpentier's learned audience in Paris.

---

[19]The two violin parts, which mainly double the two top voices, are omitted from Exx. 7.4–6.

CHAPTER 8

LATE BAROQUE OPERA

In the late Baroque—which we may equate very roughly with the first half of the eighteenth century—European musical traditions continued on the paths they had taken during previous decades. Thus French and Italian musicians maintained their distinct styles, which were imitated singly and in combination by musicians elsewhere. This was particularly true in opera, where the Lullian model remained supreme in France. Although gradually transformed by the addition of Italian elements—a controversial trend resisted by some French musicians—it retained its distinctive character and remained the only viable approach for serious operatic composers in France during the period we are studying. In Italy, on the other hand, significant changes in the nature of both texts and music led to a new form, opera seria, that would continue as the leading type of opera through most of the century. (For a table summarizing the distinctions between the two types of opera—and by extension the French and Italian styles of the later Baroque in general—see Box 8.1.)

Trends in Late Baroque Music

Naturally, developments in opera in the first half of the eighteenth century reflected broader changes that affected other genres as well. Although it is hazardous to generalize about stylistic developments across the entire repertory of European music in the early eighteenth century, a few significant trends are evident. Some are continuations of trends that we have observed from the beginning of the seventeenth century, such as the differentiation of distinct national styles and the use of idiomatically conceived instrumental parts. Others are trends that began in the later decades of the seventeenth century and continue through the eighteenth, in effect constituting the transition from Baroque to Classical style. Among these is a gradual simplification of harmony and musical texture that leads to an emphasis on tuneful melody and a corresponding reduction of interest in counterpoint and contrapuntal genres. These trends, which led to the so-called *galant* style, are taken up in Chapter 14.

Two fundamental trends seem to have been of particular importance in the later Baroque, influencing both vocal and instrumental music. These trends have been noted previously in conjunction with particular genres, but they become close to all-encompassing in the eighteenth century. The first was the use of in-

---

Box 8.1

Some Distinctions between Late Baroque French and Italian Opera

---

French
- Continued use of elaborate recitative and arioso
- Limited use of the aria
- Restrained melodic style
- Many ornaments indicated by signs; little free embellishment
- Use of chorus for both dancing and singing
- Frequent instrumental dances in *divertissements* (ballets)
- Standard dance rhythms common in airs and dances
- Main voice types: soprano, *haute-contre* (male alto), tenor, bass

Italian
- Recitative mainly limited to *recitativo semplice*
- Heavy reliance on the da capo aria
- Frequent virtuoso writing with passagework (lively figuration: rapid scales, etc.)
- Most ornaments unnotated; much free embellishment
- Chorus absent
- Few instrumental numbers; rarely any dance
- Identifiable dance rhythms less common (but by no means rare)
- Main voice types: soprano and alto (female and male castrato), bass

---

creasingly clear, distinctly articulated formal structures. In its most basic manifestation, this trend produced the increasingly clear division of works into distinct movements. In vocal music, this meant that most works came to comprise arias or arialike movements alternating with separate recitatives. The arias, moreover, tended increasingly to follow a limited number of clearly defined, clearly audible musical forms—above all, da capo form. Meanwhile, the improvisatory or through-composed designs of most earlier works tended to disappear, although they continued to be heard in certain contexts (such as improvised keyboard playing).

A second, related trend is that toward tonality in the full sense of the word. Already in the sixteenth century, most polyphonic works were tonal in the limited sense that they included what we recognize as standard functional chord progressions, such as half and full cadences. We might even consider some such works to be in major and minor keys, although many others are distinctly modal. But even those sixteenth-century pieces that can be said to lie in a major or a minor key contain few if any true modulations—shifts to new keys that govern substantial sections of a piece, which are thus said to be in foreign key areas (or tonal areas). Only when musical forms came to be organized in terms of lasting modulations to and from the tonic can we say that modality had been largely or entirely replaced by tonality as a principal formal element.

The trend toward tonality is evident in many movements of the works we have examined from the later seventeenth century. Within such movements, sections may be organized according to a symmetrical scheme that includes modulation to one or more foreign keys, followed by a return to the tonic. Thus a binary form (such as the air "Or if more influencing" in Purcell's *From Rosy Bowers*) may modulate to the dominant or relative major at the end of the first half; the second half returns to the tonic. The A section of a da capo form or ABA design, when considered apart from the B section, often has a similar bipartite form. But the middle or B section not only introduces new textual and motivic ideas but also modulates to new keys.

Tonality may seem a terribly abstract concept, yet composers of the later Baroque made it one of the bases of musical form—even in opera arias—and it would become the source of much of the power and drama of eighteenth-century music. This is one reason why keys are so often included in the titles of instrumental works, beginning in the late seventeenth century, and for this reason, too, keys and modulations will be mentioned increasingly in analytical comments here. It was tonality that helped make possible in the eighteenth century the extension of arias and other movements over much longer periods of time than in seventeenth-century music: compositions grew longer. The early Baroque concern with musical rhetoric was not abandoned, but it took a different form as composers learned to employ the longer time spans of arias and other movements for expressive and dramatic purposes.

Opera Seria

The new form of Italian opera, known as **opera seria** ("serious opera"), originated in the late seventeenth century as a reaction against the heterogeneous, half-tragic, half-comic mixture of spectacle and entertainment that Italian opera had become, particularly at Venice. An opera seria libretto was normally in three acts (without a prologue); within each act, the number and type of arias allotted to each character were strictly related to that character's social rank and significance to the plot. Opera seria's first proponents were members of some of the learned academies that continued to flourish into the eighteenth century in Italy and elsewhere. Particularly important was the poet Apostolo Zeno (1668–1750), whose first opera libretto, *Lucio Vero*, was set to music by Carlo Francesco Pollarolo (ca. 1653–1723) and performed at Venice in 1695. In this type of opera, minor comic characters and subplots (such as occur in Cavalli's *Giasone*) were eliminated and the structure of the libretto was regularized. A typical scene was constructed of many lines of recitative leading up to an aria whose text comprised just a few lines, although its music made it far longer than the preceding recitative. As in earlier opera, recitative contained dialogue and advanced the action. The purpose of the aria was to permit one character to express his or her emotional response to the events just portrayed; having done so, the character almost always left the stage, leaving those remaining to begin another such scene. In the hands of a master composer such as Handel, the aria became a means for defining the personalities and relative significance of the major figures in the drama—a form of musical characterization.

Figure 8.1 The Royal Opera House, Naples, with a performance of Giuseppe de Maio's serenade *Il sogno d'Olimpia*, from *Narrazione delle solenni feste* (Naples, 1749). This performance, on 6 November 1747, was part of celebrations of the birth of an heir to King Carlo Borbone, who is seated at the center (cf. Figure 5.1). The orchestra includes two harpsichords, one at each end facing inward.

This systematic, almost mechanical type of libretto reflected the rational, self-consciously civilized character adopted by European upper-class society for most of the eighteenth century. The violence of the seventeenth century was set aside, and rulers and their subordinates invariably behaved with tact and moderation (at least onstage). In the theater, unpleasant or intense emotions were expressed only in the most formal, stereotyped ways, and dramatic events, especially combat and death, tended to be represented only indirectly, by characters' narrating them. The regular alternation of recitatives and arias—the latter nearly all in da capo form, with the singer leaving the stage at the conclusion—led to a highly predictable format that satisfied eighteenth-century demands for the ready comprehensibility of artworks. Moreover, audiences got to know the thirty or forty most commonly used librettos, which different composers set to music over and over again, repeating the same familiar stories.

Such conditions might seem anathema to the dramatic spirit of opera, which for us may seem to require spontaneous, uninhibited action and expression. Moreover, the concentration on the aria focused attention on the great virtuoso singers, whose improvisatory embellishments in the arias were sometimes a greater attraction than the original music of the composer. Such arias became vehicles for the singers, who used them as much to display their own impressive vocal technique as to express emotions appropriate to the drama or to advance the plot. Eighteenth-century writers, including singers and composers such as Pier Francesco Tosi and Benedetto Marcello, occasionally criticized these aspects of opera seria, and from the perspective of the very different types of opera favored in the nineteenth and twentieth centuries they may appear to be fatal flaws. Yet composers from Alessandro Scarlatti to Gioacchino Rossini (1792–1868) gladly accepted the conventions of opera seria. In part this must have been due to its enormous popularity, which no musician seeking to earn a living could ignore. But it was also because in the hands of the most skilled poets and composers opera seria was a remarkable achievement. Its best librettos, many by the influential poet Pietro Metastasio (1698–1782), provided composers with verbal phrases and images that Baroque musical rhetoric was well equipped to handle. Moreover, the alternation of recitative and aria furnished a pattern whereby dramatic tension built up during a recitative could be relieved in the following aria. The largest, most impressive arias, in which singers displayed their greatest feats of both technique and expression, were not randomly disposed. Rather, they served as climaxes to particularly crucial series of events in the plot and thus were frequently placed at the ends of major scenes or whole acts. Occasionally, too, conventional patterns could be broken—for example, an aria apparently in da capo form might be broken off, left unfinished—to achieve a special dramatic effect.

Most recitative in opera seria is in the simple style that we observed in portions of the Scarlatti cantata. Unusual harmonies, remote modulations, and melismas are reserved for only the most emotionally or dramatically crucial moments in a dialogue. Accompanied recitative—that is, recitative with fully scored orchestral accompaniment—is used occasionally for particularly impassioned or dramatic speeches, especially monologues or soliloquies by major characters that are crucial to the plot. With the important exception of Handel, the arias of most composers use a homophonic texture that focuses attention on the melodic line—an important feature of the emerging *galant* style (see Chapter 14). In addition to employing da capo form, virtually all arias can be described as being in *ritornello* form, with an orchestral introduction that is now firmly integrated into the body of the aria.

Among the most important composers of opera seria active during the first half of the eighteenth century were Alessandro Scarlatti, Handel (discussed below), Vivaldi (discussed below), and Johann Adolph Hasse (1699–1783). Hasse's career extended well into what we call the Classical period, during which opera seria remained an important genre; Haydn and Mozart, as well as Bach's youngest son, Johann Christian Bach (1735–87), were among those who contributed to it.[1] Handel, Hasse, J. C. Bach, and Mozart were all German-speaking musicians who nevertheless achieved great success as composers of Italian opera. Indeed, each was widely regarded as the leading Italian opera composer of his generation, enjoying an international career and directing performances in major cities throughout Europe. Not only did their operas influence those of other composers; instrumental music also reflected elements of oper-

---

[1] Mozart's most important contributions to opera, however, lie in his *opere buffe*: works such as *Don Giovanni* and *The Marriage of Figaro*, which are essentially comedies.

atic style. This was especially true of the instrumental concerto, which developed during the same period as opera seria and, as we shall see in Chapter 13, eventually employed related types of form, scoring, and means of expression.

The Performers of Opera Seria

Eighteenth-century opera seria differed from seventeenth-century Italian opera in the reduced number of singing characters, who might number as few as four or five. Moreover, it was dominated even more than previously by high voices, especially sopranos. Through a convention that now seems strange, soprano and alto voices were employed for most adult male as well as female roles. Thus, throughout the eighteenth century, the heroic character of kings, princes, and warriors and other leading male figures was expressed in opera primarily by the virtuosity of soprano and, less frequently, alto voices.

Although women and male falsetto singers sometimes took such roles, the most frequent singing voice used for them—and for some female roles as well—was the **castrato**. Through a surgical procedure carried out before the onset of

Figure 8.2 *Rehearsal of an Opera*, oil on canvas by Marco Ricci (1676–1729), 19 × 22 in (48.5 × 58.0 cm), Yale Center for British Art, Paul Mellon Collection (B 1981.25.523). In this satirical painting, the standing figure at the harpsichordist's left, sometimes thought to be Handel, may actually be the castrato Nicolini (Nicolò Grimaldi, 1673–1732), who sang in Handel's opera *Rinaldo*.

puberty, a boy's physical maturation could be prevented. By long tradition going back to the sixteenth century, boys from poor families who showed sufficient musical talent could thus retain their high voice; contrary to modern belief, the operation appears to have been perfectly legal and socially acceptable, even encouraged, in the regions of Italy where it was practiced. Most castrati wound up as priests singing in parish churches; few achieved fame as opera stars. In addition to preventing sexual maturation, the operation appears to have had other physical effects that favored the development of unusually strong wind support. Although at first confined mainly to the performance of sacred music at Rome, Venice, and other Italian centers, by the mid-seventeenth century the castrato voice had entered opera. By the eighteenth century the most accomplished of the castrato singers had become the greatest stars of opera.

Modern notions about gender and sexuality are apt to cloud our understanding of the castrato phenomenon. Although incapable of producing children, castrati were adults, able to understand the emotions of the characters they portrayed, women as well as men. The best ones were praised for their acting as well as their singing, and although occasionally ridiculed—as all public figures are likely to be—some, such as the soprano Carlo Broschi (1705–82, known as Farinelli), were widely respected and even took on important political and diplomatic roles.[2] Women could and did sometimes substitute for castrati in male roles; it distorts the music far more to transpose a soprano part down an octave, allowing it to be sung by a tenor, than to substitute a female voice. Use of the castrato was hardly confined to the early eighteenth century; castrato roles remained a regular feature of Italian opera through the early nineteenth century, and castrati sang in the Cappella Sistina—the pope's personal choir at Rome—until 1902.[3]

Instrumentation

As the number of singers diminished, the orchestra grew: indeed, it *became* an orchestra in the modern sense. Eighteenth-century opera seria normally employed a relatively large string section of as many as two dozen or more players, joined regularly by winds—at least two oboes, and frequently other woodwinds and brass—as well as a continuo section composed minimally of two harpsichords. One of the latter was normally played by the composer, who coached the singers and directed the ensemble from the keyboard. All of the *recitativo semplice* was, as before, accompanied by the continuo, but by now it was rare for an aria to have only continuo accompaniment. Many arias, especially those of particular importance within the work, are scored for the full or-

[2]The exotic, unnatural character of the castrato has fascinated many writers, artists, and others. The French novelist Honoré de Balzac (1799–1850) wrote his novella *Sarrasine* at a time when castrati were still heard in opera. More recently, the film *Farinelli* (directed by Gérard Corbiau, 1995) presented an imaginative account of the singer's life that, although largely fictional, is worth seeing for its relatively accurate portrayal of a number of Baroque opera scenes (the musical performance practices heard and depicted in the film are less strictly historical).

[3]Early recordings of the Sistine Chapel choir include several castrato singers, notably its director and principal soloist Alessandro Moreschi (1858–1922).

chestral ensemble, and special orchestral colors are given prominence in particular sorts of arias (e.g., recorders in quiet scenes or lamentation, horns or trumpets in hunting or military scenes). Accompanied recitatives are reserved for only the most important dialogue, but they too frequently employ special orchestration and effects.

Performance

The conventions of opera seria included numerous rules of stage deportment and gesture that were generally known and agreed upon by actors as well as singers. Many of the poses and gestures used can be seen in paintings of the period, which when depicting historical or mythological events may even derive from operatic representations of the scenes depicted. Movement onstage closely resembled ordinary, everyday deportment in polite society, which was equally governed by rules and protocols. For this reason, trained singers rarely required stage directors as such. Each type of character and each event in an opera called for a particular vocabulary of movements and gestures that, with variations, could be adopted to each individual role.[4]

Figure 8.3 A modern performance in period style of Handel's opera *Ariodante*, from the 1995 Händel-Festspiel, Göttingen (Germany): the Furies' Dance (New York Baroque Dance Company). The costumes, gestures, movement, and positioning of the figures on stage are in close imitation of eighteenth-century style, as is the stage set. Photograph by courtesy of Drew Minter.

---

[4]On the use of stylized gesture and other aspects of historical acting, see Dene Barnett (with the assistance of Jeanette Massy-Westropp), *The Art of Gesture: The Practices and Principles of Eighteenth-Century Acting* (Heidelberg: Winter, 1987).

On the whole, there was probably less movement than in modern operatic productions. As in the spoken theater of the day, lengthy speeches (that is, arias) might be delivered with only small gestures varying each character's basic pose; the audience's attention was instead directed on the singing itself. During the singing of an aria there was no need for the fussy stage business that modern directors often introduce in an effort to keep the audience's attention. Eighteenth-century audiences were accustomed to listening carefully to details in the music, paying particular attention to the embellishments and cadenzas that a virtuoso singer was likely to introduce.[5]

The second A section, that is, the "da capo" of a da capo aria, was the most frequent locus of embellishment, but this aspect of performance has probably been exaggerated in some modern discussions. Modern singers unfamiliar with historical style sometimes distort the music grotesquely by transposing final notes up an octave or rewriting the passagework of virtuoso arias, while leaving out or performing incorrectly trills and other ornaments that were considered essential in standard cadential formulas.[6] Instrumentalists are sometimes guilty of similar things as well. It is true that eighteenth-century virtuosos such as Farinelli sometimes embellished arias beyond all recognition, but they did so only in certain types of aria. Moreover, Farinelli and other great singers had substantial training in theory and composition that guided their improvisations. Only fully thought-out and cleanly executed embellishments were approved by eighteenth-century connoisseurs, who might have been more impressed by the addition of a single expressive appoggiatura at the right place than by cascades of banal passagework. Many arias, particularly among those of master composers such as Handel, require nothing more than the addition of a few standard ornaments. The best candidates for embellishment are slow arias and other movements in which an unusually simple melodic line suggests that the composer purposely created an opportunity for improvisatory embellishment. Other suggestions for improvisation are provided by pauses and fermatas, which often signal a cadenza—two different cadenzas, if the pause or fermata occurs in a repeated section. A number of singers and composers, including Farinelli and Handel, left written-out examples of embellished arias; these provide clues to the nature of singing in opera seria, as does the comprehensive singing treatise by Tosi, already mentioned in Chapter 3.[7]

GEORGE FRIDERIC HANDEL

George Frideric Handel (1685–1759) was, with J. S. Bach, one of the two late Baroque composers who achieved the greatest renown in later centuries. Han-

---

[5] Opera seria was later criticized by observers who noted the conversations, card playing, and other diversions that went on in the audience, but such behavior was probably more common during poor productions of second-rate works.

[6] Composers of Italian music, unlike the French, rarely wrote ornament signs; performers were expected to know where to apply trills in cadences.

[7] See bibliography under "Baroque Vocal Technique."

del was the more famous during his own lifetime, although his fame was due largely to his operas and not to what are now his better-known English oratorios. Handel's career followed a path considerably different from those of the musicians whose lives we have hitherto examined. Born in the eastern German city of Halle, as a boy Handel seems to have studied music—chiefly keyboard playing—only as an avocation; his father was a surgeon-barber (the two occupations were commonly joined at the time) and evidently did not intend his son to pursue a musical career. Nevertheless, Handel studied with the Halle organist Friedrich Wilhelm Zachow (1663–1712), a composer of some significance, and in 1702 gained an organist position there himself. He seemed headed for the type of career that Bach, growing up under similar circumstances less than a hundred miles away, would pursue. But a year later he left Halle for Hamburg—the most important city in northern Germany—where within two years he had established himself as an opera composer (see Box 8.2).

Handel's Early Career in Hamburg and Italy

As the only city in Germany with a flourishing public opera, Hamburg would have been a natural destination for a talented musician whose ambitions lay in the theater, as Handel's evidently did. Initially he played second violin in the Hamburg opera orchestra, under Reinhard Keiser (1674–1739), then the leading German opera composer. But his talent must have been immediately apparent, for the first of his three or four Hamburg operas was premiered before his twentieth birthday. He also made the acquaintance of Johann Mattheson (1681–1764), a singer, dancer, and composer who would soon become an influential and prolific writer. Mattheson's writings on music are still consulted as important sources of information on eighteenth-century music and musicians; they include an account of a trip Mattheson and Handel made together to Lübeck, another northern port city, where both were interested in succeeding to the organist position then occupied by Dietrich Buxtehude (see Chapter 11) until learning that they would have to marry the latter's daughter.[8]

Despite its location on the northern shore of Continental Europe, the Hamburg opera was predominantly Italian in style. It included French overtures and dance scenes, but the texts of most works were either all Italian or a mixture of Italian for the arias and German for the recitative (a compromise intended to help the audience follow the dialogue). In 1706 Handel left Hamburg, traveling to Italy at the invitation of a Florentine prince. He spent four years there, writing Italian operas for performance in Florence and Venice as well as two Italian oratorios, a substantial amount of Latin church music, and over one hundred secular cantatas with Italian texts.

During these years Handel met many of the important composers in Italy, including the violinist Arcangelo Corelli and Alessandro Scarlatti and his son Domenico. He possessed the facility, melodic imagination, and virtuosity nec-

---

[8]Marriage arrangements such as this were common at the time; Handel's father, at his first marriage, had taken over the business that had belonged to his new wife's recently deceased first husband.

BOX 8.2

George Frideric Handel (1685–1759)

1685. Born at Halle, in eastern Germany. Early studies with Friedrich Wilhelm Zachow, organist in Halle.

1702. Appointed organist at Halle Cathedral.

1703. Leaves for Hamburg (northwest Germany); his first opera, *Almira*, performed two years later.

1706. Travels to Italy; goes first to Florence, later to Venice and Rome; composes cantatas, two operas, two oratorios.

1710. Heads north to Hanover, in Germany; his opera *Rinaldo* performed in London the following year.

1712. Moves permanently to England; thirty-five more operas composed and performed there (1712–41).

1716. Visits Germany (*Brockes-Passion* performed in Hamburg). Returns to England under the patronage of the duke of Chandos, for whom he writes anthems, the masque *Acis and Galatea* (1718), and the first version of the oratorio *Esther* (1718).

1719. Visits Germany to recruit singers for the Royal Academy of Music, newly founded London opera company.

1720. Handel's first Royal Academy opera, *Radamisto*; the company continues through the spring 1728 season, producing thirteen new Handel operas in all, plus works by other composers.

1729. Visits Italy and Germany recruiting singers for new company (the "Second Academy"); first season opens December 1729. The company lasts through spring 1737, producing a total of fourteen new Handel operas.

1732. Revised version of *Esther* performed publicly: Handel's first English oratorio. *Deborah* follows the next year.

1733. Rival company, Opera of the Nobility, founded; both fold after four seasons.

1737. Suffers an undiagnosed crippling illness; vacations at Aachen (Germany) and recovers. During the seasons from 1737–38 to 1740–41, produces both operas and oratorios, including his five last operas and three oratorios.

1742. *Messiah* premiered in Dublin; fifteen more oratorios follow.

1750. Last visit to Germany.

1751. Composes *Jephtha*, his last complete work; its composition interrupted by blindness. Completely blind by 1753; subsequently composes only revisions and a few insertions to existing works, dictated to his assistant.

1759. Dies at London, a week after his final performance (*Messiah*).

essary for writing the tuneful, gracefully expressive, easily singable music that had been made popular by Scarlatti and others. Yet he retained an interest in chromatic harmony and a mastery of counterpoint that reflected the German tradition in which he had been trained at Halle. Thus, although his own style became thoroughly Italian, his music has a complexity and richness lacking in that of his Italian contemporaries.

Handel in England

Like Schütz and other earlier Germans who had undertaken extended visits to Italy, Handel probably never intended to stay there. In 1710 he headed back north for Germany. But after a brief stay at Hanover—whose ruler was soon to become king of England—he went to London, which would be his home for the rest of his life. At the time, moves were afoot to establish a permanent public theater for Italian opera in London, and Handel's *Rinaldo*, first performed there in 1711, proved a resounding success. For the next thirty years Handel continued to write operas—thirty-five new ones in all. Meanwhile he produced instrumental and church music of various sorts, as well as several English oratorios—a genre that turned out to be surprisingly popular.

In 1741 the expenses of Italian opera and its failure to turn a profit finally forced Handel to abandon the composition of such works. He was able to continue his career in London by focusing thereafter exclusively on oratorio, although of a type that differed substantially from the earlier ones we have examined at Rome and Paris. Since 1732 Handel had been producing oratorios of this new type, with English text, at a rate of approximately one new work per year. He continued to do so through 1752, presenting the works in public concerts during Lent, when plays and other staged dramatic works were banned. Blindness forced him to cease active composition after 1752, but until a few weeks before his death he continued to direct his Lenten concert series from the harpsichord.

By 1759, when Handel died, Haydn was already composing symphonies, and many of the Baroque traditions in which Handel had been brought up had become outmoded. He had few students as such, and only some minor English composers directly imitated his style. Yet it would be wrong to regard Handel simply as an old-fashioned "Baroque" composer, for the opera seria tradition that governs both Handel's operas and his oratorios was in many respects as much a pre-Classical as a Baroque tradition. Handel's operatic style is close in many respects to that of his younger contemporaries Hasse and J. C. Bach—who in 1763 succeeded Handel as the reigning German composer of Italian opera in England. When, a year later, Mozart met J. C. Bach in London, both composers might have viewed themselves as continuing the tradition that Handel had represented. In later years, Mozart would certainly be influenced by Handel, some of whose works he performed in his own arrangements (notably the oratorio *Messiah*).

Handel's Works

As his biography suggests, Handel's most important works fall into two large groups: the Italian cantatas and operas composed from the early years through

1741, and the English oratorios that followed. He wrote numerous other vocal works as well, including a few motets and other Latin sacred music composed in Italy, as well as sacred anthems and secular odes with English texts.[9] In addition, Handel was active throughout his life as a virtuoso keyboard player and left many harpsichord pieces and works for instrumental ensemble. These appeared in several published collections, including eight harpsichord suites (1720), two sets of concertos for organ or harpsichord, solo and trio sonatas, and a dozen concerti grossi composed during a four-week period in autumn 1739. Among his other orchestral works are the French overture, dances, and other pieces known collectively as the *Water Music*, composed in 1717 for royal boating outings on the Thames River in London, as well as the *Music for the Royal Fireworks*. The latter was intended for outdoor performance by a large wind ensemble during celebrations marking the peace treaty of Aix-la-Chapelle (1749). His most important instrumental works, however, are probably the overtures and related movements, numbering close to one hundred, in his operas, oratorios, and cantatas. (For a detailed account of the suite, concerto, and other late Baroque instrumental genres, see Chapters 10–13.)

Handel's *Orlando*

All of Handel's operas are of the opera seria type. The best known include *Rinaldo*, his first London opera, as well as *Giulio Cesare*, *Tamerlano*, and *Rodelinda*, composed during a particularly inspired period in 1724–25, and *Orlando*, first performed in 1733. *Orlando* (anthology, Selection 18) marked a somewhat unfortunate milestone in Handel's professional life, for it was the last work of several that he wrote for a cast that included the great castrato known as Senesino (Francesco Bernardi). During the following years Senesino joined a newly established opera company, called the Opera of the Nobility, which had been founded to compete with Handel's. The financial strains produced by the competition contributed to Handel's abandonment of opera eight years later.

The plot of *Orlando* derives indirectly from the *Orlando furioso*, an enormously popular epic poem by the Italian Renaissance writer Lodovico Ariosto (see Box 8.3).[10] Like the later *Gerusalemme liberata* by Tasso, Ariosto's poem is on topics from medieval history: the wars of the Frankish king Charlemagne and the hero Roland ("Orlando" is the Italian form of Roland's name). The tone of Ariosto's poem is less serious, and it includes a greater variety of minor characters and subplots. Two centuries later, this feature proved convenient for opera librettists, who frequently adapted Ariosto's stories, particularly those with a magical element. Magic is especially important in *Orlando*, in which the small size of the cast—just five singing characters—would have been compensated for by

---

[9]Handel's anthems and odes are in the tradition of Purcell's sacred and secular vocal works for soloists, chorus, and orchestra. Like Purcell's, most of these were written for the English royal court.

[10]Handel's libretto was an anonymous reworking of a text by Carlo Sigismondo Capeci (1652–1728) that had been previously set by Domenico Scarlatti, son of Alessandro (see Chapter 11 for Domenico's keyboard sonatas).

Box 8.3

Handel: *Orlando*

Anonymous libretto after *L'Orlando* by Carlo Sigismondo Capeci (1652–1728), previously set to music by Domenico Scarlatti (Rome, 1711, lost). The source of the story is the *Orlando furioso* of Lodovico Ariosto (1474–1533).
First performed 27 January 1733 at the King's Theatre, London.

Chief Characters

Orlando (alto), a heroic defender of France under the medieval emperor Charlemagne.

Angelica (soprano), queen of Cathay (China).

Medoro (alto), an African prince, lover of Angelica.

Dorinda (soprano), a shepherdess.

Zoroastro (bass), a sorcerer.

SYNOPSIS

Orlando, wandering in a strange land, is warned at the outset of Act 1 by Zoroastro that he must choose between love and conquest. Orlando, however, declares that like Hercules he can succeed at both—a big mistake, of course. He is already in love with Angelica, who is, however, in love with Medoro. Angelica, moreover, has seen Orlando in the company of a certain princess (whom he has previously rescued from danger). Meanwhile, the shepherdess Dorinda has also fallen in love with Medoro. As Act 1 ends, Orlando has set off to fight his enemies in order to prove his love for Angelica—while Angelica and Medoro try to convince Dorinda that her love for Medoro is misplaced.

Later in the opera, Orlando goes mad after discovering that Angelica and Medoro have been in love all along. He tries to kill them, but in the end all is set right by the magician Zoroastro, who has been watching over all of them from the beginning.

SELECTIONS DISCUSSED IN THE TEXT

Overture.

Act 1, scenes 7–8. Dorinda and Medoro meet in the woods where she lives. Medoro tries to tell her diplomatically that he loves another (aria "Se il cor mai ti dirà"), then leaves. Dorinda, alone, complains about the untrustworthiness of people: aria "Oh care parolette."

———, scene 9. Zoroastro informs Angelica that he is aware of her love for Medoro and warns her that it will anger Orlando; the latter appears, as does Medoro, but Zoroastro saves him by concealing him magically. Angelica tells

> Orlando that she can't love him without his proving his faithfulness: aria "Se
> fedel vuoi."
>
> ————, scene 10. Orlando, alone, complains that Angelica has misunderstood his
> affair with the princess; he vows to fight monsters: aria "Fammi combattere."

elaborate stage effects. The latter included the magical disappearance of Medoro during the recitative in Act 1, scene 9 (see anthology, Selection 18b), as well as the visions of the underworld that Orlando sees in the opera's climax, his famous mad scene at the end of Act 2.

Orlando opens, as do most of Handel's operas, with a French overture. The remainder of the opera is, however, thoroughly Italian in form and style, and most of the arias of the major characters fall into certain more or less standard types that had been established by the previous generation of Italian composers, such as Alessandro Scarlatti. In the portion of the work that we are studying, Orlando's aria "Fammi combattere" is an expression of heroic might, full of virtuoso passagework for the singer and imitations of trumpet calls in the orchestra (anthology, Selection 18c). Similar arias sung at moments of anger or pathos are sometimes referred to as "rage" arias. On the other hand, the aria of Angelica (anthology, Selection 18b), a somewhat ambivalent expression of love, is relatively short, lightly scored, and restrained in emotional profile. This might have been considered an *aria di mezza carattere* (aria of medium character).

Key, instrumentation, and melodic material all help define an aria's expressive character. For example, horns appear only once in the opera, to lend extra grandeur to Orlando's aria "Non fu già men forte Alcide" in Act 1, scene 3, in which he compares himself to Hercules.[11] This aria is preceded by an accompanied recitative whose string accompaniment and opening key—F minor, rarely used at this date—underline the prophetic visions that the magician Zoroastro has shown to Orlando.

Brass instruments are absent from Orlando's equally martial aria in scene 10, "Fammi combattere" (anthology, Selection 18c). But they are represented symbolically by the fanfare motives, reminiscent of trumpet calls, that are developed imitatively in the opening ritornello (mm. 4–5). Oboes, which double the first violins in the ritornellos of this aria, were also commonly used as military instruments at the time and thus reinforce the martial effect. The vocal part includes lengthy melismas on two words: *combattere* ("to do battle," mm. 14–18) and *valor* ("strength," mm. 31–35). The latter word is accompanied by the fanfare motive in the first violins, thus emphasizing the two ideas most important in the text of the aria and most representative of Orlando's personality—or, at least, of his aspirations.

---

[11]Horns had been introduced to the opera orchestra during the first two decades of the century and at the time of *Orlando* were still something of a novelty in London, employed chiefly as a special effect associated with hunting scenes, the horn still being in use as a signaling instrument during hunts.

On the other hand, Angelica's aria (anthology, Selection 18b) is distinguished by its simple (but very beautiful) vocal line. The latter is almost entirely syllabic, but for this very reason its brief melismas—the two longest, significantly, on the word *fedeltà* ("faithfulness," mm. 10 and 12)—bear considerable rhetorical weight. Apart from two brief ritornellos, this aria is scored solely for voice and continuo, a throwback to seventeenth-century texture that creates an effect here of intimacy and sincerity, in keeping with Angelica's unhappiness and uncertainty as she pleads with Orlando to prove his faithfulness to her.

Dorinda's aria "Oh care parolette" (anthology, Selection 18a) is particularly interesting as an example of musical characterization. Although its text appears to be pessimistic—a complaint about the untrustworthiness of lovers' promises—the music is a lightly scored Italian jig, with the quick triplet rhythms characteristic of that dance. Moreover, both the ritornello and the vocal part open with somewhat comic repetitions of a perky three-note motive. The juxtaposition of such light music with an ostensibly solemn text seems to characterize Dorinda as a figure who either has no profound feelings or does not take what she says seriously. The effect is one of irony—an example of the sort of sophistication that was possible within the seemingly rigid conventions of opera seria.

Ritornello Form

Despite their varying character, most of Handel's arias share the same design, illustrated in Table 8.1, which analyzes Dorinda's aria. In addition to their fundamental da capo form, most of these arias also employ **ritornello form**: a design in which all or part of the instrumental introduction, or ritornello, is repeated several times within the body of the aria. The ritornello thus becomes an integral part of the aria, not merely an external introduction or frame as in earlier arias with ritornellos.

Typically, the opening ritornello is followed by the soloist's presentation of the entire A text, which leads to a cadence in the dominant (or another closely related key). A shortened ritornello—sometimes just a restatement of the opening measure or two—may occur at this point. In the second half of the A section, its text is repeated, leading to a cadence in the tonic and another complete or partial statement of the ritornello. The B section is usually

TABLE 8.1
Handel: *Orlando*, Dorinda's aria, "Se il cor mai ti dirà"

Section A						B		A
R	1–3	r	1–3	R	4–6			1–3
Key Bb	Bb → F	F → Bb	Bb	Bb	Bb → g			Bb (dal segno)
Measure 1	9	19b	22b	34	39b	45b		9

R = ritornello
r = abbreviated ritornello
numerals = lines of text
→ = modulation followed by cadence to the indicated key

shorter—often much shorter—than the A section, and may lack instrumental participation entirely (except for the continuo). On the other hand, it may also contain several modulations to relatively remote keys. The cadence that marks the end of the B section is followed immediately by a repetition of the A section. In the repetition of the A section, Handel sometimes omits all or part of the opening ritornello, as in Dorinda's and Orlando's arias.[12]

JEAN-PHILIPPE RAMEAU

During the latter part of Handel's career in London, the leading figure on the other side of the English Channel was Jean-Philippe Rameau (1683–1764), the most important and influential French composer since Lully. Rameau's career was slow in getting started; his first opera was not performed until he was fifty (see Box 8.4). But by then he had established himself in Paris as a virtuoso harpsichordist and composer. He had also published a massive book on music theory whose principles have informed the study of harmony to the present day.

Rameau's Music

Despite his apparent inclinations toward theatrical music, the first half of Rameau's career was spent as a church organist. Although he held a number of significant positions, most were outside Paris, the one city that really counted in the French eighteenth-century musical universe. Nevertheless, prior to 1722 Rameau must have been developing a distinctive style of keyboard playing and composition, for his first substantial book of harpsichord pieces, published in 1724, reveals a virtuoso approach very different from the restrained manner of earlier French keyboard composers. The surviving motets and cantatas from these years also appear to have made significant departures from the traditional French style.

Rameau's Musical Innovations

Lully had so dominated French music during the 1670s and 1680s that his his theatrical vocal and instrumental music established the norms for the next two generations of musicians and audiences. Nevertheless, Italian-style vocal and instrumental music, including cantatas and sonatas, grew increasingly popular in France after Lully's death, and their influence eventually led to what the French composer François Couperin described in 1724 as a "reunification" of the two national styles. Nevertheless, even in those French works that employed Couperin's *goûts réunis* ("reunited styles"), the French element remained paramount, as is evident in the pervasive use of dance rhythms, the precise nota-

---

[12]Modern performances sometimes omit the entire da capo, or even both the B section and the repetition of the A section, but such practices distort the music, and Handel rarely resorted to them.

BOX 8.4

Jean-Philippe Rameau (1683–1764)

1683. Born at Dijon (about 150 miles southeast of Paris) into a musical family; presumably studies with his father, an organist, and at the local Jesuit college. Briefly in Italy (exact date unknown), afterward possibly violinist with the Lyons opera.

1702. Appointed organist at Clermont cathedral (some 200 miles south of Paris); retains title until 1708 despite moving to Paris in 1706.

1706–8. In Paris with positions as organist at two religious institutions; publishes his first book of harpsichord pieces (a single suite, 1706).

1709. Succeeds to his father's organ position in Dijon.

1713. Moves to Lyon (250 miles southeast of Paris) as organist there; composes motets and secular works.

1715. Again organist at Clermont. He is believed to have composed secular cantatas *L'impatience*, *Orphée*, and others during this period, as well as writing his *Traité de l'harmonie*.

1722. Moves to Paris; publishes *Traité de l'harmonie* and two years later *Pièces de clavecin* (harpsichord pieces; a second volume of *pièces* follows ca. 1730).

1733–44. His first opera, *Hippolyte et Aricie*, performed by the Royal Academy (1733); it is successful but controversial owing to its departures from Lullian tradition. Four theatrical works follow; also publishes a collection of chamber works with keyboard (*Pièces de clavecin en concerts*, 1741) and two more major theoretical works as well.

1745. Composes a ballet for the dauphin (crown prince); numerous theatrical works, many under royal patronage, follow.

1752–54. "Querelle des Bouffons" (Debate of the Buffoons): a series of published exchanges with leading French intellectuals, notably Jean-Jacques Rousseau (1712–78), over the respective merits of French and Italian music. The latter is judged by Rameau's critics to be more "natural" because of its simpler textures and more facile melodies.

1764. Dies in Paris.

---

tion of ornaments, and in opera and ballet, the retention of the basic conventions of Lullian style.

Rameau was probably a much greater borrower from the Italian style than Couperin ever was, yet he remained so committed to the French operatic tradition that later in life, during the so-called Debate of the Buffoons (see Box 8.4), he defended French music against younger advocates of the Italian style. The latter, with its emphasis on solo virtuosity and simple melody, was contrary to the French tradition of carefully notated and precisely performed rhythm, ornamentation, and declamation of the text. Rameau, although adhering to these ideals, nevertheless admitted a significant degree of Italian virtuosity into his music. When he first made his mark in Paris, in the 1720s and 1730s, he was thus viewed by some as a destroyer of the Lully tradition, when in fact he reinvigorated it for another generation, carrying it into the 1760s.

Rameau's Theoretical Writings

With the eclipse of the French Baroque style in the late eighteenth century, Rameau's musical compositions, like those of his contemporaries, went out of fashion. His greatness as a composer was largely forgotten, to be fully recognized only in the late twentieth century, when fully staged performances of his theatrical works began to be reconstructed with something resembling their original music and choreography. In the interim, however, Rameau's voluminous writings on the philosophy and theory of music were always studied, particularly those portions that formed the basis of subsequent theories of harmony.

Although he published significant books on all aspects of musical composition, theory, and practice, Rameau's core ideas are already present in his first book, the *Traité de l'harmonie* (Treatise on harmony, Paris, 1722), which has remained the most widely read. The book was a manifestation of that movement in French eighteenth-century thought known as the Enlightenment, which encouraged the rational, systematic examination of all scientific and cultural subjects. In Rameau's musical theory, Enlightenment thought took the form of an innovative way of analyzing chord progressions, which Rameau viewed as the basis of all musical composition.

Rameau's Theory of Harmony

Previously, chords had been regarded as the products of the voice leading of individual parts in a contrapuntal texture—the results of a linear or melodic process. This view, which had emerged from the study of sixteenth-century polyphony, had grown increasingly inappropriate for explaining later music, which tended to employ homophonic textures and to rely on tonal rather than modal types of pitch organization. In Rameau's theory, the successive vertical sonorities of a composition were viewed as constituting progressions of harmonies, which Rameau represented through a form of analytical notation which he called the **fundamental bass.** To analyze a composition, Rameau presented the fundamental bass on an extra staff beneath the actual bass line. Thus in Example 8.1 Rameau analyzed his own five-voice motet *Laboravi clamans* by adding a fundamental bass on the bottom staff. The fundamental bass was notated like a basso continuo part, using figured bass, but the only dissonant interval indicated was the seventh. The fundamental bass line consists primarily of what we would call the *roots* of the successive chords, which might appear in any of several forms or *inversions*. Rameau also employed the terms *tonic, dominant*, and *subdominant* to describe harmonies in relationship to what we would call the tonality of a composition, thereby introducing ideas from which later writers developed various theories of harmonic function.

Example 8.1 Rameau, motet *Laboravi clamans*, mm. 1–9 (soprano and *basse-taille* omitted); the lowest staff shows the fundamental bass as given by Rameau in his *Traité de l'harmonie*

Laboravi clamans.   I suffered, crying out.

Some musicians, especially in Germany, were at first reluctant to accept elements of Rameau's theory, but it eventually became the basis of later theories of tonal harmony. Nineteenth-century theorists replaced Rameau's fundamental bass with various symbols, and from these developed the modern American system of analytical chord symbols: Roman numerals to indicate the roots, and arabic numerals to indicate the inversions.[13] Other systems have been adopted elsewhere. In Germany, for example, functions are indicated by the letters *T*, *D*, and *S* (for tonic, dominant, and subdominant), with additional symbols used for other functions recognized by later theorists. Only in the twentieth century was Rameau's predominantly harmonic or "vertical" view of tonal progressions seriously challenged, notably by the Austrian theorist Heinrich Schenker (1868–1935) and his followers. Schenker derived his views from eighteenth-

---

[13]The arabic numerals are descended from the figures of figured bass.

century German theorists such as C. P. E. Bach, whose writings represent an older, "horizontal," view of harmony.

Rameau's *Les indes galantes*

Rameau's theories, although highly innovative, derived from concepts already recognizable in the French seventeenth-century tradition (notably the idea of chord inversion). The same can be said of his music, of which the dramatic vocal works are the most significant part. Unlike Lully, whose mature theatrical works are dominated by one type (the *tragédie en musique*), Rameau's stage works include a variety of additional categories: *comédies lyriques* (lyric comedies), *opéras-ballets* (operatic ballets), *pastorales heroïques* (heroic pastoral dramas), and others.

The newer types of work continue the Lullian tradition of combining sensitively declaimed poetry with extensive choral and ballet elements, but their plots and general character are less uniformly serious and heroic than those of Lully's *tragédies en musique*. This was in keeping with a loosening of conventions that had followed Lully's death in 1687. Notable among the composers of the following generation was André Campra (1660–1744; see Fig. 10.4), who wrote, in addition to operas, the *opéra-ballets L'Europe galante* (literally, Gallant Europe, 1694) and *Les fêtes vénitiennes* (Venetian carnival, 1710). These works reflect the growing influence of Italian opera, particularly the da capo aria, which continued to be felt by French composers of Rameau's generation.

Les indes galantes (anthology, Selection 19) is an *opéra-ballet*, including dialogue and action (set in Lullian recitative) but consisting primarily of dances and Italian-influenced arias. It originally comprised three acts, called *entrées*, that are only loosely related to one another (see Box 8.5).[14] First produced in 1735, it was revived the following year with the addition of a fourth *entrée*. Each act or *entrée* takes place in a different exotic locale; the added one is set in what later became the Louisiana Purchase of the United States.[15] The music of the final scene incorporates a reworking of a well-known harpsichord piece, *Les sauvages*, which Rameau had published in a collection of about 1730 (see Chapter 11); it had been inspired by a performance of ethnic dancing by two Illinois Indians in Paris in 1725.

The plot of the fourth *entrée* emphasizes the supposed "naturalness" of the Native Americans, who are viewed in the libretto as ethically superior to their more civilized French and Spanish rivals. This view reflects a romantic way of thinking common among eighteenth-century Europeans, who idealized the natives of North America as "noble savages" unafflicted by the pathologies of European civilization. Although this view may seem patronizing, it must be understood in its cultural context. The French poet Fuzelier's stereotyped impression of the Indian people parallels his stereotyping of the Europeans as

---

[14]The word *entrée* in this sense is to be distinguished from the use of the same term for a dance in dotted rhythm (see Chapter 5).

[15]The region in question was held in succession by France and Spain and acquired by the United States in 1802.

BOX 8.5

Rameau: *Les indes galantes*

Opéra-ballet, composed Paris, 1735. Revised, with addition of fourth act or
entrée (originally called the *nouvelle entrée*), 1736.
Libretto by Louis Fuzelier. Comprises overture, prologue, and four acts
or *entrées*. The *entrées* take place in four different exotic (i.e., non-European)
locales, which are visited in turn by several European adventurers. Each
entrée constitutes a self-contained dramatic ballet, with singing
and dancing.

Characters (fourth [*nouvelle*] *entrée*, titled *Les sauvages*)

Zima (soprano), Indian princess
Adario (baritone), Indian commander
Damon (tenor), French commander
Don Alvar (bass), Spanish commander

SYNOPSIS

Two Europeans, one French, one Spanish, are signing a peace treaty mediated by
Zima's father, an Indian king (called the *grand Calumet*). Both woo Zima and in
so doing reveal their supposed national traits: flirtatiousness for the French, jeal-
ousy for the Spanish. But the Indian commander Adario wins Zima by his strength
and constancy.

SELECTIONS DISCUSSED IN THE TEXT

Overture.

Fourth *entrée*, scene 4. The arrival of the European and Indian armies is signaled
by a brief orchestral *prélude*, interrupting the confrontation between Adario, on
the one hand, and Damon and Alvar on the other, who now express their hopes
for peace (recit.)

————, scene 5. Adario expresses his love for Zima (recit.). She accepts in a brief
arioso in sarabande rhythm ("De l'amour le plus tendre," mm. 10–15), then
rejects his two rivals (recit., mm. 16–25) and comments on the Indians' "natural" moral superiority in an air, "Sur nos bords l'amour vole" (mm. 26–55).
Adario looks forward to their marriage in a brief recitative (mm. 56–58), and
they celebrate with a duet, "Hymen, viens nous unir" (mm. 59–96).

————, scene 6. Final scene, celebrating their wedding; corresponds with the *divertissements* in Lullian opera. Opens with air, "Bannissons les tristes alarmes,"
for Adario, repeated by a chorus of Indians.

Long *rondeau* follows: opening instrumental version (arranged from Rameau's harpsichord rondeau *Les sauvages*), followed by vocal version "Forêts paisibles," set as duet with chorus.

Two alternating minuets (instrumental dances, "for the warriors and Amazons"—presumably male and female Indians).

Zima then sings a virtuoso air in da capo form, "Régnez, plaisirs et jeux," introduced by a lengthy ritornello.

The work concludes with a great chaconne.

well; his way of understanding national character was in keeping with Enlightenment understanding of culture and ethnography in general.

Rameau's Music Contrasted with Lully's

Rameau's work is structured much like one of Lully's, opening with a French overture and prologue. The action and dialogue of each *entrée* are presented in recitatives whose frequent changes of meter and precisely notated rhythm closely reflect the rhythms of the French text. The characters frequently break into short airs, many of which employ standard dance rhythms. Each *entrée* culminates in a large ballet scene that combines singing and dancing as in a Lullian *divertissement*.

Unlike Lully, however, Rameau includes relatively lengthy airs that are really Italianate da capo arias; these were known in France as *ariettes*. Among these is the air "Sur nos bords l'amour vole," sung in scene 5 by the Indian princess Zima. Despite its Italian formal design, this air continues to employ the French style. The latter is recognizable in the ornaments notated in both the vocal and the instrumental parts and in the recurring use of rhythms characteristic of a French dance, the gavotte (see Chapter 10).

Another Ramellian innovation is the virtuoso instrumental and vocal writing in the sixth and final scene, where Zima has a large da capo aria or *ariette* ("Régnez, plaisirs et jeux"), incorporating brilliant melismas and lengthy ritornellos unheard of in the Lully style. In addition, the instrumentation is far more flexible than Lully's, especially in the frequent use of specified instrumental sonorities other than those of the basic string ensemble, such as trumpet and timpani in the brief instrumental prelude heard in scene 4. In Zima's aria "Sur nos bords l'amour vole," the two accompanying violin parts provide imaginative counterpoint that weaves about the voice in expressive triplets and "sigh" motives—two-note descending slurred figures, especially in the B section (mm. 41–55).

Not surprisingly for a composer also known for his contributions to the theory of harmony, Rameau goes far beyond the relatively narrow variety of harmonic progressions and modulations employed by his seventeenth-century predecessor. Although *Les indes galantes* is fairly conservative in this respect, a number of Rameau's operas contain passages of considerable harmonic audacity. The most famous such example, from the Second Trio of the Fates in his first opera, *Hippolyte et Aricie*, includes a stunning chromatic sequence for which Rameau later provided a harmonic analysis in one of his theoretical works.[16]

On the other hand, Rameau's recitative remains close to the Lully style, accompanied only by continuo and using changes of meter for accurate declamation of the text. Occasional lines are set in regular dance rhythms, as when Zima describes "the most tender love," using the rhythm of a sarabande (scene 5, mm. 10–15). The two lovers rejoice in an intimate duet, still accompanied only by continuo, as in similar lovers' duets in Lully's works.[17] Only then does the final scene begin, a lengthy *divertissement* celebrating their impending wedding. After a series of dances, airs, and choruses, the work concludes with a grand chaconne, distinct in sonority but identical in rhythm and similar in form to the great *passacailles* of Lully's operas. This chaconne lacks a regular ostinato bass, instead employing a free form related to the *rondeaux* of Rameau's keyboard pieces (see Chapter 11). But it retains Lully's basic conception of presenting a magnificent succession of contrasting musical and choreographic ideas.

---

[16]The *Génération harmonique* of 1737.

[17]An ironic example for Rinaldo and Armide occurs in Act 5 of *Armide*, just before the famous *passacaille*. The Indians in Rameau's work address their duet to Hymen, the Greek god of marriage—suggesting that the French poet identified the Native Americans with ancient Greek nymphs and shepherds.

CHAPTER 9

LATE BAROQUE SACRED MUSIC

Developments in late Baroque theatrical music found close parallels in religious vocal works. In particular, opera seria's regular yet dramatic alternation of recitatives and arias was adopted by many composers of sacred music. Individual movements, that is, the successive recitatives and arias of a sacred work, similarly tended to fall into forms and styles close to those of secular works.

The introduction into sacred music of what had originated as secular dramatic forms may strike us as an anomaly, particularly when we consider that the opera theater of the time was a world dominated by castrato singers, often portraying the pagan heroes of antiquity. This development represented a breaking down of a division recognized since the early seventeenth century between a conservative church style and a freer "theatrical" style. Yet, from the beginning of the Baroque, composers such as Monteverdi, Carissimi, and Schütz had been quick to employ elements of the theatrical style, such as recitative and the *stile concitato*, to render the presentation of a sacred text more vivid or expressive. Moreover, the even older principles of musical rhetoric recognized no distinction between secular and sacred music. Hence, although eighteenth-century critics did occasionally complain about the presence of theatrical forms in church music, most musicians and listeners regarded theatrical musical devices as a desirable means of making sacred texts more accessible and meaningful to contemporary audiences.

The introduction of new types of sacred music did not mean that older ones were abandoned. Particularly in Roman Catholic countries, polyphonic music in the *stile antico* continued to be performed. Thus Alessandro Scarlatti, his son Domenico, and others still produced masses and motets in contrapuntal style. These works resembled those of Palestrina—whose music also was still performed—save for the presence of a basso continuo part. Perhaps the most influential composer of such music was the Austrian Johann Joseph Fux (1660–1741), whose book *Gradus ad Parnassum* (Vienna, 1725) has served as a counterpoint textbook to the present day.[1] It was read carefully by the mature

---

[1] The title of Fux's book can be translated as "Steps to Parnassus," referring to the mountain home of Apollo and the Muses in southern Greece, a symbol of artistic perfection. The bibliography lists several modern editions under "Baroque Theoretical Treatises."

Bach—in a German translation by his pupil Lorenz Mizler—and later by Haydn, Beethoven, and Brahms during their student years. In Lutheran Germany, *concertato* motets in the manner of Schütz continued to be composed well into the eighteenth century. Such works might still be through-composed, consisting of line-by-line settings for chorus or smaller ensembles of texts derived from the Bible or from chorales, the congregational hymns of the Lutheran church. Such was the most common type of sacred vocal work composed by Dietrich Buxtehude (ca. 1637–1707) and, until about 1708, the young J. S. Bach.

But in general, although composers continued to set to music the sacred texts traditionally used in masses and motets, the musical style and scoring of these works came to be similar to those of contemporary secular music. Motets in this up-to-date style are frequently monodic works, alternating between recitatives and arias, although some also include choral movements, as do most mass settings and such regional forms as the English anthem. The oratorio, which in the mid-seventeenth century had taken the form of a special type of polyphonic motet (see Chapter 7), by 1700 was practically indistinguishable from an opera, at least as far as the music was concerned. Italian oratorios even dispensed with the chorus, as opera seria did.

New Types of Sacred Music by German Composers

In the Lutheran regions of Germany, the adoption of theatrical forms for sacred music produced a distinct new type of religious work. The influential theologian and poet Erdmann Neumeister (1671–1756) introduced around the turn of the century a type of sacred cantata text modeled on that of the Italian secular cantata, serenata, and other quasi-operatic works. Paradoxically, the cantata's emphasis on the dramatic expression of individual emotion found a sympathetic resonance during a period that also saw the widespread influence of **pietism** in Lutheran Germany. Pietism had originated in the early seventeenth century as a movement toward individual piety and religious expression; it discouraged elaborate (and therefore expensive) forms of church music such as the cantata.

Nevertheless, the first half of the eighteenth century saw the widespread writing of pietistic poetry in dramatic form which was set to music in the current Italian style. Among the most important composers of such works were Georg Philipp Telemann (1681–1767) and J. S. Bach. Both, following the practice of Neumeister, organized their church cantatas into annual cycles: yearly series of works, one for each Sunday and holiday in the church calendar. The enormously prolific Telemann produced at least thirty-one such cycles—over two thousand individual cantatas—as well as numerous other sacred works. Bach's extant cantata cycles number only three, still a considerable quantity of music.[2] Bach and his contemporaries did not usually call these works cantatas, using instead such older titles as *concerto* and *motetto*. Nevertheless, it is convenient for us to em-

---

[2]Fragments of one or two additional cycles by Bach survive, but documentary evidence for the oft-repeated claim that he wrote five complete cycles is inconclusive.

ploy the expression *cantata*, which was used at least occasionally for those examples that involved only a single singer.

The German Eighteenth-Century Sacred Cantata

Most German sacred cantatas differ from their Italian secular models in several
respects. First, the language is, of course, German, whose particular pronunci-
ation and accentuation influence the style and sound of the music, especially in
the recitatives. Second, whereas the Italian cantata is essentially a genre for a
solo singer, many German sacred cantatas include movements for several different solo voices as well as choruses for four-part vocal ensemble. Finally, not
all sacred cantata librettos in Germany are composed solely of free poetry; many
also include biblical verses and stanzas from chorales. Bach's cantatas are particularly rich in their use of chorale, scripture, and free poetry to produce a com-
posite textual and musical form.

Eighteenth-Century Oratorio

The oratorio also took a distinct northern European form, particularly in the
English works of Handel, which therefore are usually referred to more specifically as *English* oratorios. Although the young Handel had composed two oratorios to Italian texts during his years in Italy, these followed the current Italian form. Like similar works by Alessandro Scarlatti or the Roman composer
Bernardo Pasquini (1637–1710), Handel's oratorio *La resurrezione* (The Resurrection, 1708) differs little musically from an opera seria on a sacred theme, including elaborate da capo arias for such figures as Mary Magdalene and even
Satan. In Germany, a different sort of Baroque sacred drama emerged in the **oratorio passion**—a musical setting of the passion narrative, that is, the story of
Jesus's arrest and crucifixion, traditionally read in churches on Good Friday.[3]
Seventeenth-century Lutheran oratorio passions had already incorporated
strophic arias and chorales alongside biblical recitative and choruses. Eighteenth-
century examples by Reinhard Keiser (1674–1739) and J. S. Bach took the logical step of including operatic recitative and aria as well. Bach wrote at least
three oratorio passions, as well as oratorios of a similar type on other subjects,
including the Christmas and Easter stories.[4]

Handel's English Oratorios

The German oratorio passion was usually performed as part of a church service, and as we have seen, Italian oratorios were frequently performed in quasi-

---

[3]The word *passion* comes from the Latin *patior* (to suffer), hence the special meaning of the word
as a term for a musical genre.

[4]Some music historians make a distinction between the oratorio passion, which is essentially Good
Friday music composed in *concertato* style and performed as part of a church service, and the *passion oratorio*, which can be any oratorio on the subject of the passion.

liturgical settings. But in certain places the oratorio also found an audience in the public theater, as Handel discovered in London during the 1730s. Not requiring elaborate sets, costumes, or lighting, nor expensive imported Italian singers, English oratorio could be produced at a fraction of the cost of opera, and for larger audiences as well. Handel's works in this form incorporate recitatives and arias whose English texts are modeled on those of Italian opera; his musical settings are, naturally, in a similar vein. But his English oratorios include the chorus, which, as in Lullian opera, plays an essential role as an active participant in the drama.

Handel's best-known English oratorio is *Messiah*, which he composed in 1741 (the year of his last opera). Yet *Messiah*, with its text drawn almost entirely from the Bible and without any individual roles, is a different sort of work from most of his other English oratorios; indeed, it was originally termed a "sacred entertainment," not an oratorio. Most of Handel's other oratorios, although intended for concert performances without staging, include named characters whose roles are genuinely dramatic, if not acted. *Messiah*, as well as *Israel in Egypt*, Handel's popular English oratorio of 1739, is in effect a large-scale English anthem, the principal type of Anglican church music. Both works contain much powerful music, but neither includes actual dramatic roles, achieving its effects instead through choruses interspersed with movements for soloists (the latter being far more prominent in *Messiah*). In addition, both choruses and solos in these works use chiefly biblical texts, unlike the newly written poetry employed in Handel's other oratorios.

JOHANN SEBASTIAN BACH

J. S. Bach (1685–1750) is now recognized as one of the greatest musicians in Western history (see Box 9.1). During his lifetime, however, Bach's fame was largely confined to Germany, especially the southeastern regions of Saxony and Thuringia, where he spent most of his life. He was known primarily from his occasional public appearances as an organ virtuoso; familiarity with his vocal compositions was largely confined to the cities in which he performed them, and his instrumental music was for the most part known only to other professional musicians who had performed or studied with him. Unlike his almost exact contemporary Handel, Bach never left Germany, settling for a series of positions that, with one exception, involved the composition and performance of church music. This has led to a view of Bach as primarily a composer of sacred music, and indeed the latter constitutes the majority of his surviving output. Yet like many other eighteenth-century musicians, he was equally active in both sacred and secular spheres, making little distinction between them insofar as musical style is concerned. Bach, moreover, was as willing as any of his German contemporaries to adopt the most up-to-date musical fashions emanating from France and Italy. Where he differed from most contemporary musicians was his strong interest in counterpoint and in sometimes highly dissonant, chromatic harmony—both survivals from the late seventeenth-century tradition in which he was brought up.

Box 9.1

Johann Sebastian Bach (1685–1750)

1685. Born at Eisenach (western Thuringia, in central Germany).

1695. Father dies; moves to nearby Ohrdruf to live and study with his older brother Johann Christoph.

1700. Enters St. Michael's School (choir school) in Lüneburg, 150 miles to the north. While there hears French dance music played by the court band of the ruling duke of Celle, possibly also opera and organ music at Hamburg, 25 miles away. Also presumably hears works by Lüneburg organist and composer Georg Böhm (1661–1733).

1702. Wins competition for organist at Sangerhausen (Thuringia) but is denied position.

1703. Briefly hired as "lackey" at Weimar (to serve as a musician).

1703–7. Organist at Arnstadt (east of Eisenach); composes keyboard music and possibly his earliest surviving vocal works.

1705–6. Visits Lübeck (200 miles north) for about four months to hear music by and possibly study with Buxtehude.

1707–8. Organist at Mühlhausen (north of Eisenach). Composes his first datable vocal work (Cantata 71).

1708–14. Organist at Weimar (40 miles southeast); composes organ and harpsichord music, probably vocal works as well.

1714. Promoted to *Concertmeister* at Weimar; begins monthly composition of church cantatas (through 1716, with interruptions).

1717. Visiting Dresden, challenges French harpsichordist Marchand to public contest; latter fails to show.

1717–23. Kapellmeister at Cöthen; composes or revises secular cantatas and instrumental works, including Sonatas and Partitas for unaccompanied violin (1720), Brandenburg Concertos (1721), *Well-Tempered Clavier*, Part 1 (1722).

1720. Visits Hamburg; his organ recital is praised by the aged organist and composer Jan Adamszoon Reinken.

1723–50. Cantor at the St. Thomas School and director of church music, Leipzig.

1723–27. Composes church cantatas on a regular basis (roughly one per week), also *St. John Passion* (1724), *St. Matthew Passion* (1727 or 1729), *St. Mark Passion* (1731, lost).

1726. Publishes first partita of *Clavierübung*, Part 1 (keyboard music); the six partitas constituting Part 1 are reissued in a collected edition in 1731; Parts 2–4 follow in 1735, 1739, 1741.

1729–37, 1739–41. Directs Leipzig Collegium Musicum; regular concerts at Zimmermann's coffeehouse.

1733. *Missa* (early version of B Minor Mass) sent to the new elector of Saxony; Bach receives honorary title from him three years later.

1737. Johann Adolph Scheibe publishes famous criticism of Bach's music; Bach defended by Johann Abraham Birnbaum.

1741. Visits his patron Count Keyserlingk in Dresden; publishes Goldberg Variations, so called after Keyserlingk's harpsichordist Johann Gottlieb Goldberg, a pupil of Bach.

1747. Travels to Berlin, plays for King Frederick II, improvising fugues on a subject proposed by the latter; later that year publishes the fugues (called ricercars) and other works as parts of the *Musical Offering* dedicated to the king.

1749. B Minor Mass completed; blindness forces curtailment of composing and performing.

1750. Dies at Leipzig. *Art of Fugue* published (incomplete) one year later.

At a time when the simple *galant* style of opera seria was increasingly in vogue, this made Bach appear old-fashioned to his contemporaries, a few of whom criticized him for writing music that was, in their view, archaic and difficult to perform.[5] The image of Bach as a conservative writer of complicated contrapuntal forms has persisted. This is partly due to his indeed having composed many fugues and other contrapuntal works, and to this day his contrapuntal keyboard works form part of the elementary training of many music students, as they did for Bach's own pupils. But such works constitute only a fraction of Bach's output. Indeed, perhaps the most remarkable aspect of Bach's music is its diversity, which in this respect eclipses the music of any contemporary composer, including Handel. Bach composed substantial examples in all the genres of his time; even operatic music is represented by several dramatic secular cantatas. Moreover, Bach's music successfully blends elements of both French and Italian styles with his own distinctive musical personality. The latter is evident in the elaborate formal architectures, unusual chromatic harmonic progressions and modulations, and profound contrapuntal element present in many works. His music also requires a degree of technical skill from the performer that is higher than in most of the music of his contemporaries. The result is music of great complexity that challenges both performers and listeners yet possesses enormous emotional depth and, frequently, immediate melodic and rhythmic appeal as well.

Bach's Life and Works

Bach's output, like that of most musicians before the nineteenth century, was largely determined by where and for whom he worked at any given time. Most of his organ music was written during his early years as a church organist, and much of his secular vocal music and music for instrumental ensemble dates from

---

[5]See the exchange between Bach's critic Scheibe and his defender Birnbaum, reprinted in *The New Bach Reader* (see bibliography under "J. S. Bach").

Figure 9.1 Portrait of J. S. Bach by Elias Gottlob Haussmann (1748, copied by the artist from his painting of 1746). William H. Scheide Library, Princeton. Bach holds a copy of his *Canon triplex* in six parts BWV 1076, which, following an old tradition, serves as an icon of the composer's skill and learning.

six years in the middle of his career when he directed the court orchestra at Cöthen. The sacred vocal works were mostly written during two relatively short periods during which Bach was particularly active as a church composer. The one sphere in which Bach remained steadily active throughout his life was keyboard music, especially music for stringed keyboard instruments (primarily the harpsichord).

Despite following a fairly conventional career path, Bach nevertheless exerted more self-determination than was typical of his contemporaries. Although he never traveled as widely as Handel, his frequent journeys within Germany and his life-long interest in collecting music—much of it in manuscript copies that he made himself—kept him informed about the latest trends in both French and Italian music, which he enthusiastically if judiciously adopted in his own music. Although a prolific composer by modern standards, his output is smaller than that of Telemann and other contemporaries. In part this is because when an occasion demanded a composition from him, rather than writing a new work he often preferred to revise an existing one for the particular performance at hand. Indeed, throughout his life he would return to previously composed pieces, elaborating and correcting them to bring them to a state of perfection rarely sought by other composers. As with all eighteenth-century musicians, the outward characteristics of his works were determined by conventions of genre and style. Yet in virtually every work Bach combined diverse stylistic elements and created new formal designs, belying his popular image as a conservative composer.

Bach's works were assigned "BWV" (*Bach-Werke-Verzeichnis*) numbers by the German scholar Wolfgang Schmieder; despite Schmieder's own wish to the contrary, these are sometimes called "S" numbers. The numbering is nonchronological. The first two hundred works correspond to the traditional numbering (also nonchronological) of the sacred cantatas; thus Cantata No. 127, the first of Bach's compositions that we shall be examining is depth, is also BWV 127. A more recent and more detailed catalog of Bach's works, the *Bach Compendium*, has its own numbering system, but this is not expected to replace the BWV numbers.

Early Years

Bach was born in 1685 in Eisenach, in central Germany, a region then noted for the unusually large number of talented musicians in its many towns and small cities. For several generations, members of the large extended Bach family had been particularly numerous among these musicians. Hence it was taken for granted that a boy such as Bach would become a musician like his father. After the latter's death in 1695, Bach studied music first with his older brother Johann Christoph and then at the choir school—a boys' school attached to a local church—in Lüneburg, 150 miles to the north. At the age of eighteen he received his first substantial position as church organist, at Arnstadt (1703–7). In this central German town he probably composed his earliest surviving compositions: mostly organ music, but also possibly several sacred vocal works in the old *concertato* style. During this period he also visited Lübeck, a major city on Germany's northern coast. There he probably studied with the city's organist Buxtehude, then the leading composer of organ and church music in northern Germany; like Mattheson and Handel, however, he appears to have had no interest in taking over Buxtehude's position.

Weimar: Organ Works and Cantatas

Two more organ positions followed, one held briefly in the small independent city of Mühlhausen (1707–8), the second at Weimar (1708–17). Weimar was the seat of a small duchy whose music-loving rulers had made their court a center for the performance of up-to-date vocal and instrumental music. In addition to his official duties as organist in the ducal chapel, Bach also participated in court chamber music. His promotion in 1714 to the office of *Concertmeister* (concertmaster) led to his composing church cantatas in the modern Italian style, one each month. At Weimar, too, he probably composed most of his organ works, many harpsichord pieces, and concertos and other compositions for instrumental ensemble.

Cöthen: Instrumental Compositions and Secular Cantatas

In 1717 Bach took a position as kapellmeister at the court of Cöthen, another small princely town. It was here that he composed, or at least revised, many of his now-famous works for solo keyboard and for instrumental ensemble. He eventually gathered most of these works into collections that, although not published during his lifetime, resembled contemporary music publications in containing half-dozens of similar pieces. Such was the case with the six Brandenburg Concertos (see Chapter 13), the six suites for solo cello, and the six sonatas and partitas (suites) for solo violin. Both of these latter collections followed a seventeenth-century German tradition of music for unaccompanied string instruments, without continuo. Bach, as usual, surpassed his models in the length and complexity of the resulting works.

Among the most important works that Bach probably composed mainly at Cöthen are the inventions, suites, and other pieces for keyboard instruments, written primarily for his students. The most famous of these Cöthen works is Part 1 of the *Well-Tempered Clavier*, an anthology of twenty-four preludes and fugues for keyboard, one in each of the twenty-four major and minor keys. The title refers to the system of keyboard (clavier) tuning or *temperament* that made this possible (see Chapter 11 for further discussion). Later, at Leipzig, Bach added a second volume containing another twenty-four preludes and fugues.

Bach was not required to write sacred vocal music at Cöthen. He did, however, compose an unknown number of secular cantatas for such events as princely birthdays and weddings. Similar in poetic and musical form to his sacred cantatas, Bach later adapted many of these works for church use at Leipzig through the substitution of new texts and revision of the music; this process, common at the time, is known as *parody*.

Leipzig: Church Cantatas and Other Works

In 1723 Bach moved to Leipzig—after Dresden, the second most important city in Saxony (in southeastern German). Here he served both as cantor of the St. Thomas School—a choir school—and director of music at the city's five main churches. In German schools, the position of cantor was primarily an educational one. Thus Bach was responsible not only for training the boys for participation in church music, but for teaching them Latin (a job that he assigned to a deputy). The music they were required to sing included hymns (called chorales) as well as the more elaborate types of church music we have been considering. During Bach's first few years at Leipzig his main creative focus lay in the composition of cantatas for performance at the two main churches, those of St. Nicholas and St. Thomas (next door to the school). At Leipzig Bach also

1 . Die St Thomas Kirche, 2. Die Thomas Schule.
3 . Der Steinerne Waßer-Kasten .

Figure 9.2 The St. Thomas Church (center) and School (left), Leipzig, by Johann Gottfried Krügner, Sr. This engraving appeared as the frontispiece to *Ordnung der Schule zu S. Thomae* (Leipzig, 1723), a publication containing the rules and regulations that governed the faculty and students of the St. Thomas School. Bach and his family occupied the nearest portion of the school building, shown as Bach would have known it during his first nine years at Leipzig; renovations in 1732 added two additional stories. The building was torn down in 1908.

composed and directed performance of secular cantatas for weddings and other private events, as well as for public ceremonies such as the annual installation of the city council and occasional visits by the duke (elector) of Saxony, whose domains included Leipzig.

For about four years, from 1723 to 1727, Bach produced sacred cantatas on a fairly regular basis, writing new works or revising existing ones for performance on almost every Sunday and holiday. Bach also composed two large oratorio passions based on the gospels of John (1724) and Matthew (1727).[6] There-

---

[6]Bach's later *St. Mark Passion* (1731) is lost; portions of it were parodies of movements in Cantata 198, from which scholars have reconstructed the passion version.

after, however, Bach seems to have abandoned the regular composition of church music, turning to other projects. These included a series of publications for keyboard instruments, modestly entitled *Clavierübung* (Keyboard practice), beginning in 1726. Apart from two early cantatas, these keyboard volumes were Bach's first publications; the great majority of his music remained in manuscript until the nineteenth century. In 1729 Bach became director of the Leipzig Collegium Musicum, an organization that gave regular public concerts at various places, including a local coffeehouse. Most of Bach's music for instrumental ensemble survives in versions thought to have been prepared for these performances, although in many cases it had been composed earlier. The Collegium Musicum also performed secular cantatas, including works in honor of the Saxon ruling family as well as (in all likelihood) the little comedy known as the Coffee Cantata.

Late Works

In 1741, when Bach ceased direction of the Collegium Musicum, his musical thought seems to have been turning toward encyclopedic collections that would demonstrate the arts of musical composition and performance in a comprehensive, systematic way. One product was the final installment of the *Clavierübung*, a work known as the Goldberg Variations. Published in 1741, this is a large, technically challenging set of variations for harpsichord, reportedly composed for the talented young harpsichordist and composer Johann Gottlieb Goldberg (1727–56), who had apparently studied with Bach. At about the same time Bach also wrote the *Art of Fugue*, a set of fugal compositions all on the same theme or subject, which was published posthumously in 1751. A trip to Berlin in 1747, during which Bach improvised keyboard fugues for the young king of Prussia, Frederick II (the Great), led to a volume of keyboard and chamber music dedicated to the king, the *Musical Offering*.

Perhaps the most impressive work of these years was the B-Minor Mass, which Bach completed in about 1749. A major portion, the Kyrie and Gloria, had been composed by 1733, when Bach had presented it to the elector of Saxony.[7] In return, Bach had received the honorary title of electoral Saxon and royal Polish court composer.[8] Both the original portion and the remainder added in the 1740s include parodies of movements from Bach's sacred and secular cantatas, ingeniously reworked to fit the words of the mass. Bach cannot ever have performed the work in its final form. It seems instead to have served as a compilation of vocal movements intended for study, like those which Fux had included in his *Gradus ad Parnassum*. The individual movements range from choral fugues in *stile antico* to *galant* arias and duets, although even the latter are permeated by strict counterpoint and chromatic harmony.

---

[7] The Sanctus and other sections of the B Minor Mass also were completed earlier; only a few movements were newly composed in the 1740s.

[8] The elector of Saxony was also king of Poland; Elector Friedrich August II (also known as King Augustus III) was crowned in 1733 but did not grant Bach his title until three years later.

The Performance of Bach's Cantatas

Since its rediscovery and publication in the nineteenth century, Bach's sacred music has been a central part of the European musical repertory, particularly in Germany. For this reason its performance practice has been investigated with particular care, and despite the loss of many essential sources and the difficulty of reaching firm conclusions about many matters, probably more is known about the historical performance of Bach's cantatas than any other comparable repertory.

Bach's sacred cantatas were performed in church, during worship services; the secular works had various venues, including outdoors in Leipzig's central square. Soprano and alto parts were sung by boys or adult male falsettists, at least in the church works; women did sing in some German churches by this time, but not in any locale where Bach regularly worked. Although the exact makeup of Bach's vocal forces has been a matter of debate, it appears increasingly likely that most of Bach's vocal works were composed for a "chorus" comprising a single singer on each part. Orchestral parts, too, were rarely doubled, except for the violin and continuo lines. Thus what many modern listeners have come to regard as massive choral movements for large choir and orchestra are in fact examples of chamber music for vocal soloists and a small instrumental ensemble. Bach himself originally must have directed most of these works, in some cases while seated at the harpsichord and playing continuo, in others possibly while playing violin or beating time in the modern sense.[9]

Although Bach complained several times to his Leipzig employers about the inadequacies of the student members of the ensembles he directed, it seems unlikely that most performances would have been as unsuccessful as is sometimes supposed. Bach was clearly an inspiring teacher, attracting numerous talented pupils, a number of whom went on to become some of the finest musicians in Europe. Even as boys studying at the St. Thomas School, the best of them would have been well acquainted not only with Bach's own music, which they sang and played on a daily basis, but also with the performance conventions of both the French and Italian styles. The same would have been true of the adult musicians who also participated, among them students from the Leipzig university and possibly visiting virtuosos. Nevertheless, Bach, like his French contemporaries, generally notated ornaments and embellishments with great precision; thus there is rarely any need for substantial improvised additions. Bach's precision extended to specifying, more often than not, the exact choice and number of instruments; modern performances on "original" instruments have revealed the care with which his ensemble works were scored, using specific colors that can be closely matched only with eighteenth-century techniques and instruments.

The Cantata *Herr Jesu Christ, wahr' Mensch und Gott,* BWV 127

This work (anthology, Selection 20) was composed for performance at Leipzig on 11 February 1725, the Sunday in the church year known as Quinquagesima

---

[9]The organ, the main continuo instrument in Bach's sacred music, would normally have been played by someone else, at least at Leipzig.

(the last Sunday before Lent, during which few cantatas were performed). Like most of the Leipzig cantatas, it was probably written during the week immediately preceding its performance. As soon as Bach's score had been completed, he, together with his assistants, copied out individual parts for rehearsal and performance, afterward putting them away for reuse on the same Sunday in subsequent years.

Cantata 127 belongs to Bach's second yearly cycle of cantatas, composed mainly at Leipzig between June 1724 and February 1725. The works of this cycle are all **chorale cantatas**: cantatas whose texts and music are derived primarily from those of a single chorale.

A **chorale** is one of the hymns of the Lutheran church. It is both a textual and a musical form: a melody joined to any number of stanzas of rhyming poetry. Many chorales were the products of Martin Luther, the sixteenth-century church reformer, who created the chorale to encourage congregational participation in the service. Luther attached German poetic verses to traditional Gregorian and popular melodies; many later German poets followed his model, and

Figure 9.3 The opening page of Bach's manuscript score of Cantata 9, *Es ist das Heil uns kommen her*, Library of Congress, Washington (ML96.B186case). A chorale cantata, this work was composed in the 1730s to fill a gap in the series of chorale cantatas written in 1724–5. The six instrumental parts are (from the top down) for flute, oboe d'amore, violins 1–2, viola, and basso continuo. Like most of his contemporaries, Bach composed in ink, making his first draft directly into what would become his finished score; note the corrections in the oboe part, m. 10. The voices do not enter until the following page (not shown), but in the last full measure on this page Bach sketched in the entrance of the bass voice; the word "Es" at the foot of the page is the opening word of the text.

musicians added many new melodies, so that by Bach's day there existed a large repertory of chorales for librettists and composers to draw on. In addition to serving as popular hymns for congregational singing, chorales formed the basis of more elaborate vocal and instrumental compositions, fulfilling a function much like that of Gregorian chant in Roman Catholic church music.

Bach's chorale cantatas thus drew on a two-century-old tradition of Lutheran sacred music and poetry. The text of each such cantata is borrowed in whole or, more often, in part from the stanzas of a given chorale poem. In addition, the chorale's melody plays a prominent role in at least two of the work's movements. In the present work, the chorale melody is heard complete in the soprano part of the first and last movements, and is alluded to elsewhere as well (Ex. 9.1). Although many other German composers wrote chorale cantatas, few produced compositions approaching Bach's in their varied and complex contrapuntal elaborations of the chorale melody or the subtle integration of the chorale melody and text throughout the work.

Example 9.1 Some appearances of the first line of the chorale melody *Herr Jesu Christ, wahr'r Mensch und Gott* in Bach's cantata of that title: (a) movement 1, soprano, mm. 18–21; (b) movement 1, oboes, mm. 1–2; (c) movement 1, tenor, m. 17; (d) movement 2, basso continuo, mm. 13–14; (e) movement 4, bass voice, mm. 13–15; (f) movement 5, soprano, mm. 1–2

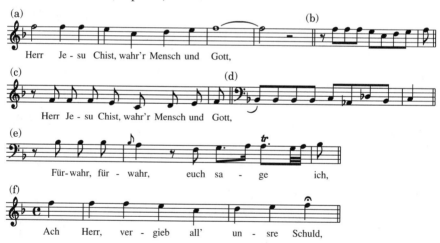

Virtually all of Bach's church works include at least one chorale movement in a relatively simple style. Often coming last in the cantata, these four-part settings are the "Bach chorales" that harmony students have studied since the late eighteenth century. A collection of them was published in the 1780s, extracted from his cantatas and other works. Since the melodies in most cases are traditional, only the harmonization—the lower three parts—is actually by Bach. The *chorale* cantatas are distinguished by not only closing with a "simple" four-part chorale movement of this type but also opening with a much larger, more complex choral movement also based on the chorale melody. Usually the text of this opening movement is the first of several stanzas traditionally associated with the chorale melody; another stanza was used for the concluding movement. In between, the librettist provided a series of recitative and aria texts. These texts usually contain extracts from additional stanzas of the chorale, as well as references to or quotes from appropriate Bible verses.

Chorale Cantatas

The Text of Cantata 127

The chorale verses used in Cantata 127 are by Paul Eber and were first published in 1560. The melody to which Eber attached his poem had already appeared a few years earlier, in 1555. The name of the librettist who adapted Eber's chorale text for Bach's use is unknown, as is the case for all of the chorale cantatas of 1724–25.

The text of the cantata as a whole is concerned with the journey of Jesus and his disciples to Jerusalem, one of the events that eventually led to Jesus' crucifixion. Jesus' entry into Jerusalem is understood in the Christian tradition as prefiguring the coming of the Messiah as ruler of the world at the Last Judgment, and thus the cantata text includes a vivid description of the end of the world, when each individual is expected to be judged for his or her sins. In addition, however, it refers to the Christian belief that the bodies of those having faith in the divinity of Jesus will be raised from the dead when he returns. It closes with a prayer that encourages the listener to remain faithful to this belief until death.

The Music

As in most of Bach's chorale cantatas, the full ensemble is used only in the opening and closing chorale movements. Both movements employ the traditional chorale melody as a *cantus firmus* (see below) in the soprano. But the first is a large, elaborate movement; only in the final movement do we hear a "simple" four-part setting of the chorale melody. The congregations of Bach's Leipzig churches would have been familiar with this and other chorales and would have recognized the tune and its poem at the outset. Today, however, it is helpful to examine first the simpler setting of the chorale in the final movement.

Movement 5: Four-Part Chorale Setting

The concluding movement is for the entire ensemble, the instruments doubling the voices as indicated.[10] The continuo, which in this work originally comprised organ, cello, and probably double bass, differs slightly from the vocal bass line and therefore is set out on a separate staff. The chorale melody is sung by the soprano (Ex. 9.1f); the other parts were added by Bach and constitute his harmonization. The setting of the text is syllabic, the musical texture homophonic—but this does not mean that the music is simple or lacking a contrapuntal aspect. The bass and inner voices retain some rhythmic independence;

---

[10]Only the trumpet is silent here, being a "natural" instrument (see below) that could not play all of the notes of the soprano part in this movement.

note, for example, the moving eighth notes of the lower parts throughout the first two phrases (mm. 1–4). Moreover, Bach's harmonization reflects the words of the specific stanza of the chorale used here. For example, the second-to-last word (*einschlafen*, "to sleep") is set to a chromatic progression—text painting that serves as a reminder that "sleep" here is a metaphor for death.

A peculiarity of this chorale tune is that it opens in F but ends with a cadence on C, apparently the dominant. Tonally ambiguous structures such as this are not unusual in chorale tunes, many of which date from the sixteenth century or earlier, prior to the period of common practice tonality. Among the modal characteristics of this type of tune is the possibility of ending on a tone other than the final, as in the present case. Such a tune presented an interesting challenge to a later composer who wished to use it in what we would call a tonal composition.

Movement 1: Chorale Fantasia

The first movement employs the same chorale melody in a much larger setting with obbligato instrumental parts. The movement resembles a **chorale fantasia,** a type of organ piece in which each phrase of a chorale melody is developed at length in various ways. Bach had written many such organ works at Weimar, and most of the Leipzig chorale cantatas open with comparable choral movements. In this case the chorale tune is sung in its entirety as a *cantus firmus* in long notes by the soprano, beginning at measure 18 (see Ex. 9.1a).[11]

The entrance of the soprano and the three lower voices is preceded by a ritornello (mm. 1–16), as is each of the five subsequent phrases of the chorale. In this respect, then, Bach treats the vocal entries just like the solo sections of an aria. He makes an exception at the very end, however: before the instruments have finished stating the final ritornello (mm. 76–80), the voices reenter, repeating the final line of the chorale stanza. In this final vocal passage the soprano part is free, having already presented the last phrase of the chorale cantus firmus—which ends on the dominant, C major—in the previous vocal passage (mm. 68–71).

The opening ritornello is a substantial musical section in itself, combining three distinct thematic ideas in a complex contrapuntal texture. At the outset, the three ideas occur as follows: (1) the oboes present a motive derived from the first eight notes of the chorale tune (Ex. 9.1b); (2) the recorders (*flauti*) present a motive in dotted rhythm; and (3) the strings present a theme in half notes. The latter is the first phrase of a second chorale melody, "Christe du Lamm Gottes" (Christ, Lamb of God). The use of two chorale melodies in one movement is very unusual but entirely appropriate, as the text of the second chorale points to the Crucifixion. It is an example of Bach's inventive use of an unprecedented musical idea—the combination of two chorales in an elaborate con-

---

[11] A **cantus firmus** (Latin, literally "fixed song") is a preexisting melody used in its entirety as a framework for a new polyphonic composition. Cantus firmus compositions based on Gregorian chant had been an important form of Western polyphony from the Middle Ages through the Renaissance.

trapuntal texture—in a way that is at once expressive, technically skillful, and directly related to the work's theological subject and religious purpose.

After the initial presentation of the ritornello's three thematic ideas, Bach recombines them, using the device known as **invertible counterpoint.** When the three thematic ideas are restated at measure 9, the recorders now have the main chorale line and the violins have the dotted motive. Invertible counterpoint allows the various thematic ideas to cycle between the various instrumental parts—a technique frequently used in Bach's music and that of his contemporaries. The three thematic ideas return in subsequent ritornellos and as counterpoint to the voices after the latter have entered.

At the conclusion of the movement, as we have seen, the end of the ritornello is combined with newly composed choral parts. The contrapuntal combination of one or more independent melodic lines with the ritornello is another common device in Bach's music, known by the German word *Einbau* ("insertion" or "installation").[12] An example for solo voice occurs in measures 21–26 of the third movement, where the solo soprano sings in combination with the last six measures of the ritornello. In both cases the device creates a sense of climax or heightened expressivity by increasing the complexity of the contrapuntal texture.

Elsewhere in the opening movement, the three lower voices develop in imitation motives from the chorale melody that the soprano simultaneously presents as a cantus firmus. For instance, in measure 17 the tenor enters with the eight notes of the first chorale phrase (Ex. 9.1c). These notes are treated as an imitative subject, subsequently appearing in the alto and the bass. Such use of a preexisting melody is an instance of **paraphrase** technique, whereby the chorale (or another tune) is broken into fragments that can then be developed through imitation or other means. Paraphrase had been an important technique in vocal polyphony since the fifteenth century; Bach was doubtless well aware of its use in chorale fantasias by Buxtehude and other older German composers (see Chapter 10).

The lower three vocal parts are often highly expressive, following the principles of musical rhetoric. For example, in measure 56 the alto has a so-called **sigh motive,** a slurred two-note descending figure. This occurs, appropriately enough, on the word *Leiden* ("suffering"), where the note (a♭') acts as a dissonant appoggiatura, forming a diminished seventh with the tenor (b♮). This type of accented, unprepared dissonance—a survival of Monteverdi's *seconda pratica*—is a fundamental element in Bach's harmonic style.

Movement 2: Recitative

This movement illustrates Bach's adaptation of Italian *recitativo semplice*. Even this "simple" recitative is a masterpiece of musical rhetoric, highlighting important words through high notes, striking harmonies, and changes of key. For

---

[12]More specifically, *Choreinbau* refers to the addition of choral parts, *Vokaleinbau* to that of a solo voice, and *Soloeinbau* for that of any soloist, vocal or instrumental.

instance, in measure 6 the word *Seufzer* ("sigh") is emphasized by being sung to a relatively high note (e♭'); moreover, the word is interrupted by a rest to represent the idea of a distressed sigh or groan (a common type of Baroque text painting). In addition, the harmony at this point is a diminished seventh chord, as indicated by the figured bass.

Through most of the movement the basso continuo, which provides the sole accompaniment, is notated in long notes. As in Italian recitative, these notes were probably not held out for their full length (see Chapter 6). But near the end of the movement (m. 13), the style shifts to arioso on the word *Ruhe* ("rest"), where the soprano momentarily "rests" on a quarter note. At the same point, the continuo has eighth notes in a motivic pattern borrowed from the opening of the chorale melody (Ex. 9.1d)—a subtle means of connecting the recitative musically to the other movements of the work. At the same time, the highlighting of this word—literally "rest," but again meaning death—points forward to the next movement.

Movement 3: Aria

The soprano aria, which falls at the center of the work, reveals Bach's attention to both tone color and the symbolic associations of the instruments. The aria is in C minor and is set in standard da capo form. Bach's instrumentation heightens the expected contrast between A and B sections; the A section is scored for woodwinds and continuo, with violins and viola entering in the B section.

The ritornello is dominated by the oboe, whose line contains many melodic embellishments, such as the scale in thirty-seconds in measure 2. The style of these written-out embellishments is derived from the improvised embellishments of the Italian adagio (see Chapter 12). The voice takes up this embellished style in the A section, where it combines contrapuntally with the oboe. Meanwhile, the recorders and continuo provide a staccato accompaniment, the cello and double bass playing **pizzicato** (plucking the strings).

Precisely what the short repeated notes of the recorders and continuo signify is revealed in the B section: bells. The word *Sterbeglocken* ("death bells," m. 31) coincides with the dramatic entry of the upper strings, which up to now have remained silent; now they begin playing pizzicato, like the cello and violone, but in sixteenth notes. Bach's listeners would have recognized this texture as a representation of special funeral bells, which were distinguished by their relatively high pitch and rapid ringing. Contrary to customary Baroque word painting, the grim image of death is intentionally cast in a delightful musical setting that coincides with the modulation to a major key, A♭. Death is thus depicted as the joyous attainment of heavenly peace, in keeping with Christian belief.

Movement 4: Recitative and Aria

Bach labeled movement 4 as a recitative; in fact it opens as *accompanied* recitative, the bass voice and continuo being joined by parts for trumpet and upper strings. The movement then departs from conventional forms by proceeding without a break to a sort of aria comprised of two alternating types of music (mm. 14–67).

The movement as a whole is a vivid representation of the Last Judgment. The trumpet, used nowhere else in the cantata, refers not only to the biblical sounding of the last trumpet but also to the military imagery inherent in the idea of a battle between good and evil that brings an end to the physical world. As in Orlando's aria "Fammi combattere" and innumerable other Baroque works, the broken-chord motives and the repeated notes of both trumpet and strings derive from actual trumpet calls used for military signaling.

The trumpet used here is a so-called **natural** brass instrument, lacking valves and thus normally confined to the natural harmonics of the instrument's fundamental tone. For instance, a trumpet in C was limited essentially to the notes shown in Example 9.2; certain notes were out of tune and rarely used, and only in the top octave of its range could the instrument readily produce a complete diatonic scale. Virtuoso trumpeters nevertheless had various techniques for improving the naturally out-of-tune notes. Bach calls for one of these, bb′, in mm. 6–7. The slightly muffled sound of that note on the natural trumpet, far from being a technical deficiency, is part of the otherworldly sound that Bach evidently desired at this point.

Example 9.2 The harmonic series: "natural" notes on a valveless trumpet in C; notes marked * are noticeably out of tune or for other reasons difficult to use

Following the initial accompanied recitative, the movement turns first to arioso (mm. 14–20) and then to full-fledged aria style, including a short ritornello (mm. 21–22). The arioso opens with another melodic reference to the opening of the chorale tune (sung to the words "Fürwahr, fürwahr"; see Ex. 9.1e); this is imitated by the continuo (mm. 15–16). Arioso and aria continue to alternate through the remainder of the movement—an unusual procedure, but again typical of Bach's originality in response to a vivid text. Underlying the surface irregularity is a deeper and more regular pattern, for this entire portion of the movement falls into a modified da capo design: the first arioso and the following aria section (mm. 14–31) together constitute the A section, which returns as a modified da capo or A′ section at the conclusion of the movement (mm. 54–67).

After this unprecedented movement, the closing four-part chorale setting serves as a moment of repose. Yet its final cadence is, as we have noted, in C major, the dominant of the tonic F major. Although conditioned by the structure of the preexisting chorale tune, this ending also reflects the fact that the drama narrated in the text of the present work is not yet completed, even though the cantata itself is finished. Through its "open" ending on the dominant, it looks ahead to the drama that would have been reenacted a few weeks later in the passion oratorio performed on Good Friday.

GEORGE FRIDERIC HANDEL: *JEPHTHA*

Handel's English oratorios represent sacred drama of a quite different and more literally theatrical kind. *Jephtha*, the last newly composed work among Handel's twenty-two English oratorios, was begun early in 1751. But the composer's deteriorating vision forced him to interrupt work on it before completing the second act. He was able to finish the oratorio by August, but, although he continued to perform publicly, he did little further composing. His one later English oratorio, *The Triumph of Time and Truth* (1757), is a reworking of his very first Italian oratorio, composed half a century earlier.

Performance of Handel's English Oratorios

As concert works, Handel's English oratorios lacked the elaborate staging of his Italian operas; they differed too in the inclusion of a chorus. The latter comprised four to six boy sopranos, plus about a dozen male altos, tenors, and basses. The soloists evidently sang from the choir, stepping forward when their roles required it. It is not entirely clear where the singers stood in relation to the instruments, but Handel would have directed from the harpsichord, perhaps facing them and the other musicians (hence with his back to the audience).

Beginning with the first public performance of his first English oratorio, *Esther*, in 1735, Handel also performed organ concertos with the orchestra between the acts of the oratorios. Although Italian composers had been writing concertos for solo violin and orchestra for some thirty years, concertos with a solo keyboard part were a novelty; Handel continued to play them to the end of his career.[13] Handel's solos in the organ concertos included substantial quantities of virtuoso improvisation, sometimes amounting to entire movements. As published, however, the concertos are easy to play and no doubt contributed to the popularity of the genre.

The Music of *Jephtha*

Much of *Jephtha* (anthology, Selection 21) is unusually vehement in expression, reflecting its dark story (see Box 9.2). The libretto by Thomas Morell provides a biblically unauthorized happy ending, absent from the anonymous Latin version of the story set by Carissimi (see Chapter 7). But as Handel was completing the end of Part 2, he must have been reflecting deeply on his failing health and weakening eyesight. In place of Morell's final verse, Handel substituted a line by the English poet Alexander Pope (1688–1744): "Whatever is, is right." But the gloomy chorus that Handel composed at this point is hardly reassuring.

---

[13] Among the few earlier concertos with solo keyboard parts was J. S. Bach's Fifth Brandenburg Concerto for harpsichord, flute, violin, and strings, composed by 1721; his concertos for solo harpsichord and strings date from the 1730s.

BOX 9.2

Handel: *Jephtha*

Text by Thomas Morell (after Judges 9).
First performed at Covent Garden, London, 26 February 1752; revived
in 1753, 1756, and 1758.

Characters

Jephtha (tenor), leader of the Israelites
Storgè (alto), his wife
Iphis (soprano), their daughter
Hamor (alto), in love with Iphis
Zebul (bass), Jephtha's brother

SYNOPSIS

The action takes place during the early history of the Israelites, when they are
at war with their neighbors the Ammonites. Jephtha has sworn that if he is
successful in battle against the latter he will sacrifice the first thing he sees
upon his return to the Israelite camp. Unfortunately, it is his daughter—here
named Iphis—who greets him. He reacts in horror, but despite the entreaties
of his wife, his brother, and Iphis's fiancé, Hamor, he refuses to break his vow.
Iphis cheerfully accepts her fate, but just as she is about to die an angel appears, sparing her life.

SELECTIONS DISCUSSED IN THE TEXT

Overture.

Part 2, scene 3. Jephtha arrives and sees Iphis; after a brief recitative ("Horror!
confusion"), he sings a da capo aria violently expressing his anguish, "Open thy
marble jaws."

———, same (later in scene 3). In the quartet "O spare your daughter," in which
all four adult characters sing, Jephtha turns down the request of the three others to revoke his vow.

———, same (later). Jephtha sings an even more agitated accompanied recitative, "Deeper and deeper still," to which the Israelites respond with the chorus "How dark, O Lord, are thy decrees."

Part 3, scene 1. The scene opens with Jephtha and Iphis preparing for the sacrifice, surrounded by Israelite priests. Jephtha sings a bitter accompanied recitative, "Hide thou thy hated beams," followed by a resigned da capo aria, "Waft
her angels, through the skies."

Jephtha, like his other English oratorios, retains many elements of Handel's *opere serie*, including the French overture at the beginning and the inclusion of a considerable number of da capo arias. But there are fewer of the latter than in earlier works; many arias now consist of simply an A section in bipartite form. The choral movements, which range from grand celebrations of the Is-raelites' military victories to the grim final chorus of Part 2, are closer in style to church music than to anything in either the Italian or French operas of the period. The choruses include impressive contrapuntal sections in fugal form as well as declamatory passages in homophonic texture. Unlike the arias, most are accompanied by the full orchestra, lacking only brass, which, as in most Baroque works, is reserved for a few choruses in major keys that have a particularly grand or military character.

The most remarkable music in the work occurs in Part 2, beginning shortly after Iphis makes her unfortunate appearance to greet her father as he returns from battle. Jephtha's initial response, after a brief recitative, is the aria "Open thy marble jaws" (anthology, Selection 21a). In C minor, its fragmented melodic line and unharmonized unison writing for voice and strings suggest his emo-tional trauma.[14] Although the aria employs the traditional da capo form, in its melodic harshness and barren harmony it is as far as one could imagine from the fashionable *galant* style of most contemporary opera seria.

Equally dramatic effects occur in Jephtha's accompanied recitatives "Deeper and deeper still" and "Hide thou thy hated beams," from Parts 2 and 3, re-spectively. The first of these contains chromatic modulations that range widely from F♯ minor to A♭ major and F minor, ending in G minor. When the text mentions "a thousand pangs that lash me into madness," Handel writes string tremolos that bear the unusual marking *concitato* (agitated), recalling Monteverdi (Ex. 9.3).[15] Only when Jephtha, reconciled to his daughter's death, bids her farewell in the serene G-major da capo aria in Part 3, "Waft her, angels, through the skies," does his music return to something that would have been regarded as normal mid-eighteenth-century style (Ex. 9.4). Here the dotted rhythms of the first violin are slurred, suggesting not a vigorous effect as in a French over-ture but the gentle beating of angel wings.[16]

Ensembles—movements for more than one soloist—are rare in opera seria and oratorio. An example is the quartet "O spare your daughter" in Part 2, in which Jephtha's wife, brother, and potential son-in-law beg him to "recall the impious vow"—that is, to take back his oath and spare his daughter's life (Ex. 9.5). Handel's music clearly sets the tenor Jephtha apart from the other three figures (soprano, alto, and bass), who sing as a group in antiphony against him.

---

[14]The unharmonized unison texture found here occurs in many other arias by Handel from throughout his career; these are of greatly varying expressive characters, making it difficult to at-tach any one meaning to this type of writing.

[15]Monteverdi, however, used the word *concitato* to describe battle music.

[16]Handel does not write out the dotted rhythm in every measure, nor the slurs, but both can be understood as applying throughout the aria—a notational abbreviation common in the Baroque and especially in Handel's music.

Example 9.3 Handel, *Jephtha*, Part 2, scene 3: recitative "Deeper, and deeper still," *concitato* passage

'Tis this that racks my brain,
And pours into my breast a thousand pangs,
That lash me into madness!

Meanwhile the accompanying string parts accelerate to repeated sixteenths as Jephtha restates the words "her doom is fixed"—that is, her fate is already cast.

The most powerful writing may be in the chorus that closes Part 2 (anthology, Selection 21b). Handel's oratorio choruses generally employ the old line-by-line form of the seventeenth-century *concertato* motet, updated by the inclusion of instrumental ritornellos and other devices. Style, texture, motivic material, and instrumentation all may change radically in the course of a single movement, always in response to the text. Some choruses are unified by a common ritornello theme or recurring accompanimental motives. Others are integrated only by maintaining one expressive character or key. The latter is the

Example 9.4 Handel, *Jephtha*, Part 3, scene 1: aria "Waft her, angels, through the skies," mm. 9–12

Waft her, angels, through the skies,
Far above yon azure plain—

case in the chorus "How dark, O Lord, are thy decrees," which falls into four sections, as shown in Table 9.1.

The first section is dominated by a repeating dotted rhythm in the string accompaniment. Far from signaling a French overture, the relentless dotted accompaniment is an effect that Handel would have found in choruses by Italian contemporaries (such as Antonio Vivaldi, discussed in Chapter 13); it lends extra energy to the voices' more sustained, homophonic declamation of the text. The second section switches to imitative style, and the instrumental parts now double the voices. This, too, is a type of writing familiar from earlier Italian choral writing; both features are reminiscent of the *stile antico*, used here to suggest the seriousness of the text.

The style grows more severe in the third section, a fugue. This section is even closer to the *stile antico*, since, unlike the preceding section, it is in the duple meter characteristic of sixteenth-century polyphony. A **fugue** is a movement in imitative texture based on a single theme; the latter, called the **subject,** is initially presented by one voice and immediately imitated by each of the others, entering in different keys (more precisely, at different pitch levels; see Box 11.1). Here the subject is heard in the soprano, alto, tenor, and bass in turn, each voice being doubled instrumentally. Not all eighteenth-century fugues are as archaic in style as this one. Indeed, even here, the style is less that of the Renaissance than of the Baroque, for in addition to employing specified

Example 9.5 Handel, *Jephtha*, Part 2, scene 3: quartet "O spare your daughter," mm. 23–25

Storgè, Hamor, and Zebul: Recall the impious vow, ere 'tis too late . . .

Jephtha: [I'll hear no more;] her doom is fix'd as fate.

instrumental parts, including the basso continuo, the fugue uses a subject containing several chromatic steps (G–A♭–A–B♭), a type of writing absent from sixteenth-century music except in radical works such as those of Gesualdo. This chromatic motive is used for the phrase *no solid peace*—an instance of word painting that, because it is present in the subject of the fugue, permeates the entire section.

The concluding section of the movement presents Pope's "maxim," added by Handel at the end of Morell's text. The first added clause ("Yet on this maxim still obey," mm. 114–20) is presented in imitative style. As in the first section of the movement, the string accompaniment has a persistent rhythmic figure, here comprising repeated eighths. But the string accompaniment ceases for the maxim itself, "Whatever is, is right" (mm. 121–24), which is stated in uncompromising declamatory style by the chorus, its two two-word phrases separated by rests—a particularly austere manifestation of classic Baroque musical rhetoric.

Figure 9.4 Handel's manuscript composing score for *Jephtha*, act 2, final chorus, mm. 16–24. By Permission of the British Library. Having completed this first section of the chorus, Handel wrote the date 13 February 1751, at the bottom right corner, adding in German that he had had to stop work at this point after losing sight in his left eye. Handel had just set to music the words "How dark, O Lord, are thy decrees, all hid from mortal sight"; as grimly ironic as this might have seemed, it is conceivable that Handel might have found in these lines a ray of hope: it is impossible to know what the future will bear, for worse or for better.

TABLE 9.1
Handel: *Jephtha*, **Part 2, scene 3, final chorus**

Section	Measure	Tempo	Style, Texture, Form	Keys
1 How dark, O Lord, are thy decrees	1	Largo	homophonic	c → A♭
2 All our joys to sorrow turning	25	Larghetto	canonic	f → g
3 No certain bliss	98	A tempo ordinario	fugue	c → V
4 Yet on this maxim still obey	114	Larghetto	alternatingly contrapuntal, declamatory	c → f → E♭ → c

Handel's Borrowings

An oddity of Handel's compositional process in this work and elsewhere was his borrowing of music both from himself and from others. Already noted during his lifetime, Handel's borrowings ranged from the reuse of individual themes or motives to the appropriation of entire sections or movements, sometimes without substantial alteration. Handel's borrowings went beyond conventional types of paraphrase and parody, extending even to his secular instrumental works. He seems to have borrowed for his own convenience in composing, rarely implying any meaningful reference to an earlier work. Thus Handel's *Jephtha*

Example 9.6 Handel, *Lotario*, Act 2: Matilde's aria "Arma lo sguardo," mm. 4–12

Arma lo sguardo	Arm your glances
D'un dolce dardo;	With a sweet arrow;
La donna altera	Then a proud
E lusinghiera	And flattering woman
Poi nel suo core	In her heart
Del folle amore	At foolish love
Si riderà.	Will laugh.

does not borrow from Carissimi's work of the same title, although Handel certainly knew at least its closing chorus, having quoted from it in his earlier oratorio *Samson* (1743).

Instead, Handel reused a theme from his opera *Lotario* (1729) for Jephtha's aria "Open thy marble jaws" (Ex. 9.6). Handel's borrowing reflects the flexibility of the associations that can be drawn between music and meaning or emotional expression. The two arias are very different in dramatic context and feeling; in the opera, Queen Matilda is counseling seduction! Yet the unison textures that perhaps expressed something sinister or threatening in her music seem equally appropriate in Jephtha's distraught aria.

In addition, the second part of the chorus "How dark, O Lord" (mm. 25–88) borrows both its melodic material and its imitative technique from a mass published a few years earlier, in 1747, by the Bohemian composer Franz Habermann (1706–83; see Ex. 9.7). In this instance there is a clear similarity in expressive character between the texts set by the two composers. Moreover, Handel elaborated upon his model's use of two-part **canon**: the precise imitation of one voice by another. Following Habermann, Handel uses canonic pairs of voices in the "All our joys" section of the chorus. It is unknown whether Habermann knew of Handel's borrowing, but if so Habermann ought to have been flattered by Handel's interest in his music—even though Handel significantly transformed the borrowed material.

Example 9.7 Franz Wenzel Habermann, Missa III from *Philomela pia* (Graslitz, 1747): Crucifixus

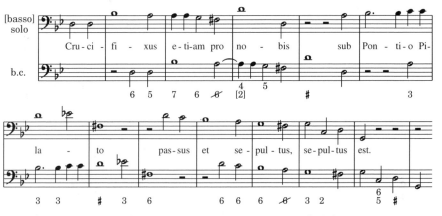

Crucifixus etiam pro nobis   Also he was crucified for us
sub Pontio Pilato, et sepultus est. under Pontius Pilate and was buried.

CHAPTER 10

BAROQUE KEYBOARD MUSIC I
Toccata and Suite

Instruments, which played roles in both domestic and sacred music making in
western Europe during the Renaissance, came to be of central importance for
the first time during the Baroque. The seventeenth century appears to have seen
a substantial increase in innovative activity by instrument makers, which continued in the early eighteenth century. Certain types of instruments, notably
strings, woodwinds, and keyboard instruments, underwent extensive changes in
both construction and technique during the period, with corresponding developments in the types of music written for them. To some degree these developments reflected general trends in seventeenth- and eighteenth-century European music, when, for the first time, composition for instruments came to be
equal in stature and significance to that for the voice.

Idiomatic Writing for Instruments

Developments in Baroque instrumental writing paralleled those in vocal writing in certain important ways. Let us recall the changes in musical texture that
led to new types of vocal writing in the early seventeenth century. First, the
adoption of the basso continuo made possible monody, that is, music consisting of a single melodic line and a bass, with improvised inner voices. In addition to new Baroque vocal genres, this led to new instrumental forms in which
one or two solo parts—usually soprano-range melody instruments of the string
or woodwind families—are accompanied by continuo. Such textures became predominant over older types of instrumental writing for ensembles of four or five
instrumental parts, although the latter continued to be used throughout the
Baroque. Even then, however, the top one or two parts tended to be much more
important than the others, as in the violin-dominated five-part string band of
Lully.

Second, much of the new monodic vocal music was soloistic, employing ornaments and virtuoso passagework or figuration and providing opportunities
for individual expression and display by the soloist. Instrumental writing developed in a similar direction, sometimes imitating the types of figuration used
by singers but increasingly employing writing that grew out of the unique

209

sound and technical capabilities of each instrument. Earlier instrumental music had rarely called for specified instruments or made use of the particular qualities of individual instruments, although music for solo lute and solo keyboard represents an important exception.

Music that calls for the particular characteristics and performance techniques of a specific instrument (or voice) is said to be **idiomatic** to that instrument (or voice). Before 1600 most European music was conceived vocally. Features idiomatic to a given instrument were added improvisatorily, as when an ensemble of viols or violins played a set of dances originally composed for unspecified instruments, each player improvising idiomatic ornamentation. In the Baroque, as composers began to specify instrumentation or write out embellishments, it became customary to write instrumental parts that are idiomatic to particular instruments. Today this seems like an obvious necessity. In 1600, however, it represented a major change: for the first time, defining the instrumental sonorities and techniques to be used in the performance of a work was part of the composer's job, not an optional detail left to the performers, and understanding the nature and capabilities of common instruments became part of the training of every composer. Consequently, the seventeenth century saw the emergence of many new genres of music that exploited the idioms of specific instruments.

Instrumental music can be divided between music for single instruments and music for ensemble. The largest and most important repertory of Baroque music for single instruments is for keyboard instruments, with smaller repertories for the lute, harp and their relatives. Ensemble music is dominated by that written for strings, especially the violin, and not until the later seventeenth century do distinct repertories for the major wind instruments begin to emerge.

Baroque Instruments

Actual instruments from the Baroque period survive in varying degrees of preservation. Some are mere broken-down fragments in museums, although even these can present a surprising amount of information to a trained **organologist: a scholar specializing in the study of instruments.** Surviving instruments from the Baroque include organs still in use in many European churches,[1] as well as numerous violins and other bowed string instruments, including those of such famous Italian makers as Antonio Stradivari (1644–1737), which can be valued in the hundreds of thousands of dollars. Functioning harpsichords and other stringed keyboard instruments are somewhat less common, brass and woodwind instruments even less so, especially those from before 1700. Virtually all surviving instruments have been altered over the centuries, often in ways that obscure their original sound and playing characteristics; this is especially true of organs and bowed strings. Nevertheless, modern instrument builders specializing in the reconstruction of historical instruments have rediscovered many of

---

[1] A few Baroque organs are also preserved in the Americas, including examples in colonial churches in the United States and Mexico.

the secrets of materials and construction used by earlier makers. When based closely on originals, modern copies of antique harpsichords, violins, and other instruments can come quite close to their historical prototypes in sound and playing capabilities—sometimes closer than actual surviving instruments that have undergone ahistorical remodeling or renovation.

Of course, playing such instruments is another matter. Seventeenth- and eighteenth-century treatises on musical performance gave increasingly specific instructions for performance, but many details remain uncertain. Moreover, there was never any one way of using a particular instrument (or of singing); one cannot produce hard and fast rules for historically authentic performance, and books that purport to do so must be read with circumspection. Still, enough is known about old instruments and their techniques to show that Baroque composers called for specific sounds and effects that can be only approximated with modern techniques and instruments.

KEYBOARD INSTRUMENTS OF THE SEVENTEENTH AND EIGHTEENTH CENTURIES

The keyboard instruments of the Baroque include the organ, which is actually a type of wind instrument, and the harpsichord and the clavichord, which are the chief stringed keyboard instruments of the period. During the Baroque, all underwent important changes, and they were joined in the eighteenth century by a third major stringed keyboard instrument, the piano. Composers often failed to specify for which instrument a given keyboard piece or part was intended; nevertheless, it is often possible to distinguish music for one instrument or another, based on style, genre, or technical considerations. For example, works for organ often include a separate pedal part, whereas French harpsichord music can be recognized by the presence of designated dance movements. Much Baroque keyboard music can be readily appropriated to the modern piano, yet it remains helpful for the player to understand the sounds, conventions, and techniques that the composer expected to be applied in each work.

The Clavichord

The clavichord remained the simplest and least expensive keyboard instrument throughout the Baroque, and for this reason it was widely used as a practice instrument by both professionals and amateurs.[2] Nevertheless, composers made little use of its capability for dynamic inflection by the player, and in any case most Baroque clavichords were limited in dynamic capacity and compass (keyboard range). Only in the second half of the eighteenth century did certain German and Scandinavian instrument makers produce clavichords whose expanded range matched that of contemporary harpsichords and pianos. A few composers, notably Carl Philipp Emanuel Bach (1714–88), a son of J. S. Bach, wrote im-

---

[2]The playing mechanisms of the clavichord and harpsichord were discussed in Chapter 3.

portant works intended primarily for the clavichord, but most of these were composed after 1750 and thus lie beyond our consideration.

The Harpsichord

The chief stringed keyboard instrument of the Baroque was the harpsichord, prominent as both a solo instrument and a member of various types of ensemble. It gradually replaced the lute as the most common domestic instrument in well-off households, and it was, together with the organ, one of the two chief continuo instruments, indispensible in both vocal music and music for instrumental ensemble. By the mid-seventeenth century, French harpsichordists, playing French and Flemish instruments, had developed a distinctive performance style that became the basis of an important repertory of idiomatic harpsichord compositions. At the same time that the Lullian style of vocal music was being adopted in England and Germany during the later seventeenth and early eighteenth centuries, composers in those countries, such as Purcell and J. S. Bach, were taking up elements of the French harpsichord style in their own playing and in their compositions.

Reflecting the distinct national styles of performance and composition, harpsichords of different countries took various forms, differing, for example, in the number of keyboards and **registers** or sets of strings that they contained. Many harpsichords in the sixteenth century already had two sets of strings, sometimes tuned an octave apart. These could be played separately or together, permitting some variation in volume and sonority. The choice of a particular sonority on such an instrument—that is, the selection of a given register or combination of registers—is referred to as **registration.**

In the course of the seventeenth century, it became common for French and Flemish harpsichord makers to include a second (upper) keyboard, playing its own set of strings, which could be combined with or played separately from those controlled by the main keyboard. German and English makers followed course in the eighteenth century, but Italian and Spanish instruments rarely had more than a single keyboard. The sonorities, touch, and other characteristics of the various types of harpsichord varied as well. For example, Italian instruments tended toward a brilliance and clarity of attack well suited for accompanying operas and other ensemble works in public spaces. Flemish and French harpsichords, on the other hand, tended toward a relatively restrained sonority ideal for the sustained type of sound called for in many French pieces for solo harpsichord.

German harpsichord builders, maintaining traditions inherited from the Renaissance, retained individual elements found in both French and Italian types, producing distinctive instruments that proved especially suitable for projecting the contrapuntal textures of composers such as Bach and Handel. They also built various exotic types of stringed keyboard instruments such as the *Lautenklavier*, a harpsichord whose undamped gut strings made it sound like a lute. Certain smaller types of harpsichord, referred to as virginals and spinets, continued to be built as well, especially in Italy and Germany. Increasingly, however, the limited ranges and registrational possibilities of these instruments were inade-

Figure 10.1 Harpsichord by Jacques Germain, Paris, 1785. America's Shrine to Music Museum, Vermillion, South Dakota, Rawlins Fund, 1983 (no. 3327). This instrument, with its two manuals and five-octave keyboard range, is characteristic of French eighteenth-century harpsichords. The expensive painting and other decoration of this instrument was a mark of ownership by a wealthy amateur or aristocrat. Photograph by Simon Spicer.

quate to the technical and expressive demands called for in works by French and German composers.

Harpsichordists evidently developed techniques for playing with both expression and brilliance, for the lack of variable dynamics—an obvious limitation of the instrument—seems not to have been regarded as a significant deficiency until the mid-eighteenth century. Only then did general changes in musical style, which affected vocal and orchestral music as well, begin to render the harpsichord obsolete. Such instruments nevertheless continued to be built into the early nineteenth century, as were clavichords.

The Fortepiano

Around 1700 the Italian instrument maker Bartolomeo Cristofori (1665–1731) perfected a type of stringed keyboard instrument whose strings were struck by hammers instead of being plucked by plectra. The result was an instrument capable of variable dynamics, like the clavichord, but larger and thus more suited to playing with other instruments or for listeners other than the player himself or herself. It was referred to as a *clavicembalo col piano e forte* ("harpsichord with softness and loudness"), or *pianoforte* for short. Later this was further abbreviated, somewhat irrationally, to *piano*. Sometimes the two elements of the name were reversed, and today, by convention, early pianos are often called *fortepianos*.

Christofori's fortepiano was only one of many new types of keyboard instruments invented in the eighteenth century, and only after 1750 did it find widespread use. Apart from its action and dynamic variability, the early piano closely resembled contemporary Italian harpsichords in construction, range, and sound. Moreover, most eighteenth-century fortepianos are, like the clavichord, fairly soft instruments, better suited for solo practice and quiet chamber music, not for public performance in large halls. Fortepianos were not generally employed in public concerts until the 1760s or later, and Haydn, Mozart, and their contemporaries in the Classical period still often used the harpsichord in their keyboard concertos. They also often did so when directing operas and other ensemble works, which for the most part continued to be conducted from a keyboard continuo instrument until the nineteenth century. For these reasons the fortepiano, although familiar to some late Baroque musicians, including J. S. Bach, was rarely called for explicitly. Before 1750 it is demanded specifically in only a few works by minor composers, such as the Italian Ludovico Giustini (*fl.* ca. 1732.)

The Organ

By the end of the Baroque, most significant churches and monasteries in western Europe contained an organ of some sort, and in many places the presence of large, innovative instruments become a matter of civic or institutional pride. Smaller instruments were widely distributed as well, not only in churches but in private homes and aristocratic palaces. Each region developed distinctive types of organs; larger instruments, which were more typical of France, Spain, and northern Germany, as opposed to Italy, southern Germany, and England, were characterized by a considerable proliferation of sets or **ranks** of pipes, each containing all the notes of the keyboard. A rank is also often referred to as a **stop**, although the latter more properly refers to the mechanism that turns a rank of pipes on or off. Since each rank contains pipes of a distinctive size and sonority, a single organ is in effect an entire orchestra of distinct wind instruments. These can be played alone or in endless combinations; as on the harpsichord, the selection of specific sonorities is referred to as **registration**. Every organ differs in the number and type of stops available. Moreover, although many small Baroque organs continued to have but a single keyboard, larger instruments may have two, three, or even more; in addition to the **manuals**—the keyboards played by the hands—there may be a **pedalboard** played by the feet.

Many Renaissance organs, particularly in Germany, had already offered pedalboards and diverse possibilities for registration. By 1600 some virtuosos had developed an advanced organ technique distinguished from that of other keyboard instruments by the use of the feet to play an independent pedal part. Pedal parts, usually but not always identical to the bass line, remained rare in Baroque organ music outside Germany and France. But in northern Germany

Figure 10.2 The organ of the church of St. Severin, Paris. Engraving, ca. 1750. John Koster Collection. An organ such as this comprises many sets of pipes (ranks) of different sizes, materials, and designs, each producing a distinct sonority. The organs placed in major northern European churches during the seventeenth and eighteenth centuries were among the period's greatest technological achievements.

the presence of an independent pedal part became by 1700 the most distinctive feature of music for the organ. Organists there, as well as in France and Spain, invented genres of organ music that exploited the distinctive registrational possibilities of the instruments built in each national tradition. Among these genres were various types of pieces played on two or three keyboards simultaneously, each registered to produce a distinctive sonority. In some cases one manual plays a solo role and employs pipes imitating a particular orchestral instrument, such as the trumpet or cornetto, while the other keyboard or keyboards furnish a less prominent accompaniment using flutelike stops. In other genres the keyboards may play equal roles in a polyphonic texture, as in Bach's trio sonatas for two manuals and pedals.

Today we associate the organ primarily with church music, although as recently as the mid-twentieth century organs were frequently found in theaters, where they accompanied plays and films. As a continuo instrument, the organ was a nearly universal component of Baroque sacred music. Much of the solo repertory of the Baroque organ is also sacred, in the sense that it was played during church services, consisting of settings of chant or hymns. But small portable organs were also often used in secular works, mainly as continuo instruments. Moreover, in some cities it was customary through much of the Baroque for organists to perform public recitals. These naturally took place in churches, since that is where the larger instruments were located. The works performed often included settings of chorales and other sacred vocal music, but the Baroque organ repertory also includes purely secular works, many calling for the same virtuosity as in other Baroque instrumental music. Even explicitly sacred works employ much the same styles and techniques as do secular ones—just as sacred vocal concertos and oratorios borrowed the manner of secular opera and cantata.

THE USES OF KEYBOARD MUSIC

At the beginning of the seventeenth century, keyboard playing and composing were confined largely to professionals. Professional keyboard players most often were employed as church organists, although some also held positions specifically as harpsichordists, particularly in the courts of France and Germany. A few wealthy amateurs who could afford instruments and teachers did play the clavichord and harpsichord, and in the course of the seventeenth and eighteenth centuries their numbers increased, as did the number of works written (and published) for amateur players.

Like members of other professions in the Baroque, instrumentalists, including keyboard players, usually learned their craft and passed it on within their own family circles. Professional keyboard players differed from most other musicians, however, in that their instruments were capable of furnishing self-sufficient music on its own. Paradoxically, however, they were called upon only rarely to play such music publicly. Although it was customary in some places for organists to provide preludes or interludes during church services, most of the time keyboard players were kept busy accompanying other musicians, through improvised figured bass realizations. Hence the education of keyboard players emphasized the skills needed to accompany others and to improvise preludes, including training in counterpoint and figured bass realization. For this reason a large portion of the solo keyboard repertory of the Baroque consists of works that were intended not for public performance but for private study and practice, as models or examples of correct improvisation or counterpoint.

Although such music was sometimes published, printed keyboard music was even more expensive than other types of published music. Early typesetting processes were inadequate to the inherently polyphonic nature of solo keyboard music, which until the 1760s was usually printed from specially engraved copper plates, like fine art prints. Hence professional keyboard players generally played not from printed music but from their own manuscript copies. They began their collections of manuscript music as part of their training, copying from scores that they borrowed (often for a price!) from teachers or colleagues. Most organists and harpsichordists thus came to own personal collections of music that constituted their own private repertories; they had little need for published music. To be sure, a number of Italian composers at the beginning of the Baroque and some French composers toward the end published significant numbers of keyboard works. But many, including J. S. Bach, left most of their keyboard music unpublished during their lifetimes. The situation changed significantly only in the mid-eighteenth century, when the growing number of amateur players finally made the widespread publication of keyboard music economical.

Baroque Keyboard Music in Italy

As with vocal music, distinctively Baroque types of keyboard music emerged first in Italy in the early seventeenth century, especially in various improvisatory types of compositions that incorporated elements of the *stile moderno*, such as a relaxed approach to voice leading and dissonance treatment. But Italian composers throughout the Baroque also continued to compose relatively strict contrapuntal pieces under such titles as *fantasia, ricercar, canzona*, and *capriccio*. These represented the keyboard version of the *stile antico*, often employing a quasi-vocal style little changed from that of the sixteenth-century motet.

The Toccata

Of the many genres of early Baroque keyboard music, the toccata was particularly distinctive as well as especially idiomatic to the keyboard. A **toccata** is most often an improvisatory work for organ or stringed keyboard instrument that may include not only virtuoso figuration but also constrasting passages consisting of imitative counterpoint or sustained, frequently dissonant, chords. The word *toccata* comes from the Italian verb that literally means "to touch" but was used to refer to the playing of keyboard instruments—hence the modern idea of the "touch" of a piano keyboard. Toccatas vary greatly in form, character, and length, some falling into distinct contrasting sections, others being short and homogeneous. All are normally through-composed, reflecting their improvisatory character. In the early Baroque, toccatas were also written for lute and for harp; as self-sufficient instruments requiring no accompaniment, the lute and especially the harp possessed solo repertories that overlapped to some degree with that of the keyboard instruments.[3]

The toccata had originated in the sixteenth century; among the important early composers of toccatas were Andrea and Giovanni Gabrieli, who probably performed them as preludes or interludes during church services at Saint Mark's Basilica in Venice (see Ex. 10.2 below). These works employ the same types of written-out embellishment—scale fragments, turning figures, and various types of trill—that we observed in early Baroque vocal music (see Chapter 3). These figures remained important in seventeenth-century keyboard writing, in which

---

[3]The word *toccata* was also employed for a few special types of music for instrumental ensemble, such as the trumpet fanfare that opens Monteverdi's *Orfeo*.

they were joined by additional types of idiomatic instrumental figuration. The Baroque toccata, moreover, incorporated many of the expressive devices found in vocal music of the period, including elements of what Monteverdi called the *seconda pratica*. In the course of the seventeenth century, it became increasingly common for toccatas and related works to comprise distinct sections, which eventually, in the works of J. S. Bach and other late Baroque composers, became separate, self-contained movements.

Girolamo Frescobaldi

The most important composer of keyboard music in Italy—and indeed throughout Europe—in the first half of the seventeenth century was Girolamo Frescobaldi (1583–1643). He was born in the northern Italian town of Ferrara, whose ruling dukes had made their court a center of the musical avant-garde, home to the so-called Three Ladies of Ferrara and visited by Gesualdo and other musicians. Frescobaldi studied with Luzzaschi, the court organist and composer of madrigals for the Three Ladies. Unfortunately, the only keyboard works of Luzzaschi that survive are a number of conservative contrapuntal pieces. But we must presume that he also composed, or at least improvised, more up-to-date

Figure 10.3 Portrait of Frescobaldi, engraving after drawing by Claude Mellan. John Koster Collection.

keyboard music that would have provided an inspiration for the works that Frescobaldi would eventually publish. Certainly this was the case with another Ferrarese organist, Ercole Pasquini (*fl.* ca. 1585–1608), whom Frescobaldi would succeed as organist at St. Peter's Cathedral at Rome.

Thus, Frescobaldi evidently grew up in an environment full of musical innovation and experimentation. Sometime around 1600 he came to Rome, where he subsequently held a number of prestigious positions, including that of organist at St. Peter's. In addition to providing organ music for services, he performed occasional public recitals, which presumably consisted largely of his own compositions and improvisations. Like Giovanni Gabrieli at Venice, he was also at the center of an important circle of students, among whom were some of the leading keyboard players and composers of the next two generations.

Frescobaldi appears to have been so overwhelming a presence in Italian keyboard music that no composer or player of equal stature emerged for over one hundred years afterward. His successors in Italy published few keyboard works of importance, apparently directing their energies toward improvisation or toward composition in other genres. Hence, his influence is most clearly documented on later music in other countries, especially France and Germany.

Frescobaldi's Music

Frescobaldi's career, like Monteverdi's, straddled what is for us the division between Renaissance and Baroque style, and his music likewise contains elements of both styles. Although an innovator, like Monteverdi he seems also to have endeavored to prove as well his ability to write old-fashioned counterpoint, and thus his first keyboard publication was a set of four-part fantasias (1608). The word **fantasia** was used during the late Renaissance and Baroque for various types of composition for solo keyboard, solo lute, or ensemble. The fantasias of William Byrd and other late Renaissance English composers generally fall into several sections ranging in style from austere counterpoint, resembling contemporary vocal polyphony, to lively dances and virtuoso figuration. Frescobaldi's fantasias are composed entirely of music of the first type—archaic imitative counterpoint—as is his 1615 collection of **ricercars,** another name for essentially the same type of conservative imitative piece. This was followed by set of somewhat more modern but still severely contrapuntal *capricci* (capriccios, 1624). Frescobaldi also published a book of polyphonic madrigals (1608) and two books of more up-to-date monodies and other vocal chamber music (both in 1630). An important collection of instrumental chamber works appeared in 1628, comprising thirty-five *canzoni* for one to four unspecified instruments plus continuo.

Frescobaldi's most innovative keyboard compositions are found in his two volumes of toccatas and partitas, published in 1615 and 1627. The toccatas follow in the tradition of earlier such pieces by the Gabrielis and others, but with Frescobaldi their style is clearly allied with that of Luzzaschi, Caccini, and other composers of the emerging Baroque. Published in the same volume as the toccatas were several **partitas,** Frescobaldi's term for keyboard **variations.** The latter refers to a series of contrasting settings of a given melodic line, which may be a hymn or chorale, a popular tune, or even a bass line such as the Romanesca, one of several ostinato basses that served as foundations for numerous variation sets by early Baroque composers.[4] An instance of the latter occurs in Example 10.1, which shows the ostinato itself and the first few measures of several variations from Frescobaldi's set of partitas on it. Keyboard partitas of this sort constituted an instrumental version of the strophic-variation aria (see Chapter 4), for which Frescobaldi, Monteverdi, and other early Baroque Italian composers often used the same traditional ostinato basses.[5] Frescobaldi's keyboard varia-

Example 10.1 Frescobaldi, *Partite sopra l'Aria della Romanesca*: (a) the underlying melody and ostinato bass; (b) *sesta parte* (variation 6), mm. 1–3; (c) *nona parte* (variation 9), mm. 1–5

[4]The origins of the Romanesca are uncertain; it may originally have been a Spanish tune with the melody shown in Ex. 10.1a. Other traditional ostinati went by the names Ruggiero, Follia, and Monica.

[5]For example, Monteverdi's Seventh Book of Madrigals (1619) contains an *aria di Romanesca* for two sopranos and basso continuo, *Ohimè, dov'è il mio ben?*, which uses the same ostinato bass line as Ex. 10.1.

tions greatly embellish the traditional Romanesca bass line; in addition, they resemble his toccatas in their use of embellished melody and expressive dissonances. Nevertheless, like Monteverdi, Schütz, and J. S. Bach, Frescobaldi never abandoned the older contrapuntal style, and his last major publication is a collection of relatively conservative organ pieces for church use, the *Fiori musicali* (Musical flowers, published 1635).[6]

The style of Frescobaldi's published toccatas undoubtedly reflected that of his own improvisations, which in turn must have been inspired by both vocal and keyboard music he had heard at Ferrara. This type of music must still have been unfamiliar to many players when Frescobaldi published his first book of toccatas in 1615. Consequently, the volume includes a preface that, like the preface in Caccini's *Nuove musiche* (1601), explains the music's performance and notation. Particularly notable is Frescobaldi's mention that the tempo of the toccatas should vary as in "modern madrigals," which might refer as much to the monodic solo madrigals of Caccini and Monteverdi as to the older polyphonic type. Despite Frescobaldi's concern with the proper performance of these pieces, he did not discuss their instrumental medium. Although the title of the 1615 collection originally specified that it was for harpsichord, the revised edition of 1637 changed this to "harpsichord and organ." Following a convention that continued in many Baroque genres into the eighteenth century, Frescobaldi evidently expected performance of most of the pieces in the volume on both organ and harpsichord.[7]

Toccata IX

This work (anthology, Selection 22) from Frescobaldi's 1615 book stands apart from the others in the volume in that it falls into three clearly defined sections; in this respect it resembles a number of the presumably later toccatas published in the 1627 volume. These sections can be characterized as: (1) an improvisatory opening (mm. 1–29a); (2) a more highly structured imitative middle section (mm. 29b–43); and (3) an improvisatory close (mm. 44–50). The outer sections are improvisatory in the sense that the music at first appears to be almost formless, moving without pattern or structural articulation. In fact, however, the opening section treats several recurring motives in imitation, up to the half cadence on V of C at the end of measure 10. At that point the quasi-contrapuntal texture is replaced by a freer, more homophonic texture characterized by figuration or passagework.

Particularly in measures 11–19 the passagework resembles that of Venetian keyboard music of the previous century in its use of running figuration in one hand accompanied by sustained notes in the other. Moreover, Frescobaldi uses some of the same types of written-out trills and other ornaments that occur in Example 10.2, taken from an *intonazione*, a sort of prelude or miniature toccata,

---

[6]Frescobaldi's *Fiori musicali* is particularly famous because J. S. Bach is known to have made a manuscript copy.

[7]The same option is given in the title of Frescobaldi's second collection of toccatas and partitas, first published in 1627.

Example 10.2 Giovanni Gabrieli, *Intonazione del secondo tono* (complete)

by Giovanni Gabrieli. Yet Frescobaldi's figuration is on the whole more irregular, containing frequent leaps and surprising twists and turns, such as the rhythmically odd figure in measure 19. Moreover, Frescobaldi occasionally uses expressive devices reminiscent of Monteverdi's *seconda pratica*. Among these are harsh melodic intervals such as the diminished fourth (mm. 1–2: F–C♯, in alto, then bass) and occasional chromaticism (m. 2: f′–e′–f♯′), as well as sharply exposed dissonant passing tones (m. 17: both c″ and b′ in the right hand's written-out trill).

The middle section of the toccata seems to revert to an older style (mm. 29b–43). The use of a more reserved, polyphonic style following an introductory improvisational section is derived from toccatas by Andrea Gabrieli (uncle of Giovanni and also an important Venetian composer and keyboard player). Only a few details suggest that the present passage indeed belongs to the early Baroque—for instance, the diminished fourth in the lowest voice in measure 35. Later Baroque toccatas and other works would continue to introduce references to sixteenth-century style through sections or movements written in imitative texture.

BAROQUE KEYBOARD MUSIC IN FRANCE AND GERMANY

Frescobaldi's immediate influence is strongest in the music of Johann Jakob Froberger and later German composers. There are also traces of it in France, although by 1650 or so a distinctive French style of keyboard composition had emerged. Moreover, in both France and Germany clear distinctions soon emerged between music for organ and music for stringed keyboard instruments. The harpsichord was the stringed keyboard instrument of choice, and French harpsichord music came to be highly idiomatic to that instrument. German composers, notably J. S. Bach, imitated this music while combining with it elements of the Italian style and adding their own special interest in complex counterpoint. In France, the standard term for keyboard compositions was simply *pièces*—"pieces." This could be qualified as *pièces d'orgue* ("organ pieces") or *pièces de clavecin* ("harpsichord pieces"). German composers often used similar French titles for works in the French style, especially in the eighteenth century, although they retained Latin or Italian titles for the genres that had been cultivated by Frescobaldi.

French Baroque Organ Music

Following a tradition established by the sixteenth century throughout Roman Catholic countries, French Baroque organ music consists primarily of pieces composed for performance during, or rather in place of, certain portions of the sung mass or office. The practice is referred to as ***alternatim*** performance. For example, in the performance of a hymn, the odd-numbered verses might be replaced by short organ pieces alternating with the chanted even-numbered verses. In an **organ mass,** the Kyrie, Gloria, and so forth might be similarly treated. Many *alternatim* organ pieces are based on the chants for which they substituted; the chants are used as cantus firmi or in paraphrase settings, much as in sixteenth-century vocal (and organ) music.[8] Increasingly, French organists employed freely composed pieces as well, that is, pieces not based on preexisting material. Among the most important French organ composers of the seventeenth century are Nicolas Lebègue (1631–1702), one of Louis XIV's court organists, and Nicolas de Grigny (1672–1703). J. S. Bach made a manuscript copy for his own use around 1714 of Grigny's *Livre d'orgue* (Organ book), published in 1699.

Most French Baroque organ music is highly idiomatic, composed to take advantage of the specific sonorities available on French instruments, such as the distinctive reed stops, used to imitate woodwind soloists or, in fugues and other contrapuntal pieces, a four- or five-part woodwind choir. This music is also carefully notated, the ornaments in particular being indicated with considerable precision. The same is true of French harpsichord music.

French Harpsichord Music

At first, the repertory of French harpsichordists probably consisted largely of improvised arrangements and adaptations of dance music composed for the Twenty-Four Violins of the King and similar bands. Little of this music survives, probably because it was rarely written down. But by 1650 or so there had emerged a repertory of **stylized dances:** instrumental pieces whose tempo, rhythm, and general style were still borrowed from music used for the actual dances of court and theater—courantes, sarabandes, minuets, and the like—but which were now independent compositions, not used for dancing. For the next hundred years, French harpsichord music—as well as music in the French style for the lute and other instruments—consisted largely of these stylized dances. At first these were composed individually and collected together in fairly random assortments, from which players would presumably make their own selec-

---

[8]*Paraphrase* technique involves taking a preexisting chant or hymn melody, breaking it up into individual phrases, and developing each phrase in imitation or through some other device; see the discussion of Buxtehude's organ chorales in Chapter 11.

tions. But by 1700 or so it had become customary for composers to organize their dances into **suites**: sets of dances (and, increasingly, other types of pieces) in a specific order and in a single key. Hence the suite became the most characteristic genre of French instrumental music.

The chief exception to the dance-based character of instrumental music in the French style was the prelude, which took an improvisatory form related in a general way to the Frescobaldian toccata. At first, French harpsichord preludes were rarely written down. When composers began to notate them, in the 1650s or 1660s, they found that the free rhythm of their improvisations did not permit precise notation. The result was the **unmeasured prelude**, a type of piece written largely in whole notes and without barlines. The note values must be determined by the player, guided by convention and his or her understanding of the appropriate style.

Both the unmeasured prelude and the dance suite of the French harpsichordists are closely related to similar compositions by French lutenists of the same period, such as Ennemond Gaultier (1575–1651) and his nephew Denis Gaultier (1603–72). Indeed, it was once thought that the French harpsichord style developed through imitation of somewhat earlier French lute music. But certain devices of French keyboard music that were once thought to be derived from lute music, such as the *style brisé* described below, more likely originated independently as idiomatic keyboard techniques. It may be that the lutenists only *appear* to have preceded the keyboard players, since the latter were at first fewer in number and their music, up until the mid-seventeenth century, has been largely lost.

Among the first important French keyboard composers whose works survive is Jacques Champion de Chambonnières (ca. 1602–1672). A musician active at the royal court, in 1670 he published the first two volumes of harpsichord music printed in France. These were followed during the next three decades by a small number of additional volumes; one was the single book of pieces published in 1689 by Jean-Henri D'Anglebert (1628–91), Chambonnières's successor at court and harpsichordist at the French opera under Lully. D'Anglebert's harpsichord works include not only original pieces but idiomatic arrangements of dances from Lully's operas and ballets. Among these is the arrangement of the *passacaille* shown in Example 10.3 (compare the original, illustrated in Ex. 5.9). D'Anglebert's volume followed by two years the first volume of pieces by Elizabeth Jacquet de La Guerre, whose music is discussed below. Her 1687 collection was the first keyboard music of any sort published by a woman.

Example 10.3 D'Anglebert, *Passacaille* from *Armide*, mm. 1–9

Froberger

In a sense, all of these French composers were preceded by the German composer Johann Jacob Froberger (1616–67). Although virtually none of his music was published during his lifetime, by 1649 he had already produced two definitive manuscript collections of his keyboard works; three more followed (two are lost). Although a German and, probably, a student of the Italian Frescobaldi, Froberger is of great significance to the history of French keyboard music. The keyboard suites in his 1649 manuscript are the earliest such works to survive. Moreover, through one or more visits to France, Froberger appears to have deeply influenced his contemporaries there. German keyboard music as late as that of J. S. Bach also shows his influence. Like most later German composers, Froberger wrote in both the French and the Italian styles, employing each in its appropriate genres. We shall examine one of his suites, a work in the French style. He also composed improvisatory toccatas as well as fantasias, ricercars, and other contrapuntal works modeled on those of Frescobaldi.

Froberger was born in Stuttgart, in western Germany. Little is known about his early training, but by 1637 he was working as an organist at the court of the Austrian emperor in Vienna. By 1641 he had visited and returned from Rome, where he is thought to have studied with Frescobaldi. During a second visit in the late 1640s, he made the acquaintance of Carissimi and other prominent musicians. Later travels apparently included visits to Paris (in 1652) and possibly to England and the Netherlands. During these trips he probably met and played for many of the local musicians and their patrons. He nevertheless retained his Viennese position until 1658, when he was dismissed. He spent the remainder of his life as the teacher and court harpsichordist of Princess Sybilla of Württemberg-Montbéliard, the German ruler of a small enclave in what is now eastern France.

Froberger's Music

Froberger's surviving works are almost exclusively for keyboard. A majority of them are preserved in the three manuscripts mentioned above, which the composer himself wrote out and presented to his employers, the Austrian emperors, in 1649, 1656, and 1658, respectively. These manuscripts include both toccatas and other works in the Italian style and suites in the French style. The toccatas are similar to those of Froberger's teacher Frescobaldi, but, illustrating a trend that would continue with later German composers, they tend to include longer and more distinct contrapuntal sections, some of which constitute self-contained fugues (see Chapter 11).

The suites must reflect Froberger's knowledge of works by Chambonnières and other French composers, although their music was not published until after Froberger's death. Since he had clearly mastered the French style long before, he might have gained access to it through manuscript copies, now lost, that circulated during Froberger's formative years. Nevertheless, his own music in French style often includes distinctive elements that might have derived from the Frescobaldi style. Among these are (1) a highly expressive type of writing marked by irregular dissonances and other elements of the *seconda pratica*; and (2) the use of fairly strict imitative counterpoint. The first of these elements is particularly prominent in the allemande, invariably the first dance in each of Froberger's suites. The second characteristic, imitative counterpoint, occurs in many of Froberger's examples of another dance, the gigue.

Suite X in A Minor

Froberger's manuscripts of 1649 and 1656 each contain six suites. Modern scholars have assigned them numbers based on their order in these manuscripts. Thus, Suite X (anthology, Selection 23) is the fourth suite in the 1656 manuscript. Like all the suites in that collection, it consists of four dance movements: allemande, gigue, courante, and sarabande.

These four dances were, and would continue to be, the most common components of Baroque suites for harpsichord (as well as for lute). Froberger was apparently the first, however, to organize them in such a regular manner. Although many later German composers (including Bach) followed him in this practice, it was by no means universal and was rare in France. Moreover, by the end of the seventeenth century it had become more common for the gigue, if present at all, to come at the end of the suite instead of after the allemande, and other dances, such as the minuet, might be included as well. Hence it would be wrong to think of the Baroque keyboard suite as having a specific form. It is likely that players picked and chose the pieces they wished to perform even from among the regularly ordered suites of Froberger and, later, Bach.[9]

The four movements of the A Minor Suite reveal the characteristic features of each of its four stylized dances. All are in **binary form**, consisting of two halves, each repeated. As in most Baroque binary forms, the first half usually modulates to a new key (most frequently the dominant or the relative major) while the second returns to the tonic. Each movement also employs the traditional rhythmic and other musical characteristics of its particular dance type. These characteristics recur in later Baroque instrumental music and, as we have already seen, in many vocal works. By identifying elements in a piece that correspond to a particular dance, it is possible to determine the appropriate tempo and expressive character of the piece; this is true even in many works that are not explicitly identified as dances by their titles.[10]

The Allemande

The first dance movement of most Baroque keyboard suites is the **allemande**. As with many dances, the name is derived from that of a place or region in Europe; in this case it is the French word for Germany. But by the mid-seven-

---

[9]A number of Froberger's suites in which the gigues originally followed the allemande were published after his death with the gigues moved to the end. Bach and other composers similarly altered the order and number of movements in their keyboard suites in the course of revising them.

[10]The descriptions of the dances given below apply to the French Baroque versions of these dances; Italian composers used similar titles for sometimes very different types of music.

teenth century the allemande had lost any association it may once have had with the country of its origin. Moreover, although the allemande had been a common dance from around 1550 to after 1600, the stylized allemandes of the French harpsichord and lute repertory have almost nothing in common with the actual dance. The allemande of the harpsichord or lute suite is a slow movement in common time $\left(\frac{4}{4}\right)$ employing a more or less improvisatory style. Many allemandes, including this one, lack regular themes or even melodies in the usual sense. Instead, like a French harpsichord or lute prelude, they tend to be composed largely of broken chords—that is, chords whose notes are played one-by-one or **arpeggiated,** as on the fourth beat of measure 1. There the four notes of the chord—D, A, B, and F—are struck one at a time and held. Other chords, such as those on the downbeats of measures 1, 2, and 9, are not fully arpeggiated, but one or more notes are delayed, so that they are spread out instead of being struck all at once.

The careful writing-out of this type of arpeggiation is now known as the *style brisé*, a French expression meaning "broken style."[11] The *style brisé*, although particularly common in allemandes, is employed throughout the French harpsichord repertory. Its intricate rhythmic notation often makes the music look more complex than it actually is. The first two measures of Froberger's allemande appear to comprise four rhythmically independent voices, but in performance the texture sounds largely homophonic. The invention of this type of notation was a major achievement, marking the composer's specification of an element of performance—the expressive arpeggiation of chords—that had previously been left up to the player. Such precision was typical of the French style. It is curious, then, that Froberger rarely specified the ornaments that were an equally essential part of the French style. Later composers would mark them with great care.

In addition to specifying explicitly which chords were to be arpeggiated, the composer also implicitly specified which chords were *not* to be audibly broken. Thus the four-note dissonant chord on the downbeat of measure 7 is struck as a single unit. On the harpsichord, this is the equivalent of a dynamic accent, producing a more forceful attack than the gentler two-note chord struck on the next beat, which therefore sounds like a relatively quiet resolution of the dissonance. Froberger's allemandes are particularly rich in such idiomatic, expressive harpsichord devices. They also contain devices familiar from the monodic style of contemporary vocal music. Among these are the chromaticism in measure 6 (d$\sharp$'–d$\natural$') and the repeated g's in measure 15, which suggest the declamatory style of recitative.

The Gigue

The French **gigue** is a version of the dance referred to in England as the jig. The gigue of this suite and in most later ones is a relatively quick movement

---

[11]Another term sometimes used for keyboard music in this style is *luthée*, referring to its resemblance to or its supposed origin in lute music.

in compound duple time ($^6_4$ or $^6_8$). French gigues often employ skipping rhythms, as in the second half of measure 1.[12] This gigue resembles many by Froberger in its fugal texture, a practice followed by many later Germans (including Bach) and, less frequently, in France.

As in many fugal gigues, the binary form of the dance is reflected in the treatment of the subject, which is heard unaccompanied at the beginning of the first half. The second half employs an upside-down version of the subject, that is, the **inversion**: for each melodic interval in the subject, the inversion employs the same or a similar interval in the opposite direction. For example, the initial downward leap of a minor sixth (e″–g♯′ in m. 1) is converted into an upward leap (e′–c″ in m. 16).

Inversion is one of several compositional devices that were more commonly associated in the Baroque with the ricercars and other strict contrapuntal forms of the *stile antico*. Froberger's inclusion of such a device in a stylized dance represented the intrusion of learned style into a popular form. Such a mingling of styles appears to have been a special interest of German composers; Bach would use it particularly often (as in the gigues of his keyboard suites).

This gigue is unusual in that the last four measures shift to common time ($^4_4$); moreover, the style of this closing passage returns to that of the allemande. The ending has the effect of joining the allemande and the gigue into a single larger unit, somewhat like the two halves of a French overture. Such passages are rare in suites by later composers, where the gigue normally is separated from the allemande by several other movements.

The Courante

In many suites, the allemande is followed immediately by one or more courantes. The **courante** resembles the gigue in being written primarily in compound duple time ($^6_4$ or $^6_8$). But its tempo is more moderate and the meter is elaborated by the presence of frequent **hemiola**: the substitution of one division of a triple measure by another. Thus in measure 4 the presence of three half notes in the bass marks a momentary shift to triple meter ($^3_2$). Hemiola is common in Baroque vocal and instrumental music in triple meter; its frequent presence in courantes made the latter one of the more complex and subtle of the French Baroque dances.[13] It was the most popular one at the court of King Louis XIV, who was something of a dance connoisseur; under his successor Louis XV the simpler minuet was preferred.

---

[12]The skipping rhythm was particularly characteristic of the type of gigue known in France as the *canarie*, after the Canary Islands, where it was supposed to have originated.

[13]For examples of hemiola from Baroque vocal music, see Schütz, *Neige deine Himmel* (anthology, Selection 14), m. 55, and the opening passage of *Saul, was verfolgst du mich* (anthology, Selection 15), which alternates repeatedly between $^3_1$ and $^6_2$.

The Sarabande

The **sarabande** is in triple time $\left(\frac{3}{2} \text{ or } \frac{3}{4}\right)$ and employs a moderate or, particularly in eighteenth-century examples, a slow tempo. Often the second beat is strongly marked, as in the first and last measures of our example, where the note or chord on the downbeat is repeated on beat 2. The sarabande is usually simpler in rhythm, melody, and texture than the other dances, and it often contains numerous block chords, as is the case here. This simpler texture does not preclude expressive effects, such as the dissonant suspensions on the downbeats of measures 5 and 7 and the chromaticism of measures 13 and 16. The weighty chords of many sarabandes seem to give them a grand or noble character. The dance's position at the end of this suite emphasizes the grave, expressive character with which Froberger imbued the genre; many later suites conclude with the livelier gigue or a simple minuet, reflecting fashions that favored a progression toward increasingly lighter, less serious music in the course of a suite or other multimovement work.

Jacquet de La Guerre

Among the numerous French keyboard players of the generations following Froberger was Elizabeth-Claude Jacquet (1665–1729), who became Jacquet de La Guerre after her marriage in 1684. She soon published her first book of harpsichord pieces (in 1687); another followed in 1707.[14] A child prodigy, she enjoyed the patronage of King Louis XIV while still in her teens. She went on to become the first and only woman to compose a full-length opera produced by the French Royal Academy of Music (*Céphale et Procris*, 1694). Among her other vocal and instrumental works were some of the earliest published French cantatas and violin sonatas—excursions into Italian genres at a time when these were considered somewhat controversial in France.

Women in Baroque France enjoyed somewhat greater opportunities and freedoms than those in most other European countries. They remained barred from the clergy and therefore from most important roles in the church (and in church music), but by the eighteenth century at least a few had gained appointments as court musicians, and many others were active as composers and teachers. To be sure, most women musicians had the advantage of being born into musical families, as was Jacquet de La Guerre, or the aristocracy, but the same could be said of male musicians as well. Jacquet de La Guerre never acquired a court title or indeed any professional position as a musician. But she appears to have directed the equivalent of a public concert series in her Paris home, gaining the reputation of one of the best harpsichordists in France.[15]

---

[14]Until recently, no copy of Jacquet de La Guerre's first book of harpsichord pieces was known to have survived; for this reason it is listed in some reference works as "lost."

[15]The earlier harpsichordist-composer Chambonnières had established a concert series as early as 1641, and musical gatherings at the homes of wealthy Parisian amateurs are known to have taken place throughout the century.

Figure 10.4 Portrait of Jacquet de la Guerre from Titon du Tillet, *Le Parnasse français* (n.p.: 1732). Library of Congress, Washington (CT1002.T6). On this page from a collection of imaginary memorial medallions, Jacquet is shown facing the opera composer André Campra (1660–1744). The motto on the reverse, which shows Jacquet playing the harpsichord, reads: "I competed for the prize with the great musicians," implying that she was at least the equal of any of her male contemporaries. (The word *musicien* is grammatically masculine.)

Jacquet de La Guerre's A Minor Suite

The third of the five suites in Jacquet de La Guerre's 1687 collection includes, in addition to the four dance movements found in Froberger's suites, a second courante, a chaconne, a gavotte, and a minuet (spelled *menuet* in French). There is also an opening prelude of the unmeasured type; its style, considerably more fiery and virtuosic than most earlier French preludes for lute or harpsichord, must reflect some of the characteristics that had won the king's admiration for Jacquet de La Geurre's playing.

The Prelude

The unmeasured prelude was an attempt to capture on paper the spontaneous irregularity of an improvisation. Example 10.4 represents an attempt to render in explicit modern notation the beginning of Jacquet de La Guerre's prelude (anthology, Selection 24) as it might be played; needless to say, this is only one of an infinite number of possible renditions. Still, the example shows that, like the keyboard allemande, the French unmeasured prelude is composed primarily of broken chords, arpeggiated in a constantly varied manner. The original notation, which in the earliest examples of the genre consists solely of whole notes, is clarified here by slurs and other lines, which indicate the holding of notes, as well as occasional smaller note values. Thus the first slur in the upper staff, over the notes a'–c''–d''–$f\sharp''$, indicates that each of these notes remains held after it has been struck, forming what we would call a D^7 chord. The line beneath this, in the lower staff, signifies that the note last struck by the left hand (A) is also held, serving here as a pedal point.[16] Groups of smaller note values indicate lively passagework, as in the sixteenths at the opening. Individual notes of small value are usually dissonant passing tones, inserted into the arpeggiation of certain chords but not held out with the other notes.

Example 10.4 Jacquet de La Guerre, Suite no. 3 in A minor, *prélude*, opening (suggested "realization")

---

[16]A **pedal point** is a sustained note in one voice, usually the bass, which is held against a series of changing harmonies in the other voices. It is so called because on the organ such a note might be played on the pedal keyboard (see Chapter 11).

Despite the seemingly chaotic appearance of such music, it consists largely of the written-out embellishment of familiar chord progressions. Although the notation can make these progressions difficult to recognize, the bass notes are usually quite distinct. For example, after the initial pedal point on A and a flourish of descending figuration in sixteenth notes, the bass moves downward by step: F–E–D–C. Because each bass note tends to bear a distinct harmony— as in an early basso continuo part—identifying these bass tones is the first step toward recognizing the chords that are arpeggiated in the upper voices. Jacquet de La Guerre, like earlier composers of unmeasured preludes, employs many of the same expressive devices found in Froberger's allemandes, which derive in turn from Frescobaldi's toccatas. But she reveals her independence in the occasional inclusion of lively figuration derived from more recent Italian music. An example of this occurs with the rapid upward arpeggiation of a C-major chord by the right hand (notated in eighth notes), about two-thirds of the way through the present prelude.

The Additional Dances

Supplementing the four standard dances in Jacquet de La Guerre's suite are additional types that would appear with increasing frequency in later keyboard suites. The **chaconne** is musically similar to the *passacaille* or passacaglia (see Chapter 5), with which it shares its triple meter and moderate tempo. The chaconne of the present suite lacks the ostinato bass of most chaconnes (Ex. 10.5a). Instead it is in the form of the **rondeau,** a simple rondo form in which a single main theme (mm. 1–4) alternates with a series of contrasting phrases or couplets in the pattern ABACADA (etc.). This chaconne is notable for its exploitation of the rich sonorities of the middle and low registers of the French harpsichord.

The **gavotte** is always in cut time $\left(\begin{smallmatrix} 2 \\ 2 \end{smallmatrix}\right)$ and is usually notated so as to begin in the middle of the measure (Ex. 10.5b). The initial half-measure is an upbeat; if the first note is unduly accented in performance the barlines may seem to be drawn in the wrong place. This gavotte is typical of French examples in its moderate tempo and fairly delicate character; some German gavottes (including one or two by Bach) are more energetic. We have previously seen an example of this dance in the air "Sur nos bords" from Rameau's *Les indes galantes* (anthology, Selection 19).

The **minuet** is musically the simplest of the common French Baroque dances, and our example is particularly light in character and texture, its very simple harmony perhaps suggesting the dance's folk origins (Ex. 10.5c). Minuets are always in triple time, often moving simply in quarters and eighths like the present one, without hemiolas or other rhythmic complications. Most usually fall into regular four-measure phrases, although there is also a type composed of three-bar phrases (the *menuet de Poitou*). In the eighteenth century the first pieces learned by beginning keyboard players were frequently minuets, probably reflecting the fact that the minuet had become the most popular of the social dances and was the easiest to learn. For this reason, too, the minuet remained an important genre long after most of the other Baroque dances had been abandoned. It appears frequently as a movement in eighteenth-century sonatas and

Example 10.5 Jacquet de La Guerre, Suite in A minor, chaconne: (a) mm. 1–7 (*rondeau* and opening of first *couplet*); (b) gavotte, mm. 1–4; (c) minuet, mm. 1–8

as the third movement of symphonies and string quartets composed during the second half of the eighteenth century and into the nineteenth. By then its musical character had changed, and the minuets of the Viennese Classical composers Haydn, Mozart, and Beethoven often incorporate asymmetrical phrases containing odd numbers of measures and irregular accents.

CHAPTER 11

BAROQUE KEYBOARD MUSIC II
Fugues, *Pièces*, and Sonatas

LATER BAROQUE GERMAN KEYBOARD MUSIC

In the later seventeenth and eighteenth centuries, German composers continued, like Froberger, to create their own versions of idioms derived from existing Italian and French genres. The models provided by Frescobaldi and Froberger proved especially influential, continuing to be studied and copied into manuscripts well into the eighteenth century. German composers borrowed ideas from later Italian and French music as well, although the scarcity of published Italian keyboard music meant that composers borrowed instead from Italian-style vocal and especially ensemble music.

The North German Organ School

Northern Germany, that is, the area bordering on the North and the Baltic Seas, was linguistically, culturally, and politically a distinct region throughout our period. Dominated culturally by the port cities Hamburg and Lübeck, it was distinguished during the Baroque by a group of organist-composers now often identified as a North German "school." As in other instances (e.g., the "Netherlandish school" of the early Renaissance), the word *school* is somewhat misleading, since the music in question is related more by a general similarity of medium and style than by the presence of any central educational institution. Nevertheless, the building of fine organs and the development of an idiomatic musical repertory for them appear to have been special interests of North German musicians in the seventeenth century. The wealthier towns competed with one another in the building of large instruments, a number of which survive or have been reconstructed. Those by the builder Arp Schnitger (1648–1719) are particularly prized for their strong, clear tone and the rich registrational possibilities offered by their carefully designed sets of pipes, which are well suited to the music that was written for them.

Among the most prominent of the North German organist-composers were the Hamburg musicians Matthias Weckmann (1619–74), who had studied with

Schütz, and the long-lived Jan Adamszoon Reincken (1623–1722),[1] whose teacher Heinrich Scheidemann (1596–1663), also an important keyboard composer, had studied with Jan Pieterszoon Sweelinck (1562–1621). Sweelinck had been the leading Dutch composer and organist of the late Renaissance, like the English composer William Byrd a writer of both sacred polyphony and a distinguished repertory of solo keyboard pieces. Through Sweelinck and his many students the North German tradition thus extended back to the sixteenth century; the tradition was continued by J. S. Bach, who studied with (or at least visited) Buxtehude in 1705 and who also heard and later played for Reincken.

Unfortunately, much of the music of these composers is lost. Hardly any was published during their lifetimes, their keyboard works being preserved in manuscripts written in a form of **tablature** (a type of notation using letters instead of notes and staves) that went out of use in the eighteenth century. Much of their music may have been improvised, never written down at all. For the most part, the North German keyboard repertory is preserved in a small number of later manuscript copies, including several by J. S. Bach and other members of his family. The vocal works of these composers, which included sacred concertos and oratorios, are also scarce; many works are known to have been lost.

Buxtehude

The greatest of the North German Baroque composers was Dietrich Buxtehude (ca. 1637–1707), who served as organist at the church of St. Mary at Lübeck from 1668 until his death. The exact place and date of Buxtehude's birth are unknown; the family might have come from the North German city of Buxtehude, near Hamburg. Following local tradition, Buxtehude married his predecessor's daughter when he took the position at Lübeck. The reluctance of Handel and Bach, as well as other potential candidates, to continue the tradition apparently explains their failure to succeed Buxtehude. Both had been interested in the job, which was eventually taken by the minor opera composer Johann Christian Schieferdecker (1679–1732)—who did marry Anna Margreta, the oldest of Buxtehude's three daughters.

Buxtehude's works, like Bach's, have been listed in a modern scholarly *Werke-Verzeichnis* (catalogue of works). From this come the BuxWV numbers used to identify individual compositions. Buxtehude's organ works, like those of other North German musicians, were probably composed for use not only in church services but also in the public organ recitals that were a regular feature of musical life at the time in the major North German cities. At Lübeck, Buxtehude's predecessor Franz Tunder (1614–67) had regularly given recitals on Thursday afternoons. Buxtehude augmented this practice by including vocal works, and the concerts came to be known as *Abendmusiken* ("vespers concerts," since the evening performances took place at the time of the old liturgical office of vespers).

---

[1]Recent research suggests that Reincken may actually have been born in 1643.

Unfortunately, of the oratorios and other quasi-dramatic works that Buxtehude performed on these occasions only some of the librettos survive. The music, which presumably was Buxtehude's, appears to be completely lost, save for one anonymously preserved work that might have been performed during an *Abendmusik* concert of the 1680s, the three-act oratorio *Wacht! euch zum Streit* (Awake to the struggle!). Nevertheless, over one hundred sacred vocal works of a more strictly liturgical nature survive, giving a more complete picture of Buxtehude's vocal music than that of any other North German composer. From this it is clear that his sacred vocal works, like those of many of his German contemporaries, represent a continuation of the older type of vocal concerto such as Schütz wrote. Buxtehude combined elements of this tradition with more modern Italian elements, including various aria forms, as well as the distinctly German traditions associated with the Lutheran chorale.

Buxtehude's Organ Music

German organ music of the period falls into two main categories: compositions based on chorale melodies, and "free" works with no such preexisting element. Buxtehude's surviving chorale works number about fifty, ranging from brief preludes to longer fantasias; the free works include about thirty large *praeludia* and other compositions, all related to the Frescobaldian toccata, as well as a few separate fugues and other pieces. Both free and chorale works are written-out examples of the types of music that appear to have been routinely improvised by German organists. Prospective organists underwent auditions during which they had to improvise at length in various styles, demonstrating both their technical proficiency at the keyboard and their mastery of harmony and counterpoint. This remained true during and after the time of J. S. Bach, whose organ works parallel those of Buxtehude in general form and style.

Chorale Works

Buxtehude's chorale pieces, like those of other German Baroque composers, continued to employ the older compositional techniques of cantus firmus and paraphrase, though with the inclusion of idiomatic keyboard figuration. The shorter chorale works are now referred to as **chorale preludes**: relatively brief settings of a hymn tune (chorale) that might have preceded congregational singing of the same chorale during a church service. In the chorale prelude *Nun bitten wir den heiligen Geist* (BuxWV 208; anthology, Selection 25), the traditional melody is played once through as a cantus firmus in the soprano, with three-part accompaniment below.[2]

Buxtehude's setting focuses on his decoration of the cantus firmus. One might compare this organ setting with one of the three four-part vocal settings of the

---

[2]The melody, first published in 1524, is by Johann Walther; the words, by Martin Luther, begin "We pray now to the Holy Spirit."

same melody by J. S. Bach (BWV 385), whose soprano part contains the same cantus firmus in simpler form (anthology, Selection 26). The melody would have been familiar to Buxtehude's listeners, who would have followed it within his decorated version, no doubt appreciating the expressive ornamentation and counterpoint of Buxtehude's setting.[3] Buxtehude's decoration includes both florid embellishment reminiscent of the Italian style, written out in small note values, and ornaments typical of the French tradition, indicated by ornament signs.

The melody, in the soprano, is played by the right hand on an organ manual that would have been registered to sound a distinctive solo stop such as the *Cornet* (an imitation of the cornetto). The bass line is played by the feet on the pedals, the inner parts or voices by the left hand on a second, more quietly registered manual. The lower voices serve chiefly to accompany the melody in the soprano, but they also provide interludes and are composed throughout in contrapuntal, occasionally imitative, texture.

The interlude in measures 11–12 employs an imitative subject that derives from the third phrase of the chorale melody; thus $g'-g'-g'-f\sharp'-g'$ in the alto (mm. 11–12) corresponds to $b'-b'-b'-a'-b'$ in the soprano (mm. 13–15). The motive is played in longer note values and embellished in the soprano, but at the same time it is imitated in plain eighth notes by the tenor (m. 14). This is an example of paraphrase technique, also used alongside a chorale cantus firmus technique in the opening chorus of Bach's Cantata 127 (anthology, Selection 20) and in other German Baroque vocal works. It is typical of this type of organ chorale prelude that the imitative subject first appears in the interlude *preceding* the entry of the corresponding phrase of the cantus firmus; for this reason the technique is sometimes referred to as **preimitation.**

German Baroque organists also wrote more extended chorale works for organ; these generally make more extensive use of paraphrase technique and are therefore usually described as **chorale fantasias.** Buxtehude and Bach wrote numerous examples of such works. A third category of chorale settings for organ comprises sets of variations on chorale melodies. Buxtehude and Bach each wrote only a few of these, in which the individual variations may resemble either the prelude or fantasia types.

Free Works

Buxtehude's free keyboard compositions include suites and variations on secular tunes for clavichord or harpsichord, as well as a passacaglia and two chaconnes on ostinato basses, all for organ. There are also a number of **canzonas:** fugal works related to those of Frescobaldi and Froberger but somewhat more up-to-date in style.[4] Buxtehude's most important free works, however, are some

---

[3]Bach's harmonization of the melody dates probably from the 1720s or later and would not have been familiar to Buxtehude or his late seventeenth-century listeners.

[4]The seventeenth-century keyboard canzona is a remote descendant of the sixteenth-century keyboard canzona, which was usually an arrangement of vocal polyphony; on Giovanni Gabrieli's canzonas for instrumental ensemble, see Chapter 7.

two dozen *praeludia*. Popularly known as a prelude and fugue, a *praeludium* of this type incorporates both improvisational and fugal sections descended from those of Frescobaldi's and Froberger's toccatas.

The term **praeludium** is, in origin, the Latin equivalent of English *prelude*. In Germany it came to refer to a distinct genre of organ music that arose in the seventeenth century. It generally includes improvisatory opening and closing sections, similar in style to those in the toccatas of Frescobaldi and Froberger. But the main substance of the work is usually one or more fugal sections that come at the center. Most of Buxtehude's *praeludia* include pedal parts and therefore achieve their full effect only on a large organ. Indeed, many of these works contain virtuoso passages for the unaccompanied bass line, intended to demonstrate both the power of the North German organ's pedal division—those pipes reserved for the pedals—and the organist's mastery of pedal technique (see the *praeludium* in the anthology, Selection 27, mm. 64 and 115).

The organ *praeludia* of Buxtehude and other German composers nowadays are played frequently as preludes or postludes to church services. Many, however, were originally used probably for recital performance, like the chorale fantasia. The *praeludium* was the organist's equivalent of the sonatas that were being written at the same time for instrumental ensemble. Indeed, Buxtehude also wrote about twenty sonatas for instrumental ensemble that are comparable in form and style to his organ *praeludia*.

The Praeludium in A Minor, BuxWV 153

Like most of Buxtehude's organ music, this work (anthology, Selection 27) remained unpublished until after his death. The manuscript copies in which it is preserved date from long after its composition, making it impossible to determine for what circumstances it was written, although the composer presumably wrote it for his own recital use at Lübeck. It is typical in comprising (1) an opening improvisatory or free section in common time: the "prelude" proper (mm. 1–21); (2) a four-part fugue also in common time (mm. 21–67); (3) a second fugue, also in four parts and using a variation of the subject of the first fugue, in compound time $\binom{6}{4}$ (mm. 67–104); and (4) a **coda** or closing section that returns to the free style of the prelude (mm. 105–25).

The opening and closing sections make much use of certain motives in small note values that are found throughout the North German repertory. These must have been formulas frequently heard in improvisations. For example, in measures 5–6 the two manuals and pedal each have statements of a four-note motive that is developed imitatively (it appears initially as d′–e′–b–c′ in the tenor). Not surprisingly, pedal points are common in pieces such as this one that employ actual pedal parts. The opening section ends with a cadence prepared by a lengthy dominant pedal point (mm. 15–20). The coda ends with another pedal point on the tonic (mm. 118–25). Such pedal points serve to build up tension and are one of the chief sources of drama in works of this sort. Another source of drama is written-out arpeggiation, as in the last full measure of the prelude (m. 20). The notation is borrowed from the *style brisé* of the French harpsichordists. But because the organ, unlike a plucked string instrument, is capable of sustaining notes indefinitely, the effect is that of a crescendo, as more and more notes are added to the sounding texture.

The presence of two fugues employing versions of the same subject in different meters derives from the archaic contrapuntal works of Frescobaldi and Froberger—especially their capriccios and canzonas. This work is more up-to-date in style; its first fugue—which begins with the second note of the soprano in measure 21—is characterized by the numerous repeated notes in its subject, which exemplifies a type especially favored by German Baroque organists (sometimes termed "repercussive"). Unlike the imitative sections of certain other types of Baroque keyboard works, such as the toccatas of Frescobaldi, the present fugue strictly maintains its four-voice texture—a practice typical of the contrapuntal works of Bach as well. Of course, the number of voices present at any given moment varies, just as in vocal polyphony. The full "ensemble," including the bass—played on the pedals—is employed only occasionally. By adding or subtracting voices from the texture, the composer could produce the effect of a crescendo or a diminuendo. Particularly dramatic results are achieved when, for example, the bass enters after a rest to complete the four-part texture (as in m. 28).

The first fugue ends with a short coda in free style (mm. 64–66). The passage includes a written-out trill in thirds (g♯–b) for the pedals, an example of the type of virtuoso pedal writing typical of the North German organ style. This trill in thirds also exemplifies a sort of playful oddity in which these musicians occasionally indulged, an imitation of the *bizzarria* ("extravagance," "oddity") favored by composers of seventeenth-century Italian instrumental music.

In the second fugue, some of the repeated notes of the original subject are replaced by a chromatic idea. Nevertheless, the shape of the subject remains recognizable, opening with an upward leap of a fourth or fifth and concluding with a larger upward leap to a syncopated or suspended note.

Fugue Analysis

The analysis of fugues has interested musicians since the seventeenth century, when a number of musicians, among them Schütz's student Bernhard, wrote treatises on counterpoint and related topics. These were the ancestors of such eighteenth-century works as Fux's *Gradus ad Parnassum*. Such works were practical rather than theoretical in nature; their primary aim was to instruct composers in the writing of works that would be used in actual performance, especially church music.

The modern analysis of fugue employs terms and concepts that have been developed largely from the study of Bach's fugues by nineteenth- and twentieth-century theorists. One sometimes gains the impression from such writings that fugue was a fixed form that can be understood by reference to a few frequently cited examples by Bach. There is, however, no one form or style for fugue. For Buxtehude, Bach, and other Baroque composers, fugue was simply one of several types of contrapuntal texture that might be employed in diverse ways within any vocal or instrumental piece.

Box 11.1 summarizes some terms used in the present-day analysis of fugues, including the two fugal sections of the Buxtehude *praeludium*. Modern analysts

Box 11.1

Fugue

This box introduces a number of terms used in the modern analysis of fugue. Not all writers use these terms in the same way, nor do all these terms apply to all fugues.

Strict Fugue

In a **strict** fugue, the texture consists of a set number of voices or parts, often specified in the title (e.g., *Fuga a 3*, three-part fugue). In a keyboard fugue, these voices move within distinct ranges, just like real voices. They rarely cross, and the number of voices remains constant throughout the movement (although individual voices may rest from time to time). Needless to say, the rules of counterpoint, such as the injunctions against parallel fifths, are strictly followed. One purpose of a strict fugue is to demonstrate technical mastery using limited musical means. Hence, in a strict fugue most of the motivic material is derived from that of the subject and its countersubject(s) (see below).

Subject

Most instrumental fugues begin with the monophonic statement of a **subject**, the theme that will be developed through imitation and other means throughout the movement. The subject is initially presented by a single voice; as each of the remaining voices enters in turn, the preceding one continues with new material. It is not always clear precisely where each entry of a subject begins or ends, nor is it necessarily important to reach such a decision. Fugues, unlike dances and other homophonic genres of the Baroque, comprise numerous overlapping phrases; as a result, fugues frequently lack the clear-cut articulations that mark off segments or sections in other types of music.

Exposition, Episode, and Bridge

A section of a fugue containing entries of the subject constitutes an **exposition**. A fugue is likely to contain several expositions, and in a strict fugue these will tend to contain a single entry of the subject in each voice. Some fugues consist of nothing but expositions; in such fugues, at any given point the subject is being stated by one voice or another. Usually, however, there are connecting passages and interludes from which the subject is absent (although motives extracted from the subject may be present). All such passages can be called **episodes**, although it is best to reserve this term for distinctly articulated sections—that is, interludes of significant length from which the subject is absent. Shorter passages that merely connect entries of the subject can be termed **bridges**. Within an exposition, there may be bridges connecting one entry of the subject to the next. But an episode is best regarded as a relatively lengthy passage that falls *between* two expositions.

Tonal Design (Keys)

Fugal imitation differs from other types in that successive entries of the subject are usually in different keys. The first entry of a fugue is usually in the tonic, followed by one in the dominant. Within the first exposition, the keys of the entries alternate in this manner until all the voices have entered. In subsequent expositions the order of keys, like the order of voices, is likely to vary from that of the first exposition. Moreover, the keys used are likely to range more widely, including entries in the relative major or minor.

More precisely, the even-numbered entries of the first exposition are not *in* the dominant; they are *on* the dominant. The latter expression indicates that the modulation from tonic to dominant is only momentary, and indeed the music usually returns immediately to the tonic in the next entry. Subsequent modulations within a fugue may also be of a temporary nature. Indeed, fugues composed before the eighteenth century, including most of Buxtehude's, rarely contain any lasting modulations, merely alternating between tonic and dominant and one or two other keys.

Stretto

An answering or imitating voice need not wait until the previous entry has been completed to make its own entrance. A fugue subject can often be combined with itself through the technique of **stretto**. For example, in the second fugue of the Buxtehude *praeludium*, the bass entry in measure 100 is followed at a distance of only half a measure by an entry in the soprano. This is an isolated stretto entry, but it is possible to have an entire exposition composed through stretto. The word *stretto* literally means "acceleration"; it refers to the diminished time interval between entries. Stretto entries usually represent an intensification of the drama that is often present in a fugue, and they are likely to occur near the end of a movement, as is the case here.

Tonal Answer

Not every statement of the subject need take precisely the same melodic or rhythmic form. Indeed, sometimes it is necessary to alter certain melodic intervals in the subject, especially leaps, to insure that a given entry will end up in the right key. In Buxtehude's A-minor *praeludium*, for example, the first statement of the subject (soprano, m. 21) opens with an ascending fifth (a'–e''). In the next entry, however (alto, m. 23), the initial leap turns into a fourth (e'–a'). This type of altered entry is called a **tonal answer**, since the alteration affects the tonality of the entry and prevents it from modulating too far from the tonic. The next entry (tenor, m. 26) is termed a **real answer** because it reverts to the original form of the subject.

Inversion

Another type of alteration occurs in measure 30 of the same fugue, where the subject is **inverted**: every melodic interval is turned upside-down, moving upward where it originally moved downward (and vice versa). Indeed, measure 30 marks the beginning of an entire exposition using the inversion, as opposed to the original or **upright** form of the subject. (The Latin word *rectus* is also used for the original form of the subject.)

Thematic Variation and Motivic Development

Fugue subjects may also be varied and developed through the usual devices of thematic variation and motivic development. **Thematic variation** includes such procedures as melodic embellishment and rhythmic alteration. A subject that is varied retains its original length and basic shape. **Motivic development** involves detaching an isolated figure from the subject, such as an opening leap or a repeated note, and using it in sequence or some other type of passage outside of the context of the subject itself. This is a commonly used technique in episodes, as in measures 94–99 in the second fugue of the Buxtehude *praeludium*. Sometimes a statement of a subject is simply truncated, its end left off. In such cases it may be hard to say (and unnecessary to decide) whether one is dealing with a shortened entry of the subject or merely a statement of its opening motive.

Countersubject

Many fugues contain more than one subject. For example, in the Buxtehude fugue the soprano, having introduced the subject, continues (m. 23) with a second idea that is later combined with subsequent entries of the subject as well. A secondary subject that combines repeatedly with the main subject constitutes a **countersubject**. A fugue may have any number of countersubjects—or none at all. Countersubjects, like subjects, may undergo various types of alteration. It is rare, however, for the countersubject(s) to be treated as rigorously as the subject. In the Buxtehude fugue, the countersubject disappears after the first exposition, and even within the latter it undergoes greater variation than does the subject.

Second Subject

At some point after the first exposition, a fugue may contain another exposition employing an entirely new subject. Such a subject is termed a **second subject**. This differs from a countersubject, which serves chiefly to accompany the main subject, without receiving an exposition of its own. A second subject may even have its own countersubject(s).

Double Fugue

Usually, after a second subject has been thoroughly worked out in its own exposition, there is yet another exposition in which it is combined with the first subject. A fugue in which this occurs is termed a **double fugue**. It is also possible to have triple and quadruple fugues with corresponding numbers of subjects.*

Types of Fugues

Most fugues use only a selection of the devices described above. A few strict fugues by Bach and other composers intentionally incorporate many such devices in order to demonstrate the techniques of fugal counterpoint. But even in pedagogical works, such as Bach's *Well-Tempered Clavier*, the emphasis is usually not on fugue as a contrapuntal exercise but on fugue as a texture that permits expressive or dramatic music that is idiomatic for its chosen medium. Fugue was favored by Baroque composers not because of its rigidity or severity—characteristics that were attributed to it only after Baroque traditions of composition had died—but because of the freedom that it permitted. Fugues could even be improvised; indeed, the improvisation of fugues was one of the required skills in which organists such as Bach were tested when they underwent auditions—a tradition that continues in some schools of organ playing today. Naturally, an improvised fugue would have been less strict than the rigorous examples in a pedagogic work such as Bach's *Art of Fugue*. Both types, however, would have manifested the Baroque love of variety, technical virtuosity, and expressive intensity.

Symbols for the Analysis of Fugue

Tables 11.1 and 11.2 illustrate the use of certain symbols in the analysis of fugue. The meaning of the symbols is explained in the key that follows each chart. Different symbols are used in different charts, since differences in the structure of the fugues require different analytical approaches.

*Some writers use the expression *double fugue* for any fugue that contains a regularly occurring countersubject. But the term is better confined to works in which a second subject receives its own separate exposition, as in the fugue in C♯ minor from Part 2 of Bach's *Well-Tempered Clavier*.

do not always use the same terms in the same ways, however, and not all terms are relevant to all fugues. Some Baroque fugues are pedagogic pieces that were intended to demonstrate to students the use of particular contrapuntal techniques. But most, including the two fugal sections of the Buxtehude *praeludium*, are first and foremost virtuoso pieces that use imitative counterpoint for its expressive and dramatic possibilities.

Table 11.1 provides an analysis of the first fugue in Buxtehude's A minor *praeludium*. The table divides the fugue into four **expositions**: sections in which the subject is present and treated in imitation. The first and third expositions employ the subject in its upright or *rectus* form; its inversion forms the basis of the second and fourth expositions, although in the last exposition all but one of these entries is abbreviated. It is in the nature of fugue that the divisions between these sections are somewhat blurred. For example, the table identifes the inverted entry of the subject by the soprano in measure 30 as marking the beginning of the second exposition. Yet this moment comes slightly *before* the ca-

TABLE 11.1

Buxtehude: Praeludium in A minor, BuxWV 153, first fugue

	Expositions			
	1	2	3	4
Soprano	a x (x)	{a} + ({e})	[d]– [a]	({a})
Alto	[e]— x	{[e]} +	a x′	[e]—
Tenor	a	{a}	[e]	({e})—
Bass	[e]	{[e]}—	a	({a})
Measure	21b	30 31b	42b	54
Cadences		a	a	a

letters = keys of normal fugal entries (real answers)
[letters in brackets] = initial keys of tonal answers
{letters in curly brackets} = inverted entry
x, + = countersubjects
(symbols in parentheses) = incomplete or substantially altered entry
′ (prime) = varied (embellished) version of entry
— (dash) = bridge (free continuation of an entry)

dence to A minor in measure 31, which brings the first exposition to a conclusion. Thus the first and second sections overlap, maintaining a fluid continuity typical of the imitative counterpoint of both the Renaissance and the Baroque.

Other German Keyboard Composers

Buxtehude was only one of many German organist-composers active during the seventeenth and early eighteenth centuries. In addition to his North German contemporaries mentioned at the outset of this chapter, there were important earlier figures such as Samuel Scheidt (1587–1654), organist at Halle (Handel's birthplace) and a pupil of Sweelinck. He published an important collection of organ music, the *Tabulatura nova* (New tablature, 1624), containing fantasias, variations on chorale melodies, and other types of pieces.

Prominent among Buxtehude's younger contemporaries was Johann Pachelbel (1653–1706), who held positions as organist in the central Germany cities of Erfurt and Nuremberg. Pachelbel has become famous for a chamber work preserved under his name, a Canon for three violins and continuo composed over an ostinato bass.[5] He was more important, however, for his numerous fugues and chorale settings for organ. These, although somewhat less virtuosic in style than those from northern Germany—most lack independent pedal parts—are admired for their polished imitative technique. Typical is the opening of the

---

[5]In a **canon**, one part is imitated *exactly* by another, throughout the piece. In the work attributed to Pachelbel—his authorship is not fully documented—both the second and third violins imitate the first part canonically. There is also a second movement, a gigue (which is noncanonic).

fugue shown in Example 11.1, which is characteristic of Pachelbel's fugues in the composition of its subject from two distinctive gestures separated by a rest, producing a quasi-rhetorical effect.[6] Although less imposing than the virtuoso fugues of Buxtehude, Pachelbel's fugues may have been equally important as models for J. S. Bach, whose older brother and teacher Johann Christoph Bach had studied with Pachelbel in the 1680s.

Example 11.1 Pachelbel, Magnificat Fugue no. 3/11 in C, mm. 1–11 (entries of subject marked by brackets)

J. S. Bach's Keyboard Music

The composer who today is most closely identified with fugue is J. S. Bach. Fugue is actually only one of many contrapuntal textures employed by Bach, but he used fugue or fugal technique in nearly every genre in which he wrote. His keyboard fugues, in particular, have been closely studied by musicians ever

---

[6]This so-called Magnificat fugue is from a collection of numerous short fugues apparently composed by Pachelbel for *alternatim* performance between chanted verses of the Magnificat (Luke 1:46–55). An important part of the Roman Catholic vespers service, the Magnificat was also used in Lutheran services during the Baroque.

since his students began making manuscript copies of them in the second decade of the eighteenth century.

Bach's organ works fall into essentially the same genres as Buxtehude's—chiefly the chorale prelude, the chorale fantasia, and the *praeludium* or prelude and fugue. Composed mainly during the period 1703–17, during which Bach held a series of positions as organist at several central German towns (see Chapter 9), his chorale compositions include the *Orgelbüchlein* (Little organ book), a collection of forty-five chorale preludes assembled at Weimar around 1715, and a set of seventeen (later expanded to eighteen) larger chorale fantasias, gathered together and revised at Leipzig in the 1740s but mostly composed by 1717. He also published three volumes of organ music, including the third volume of his *Clavierübung* (Keyboard practice, 1739), which contained both free pieces and chorale settings, and the so-called Schübler chorales (ca. 1748), organ transcriptions of six of the chorale-fantasia movements from his church cantatas.[7]

Bach's free organ works consist primarily of about two dozen *praeludia* and related pieces. These too were mostly composed by 1717, although Bach subsequently revised existing works and wrote occasional new ones for the recitals that he continued to play for the remainder of his career. Many of these recitals took place in connection with the completion of a new instrument or the rebuilding of an old one in churches in and around Leipzig. On such occasions, Bach and other leading musicians would be called upon to provide expert evaluations of the builders' work. Bach was famous for the rigorous testing of the instrument that took place when he sat down on such occasions to improvise or to play one of his larger compositions.

Most of Bach's *praeludia*, unlike Buxtehude's, consist of two distinct movements. No longer musically connected—indeed, they were often composed separately—the prelude and the fugue thus constitute independent, self-contained compositions. Among Bach's organ works of this type are several that have been given popular nicknames by later musicians. These include the "Wedge" in E minor (BWV 548), named for the shape of its fugue subject, which expands through widening leaps in both directions from the tonic note, and the "Dorian" in D minor (BWV 538), so called because it lacks the one-flat key signature now customary for works in this key.[8] Another famous work of this type, the so-called Toccata and Fugue in D minor (BWV 565), is probably not by Bach but, like a number of anonymous eighteenth-century works, was apparently attributed by manuscript copyists to a well-known composer whose style it was thought to resemble.

---

[7]The Schübler collection is named after the publisher, Johann Georg Schübler of Zella, in Germany.

[8]Many Baroque works in minor keys were originally notated with fewer accidentals in the key signature than is now customary. This has no bearing on their tonality, however, since the accidentals are supplied where needed in the score. Bach's so-called Dorian prelude and fugue is as fully tonal as any of the composer's works.

Bach's "Clavier" Works

In addition to his organ *praeludia*, throughout his life Bach composed similar pieces for unspecified keyboard instrument. Lacking pedal parts, these probably were most often played on the harpsichord. But as they remain playable on other instruments they are best referred to simply as keyboard or "clavier" works. This distinguishes them from Bach's suites and a few other works that are either explicitly for harpsichord or whose French style and genre calls for the specific capabilities of that instrument.[9]

Most of the clavier pieces were composed, at least in principle, for use in teaching. Among them are the fifteen two- and fifteen three-part **inventions**— short pieces in imitative texture that Bach first gathered together, alongside other pedagogic pieces, in the Little Keyboard Book for Wilhelm Friedemann Bach. This was a manuscript collection that he presented to his oldest son in 1720, a few months after the latter's ninth birthday.[10] Two years later Sebastian completed the first of the two volumes of his more advanced collection of pedagogic pieces, the *Well-Tempered Clavier*.

The *Well-Tempered Clavier*

Each volume of the *Well-Tempered Clavier* consists of twenty-four preludes and fugues, one in each of the twenty-four major and minor keys. The title refers to any of various systems of keyboard tuning, among them modern equal temperament, that made such a work possible. It will be recalled that *clavier* means any musical keyboard; a **temperament** is any of various ways of tuning such an instrument to permit its playing in more than one key. Temperament involves the intentional mistuning of certain intervals—thirds and fifths—in order to produce pure octaves. For example, three pure thirds (C–E, E–G♯, G♯–B♯) do not yield a pure octave; B♯ is slightly lower than C unless the thirds are tempered, that is, tuned slightly wider (the upper note sharper) than pure. Likewise, the circle of fifths—C–G, G–D, D–A, and so on to E♯–B♯—produces a true circle, with B♯ the same as C, only when some (or all) of the fifths are tuned a little narrower (the upper note lower) than pure. The exact amount by which each fifth is tempered depends on the system of temperament chosen.

In keyboard temperaments from before the eighteenth century, the most frequently used intervals were tuned very purely but certain others were intentionally left audibly discordant. Such temperaments favored the use of the most commonly employed keys but forced composers to avoid keys having more than two or three flats or sharps in the key signature. "Well-tempered" tempera-

---

[9]Bach's keyboard suites include six so-called English Suites, six French Suites, and six larger suites published under the title *Partitas*. Despite the varying titles, all combine the basic French dance types with Italian and German stylistic elements, including whole movements—the preludes of the English Suites—in the style of the Italian concerto.

[10]The three-part inventions are also known as *sinfonias*, their title in J. S. Bach's revised version of 1723. Bach had designated them fantasias in the Little Keyboard Book for W. F. Bach.

Figure 11.1 Harpsichord in the Bachhaus, Eisenach (inventory no. 177), by an unknown maker, Thuringia (Germany), early eighteenth century. Bach and his students might have played his *Well-Tempered Clavier* and other works on unpretentious instruments such as this (compare with the decorated French harpsichord shown in Figure 10.1).

ments evened out these distinctions, making all keys usable; modern equal temperament is one such system, but others exist and it is uncertain which one or ones Bach used.

Previous composers, notably the South German Johann Caspar Ferdinand Fischer (ca. 1665–1746), had written collections similar in plan to Bach's *Well-Tempered Clavier*.[11] But most had stopped short of including all twenty-four keys, and none had produced a collection approaching Bach's in size or stylistic diversity. Moreover, with Bach, unlike some of his predecessors, the preludes are generally equal in length and musical significance to their accompanying fugues. Although not intended for public performance, many movements in the *Well-Tempered Clavier* provide opportunities for expressive playing as well as virtuoso display. At least some movements probably derive from earlier works that, like other surviving clavier pieces, Bach might have performed for friends or at the princely courts that he occasionally visited throughout his career.[12]

---

[11]Several fugues from Bach's *Well-Tempered Clavier* incorporate thematic material from Fischer's *Ariadne musica* (Augsburg [?], 1702), suggesting that Bach knew the latter work.

[12]Among Bach's important clavier works not included in the *Well-Tempered Clavier* are seven toccatas as well as the work known as the Chromatic Fantasia and Fugue in D minor. All probably date from before his departure from Weimar in 1717.

Contradicting later impressions of Bach as a musical conservative obsessed with strict counterpoint, the first volume of the *Well-Tempered Clavier* is characterized above all by its unfailingly rich variety. Its preludes range from the improvisatory one in B♭ to the highly symmetrical binary form of the one in A minor. Its fugues include both the short, invention-like one in E minor and the massive five-part double fugue in C♯ minor. The second volume, completed in the early 1740s, is similarly conceived. For this reason it is somewhat arbitrary to select any one prelude-and-fugue pair for study; every movement in both volumes repays careful attention.

The Prelude and Fugue in G from Book 1

This pair of movements (anthology, Selection 28) is of special interest for several reasons. First, its prelude is one of several in the first volume that retains some tenuous connections to the improvised harpsichord preludes of the seventeenth-century tradition: its motivic material consists largely of broken chords, as is true of a number of other preludes in the volume as well. Secondly, the fugue, in three voices, is one of the relatively small number by Bach that systematically illustrates a series of different fugal techniques. Table 11.2 summarizes its formal design. The first exposition (mm. 1–14) presents the subject in upright form; the second exposition uses the inversion of the subject (mm. 20–30); the third exposition uses both forms of the subject (mm. 38–46). In the final portion of the fugue, both forms of the subject are employed in stretto. (For explanations of these terms, see Box 11.1.)

Despite its methodical use of these highly technical compositional devices, the fugue is anything but a dry, pedantic exercise. On the contrary, Bach chose a subject whose rhythm seems to allude to the **passepied,** a dance in triple time that is musically a quick version of the minuet. Moreover, a bridge passage within the first exposition (mm. 9–10) introduces a lively motive in sixteenth notes reminiscent of the type of solo violin figuration found in Italian concertos of the time. In short, the fugue is a virtuoso display piece, its dramatic qualities intensified by its fugal elements.

EIGHTEENTH-CENTURY KEYBOARD MUSIC IN FRANCE

Until after 1750, keyboard composers in France largely continued in the traditions that had been established in the previous century. The chief difference was the increasing composition of pieces that did not fall into standard seventeenth-century genres. Composers of *pièces d'orgue* wrote fewer cantus firmus and paraphrase settings, favoring free compositions. The *pièce de clavecin*, although continuing to employ standard dance rhythms, more often than not bore a descriptive title—the name of a person, place, or expressive characteristic that its music was supposed to represent. Such a work, which is intended to depict or describe something or someone, is often referred to as a **character piece.**

It is not always clear how seriously the titles of French *pièces de clavecin* are to be taken. Some of the names attached to pieces may be dedications, indicating

TABLE 11.2
J. S. Bach: *Well-Tempered Clavier*, part 1, fugue in G

	Rectus (R) Exposition	Episode	*Inversus* (I) Exposition	Episode	Exposition Using R and I	Episode
Soprano	G x		{D} x		e— x	
Tenor	D +		{G} x		x {G}/e	
Bass	G—		x {G}		+	
Measure	1	15	20	31	38	47

	Stretto (R)	Episode	Stretto (R)	Episode	Exposition (I)	Episode	Stretto	Coda
Soprano	(b)		(D)				(b/G)	—
Tenor			(D)		x		({G})	
Bass	(b)				{G}		(G)	
Measure	51	56	60b	65	69b	73	76	83

letters = keys of normal fugal entries (real answers)
X/Y (slash between letters) = entry *on* note X but *in* key Y
{letters in curly brackets} = inverted entry
x, + = countersubjects (+ also used as bridge motive)
(symbols in parentheses) = incomplete or highly altered entry
— (dash) = bridge (free continuation of an entry)
R = *rectus* (upright) form of subject
I = *inversus* (inverted) form of subject

that the music was written for or commissioned by some person, but not necessarily implying that the character of the music reflects the character of that person. On the other hand, **programmatic** works—instrumental compositions that represent an idea or a narrative—were composed throughout the Baroque, in some cases with the subject of the music clearly spelled out in titles or a detailed preface.[13] Where such indications are lacking, it would be questionable to read complex narratives into these generally short pieces. But as vocal music of the period reveals, Baroque composers had at their disposal a large vocabulary of meaningful musical symbols and expressive devices. When combined with a suggestive title, these allowed the listener to draw associations between the musical events of a given piece and various extramusical ideas: images, emotions, or personal characteristics.

François Couperin

The most important French composers of harpsichord music from around 1700 and later are Rameau, whose vocal works were discussed in Chapter 8, and François Couperin (1668–1733). Couperin was a member of a musical family; his uncle Louis (ca. 1626–1661) was one of the earliest French Baroque keyboard composers whose works have survived, noted particularly for his unmeasured preludes. François succeeded to his uncle's organist position in Paris in 1685, and he soon became organist and later harpsichordist as well at the royal court. In that capacity he composed and performed chamber works for various wind and string instruments with continuo accompaniment. Among these are some of the earliest solo and trio sonatas (see Chapter 12) composed in France, as well as two collections of suites in which Couperin made a point of combining the French and Italian styles. His title *Les goûts réunis* (The reunited styles) for the second set, published at Paris in 1724, reflects the lively interest during Couperin's lifetime in the differences and relative merits of the two styles. Although Couperin and his French contemporaries must have been highly conscious of the Italian elements in these pieces, such as the use of simple "singing" melodies in some slow movements, French aspects remain predominant, notably the reliance on dance genres and the careful notation of every detail of ornamentation and rhythm.[14]

Couperin also wrote two organ masses and sacred vocal music. But he is known primarily for his four books of harpsichord music, which contain a total of 220 distinct pieces. His two daughters continued the family tradition;

---

[13] Programmatic compositions depicting battles were written by Frescobaldi and Biber (see Chapter 12), among others. Johann Kuhnau (1660–1722), Bach's predecessor as cantor at Leipzig, published a set of six Biblical Sonatas for keyboard instrument (Leipzig, 1700) on subjects such as the battle of David and Goliath and Jacob's marriage; each work is accompanied by a detailed prose account of the underlying story.

[14] Although Couperin's collection *Les goûts réunis* contains some movements in Italian style, he had made his closest approach to the pure Italian style in several sonatas for instrumental ensemble composed in the 1690s; three of these were included in his later publication *Les nations* (Paris, 1726) alongside a fourth, more recently composed, sonata.

both were musicians, the younger one (Marguerite-Antoinette) succeeding him as royal chamber musician.

Couperin bears the same relationship to the harpsichord that Frédéric Chopin (1810–49) does to the piano. No one has written harpsichord music that is more idiomatically conceived for the instrument, that uses it so imaginatively, or that is so meticulously composed and so precisely notated to take advantage of its particular capabilities. Many works of both composers are often erroneously regarded as miniatures. But although many pieces are short in duration, the great majority are so well crafted and contain such original musical ideas that they can hardly be described as trifles. This is true even when, as is often the case with Couperin, the pieces bear humorous or punning titles. Like most later Baroque composers, Couperin generally avoided strict counterpoint of the type found in the fugal keyboard works of Froberger or Bach. But there is a strong contrapuntal component in most of his music, as well as a sophistication of harmony and modulation that goes far beyond what is found in the so-called rococo or *galant* pieces of many younger contemporaries in France.

Couperin carefully oversaw the production of his four volumes of harpsichord music, insuring that, among other things, the ornament signs were precisely drawn and placed. Moreover, like Caccini and Frescobaldi one hundred years earlier, he provided a guide for the performance of his music. This took the form of a short treatise, *L'art de toucher le clavecin* (The art of playing the harpsichord, Paris, 1716), which proved widely influential. Couperin's keyboard music was influential as well, furnishing models for character pieces by the next two generations of composers, including Bach's son Carl Philipp Emanuel and other Germans. J. S. Bach, who had eagerly collected works by Couperin's French predecessors, knew at least some of his music; one piece appears in the second Little Keyboard Book for Anna Magdalena Bach, which served as a collection of study material for the Bach children.[15]

Ornaments in French Harpsichord Music

For modern performers, one of the most distinctive elements of French Baroque keyboard notation is the presence of numerous ornament signs. We may define ornaments in this music as small, stereotyped melodic figures consisting of short notes that decorate a longer one. Ornaments are best distinguished from *embellishments*, which involve greater numbers of small note values that cannot be expressed by simple signs and must therefore be written out. The presence of numerous ornaments and their notation through distinctive signs was, as we have seen, a defining feature of the French style of the later Baroque. Within this repertory, keyboard music was unique in that composers used a constantly growing number of symbols to indicate precisely which ornaments were to

---

[15]In addition to the Little Keyboard Book for his son Wilhelm Friedemann Bach, J. S. Bach presented his second wife, Anna Magdalena, with two manuscript books of keyboard music, dated 1722 and 1725; both contain suites and individual dances, including many by Bach's contemporaries in the 1725 book.

be played. The greater notational precision of French—as opposed to Italian—keyboard music in this regard might reflect the fact that much of this repertory was published for performance by amateurs, who required more guidance. But the same trend appears in French organ music, which only professionals would have played. Evidently, French keyboard composers had precise intentions about the melodic content of their works for both organ and harpsichord that they expected players to observe scrupulously—professionals as well as amateurs.

Despite the proliferation of ornament signs, the basic ornaments were few in number and, probably, quite standard in execution. But the signs and even the names for them varied from one composer to another. For this reason, most French harpsichord books included tables explaining what each ornament sign meant. These tables cannot serve as guides to the precise interpretation of the signs, since the exact rhythm of an ornament cannot be precisely notated; that is why symbols were used in the first place! Performers who specialize in this music base their interpretations of the ornament signs on published ornament tables together with information from treatises and other documents, as well as their own analysis of the music and their experience performing it.

The anthology (Selection 29) includes extracts from the ornament tables of the three most important French harpsichord composers of the later Baroque: Jean-Henri D'Anglebert (1689), François Couperin (1716), and Jean-Philippe Rameau (1724). Rameau apparently based his system on D'Anglebert's, and therefore their ornament signs occupy the first two columns of the table. There are three basic ornaments: the appoggiatura or *port de voix*; the mordent or *pincé*; and the trill or *tremblement*. Most of the remaining entries in the tables represent combinations or variations of these basic ornaments. In addition, there are various types of arpeggiation, some involving the addition of nonchord tones (acciaccaturas). Couperin used a number of further signs not shown here, including a sort of comma used to mark the ends of certain phrases (as in m. 16 of *La reine des cœurs*).

Couperin's *La reine des cœurs* and *La Couperin*

Couperin published his *pièces de clavecin* in numbered suites, of which there are twenty-seven in all. Couperin used the term *ordre* instead of *suite*. But as in the works of other French composers, there is little to unify the movements of each suite, apart from the use of the same key and perhaps a general commonality of style or tone. It is unlikely that players always performed all movements of each suite in their entirety.

The five suites of Couperin's first volume (published 1713) include the traditional dances—allemandes, courantes, sarabandes, and gigues, alongside others—in what had become by 1700 the traditional order. There are numerous character pieces as well, with such titles as "The Bees," "The Sentiments," and "Fanfare for the Followers of Diana"—this last referring to the Roman goddess, and conceivably to some woman named Diane as well. By the fourth book (1730), few untitled dances remain, and the suites are shorter. We shall consider two of the five pieces from the *Vingt-unième ordre* (Twenty-first suite; anthology, Selection 30).

The first piece, *La reine des coeurs* (The queen of hearts), is in $\frac{3}{8}$. It is in binary form and has, for the most part, the regular eight-bar phrasing of a minuet. Yet it does not exactly fit any dance type. This point is emphasized by Couperin's tempo indication, which, characteristically for him, is very precise: *Lentement, et très tendrement* (Slowly and very tenderly). The piece's title is the name of a playing card. But it might also have referred to a particular woman—perhaps one whose personality is represented by the piece's musical character (or at least by its tempo mark!).

The same playful use of titles is evident in the third piece from the suite, *La Couperin*, whose title seems to refer to the composer himself.[16] There was a tradition of musician portraits by French composers; Antoine Forqueray (1672–1745), who played viola da gamba in the royal chamber concerts alongside Couperin, wrote musical portraits not only of Rameau and the violinist Leclair but of himself (these pieces were published posthumously in 1747). Couperin's musical self-portrait bears the modest tempo marking *d'une vivacité modéré* (with moderate vivacity). But to what degree this is or was meant to be a true characterization of Couperin is impossible to say. The piece somewhat resembles an allemande, although its unusual upbeat—a measure containing $2\frac{3}{4}$ beats—is not characteristic of that dance or any other. It is, however, in the expected binary form. As in many such pieces, each half begins and ends with similar melodic gestures but is otherwise freely composed.

If one is seeking clues to Couperin's personality, one might note the chromatic bass line at the beginning of the piece (mm. 1–4), with suspensions in the upper voices. This suggests a grieving or at least a deeply emotional character. Yet, the next phrase contains a forceful sequence, the left hand striking octaves in measures 5 and 6. This is more in keeping with the vivacious character implied by the tempo mark, as are the ascending sequences in the piece's second half (mm. 13–14, 18–19). It would be reasonable to conclude that Couperin was a changeable character—or that he has been teasing us by inviting us to see him in this difficult-to-characterize piece.

Both pieces illustrate Couperin's ability to make full use of the idiomatic capabilities of the eighteenth-century French harpsichord. For example, in the second half of measure 2 of *La Couperin*, the upper note in each pair of two sixteenths is held out as an eighth note. This not only brings out the melodic line (d♯″–e″–f♯″–g″) but also creates a warmer sonority, contrasting with drier passages such as measure 7–8, where no notes are held out; instead some are marked with staccato signs to insure crisp performance.

---

[16] The fact that the title uses the feminine form of the French definite article, *la*, is irrelevant here. The word *pièce* is feminine, and *all* such titles for Baroque pieces, even those referring to men, are grammatically feminine.

OTHER EIGHTEENTH-CENTURY KEYBOARD COMPOSERS

The eighteenth century saw a tremendous increase in the composition and publication of instrumental and especially keyboard music for the public. By 1760 or so this had turned into a flood as composers and publishers catered to a growing amateur market. The later development of this trend lies beyond our scope, for the music in question is increasingly closer to what we call the Classical and even the Romantic styles than to what we recognize as Baroque. After 1740 or so, the chief genre of eighteenth-century keyboard music became the **sonata**: a multimovement work modeled after sonatas for instrumental ensemble (see Chapter 12).

The sonata was an Italian genre, but already among Couperin's younger contemporaries it was fast encroaching on French soil, and Couperin himself composed sonatas for instrumental ensemble. Although few if any French composers wrote multimovement keyboard sonatas before 1750, many earlier keyboard pieces are close in style and form to sonata movements for the violin and other instruments. This is particularly clear in the case of Rameau, whose harpsichord pieces are in some respects remarkably similar to the one-movement keyboard sonatas of his close contemporary Domenico Scarlatti. Works by the two may serve as examples of the types of solo keyboard music in vogue as the middle of the century approached.

Rameau

Having begun his career as a church organist, Rameau turned to opera only in his fifties. The sense of drama and the feeling for wonderfully evocative dance music that so animate his operas had been earlier developed in his harpsichord works, which he published in three volumes (1706, 1724, and 1729 or 1730). As with Couperin, the first volume is relatively conventional; it contains a single suite, comprising an unmeasured prelude—one of the last to be published—and a series of dances. The later volumes contain increasing numbers of character pieces. Unlike Couperin, Rameau was not averse to incorporating the unrestrained virtuosity of the Italian style into his music, as we saw from his use of the da capo aria (*ariette*) in *Les indes galantes*. His keyboard music includes virtuoso devices that might have embarrassed Couperin: flying leaps, long arpeggios and scales, even glissandos and hand crossings. Nevertheless, Rameau's keyboard music retains important elements of the French style. It is precisely notated, down to the numerous small ornaments, admitting little improvised embellishment or other alteration, and it continues to employ the traditional binary and rondeau forms and, frequently, the traditional dance rhythms as well.

Two pieces from Rameau's *Nouvelles suites de clavecin* (New harpsichord suites) of 1729 or 1730 illustrate his approach to the keyboard. *Les sauvages* (anthology, Selection 31a) is the original version of the vocal duet and chorus from the fourth *entrée* of *Les indes galantes*. Its title (The savages) refers to the North American Indians whose dancing is supposed to have inspired it. Some of the wildness that an eighteenth-century Parisian saw in their dance might be perceived in the leaps and arpeggios of the main theme, as well as in its repeated notes (m. 6), a rare device in French keyboard music. Nevertheless, the underlying rhythm is close to that of the *anglaise*, a dance in cut time similar to the gavotte. The form is that of a rondeau with two *couplets* or contrasting sections.

L'Egiptienne (The Egyptian; anthology, Selection 31b) is another piece inspired by the eighteenth-century European fascination with ethnicity; the title refers not to the actual inhabitants of Egypt but to a Gypsy woman. Perhaps the piece's G-minor tonality and twisting melodic lines suggested a slight exoticism that contemporary French listeners would have identified with the Gypsies or Roma people. Today we avoid such ethnic stereotyping, but it was an accepted way of thinking about culture in eighteenth-century Europe, applied by the French to themselves as well as others (as we saw in Rameau's *Les indes galantes*).

Whatever the implications of its title, the piece has an expressive, even plaintive character, thanks to its insistence on the half step d″–e♭″ (as in mm. 2–3 and 62–66). At the same time, it is clearly a virtuoso keyboard piece, many of its motivic ideas deriving from the technical feat of hand crossing. In measure 2, for example, the left hand enters on a note that places it more than an octave above the right hand. Similar crossings of the hands occur throughout the piece.

Also notable is the piece's form. It is essentially in binary form, like our two selections by Couperin.[17] But whereas the two halves of Couperin's pieces are largely independent of one another, here the second half is in part a restatement of the first half. Indeed, all but the first ten measures of the first half is restated a fifth lower in the second half (compare mm. 11–36 with mm. 50–76). This sort of restatement, in which material from the first section returns later, can be described as **recapitulation**; the term implies not only the restatement of material but also its transposition (where necessary) to the tonic. Binary forms by Couperin, Bach, and other Baroque composers often employ brief recapitulated passages, but those in Rameau's piece are far more extensive. Recapitulation in this sense reflects an eighteenth-century trend also found in the sonatas of the Bach sons and other younger contemporaries, and it would become an important element in the sonata-allegro form of the Classical and Romantic styles.

Domenico Scarlatti

In the preface to his 1724 volume, Rameau gave the impression that he had invented the types of hand crossing technique seen in *L'Egiptienne*. Yet comparable devices can be found occasionally in keyboard music from as early as 1600 or so, and by 1724 they must have been a familiar trick to keyboard virtuosos. Today the best known of those virtuosos is Domenico Scarlatti (1685–1757), son of the opera composer Alessandro Scarlatti.

---

[17]Couperin, like Rameau, also wrote numerous pieces in rondeau form.

Born in Naples on the southwestern coast of Italy, Domenico at first must have aimed at following in his father's footsteps, learning to play the harpsichord brilliantly while preparing for a career as a composer of operas and other vocal music. Indeed, for the first two decades of the century he was active as an opera composer in Naples, Venice, and Rome. It was at the latter city, around 1707, that he met Handel, with whom he is said to have played a competition on harpsichord and organ, reportedly winning on the harpsichord while Handel took the honors on the organ.

In 1720, however, Domenico took a position in Lisbon as the harpsichord teacher of the Portuguese princess Maria Barbara. When the latter married the Spanish crown prince Ferdinand in 1729, Scarlatti followed her first to Seville and then to Madrid, where he spent the rest of his life. Little is known about Scarlatti's activities during this period, although it has been argued that this is when he composed the bulk of his keyboard music, presumably for performance by himself or his royal pupil. He left behind some 550 one-movement pieces, each bearing the title *sonata*.

These one-movement sonatas probably grew out of a seventeenth-century tradition of improvisatory toccata-like pieces, in which Domenico's father, Alessandro, evidently excelled. It is possible that Scarlatti also absorbed ideas from the rich Iberian tradition of solo keyboard music, although his sonatas show little evidence of his having known the great organ fantasias (called *tientos*) of Juan Cabanilles (1644–1712), organist at Valencia Cathedral, whose imagination and contrapuntal rigor at times approach those of J. S. Bach. But the possibility remains of mutual exchanges with Iberian contemporaries such as Vicente Rodríguez (1690–1760), Cabanilles's successor at Valencia, or the Portuguese organist Carlos de Seixas (1704–42), a colleague of Scarlatti's at Lisbon, both of whom composed virtuoso sonatas in one to three movements.

Thirty of Scarlatti's early sonatas, published in 1738, rightly gave him the reputation of a composer of capricious, sometimes gratuitously virtuosic pieces full of hand crossing and other technical tricks. Many later pieces employ those devices as well, although the frequency of hand crossing gradually diminished. It is sometimes supposed that this was because hand crossings were made difficult by Scarlatti's increasing girth (or perhaps that of his royal pupil). But musical reasons were probably involved as well, for technical tricks are rarely the main substance of Scarlatti's mature sonatas. Like Rameau, Scarlatti might have derived the initial inspiration for a few pieces from a purely technical idea such as hand crossing. But other ideas seem to have come from visual and aural images, including the sounds of trumpets, mandolins, and guitars, all of which are imitated in his sonatas. These works also show ingenious harmonic progressions and motivic development, as well as striking effects idiomatic to the eighteenth-century Italian harpsichord. Almost every sonata is in in binary form, and many contain the same type of extensive recapitulation found in Rameau's pieces. Yet they never repeat themselves, revealing constantly varied approaches to modulation, recapitulation, and other aspects of form and style.

Because none of Domenico's own manuscripts of the sonatas survive and only a handful were published during his own lifetime, it remains quite unclear when most were composed or in what form they were meant to be played. Most are preserved within two sets of manuscripts, both of which may have been owned first by Queen Maria Barbara and later by the castrato Farinelli, who, after his retirement from opera, had served as Scarlatti's colleague at the Spanish court. In these manuscripts, most of the pieces, most of the sonatas are grouped into sets of two or occasionally three works in the same key. It is not known whether Scarlatti himself was responsible for these groupings or even whether the sonatas within each group were composed at the same time. In the twentieth century, Scarlatti's sonatas were assigned numbers by the American harpsichordist Ralph Kirkpatrick, who made them a lifetime object of study. His "K" numbers, which run from 1 to 555, are in principle chronological. But although based on certain plausible hypotheses about the development of Scarlatti's style, the ordering is largely conjectural.

The Sonatas K. 181–82

This pair of pieces (anthology, Selection 32) illustrates aspects of Scarlatti's music from perhaps the middle of his career. Both are in A major and, like the great majority of Scarlatti's sonatas, in binary form. The second (K. 182) includes a few brief instances of hand crossing (mm. 15–16, 21–22, etc.). More significant, however, are several other devices idiomatic to the harpsichord that are particularly characteristic of Scarlatti's writing.

The most distinctive of these is the simultaneous **acciaccatura**, first heard in K. 181 on the second beat of measure 3. The harmony here is V^7–a dominant seventh chord. Yet the left hand contains not the third (g♯) but the fourth (a) of the chord, a dissonance. The same device occurs on the fourth beat of measure 7, the first beat of measure 27, and elsewhere. French composers also used acciaccaturas, but only as momentary dissonances played as passing notes during the arpeggiation of a chord. Here the dissonance is struck together with the main chord tones, producing a sharp, crunching accent on a stringed keyboard instrument. The effect is particularly striking when it occurs as part of a series of repeated chords, as in measures 22–28.

Unprepared, unresolved accents were an occasional feature of the *seconda pratica* at the beginning of the Baroque. But then they were employed for expressive effects—specifically for grief and other "negative" emotions. Scarlatti, however, seems to have employed such devices simply for their startling sound, and perhaps also for the sheer pleasure of breaking rules, producing what the Italians called *bizzarria*. Elsewhere, Scarlatti often broke other rules as well, writing parallel fifths and octaves, chords that contain "incorrect" doublings, and so forth. Yet he rarely did so irrationally; often the "incorrect" idea is treated like a motive, developed in various ways in the course of a sonata.

Another notable feature of Scarlatti's style is his frequent reliance on sheer repetition, whether of single chords or whole measures and phrases. One manifestation of this, the frequent use of recapitulation in the second half of a binary form, reflects a general eighteenth-century trend. Repetition on smaller scales is also common, reflecting the general eighteenth-century preference for regular patterning. Yet Scarlatti uses repetition not merely for the sake of symmetry but as a means of dramatic intensification. For example, K. 182 contains a passage in which the right hand seems to get stuck on the note a″. The note is repeated directly or in alternation with just one other note through a whole series of chords (mm. 27–32). In the course of the passage the chords become thicker, growing from consonant four-note sonorities (m. 27) to dissonant seven-note harmonies (m. 31). This is a way of producing the effect of a crescendo on a nondynamic instrument such as the harpsichord—as Scarlatti certainly would have known from long experience of improvising at the keyboard.

Although they are called sonatas, Scarlatti's pieces are only distantly related to the sonata-allegro form of the later eighteenth century. For example, reflecting the approach used in older binary forms, Scarlatti usually avoids recapitulating the opening measures of a sonata, instead beginning the recapitulation at a point taken from somewhere in the middle of the first section, as in both of our sonatas.[18] But one feature used in many later sonata forms is present in both K. 181 and K. 182: the introduction of passages in the minor mode to provide expressive contrast or relief within a predominantly major movement. Often such a passage is part of a modulation to a new key, as in K. 181 (mm. 16–29). In this case the modulation also includes an ingenious **enharmonic** progression, that is, one involving the reinterpretation of an accidentally altered note. Here the note c″ is converted to its enharmonic equivalent b♯′ (mm. 19–20), permitting a modulation from A minor to F-sharp minor.

In Scarlatti's sonatas, sophisticated transitional passages such as this often follow seemingly innocent opening material. Indeed, both of these sonatas begin with apparently simple themes of the type often found in the *galant* works of Scarlatti's lesser contemporaries. The somewhat dim-witted simplicity of these themes hardly prepares one for what follows, but that is a part of the humor that pervades Scarlatti's music. Usually the simplicity returns in the final phrase or two, as if to say that, despite all the fuss and technical fireworks, nothing out of the ordinary has really happened. K. 182 is an exception, however. Unlike most major-key pieces, whose excursions to the minor mode are only temporary, it ends in A minor. Yet the liveliness of the closing phrase makes it unlikely that this minor-mode ending is to be interpreted as sad or otherwise "negative." Instead, this ending might be understood as yet another example of *bizzarria*, an intentional surprise meant to produce a sort of puzzled delight in the listener.

---

[18] In both sonatas K. 181 and K. 182 the second half begins with material closely derived from the opening of the first section, a common practice in Baroque binary forms. But because this material does not exactly parallel any passage in the first section and is not in the tonic, it cannot be described as a recapitulation.

CHAPTER 12

BAROQUE MUSIC FOR INSTRUMENTAL ENSEMBLE
The Sonata

The sonatas, concertos, and other instrumental genres of the seventeenth and eighteenth centuries are among the most familiar parts of the Baroque repertory. A number of them, mostly works from the first half of the eighteenth century, such as J. S. Bach's flute sonatas and the Vivaldi violin concertos known as *The Four Seasons*, have long been in the modern concert repertory and are among the first examples of "early music" encountered by many musicians and listeners. This survey has saved them for last, since the instrumental concerto, although not the sonata, was among the last distinctive types of music to emerge during the Baroque, and to a considerable degree the styles and forms of both derived from those of vocal music. Moreover, the training of most Baroque musicians began with singing, and good instrumentalists then as now learned phrasing, breathing, and other vital aspects of performance by studying vocal music and listening to good singers.

Isolated examples of polyphonic music for instrumental ensemble are preserved from the fourteenth century and perhaps earlier. But a vigorous tradition of composing such music, as opposed to various unwritten traditions, dates from only the sixteenth century. Even then, the repertory, consisting chiefly of dances and contrapuntal pieces such as fantasias, was usually written for unspecified instruments. Composers did not concern themselves with the actual instrumental sonorities, and any idiomatic instrumental effects or melodic decoration would have been added improvisatorily by the players. With the turn of the seventeenth century, composers such as Giovanni Gabrieli began not only to specify the instrumental participants in their ensemble music but also to make use of idiomatic devices particular to one instrument or another. Some composers, including Gabrieli and Frescobaldi, did so only occasionally; most of their canzonas and sonatas remain for unspecified instruments. Others, however, eagerly explored the possibility of writing music that exploited the capabilities of particular instruments.

For the first time, it became necessary for composers to be familiar with instruments—their ranges, techniques, and the types of figuration that each can and cannot play conveniently. Nowadays it is taken for granted that learning such things is part of the training of a composer, but that view emerged only gradually in the course of the seventeenth century, as the number of instruments routinely employed in serious music making increased. Although preceding chapters have included some remarks about particular instruments, it will be useful to summarize some of the main features of the instruments most frequently used in seventeenth- and eighteenth-century music for instrumental ensemble before proceeding to the works themselves.

THE CHIEF ENSEMBLE INSTRUMENTS OF THE BAROQUE

String Instruments

The violin family, already in widespread use for dance music during the sixteenth century, had become the main instrumental component of French and Italian ensemble music by the mid-seventeenth century. Music for the quieter lute and viola da gamba continued to be composed well into the eighteenth century, but these instruments could not compete in volume with the violin, which therefore dominated the ensemble genres of sonata, concerto, and overture. The viol and the violin represent distinct families of bowed string instruments that had emerged at about the same time, the late fifteenth century; the viol was not a predecessor of the violin. The Renaissance and Baroque members of the violin family were, moreover, distinct from their modern counterparts, with different construction and different performance techniques. In addition, their technique and to some degree their construction varied with time and place; for instance, distinct types of performance practice and bows were associated with the French and the Italian styles, respectively, of the seventeenth century.

The French style, which centered on the playing of overtures and dances in Lullian opera and ballet, emphasized tightly controlled ornaments, precise articulation, and rhythmic exactness. Ensembles such as the French king's Twenty-Four Violins were renowned for their rhythmic precision and unanimity of ensemble. These aspects were enforced by conventions or rules governing ornamentation and bowing that all members of the ensemble had to master; the relatively short bow used in this style made for greater ease in the frequent retaking of the bow required in playing dance music. Italian playing, on the other hand, tended to emphasize facility in embellishments and quick passagework, and sustained melodic lines in slow movements, for which a somewhat longer bow was favored. Both traditions differed from present-day playing in the more restricted use of vibrato and the more frequent use of open strings—which were of gut, not metal—and of low left-hand positions generally. Bowing in both styles involved a greater number of short strokes, French players frequently retaking the bow in order to place downbows on the strong beats of each measure. It would be wrong, however, to conclude that Baroque violin playing involved a lesser degree of virtuosity than that of later periods. Italian-style works from throughout the Baroque include difficult passagework in high positions, sometimes involving exotic bow strokes. Even in the French style, the required precision of ornamentation and rhythm makes considerable technical demands.

Figure 12.1 Violin by Jacob Stainer, Absam bei Innsbruck (Austria), 1668. America's Shrine to Music Museum, Vermillion, South Dakota, Board of Trustees in memory of Arne B. and Jeanne F. Larson, 1989 (no. 4548). The violinist-composer Heinrich Biber owned a violin by this maker, from whom he also ordered instruments for his employers at Kroměříž and Salzburg. Note the relatively short neck, which forms a straight line with the body of the instrument. On modern violins the neck is longer and angled back, and most surviving instruments from the Baroque, unlike this one, have been altered accordingly. See Figure 1.4 for a typically short Baroque bow. Photograph by Simon Spicer.

The Baroque viola, which furnished as many as three inner parts in some ensembles (including the Twenty-Four Violins), tended to be somewhat larger than later examples although normally tuned the same way, a fifth below the violin. (The four strings of the violin are tuned g, d′, a′, and e″; of the viola, c, g, d′, and a′.) The cello was a relatively late addition to the violin family, the lowest part of the ensemble originally being provided by the bass violin, a somewhat larger instrument that often descended to B♭′ (the cello's four strings are tuned C, G, d, and a). Cello-like instruments, sometimes with an additional fifth string (useful for high solo passages), became common only toward the end of the seventeenth century. Double-bass instruments, used to play bass lines an octave lower than written, were rare in Baroque ensembles before the eighteenth century. The word *violone*, found in many Baroque scores, simply means "big string instrument" and often refers to the bass violin, cello, or bass viola da gamba, not a true double bass. By the eighteenth century, however, double-bass instruments were being used in many larger ensembles. Their precise construction and technique varied, but the instrument usually retained characteristics of the viol family, such as tuning in fourths rather than fifths (as is true of the double bass to this day).

Modern players and instrument builders have reconstructed the various techniques and types of instrument and bow used in the Baroque. As with keyboards, they have relied heavily on surviving instruments and on documentary sources. Notable among the latter are the prefaces to several collections of suites and sonatas for instrumental ensemble by the organist-composer Georg Muffat (1653–1704), who had known both Lully and Corelli before taking up positions at Salzburg and later Passau in southern Germany. Thanks to his unique background, Muffat was able to provide instructions on how to play in both the French (Lullian) and Italian styles of the late seventeenth century. A treatise by another Salzburg composer, Mozart's father Leopold (1719–87), is of great value to understanding violin playing in the first half of the eighteenth century although published as late as 1756.[1]

The predominance of the violin in Baroque instrumental music gave it a vast repertory of sonatas, concertos, and other works, and violinist-composers were among the most important writers of instrumental music, especially in Italy. Sonatas and concertos with solo cello parts also were written, especially after 1700, and there is a small eighteenth-century repertory with parts for solo viola, mainly by German composers. Other string instruments continued to be cultivated alongside members of the violin family. In the early seventeenth century, composers in France, England, and Italy continued to write polyphonic fantasias and other works for combinations of one or more viols with lute, organ, or harp. There is also a later repertory of solo pieces by such composers as the Frenchman Marin Marais (1656–1728) for viola da gamba (with continuo) and the German Silvius Leopold Weiss (1686–1750) for the lute. The harp and the guitar were also employed throughout the Baroque (in distinctly Baroque forms) and have small solo repertories. But in ensemble music they were largely limited to serving as continuo instruments or for special effects in opera.

Woodwinds

Woodwinds of the Renaissance had included both flutes and double reeds. Most types were built in bass to soprano and even sopranino (piccolo) sizes, so that complete ensembles or **consorts** could be constituted from examples of a single type of instrument, as was also done in the case of the violin or viol. This

---

[1]See bibliography under "Instruments and Instrumental Practice" for editions and translations of Muffat's and Mozart's writings.

became less true during the Baroque, when the higher members of the wood-wind families came to be used as solo instruments while the lower ones, with the exception of the bassoon, were abandoned or limited to occasional use. Like their Renaissance counterparts, Baroque woodwinds were built entirely of various types of wood, metal being used only for a few keys on certain types or sizes of instrument.

In the seventeenth century, woodwinds were employed mainly to add color or contrast in works for string-based ensembles, or as optional alternates to members of the violin family in sonatas and other pieces. It is likely that woodwind consorts were also used, as in previous centuries, for impromptu transcriptions of music originally scored for voices or other instruments and in unwritten dance music. Sonatas, concertos, and other works with idiomatic solo

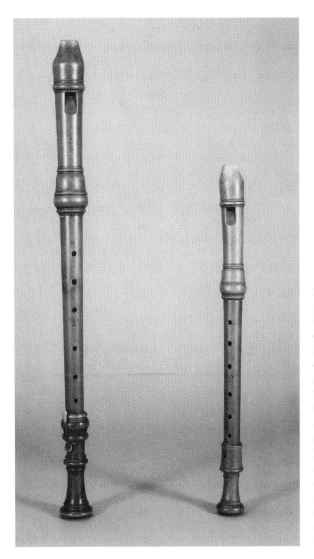

Figure 12.2 Alto and tenor recorders by Jacob Denner, Imperial City of Nürnberg (Nuremberg, Germany), ca. 1715. Ex coll.: Albrecht Kleinschmidt, Neu Ulm, Germany. America's Shrine to Music Museum, Vermillion, South Dakota. Purchase funds gift of Cindy and Tom Lillibridge, Bonesteel, South Dakota, and Linda and John Lillibridge, Burke, South Dakota, 1997 (nos. 6043–4). A single key on the larger (tenor) instrument allows the player to reach the lowest of the seven tone holes (an eighth hole for the thumb is on the back of the instrument). Photograph by Simon Spicer.

woodwind parts were first composed in significant numbers only in the early eighteenth century, using forms and styles similar to those found in music for strings.

Eighteenth-century woodwind players normally mastered more than one type of instrument and were often expected to double on two or more (e.g., oboe and recorder), sometimes switching between instruments within a single multi-movement work. As in string playing, great emphasis was placed on the precise articulation of notes and the controlled performance of ornaments. The eighteenth century saw the publication of numerous instructional manuals for woodwind instruments, especially the recorder and flute, reflecting the popularity of the latter among amateurs. Among these are the flute treatises of the French composer Jacques Hotteterre (1674–1763) and the German flutist, composer, and flute maker Johann Joachim Quantz (1697–1773).

Flutes included both **recorders,** held downward, and **transverse flutes,** held sideways like the modern flute. Both types date back at least to the early Re-

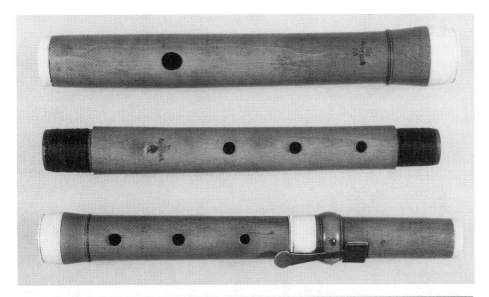

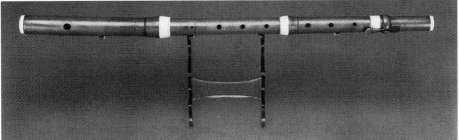

Figure 12.3 Transverse flute by Philip Borkens, Amsterdam, ca. 1725–50, its three pieces shown disassembled (a) and mounted on a display stand (b). America's Shrine to Music Museum, Vermillion, South Dakota. Board of Trustees, 1994 (no. 5795). The single key, absent on older seventeenth-century instruments, is for E♭. Photograph by Simon Spicer.

naissance. Older transverse flutes have a sweet or mellow, usually very quiet, sound, and a relatively limited range, which made them less practical for combination with louder instruments than the more brilliant and versatile recorder. But the eighteenth century saw the introduction of relatively powerful flutes that were, in addition, equal in virtuoso capability to the violin and other instruments. During the first third of the eighteenth century, composers employed both recorders and flutes in a large and varied repertory, in both solo and ensemble capacities. The early eighteenth century saw a particular proliferation of sonatas and concertos, as well as arias in operas and cantatas, with flute or recorder parts. After 1740 or so the latter instrument virtually disappeared, but until then the word *flute* most often referred to the recorder. Thus the *flûtes* or *flauti* called for in scores from Lully to J. S. Bach are usually recorders, not flutes, although both composers also used the transverse instrument, specifying it by *flûte d'Allemagne, flauto traverso*, or an equivalent expression.[2] Present-day players often substitute the nineteenth-century silver flute in both recorder and flute parts.

Both types of flute began to undergo substantial changes in the late seventeenth century, gaining expanded ranges and somewhat greater volume as well. Keys, at first entirely absent, were gradually added to the transverse flute over the course of the eighteenth period. But until well after 1750, most transverse flutes had but a single key (those built by Quantz have two), and both types of flute, like all Baroque winds, were easy to play in only a limited number of tonalities. Thus the transverse flute was most often used in tonalities that employ sharps in their key signatures, whereas the recorder was more commonly used in "flat" keys. Such patterns should not be understood as limitations; the association of an instrument with particular keys was as much a part of each instrument as its range and tone color. Composers made good use of these instrumental characteristics, occasionally writing for instruments in "bad" keys in order to create special timbral effects or to give virtuosos a chance to display their mastery of difficult keys; in his *St. John Passion* Bach included flutes in an aria in F minor ("Zerfließe, mein Herze"), using the instruments' dark, somewhat muted color when played in that key to deepen the mournful effect of the aria.

The chief double reed of the Renaissance, the **shawm,** had been a somewhat raucous instrument employed chiefly in loud dance music. Like the flutes, it was built in several sizes, and seventeenth-century shawm bands sometimes served a military function, reflected in the occasional use of double reeds for marches and similar music in theatrical works. But Lully and later composers required a more refined instrument for use in opera and ballet: the result was the **oboe,** believed to have been developed from the shawm by seventeenth-century Dutch instrument makers. By 1700 the oboe had become the chief woodwind, often doubling the violins in larger ensembles and possessing a growing chamber music repertory as well.

---

[2]An important exception occurs in works of the early eighteenth-century Dresden composers Johann David Heinichen, Johann Adolph Hasse, and others, for whom "flute" usually means the transverse flute.

Figure 12.4 Banquet for the coronation of Louis XIV with a double-reed ensemble, 7 June 1654, engraving from Antoine Lepautre, *Le sacre et couronnement de Louis XIV* (Paris, 1717). A band of oboes and bassoons or other double-reed instruments, used for military and ceremonial functions, was employed at the French court throughout the Baroque. The repertory probably consisted largely of dances from ballets and operas.

Like flutes and recorders, oboes were built in various sizes, each playing at a different pitch and favoring particular keys. The regular oboe of the later Baroque had middle C as its lowest note and was, like the recorder, especially favored in "flat" keys. A tenor form, known by the French word *taille* (which could in fact refer to any tenor part), was pitched a fifth lower; a version of the same instrument with a flaring metal bell was known as the **oboe da caccia**. German composers, including Bach, also used an alto instrument based on the note a and used primarily in "sharp" keys; this is referred to as the **oboe d'amore**.

The **bassoon,** another double-reed instrument employed since the later Baroque as the bass of the oboe family, has a distinct history, being derived from the seventeenth-century curtal and dulcian. Bach and his contemporaries in Germany knew both the *Fagott,* usually as part of the continuo group, and the *basson*; the words, used in modern German and French, respectively, for the bassoon, were apparently applied to two different instruments. The *basson,* the more modern one, joins the oboes as the bass of Bach's double-reed group, a practice derived from that of Lully. A double-bass instrument corresponding to

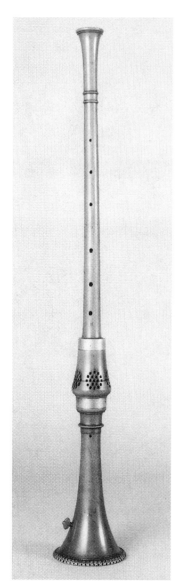

Figure 12.5 Deutsche schalmei by Richard Haka, Amsterdam, ca. 1690. America's Shrine to Music, Vermillion, South Dakota. Board of Trustees, 1988 (no. 4545). Still close in many respects to the sixteenth-century shawm, instruments similar to this one (shown without its double reed) would have furnished the upper line in the ensemble depicted in Figure 12.4 or in Lully's early ballets. Differing only in details, the Baroque oboe was already in use in France when this instrument was made by one of the leading Dutch woodwind makers of his time. Photograph by Simon Spicer.

the modern contrabassoon was occasionally used to double the bass line in works for very large ensemble.

The **clarinet**, a single-reed instrument, originated in the early eighteenth century as a refined version of the *chalumeau*. The eighteenth-century clarinet retained much of the older instrument's strident, trumpetlike character—hence the name, derived from the Italian word for a high trumpet (*clarino*). Clarinet parts occur occasionally in sonatas, concertos, and opera arias from the first half of the eighteenth century, including works by Vivaldi and Handel, who used it as a sort of substitute for the trumpet in keys unsuitable for that instrument.

Figure 12.6 Oboe by Jan Steenbergen, Amsterdam, ca. 1725. America's Shrine to Music Museum, Vermillion, South Dakota, purchase funds gift of Julie and Chris Bauer, Yankton, South Dakota, 1997 (no. 6089). A direct descendent of the instrument shown in Figure 12.5, this type of oboe (shown here without its reed) was used during the first half of the eighteenth century. Photograph by Simon Spicer.

But the clarinet did not become a regular member of most orchestral ensembles until the late eighteenth century.

Brass

Brass instruments included trumpets, horns, and trombones; each had distinct uses. Because of their role as military signal instruments, trumpets (along with timpani) were generally played by members of special ensembles that were distinct from any other musical ensembles maintained by a given court or city. The horn originally resembled a coiled trumpet; it was used for signaling during the court hunts that were an important part of aristocratic life in the Baroque, and for this reason the instrument was often referred to as the *corno da caccia* (hunting horn).

Baroque **trumpets** and **horns** were both **natural** instruments: they lacked keys or valves and thus were confined largely to playing the harmonic overtones of a single **fundamental** pitch. As a result, each example of these instruments could play essentially only in one major key, and even then the complete scale of the key was available only at the very top of the range; in lower registers the

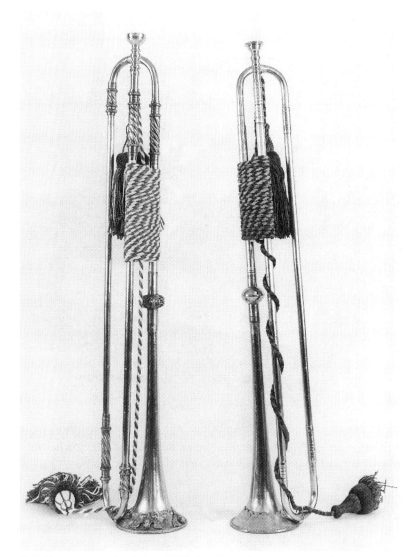

Figure 12.7 Two trumpets by Johann Wilhelm Haas, Nuremberg, ca. 1690–1710 (top) and ca. 1710–20 (bottom). America's Shrine to Music Museum, Vermillion, South Dakota, Board of Trustees, 1985 (nos. 3600–1). Note the absence of valves, typical of brass instruments before the nineteenth century. The Baroque trumpet was also made in a coiled shape. Photograph by Simon Spicer.

instrument was restricted to notes of the tonic triad (see Ex. 9.2). Individual members of the traditional trumpet ensemble specialized in playing in the high, middle, or low portion of the range; eighteenth-century orchestral parts tended to use the trumpet only in the highest part of its range, where the instrument was designated the *clarino*. As with woodwinds, the technical features of the natural instruments should not be considered limitations. Baroque trumpeters developed a sophisticated technique that permitted them to produce notes of exceptional purity throughout their range and to play complex passagework in the top register. Composers took advantage of this, occasionally using nonharmonic tones for special effect (as we have seen in Bach's Cantata 127).

Composers nevertheless tended to use trumpets only for grand or ceremonial music in major keys, especially C and D. Works with independent trumpet parts are rare until the late seventeenth century, which saw the development of a substantial repertory of works for one or two trumpets with strings, mostly from Italy but with examples from Germany and England as well. Like woodwinds, trumpets were often used in pairs, but Bach and some other eighteenth-century German composers frequently wrote for them in three parts, joined by timpani. The virtuoso *clarino* technique developed by Baroque trumpeters in Italy and Germany appears to have been largely lost after 1750; the trumpet parts in Classical works are relatively simple and in some cases even optional. By the end of the eighteenth century, instrument builders were experimenting with the use of keys and later of valves, which eventually led to the fully chromatic trumpet of the nineteenth-century orchestra. Modern players sometimes use so-called Bach trumpets for eighteenth-century *clarino* parts, but these small modern valved trumpets lack the rich sonority and pure intonation that the natural instrument possesses when properly played.

The horn underwent a development parallel to that of the trumpet, although it was rarely used in serious music before the early eighteenth century. After 1700 natural horns quickly became common members of orchestral ensembles. At first they tended to be restricted, like the trumpet, to particular keys—especially F—and to special types of piece, such as marches and arias sung by hunting characters. But through various techniques, such as the use of "stopped" tones (produced by inserting the hand into the bell of the instrument), horn players could attain a nearly complete chromatic scale, and by substituting metal tubes of varying lengths (called *crooks*) for a portion of the instrument's length they could alter the pitch of the instrument, enabling it to play in any key. By 1750 the combination of two horns and two oboes had become the standard wind complement of the Italian string orchestra, a practice that continued into the Classical style. Valved horns were invented early in the nineteenth century, but many composers continued to specify the natural instrument, and it has been revived today for use in eighteenth-century music.

The Baroque **trombone** remained close to its Renaissance version, the **sackbut**. Like the latter, the trombone continued to be built in several sizes that could constitute a complete choir, like the early woodwinds. The soprano part of the trombone ensemble, however, was usually supplied by the **cornetto**, a woodwind instrument fitted with a brass-style cupped mouthpiece. The resulting timbre blends well with that of the trombone.

In the early Baroque, especially in Italy, the cornetto was an important solo instrument, with a repertory of sonatas and other works rivaling that of the violin. It became rare in the eighteenth century, although for a time Bach and other German composers continued to use it. There exists as well a small repertory of sonatas and other works from the later seventeenth century with solo trombone parts, usually in conjunction with one or more violins or other instruments. In addition, cornetto-and-trombone ensembles had a special use throughout the Baroque in many cities of Italy and Germany, furnishing ceremonial music for civic events and playing for the public at specified times from watchtowers or other public sites. For this reason there exists a seventeenth-century repertory of dances and marchlike pieces for these instruments. They were also used in opera and ballet, although there the trombone ensemble tended to be restricted to scenes in which a solemn effect was desired, as in the underworld scenes in Monteverdi's *Orfeo*. Trombones and cornettos were also frequently used in sacred choral music, as in the works of Gabrieli (see Chapter 7); later composers used them particularly in old-fashioned works in the *stile antico*. The trombone's slide mechanism permits it to play a complete chromatic scale. Thus Bach employed cornetto and trombones to double the voices in a number of highly chromatic choral movements in his cantatas.

A number of German composers, including Bach, occasionally used a type of **slide trumpet.** Such an instrument, a hybrid between the trumpet and the trombone, could play a complete scale even in its lower register. But it lacked agility and was therefore usually restricted to playing slow-moving cantus firmus lines, as in the opening movements of Bach's chorale cantatas.

Percussion

Percussion instruments are relatively insignificant in Baroque music. Indeed, their parts were rarely written out until the early eighteenth century, and then chiefly for the **timpani** or kettledrums, which had traditionally served as the bass instrument of the trumpet ensemble. Earlier works that include trumpets—certain sacred works for large ensembles and occasional theatrical marches and battle scenes—might have included improvised timpani parts. Other percussion instruments, including various types of drum, must have been employed in dances and marches and for special effects in theatrical works, but their use was rarely specified by composers.

Scoring

The scoring of instrumental works followed the patterns we have already seen in vocal music. In particular, most instrumental ensembles included one or more continuo instruments. The continuo part in early Baroque works—especially chamber music involving only one or two other instruments or voices—was often limited to a single keyboard or plucked string instrument. Chamber works from the earlier Baroque that require an additional melodic instrument to double the bass line usually included a separate part for it. But in large ensembles, and particularly after 1700, the continuo was often a group of instruments, comprising one or two keyboards as well as cello, bassoon, and perhaps even a double-bass instrument. Naturally, the size of the continuo group varied in proportion to the size of the ensemble as a whole. Within a movement, the continuo group might be reduced for lightly scored passages; Bach, for example, often reserved the violone (string double bass) for the ritornellos of his arias, retaining only the cello and keyboard in the continuo part in passages where the voice sings.

The upper parts of most Baroque works for instrumental ensemble are dominated by violins, which, except in seventeenth-century French dance music, are most frequently used in pairs (for the Lullian string band, which remained the basis of the French opera orchestra into the 1720s, see Chapter 5). Much Baroque instrumental music, even that played by large ensembles, consists essentially of just one or two violin parts accompanied by continuo. This is true not only of trio sonatas, most often written for two violins and continuo, but also of eighteenth-century overtures and concertos for much larger ensembles, in which the upper parts were played by multiple violinists, doubled perhaps by oboes. In such pieces the viola often merely doubled the bass line an octave higher, although German composers such as Bach were more likely to give it an independent inner voice.

When composers did write for larger numbers of independent parts—as in certain types of sonata and concerto—they often employed the polychoral scoring found in the canzonas and sonatas of Gabrieli. In effect, the strings served as the main choir, to which brass or woodwind choirs might be added. For example, in the last two of Bach's orchestral suites the four-part string group is joined by a double-reed group (two or three oboes and bassoon) and a brass group (three trumpets and timpani).

Woodwind and brass players usually doubled on several different instruments. For this reason, even large ensembles rarely included more than a few wind players; as in a modern jazz ensemble, wind players were expected to switch from one instrument to another as needed. Thus the same piece rarely calls simultaneously for trumpets and horns, or for flutes, recorders, and oboes. Moreover, each of these instruments tends to be used only in certain keys; thus trumpets, for example, rarely occur outside pieces in C or D major, and neither trumpets nor horns are often used in slow movements or works in minor keys. Only in the very largest Baroque ensembles, such as that of the eighteenth-century Paris opera, could all of these instruments be employed together, as in the later symphony orchestra.

TYPES OF BAROQUE MUSIC FOR INSTRUMENTAL ENSEMBLE

We have already encountered several types of instrumental music cultivated during the Baroque. Some of these, such as the French dance pieces for violin band, represented continuations of sixteenth-century traditions. New, distinctly Baroque repertories of self-contained music for instrumental ensemble arose chiefly in Italy. The most common title for such works is *sonata*; the concerto, another Italian genre, emerged around 1700. These were joined by various other types of ensemble piece, including overtures and suites in the French style.

We are accustomed to thinking of sonatas as **chamber music,** for small ensembles with a single player to each part, and concertos and overtures as **orchestral music,** in which each string part may be doubled by a dozen players or more. But the symphony orchestra did not exist until the late eighteenth century, when public concerts of orchestral music first became common in the major cities of western Europe. Most earlier instrumental ensembles were relatively small, and thus the modern distinction between chamber works and orchestral works was rarely made explicitly. Instead, instrumental genres, like vocal ones, were more often described in terms of their purpose—whether for church, theater, or home use.

The idea of sacred instrumental music may seem a contradiction in terms. But in Roman Catholic countries, especially Italy, sections of the mass or office could be replaced by pieces for organ or for instrumental ensemble. Italian composers from Gabrieli onward wrote innumerable sonatas and other works for this purpose; indeed, most early sonatas seem to have been intended primarily for use in church. In the later seventeenth century, as the term *sonata* came to be applied to secular works as well, sonatas for the church were sometimes distinguished by the Italian expression *da chiesa,* as in the expression *sonata da chiesa* (church sonata). Church concertos (*concerti da chiesa*) were also written. Musically, there is little that is distinctly sacred or religious in character about such pieces, although a sonata or concerto *da chiesa* might be more likely to include fugal movements, whose old-fashioned contrapuntal texture might recall the quasi-Renaissance *stile antico,* used in sacred vocal music throughout the seventeenth and eighteenth centuries.

In Italy, music *da chiesa* was regarded as contrasting with music *da camera:* literally, music "for the chamber," that is, private domestic or home use, from which comes the modern expression *chamber music,* although the latter does not necessarily imply a private or amateur function. Chamber music in the Baroque sense ranges from simple sonatas, which might be played by a single amateur instrumentalist with continuo accompaniment, to concertos and other compositions played by large ensembles in princely palaces. Instrumental works originally intended for the church could also be performed at home, and thus there was a frequent blurring of the theoretical distinction between sacred and domestic instrumental music. Much music was published with titles indicating that it was appropriate for both uses, although works for the "chamber" were often distinguished by the presence of dances and other movements that had originated in opera, ballet, and other theatrical genres.

The Sonata

The term *sonata* originally referred to any piece that was played by instruments, just as the word *cantata* originally meant "sung." By the 1620s the word had become the usual term for most types of Italian instrumental chamber music, replacing the older *canzona* and *fantasia*. Early sonatas usually comprised several distinct sections; by the end of the seventeenth century most of these sections had become self-contained movements that could stand on their own, although they might be connected by short transitional passages (usually slow in tempo). One hundred years later, in what we call the Classical period, the instrumental sonata had become typically a three-movement work, with movements in the order fast-slow-fast. But only after 1720 or so did any such standardization begin to emerge. Works entitled sonata could contain anywhere from one to a dozen or more sections or movements falling in any conceivable order, ranging in length from a few measures to five minutes or more.

Baroque sonatas could be for any number of instruments, but most are for one or two high instruments—usually violins—with continuo. Sonatas for a single instrument plus continuo can be referred to as solo sonatas, although some composers, especially before 1700, distinguished true solos from duos in which upper and bass parts are of equal importance; some such works contain a separate continuo part (usually a simplified version of the bass part, with figures added), others none at all. Sonatas for two melody instruments and an independent bass part are now called **trio sonatas,** since they consist of three distinct lines of music, although the continuo part might involve two or more players. Sonatas for larger bodies of instruments might bear such Italian titles as *sonata à cinque* (sonata in five parts). In such works, one or two parts—usually for violins, but sometimes for trumpets or other wind instruments—are often predominant, taking a soloistic role. For almost a century, the sonata was almost exclusively an Italian phenomenon, cultivated in Italy and by imitators of Italian music in England and the German-speaking parts of Europe. Only around 1700 did French composers such as Couperin and Jacquet de La Guerre adopt the genre, and others such as Rameau continued to avoid it completely. But within a few decades French publishers were issuing sonatas for flute, violin, and other instruments in numbers as great as anywhere.

The Concerto

The composition of sonatas that included soloistic parts led around 1700 to a new genre, the **concerto.** In the nineteenth century, the term came to refer to a work featuring a soloist who plays in alternation with a full symphony orchestra. Eighteenth-century concertos, however, are often for much smaller ensembles.

Not all Baroque concertos contain distinct solo parts, and the latter, even when present, generally play not only in the solo sections but as part of the larger ensemble as well. Some early concertos are simply sonatas with amplified instrumentation, recalling the vocal concertos of the seventeenth century, which, as in certain works by Schütz, may include optional *capella* parts that double or accompany the soloists. But by 1720 or so the word *concerto* had acquired the modern meaning of a multimovement work for one or more soloists and a larger ensemble, most often consisting of three movements in the order fast-slow-fast, which remained the norm through the nineteenth century. The individual movements of such works most often employed a version of ritornello form, similar to that used in the arias of opera seria, which accommodated the display of the soloist or soloists.[3]

As with the sonata, the earliest concertos are for string ensembles with continuo, and in the first half of the eighteenth century concertos for solo violin and string ensemble are by far the most common type. But by 1710 or so concertos were being composed for all manner of solo instruments, both singly and in various combinations. Even more than the sonata, the concerto was regarded as an Italian genre, no doubt because of its emphasis on soloistic virtuosity. Although a few French composers, notably the violinist Jean-Marie Leclair, took it up enthusiastically, others, including Couperin and Rameau avoided it entirely (Rameau's *concerts* are actually *pièces de clavecin* with optional parts for violin or flute and viola da gamba).

Overture and Suite

Not surprisingly, music for instrumental ensemble in France focused on overtures and stylized dance movements of types familiar from the theatrical music of Lully and the keyboard pieces of Couperin and others. Indeed, Couperin was one of the first to compose original chamber pieces in France, which emerged toward the end of the seventeenth century in the form of suites for viola da gamba, flute or recorder, or other instruments, often in combinations of two or three both with and without continuo accompaniment. French composers rarely if ever wrote overtures and suites for larger ensembles outside the context of operas, ballets, or other dramatic works. But an independent repertory emerged toward the end of the seventeenth century in Germany, where the term *Ouverture* came to refer not only to the overture itself but to a complete suite in the French style, for anywhere from one to a dozen or more players. Among the composers of such music were Muffat, Fischer, and J. S. Bach, whose works for larger ensembles, such as the four *ouvertures* of Bach, are often referred to today as orchestral suites. Certain works of this sort, as well as many examples of the concerto, were composed for performance in public orchestral concerts, whose tradition begins in the eighteenth century in such major cities as Paris, London, Leipzig, and Vienna.

THE BAROQUE SONATA

The Baroque solo sonata represents the instrumental equivalent of vocal monody: a work for a single virtuoso soloist accompanied by continuo. Hence it is not surprising that the earliest such works appeared shortly after the publication of Caccini's *Nuove musiche* in 1601. By the same token, duo and trio sonatas constituted instrumental parallels to the vocal duet.

---

[3]An important category of Baroque concerto that lacks solo parts is scored for four-part string ensemble and continuo; these are sometimes termed **ripieno concertos** or *concerti a* quattro. Occasionally, works for smaller ensembles or even for a single keyboard instrument were designated concertos (as in Bach's *Italian Concerto* for solo harpsichord).

Early Sonatas

The earliest sonatas tend to be rhapsodic, through-composed pieces, similar in conception to the keyboard toccatas of the same period: full of harmonic and rhythmic surprises, sudden changes of expressive character, and occasional bursts of virtuoso figuration. Among the most important composers of such works were the Italian violinists Salamone Rossi (ca. 1570–ca. 1630), Biagio Marini (ca. 1587–1663), and Marco Uccellini (ca. 1603–80).

Rossi was active at Mantua at the same time that Monteverdi was there composing *Orfeo* and other works, in which Rossi may well have participated. Rossi was unique among the significant composers of the Baroque in being Jewish. Although Jews throughout Christian Europe were persecuted, those of Mantua and a number of other northern Italian cities enjoyed a relative degree of freedom. A number of them, including Rossi, served as court musicians and played a significant role in the early history of the violin. Rossi is known primarily for his trio sonatas and for a collection of Hebrew motets published at Venice in 1622—a unique example of early Baroque vocal polyphony for the synagogue.

The parallel between vocal and instrumental music is made explicit in such trio sonatas as Rossi's *Sonata in dialogo* (Dialogue sonata), published in 1613 with the additional subtitle *La Viena*. Like many early sonatas, it is a one-movement work for two unspecified melody instruments (presumably cornettos or violins) and continuo. Except in the final section, where they play together, the two upper parts alternate, presenting phrases whose melodic figures are reminiscent of Monteverdian monody (Ex. 12.1). Rossi also wrote sonatas that consist of variations over traditional ground basses such as the Romanesca. These same ostinato basses were employed in variation works by Frescobaldi and other contemporaries for solo keyboard as well as for instrumental ensemble and even voice (cf. Ex. 10.1).

Example 12.1 Salamone Rossi, *Sonata in dialogo La Viena*, mm. 22–36

Biagio Marini was responsible for a larger, more varied, and more influential repertory that focused intensely on inventive writing for the violin. Born in the northern Italian town of Brescia, he was active in Germany and especially at Venice, where he is said to have been a student of, or at least to have played under, Monteverdi. His most important publications are his Opus 8 (Venice, 1629), containing sixty-eight sonatas, dances, and other pieces for from one to six string instruments and continuo, and his final publication, Opus 22 (Venice, 1655), a somewhat similar assortment of twenty-five pieces.

A number of works from these collections are distinguished by such curiosities as echo effects, the avoidance of cadences, and the continuous use of **double stops** (produced by bowing two strings at once). One work in Marini's Opus 3 of 1620 even dispenses with the basso continuo: his variations for solo violin on the Romanesca bass (Frescobaldi's keyboard *partite* on the same bass are illustrated in Ex. 10.1). Later composers, notably Heinrich Biber and J. S. Bach, likewise wrote works for unaccompanied string instruments. In such works the violin (or, in some cases, cello) provides its own harmony through the use of double-stops and other special techniques.

Sonata for Violin and Continuo, *La variata*

Marini's violin works go beyond technical contrivance; many are the equivalents of Frescobaldi's keyboard toccatas in their expressive and idiomatic use of the instrument for which they are written. *La variata* (anthology, Selection 33) is a solo sonata for violin and continuo from Marini's Opus 8. Like many early sonatas, it consists of an unbroken series of short sections in contrasting tempos and meters, ranging from slow, sustained passages to virtuoso figuration and phrases in dance rhythms. The title *La variata*—later sonatas would rarely bear descriptive titles—seems to refer to this constantly changing character, reminiscent of the Venetian opera and cantata of the same period, in which recitative, arioso, and aria flow into one another in rapid succession.

As in Frescobaldi's toccatas, these sections are too brief to be considered separate movements, and the work as a whole remains short enough to serve as an interlude in a church service, its probable original purpose. The contrasts between the six or seven sections are so great that at first the sonata may seem chaotic. But an overall symmetry is readily apparent: the first and last sections (mm. 1–15 and 122–46) share a generally quiet, restrained style. Moreover, the closing section returns to a motive played by the continuo in measure 1, developing it in imitation (beginning in mm. 122–23). Measures 16–30 repeat the opening section transposed downward by a fifth—a device rare before 1600 but symptomatic of the emerging tonal thinking of the period (compare the use of transposition in Monteverdi's *Luci serene*, anthology, Selection 4). The transposition is signaled by the addition of a "key" signature of one flat, which remains in effect through a series of dancelike passages in triple time (mm. 39–80). Their tonality centers on what we would call D minor and G minor, but the sonata returns to its opening A minor for the final sections.

Marini's sonata achieves its liveliest motion in measures 88–107, especially with the violin's thirty-second notes (mm. 94–97), which form the climax of the work.[4] From here the energy gradually dissipates. A spacious effect is created in measures 107–20 through scales in both violin and bass that encompass two octaves and more; one might hear in these scales a reminiscence of mm. 31–38, which likewise contain scales in both parts. Through such fleeting motivic connections, this improvisatory piece maintains its coherence. At the same time, the sonata suggests the effect of a monodic narrative by its movement from opening tranquillity through dance and agitation, before returning to its initial character.

Later Sonatas

With Marco Uccellini and later composers, the free, rhapsodic forms of the early sonatas, which often comprised numerous short sections linked by improvisatory transitions, are gradually replaced by regular structures in which any surprises are incidental to the larger organization. Moreover, instead of the rather chaotic collections of the early sonata composers, later musicians published their works in neat dozens or half-dozens containing a single type of sonata.

Between 1650 and 1750, hundreds of composers published thousands of sonatas. Originally confined to Italy, the sonata spread first to Germany, then to England and even France, where opposition to the Italian style gave way in the eighteenth century to its embrace by composers such as Jacquet de La Guerre, Couperin, and Rameau, resulting in what Couperin called *les goûts réunis* ("the reunited styles"). In Austria, the violinist-composers Heinrich Schmelzer (ca. 1620–80) and Heinrich Biber (see below) took up the tradition of the earlier Italian virtuoso violinists. Later German-speaking composers, including Handel, Bach, and others, wrote solo and trio sonatas using the violin as well as woodwind instruments. Bach and others also wrote trio sonatas in which the harpsichordist, normally the continuo player, plays one of the melody parts as well as the bass; the result is a duo for violin, flute, or viola da gamba plus keyboard.[5]

Given the enormous output of sonatas, it is almost arbitrary to select any particular ones for close study. Two composers of the late seventeenth century, however, may be singled out: Biber, for his unusually inventive approach to the violin and the sonata; and the Italian Corelli, because of the extraordinary influence of his works, which furnished models for Bach, Handel, and virtually every other major composer through the end of the eighteenth century.

HEINRICH IGNAZ FRANZ BIBER

Heinrich Ignaz Franz Biber (1644–1704) was born in Wartenberg, Bohemia (now Straz pod Ralskem), near Liberec in what is now the northern Czech Re-

---

[4]The word *tardo* in m. 95 may signify a momentary ritard or pause, not a lasting change of tempo.

[5]Bach wrote at least eleven duets of this type for harpsichord with flute, violin, and viola da gamba; several of them are known to have originated as ordinary trio sonatas.

public. By 1668 he was working for the bishop of Liechtenstein-Kastelkorn at Kromeríz in Moravia, 150 miles to the southeast. Two years later he entered the service of the archbishop of Salzburg in western Austria, eventually becoming kapellmeister (1684) and lord high steward (1692). Hence he spent his entire life within those parts of the Holy Roman Empire that were under the direct rule of the emperor, whose capital in Vienna Biber must have occasionally visited. Like Salzburg, it was a center for Italian-style music, its churches and imperial court and opera populated by Italian musicians and by Germans (such as Froberger) who had studied in Italy.

Biber composed important church works, including a magnificent Requiem (funeral mass) in F minor and, probably, an immense polychoral mass in no fewer than fifty-four instrumental and vocal parts.[6] His instrumental music is of great significance and originality, consisting mainly of sonatas: some twenty-five for violin and continuo and another thirty or so for larger ensembles. He is best known for the solo violin works, especially fifteen early works known as the "Mystery" or "Rosary" Sonatas. These reveal not only an inventive use of the violin, including a number of advanced technical devices, but also an impressive deepening of the quasi-dramatic style of the earlier Italian sonata.

Biber's "Mystery" Sonatas have become famous because of their programmatic organization and their systematic exploration of *scordatura* or the "mistuning" of the violin. Probably composed by 1676, during the early part of Biber's Salzburg period, the works survive in a manuscript prepared for the ruling archbishop, Max Gandolph, to whom the composer's dedication, at the head of the manuscript, is addressed. Because the original title page is missing, the pieces are known today as the "Mystery" Sonatas from the fact that each sonata in the manuscript was understood to represent an event or "mystery" in the life of the Virgin Mary. The works are not actually called sonatas in the manuscript; indeed, that term is reserved for the opening movements of some of them. The set of fifteen works corresponds to the fifteen sets of rosary beads used by pious Roman Catholics to keep count of prayers during their meditations on these mysteries; for this reason they are also known as the "Rosary" Sonatas. Attached to each work in the manuscript is a small engraving (a printed picture) depicting the mystery that the music symbolizes. The manuscript also contains a sixteenth work, a passacaglia for unaccompanied violin.

Biber composed several further programmatic pieces for string instruments, including a *Battalia*—a depiction of a battle for ten string parts and continuo.[7] But, like the character pieces of the French harpsichordists, the present sonatas rarely contain more than a few musical signs linking them to their titles. In-

---

[6]This so-called *Missa salisburgensis* is preserved anonymously; it appears in a modern edition by Guido Adler in *Denkmäler der Tonkunst in Österreich*, vol. 20, with an improbable attribution to the Roman composer Orazio Benevoli (1605–72).

[7]The autograph parts are for three violins, four violas, two "violones," and harpsichord; modern edition in Heinrich Ignaz Franz Biber, *Instrumentalwerke handschriftlicher Überlieferung*, ed. Jiří Sehnel, *Denkmäler der Tonkunst in Österreich*, 151 (Graz: Akademische Druck- und Verlagsanstalt, 1997).

deed, at least one of them is preserved in another manuscript in which it bears a strikingly different title.[8] This suggests that at least some of the pieces might have been composed previously, for other purposes.

The most striking musical feature of these pieces is their use of **scordatura:** the retuning of one or more of the strings of the violin, in order to make possible the playing of otherwise unobtainable types of figuration and multiple stop (chord). Only the first sonata and the unaccompanied passacaglia employ the conventional tuning of the violin; a different tuning is used in each subsequent work. The practice was probably suggested by the Baroque lute repertory, which employed several different tunings associated with various keys. Solo string works by other composers, including Bach and Mozart, occasionally call for retuning the instrument, but never so radically or with so many different types of scordatura. Although these pieces by Biber were probably not widely known, their considerable technical demands reveal the accomplishments of seventeenth-century violinists, and their forms reveal the enormous variety possible within the sonata of the period.

"Mystery" Sonatas nos. 9–11

A portion of the series may serve to illustrate the nature of these pieces and their notation. The score of each work opens with a chord that indicates how the four strings of the violin are to be tuned. For example, in Sonata no. 9 (anthology, Selection 34) the lower two strings are raised so that the four open strings produce a chord (c′–e′–a′–e″) of A minor, the key of the sonata. In Sonata no. 10, the top string is lowered, giving the violin two D strings an octave apart (g–d′–a′–d″); D is the dominant of this piece (in G minor). Sonata no. 11, in G major, contains the most radical retuning of all: the two inner strings must be switched before being retuned to produce the remarkable tuning g–g′–d′–d″.[9]

Even the best violinist might be hopelessly confused by the varying tuning of the pieces. Rather than indicate the actual pitches, therefore, Biber's notation tells the player where to place his or her fingers. For example, in measure 4 of Sonata no. 9 the notes g♯′ and e′ are written as f♯′ and d′. Both are played on the second string, which has been tuned a step higher than usual (Ex. 12.2). The resulting notation is misleading if read at face value; chords can seem particularly bizarre, whether played simultaneously or broken (see Ex. 12.3, where part *b* is a variation of part *a* with broken chords). Fortunately, in our work the two upper strings are unchanged and thus notes from a′ upward sound as written.

---

[8]The tenth sonata, here designated "The Crucifixion," is elsewhere entitled "The Invasion of the Turks"—a reference to the Ottoman seige of Vienna in 1683.

[9]The violinist Reinhard Goebel suggests that instead of removing and exchanging the two inner strings, the latter should be loosened and then crossed over one another; see liner notes to his recording *Heinrich Ignaz Franz Biber: Rosenkranz-Sonaten,* Musica Antiqua Köln, dir. Reinhard Goebel (Hamburg: Deutsche Grammophon, 1991, Archiv Produktion 431656–2), p. 12.

Example 12.2 Biber, "Mystery" Sonata no. 9, first movement (original notation on lower two staves, "realization" of violin notation on top staff): (a) m. 4; (b) mm. 8–9

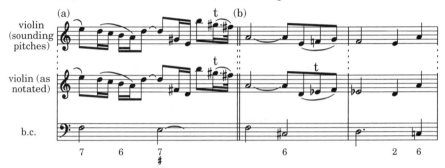

Example 12.3 Biber, "Mystery" Sonata no. 9: (a) courante, mm. 1–7; (b) first *double*, mm. 1–7

Although all three sonatas fall into distinct movements, each remains a single dramatic unity. Thus Sonata no. 9 opens and closes with improvisatory sections reminiscent of those in a keyboard toccata (these are labeled Sonata and Finale, respectively). In the middle comes a courante with two variations or *doubles*. The presence of a dance movement seems curious in view of the piece's designation as "Christ on the Way to Calvary." In the manuscript, the accompanying illustration shows Jesus carrying the cross on which he is to be crucified. Presumably Biber found something in the music that corresponded to the intense expressivity of this image. Perhaps it was the rushing passagework of the opening movement, which in measure 21 ascends to f‴—an unusually high note in a Baroque work. The closing movement is similarly intense, consisting essentially of a single dominant pedal point prolonged under irregular outbursts of figuration.

The central movement, the courante, is a faithful imitation of the French style, although the frequent chords in the solo part were a specialty of German violinists. As in most Baroque sets of variations, the two doubles each use the same bass line; the violin part grows progressively more animated in each.

Sonata no. 10, which represents the Crucifixion, consists solely of a short prelude and a set of variations. Again, there is little in the music to connect with the title, although the violin's repeated notes in the prelude might be associated with the hammering as Jesus was nailed to the cross (Ex. 12.4). Sonata no. 11, entitled "The Resurrection," consists of another prelude (designated Sonata), followed by one of the few movements in the series that clearly connect the work with its title. The movement constitutes a rare example of paraphrase composition in a violin sonata, being built around the Gregorian hymn *Surrexit Christus hodie* (Christ has risen today). The latter melody is treated first as a bass ostinato, then developed in imitation, and finally played by violin and continuo in triple octaves as in Example 12.5 (m. 130)—a unique yet characteristically Baroque symbolic representation of the Holy Trinity central to Christian belief. That the bizarre notation of the original could, thanks to the use of scordatura, produce so simple and basic a harmony was particularly symbolic of the sacred mysteries alluded to in Biber's dedication to the archbishop of Salzburg.

Example 12.4 Biber, "Mystery" Sonata no. 10, first movement, mm. 1–5

Example 12.5 Biber, "Mystery" Sonata no. 11, mm. 127–33

ARCANGELO CORELLI

Arcangelo Corelli (1653–1713) was the greatest violinist-composer of the Baroque and arguably its second most influential Italian composer after Monteverdi. Apart from a single sonata for trumpet, two violins, and continuo, he appears to have composed nothing but string music. He was born in Fusignano, near Bologna in northern Italy, but by 1675 was working as a violinist in Rome, where he spent the rest of his career. His patrons included some of the city's most important royal and aristocratic supporters of the arts, among them the exiled Queen Christina of Sweden and Cardinal Pietro Ottoboni. The latter headed the so-called Arcadian Academy, founded in 1690, a group of nobles interested in literature and the arts whose periodic gatherings included sometimes lavish musical performances. Beginning in 1706, the membership included three musicians: initially Corelli, Alessandro Scarlatti, and the Roman harpsichordist-composer Bernardo Pasquini (1637–1707). Corelli was also regularly engaged elsewhere in Rome to direct performances of operas, oratorios, and other major works, including those of Pasquini and Handel.

Corelli's chief works are his forty-eight trio sonatas, twelve solo sonatas, and twelve concerti grossi. These were published in six numbered collections of twelve works each, beginning with four sets of trio sonatas. The second set (Opus 2, 1685), bearing the title *Sonate da camera* (Chamber sonatas), contains mostly dance movements, as does the fourth set (Opus 4, 1694). Hence it has become customary to regard these two sets as collections of chamber sonatas and the other two—Opus 1 of 1681 and Opus 3 of 1689—as *sonate da chiesa* (church sonatas), although Corelli never designated the latter as such. The two subsequent collections of solo sonatas (Opus 5, 1700) and concertos (Opus 6, published posthumously in 1714) are each divided between works of the so-called church and chamber types as well.

Each of Corelli's publications was reissued throughout the eighteenth century in numerous editions. Bach imitated Corelli's *sonate de chiesa* (church sonatas) in both his trio sonatas and his sonatas for unaccompanied violin. Handel wrote a set of twelve concerti grossi (also designated Opus 6, 1739) in tribute to Corelli. Countless other Italian, German, and even French composers also wrote works modeled on Corelli's. Some even arranged Corelli's works for keyboard, recorder, and other settings.

Part of the appeal of Corelli's music must have lain in its regularity and restraint. Compared to earlier violin writing, such as Marini's or Biber's, it seems predictable. Everything is in its proper place, each gesture in one direction exquisitely balanced by one in another. This aspect of the works is evident even in superficial aspects, such as their publication in regular sets of twelve. With few exceptions, the works in each volume are constructed out of a few standard types of movement.

In fact, Corelli's works do contain harmonic surprises and even the occasional *bizzarria*. Yet these events rarely interrupt the music's continuity to the degree that they do in earlier Italian instrumental music; they often seem to represent wit and good humor rather than extreme expressivity. Corelli's own playing was reported to be extremely impassioned and full of fire. But much of this impression must have been due to improvised embellishment, for, with the exception of some of the solo sonatas, the music as written requires relatively little outright virtuosity. For this reason, string teachers ever since have tended to use Corelli's works as pedagogic pieces. Yet the music is not really easy to play. Like all well-composed works, Corelli's sonatas are more demanding than they may first appear to be, requiring sensitive and controlled phrasing, articulation, and embellishment.

Trio Sonata in D, op. 2, no. 1

Corelli's Opus 2 (Rome, 1685) is a set of twelve *sonate da camera* (chamber sonatas) for two violins, "violone," and harpsichord, the latter two instruments serving as the continuo group.[10] As in Corelli's Opus 1, published four years earlier, the twelve sonatas in the volume are all in different keys. Such planning is characteristic of late Baroque collections, which tended to be carefully laid out in such a way as to insure variety despite the homogeneous genre and scoring of the works.

Corelli's *sonate da camera* have no set sequence of movements. They consist primarily of dances, however, and many also open with a nondance movement sometimes designated *preludio* (prelude). The dances are in the Italian style, and although their names correspond to those used in the French ballet, they represent the Italian versions of those dances. In most cases these Italian dances are in the same meter and share other characteristics with the French versions. But they tend to be somewhat closer to the original versions of the dances—less stylized and more forthright.

Thus the *allemanda* is a lively movement in common time, with more strongly marked beats than the rhapsodic allemande of the French keyboard suite. The *corrente*, like the French courante, is characterized by hemiolas. But it is usually notated in $\frac{3}{4}$ (not $\frac{6}{4}$), and its tempo is quicker. Most of the other dances, including the *sarabanda, gavotta*, and *giga*, also tend to be quicker and somewhat simpler in rhythm and melodic style than their French counterparts. The *gavotta* is further distinguished by beginning on the downbeat, not in the middle of the measure as does the gavotte.

All of these characteristics hold true in the Trio Sonata in D, op. 2, no. 1 (anthology, Selection 35). Its opening prelude contains a number of the hallmarks of Corelli's trio sonata style. These recur in countless other works by him and later composers. The basic texture is freely contrapuntal, with short motives occasionally being treated in imitation between the three parts (as in mm. 4–5). Much of the movement is composed of sustained violin lines over a so-called walking bass in steady eighth notes, and in these passages one of the violin parts frequently moves in what are called **chains of suspensions**. These are usually downward-moving *dissonant* suspensions, as in measures 1–3 and 5–7. But there is also an upward-moving consonant chain of suspensions in mm. 8–10.

---

[10]It is uncertain whether this *violone* was a cello or some other low stringed instrument.

Each chain of suspensions is a type of sequence. Indeed, the prelude in large part comprises sequences of one sort or another that move to a cadence. Such music seems simple; the prelude consists of just three similarly constructed phrases (mm. 1–4, 4–8, and 8–14). Yet few other composers managed to produce music that is so unpretentious and at the same time aesthetically satisfying. This type of restraint, combined with technical perfection, insured the continued use of Corelli's music as a model of pure composition through the eighteenth century.

The *preludio* is followed by three dances. Thus the sonata, like Corelli's other chamber sonatas, is in effect a suite. As in the French style, the dances are in binary form; in this sonata, each is divided exactly in half by the double bar. Moreover, in each dance the first half ends with a cadence in the dominant, and the second half begins with material derived from the opening of the first half. This is true even in the *gavotta*, despite its extreme brevity. Indeed, its exaggerated brevity was probably an instance of Italian *bizzarria*. One is surprised to find that the movement is over almost before it began, yet it is pleasing to discover that it contains in miniature the same complete binary form as the two preceding dances.[11]

The allemanda and the corrente stand in a particularly close relationship to one another, for the opening phrase of the corrente (mm. 1–7) is a variation of the corresponding phrase of the allemanda (mm. 1–4). Less exact parallels continue throughout the two movements. Both, for example, modulate to the relative minor (B minor) in the phrase after the double bar. This type of relationship is rare in Corelli's works. It is common, however, in German keyboard suites of the period. In such works an entire courante might be a variation of the preceding allemande, resulting in a so-called **variation suite**; examples occur among the early works of Froberger, Handel, and Bach.

The tempo marks of these movements call for some comment. At the time of their publication the use of tempo marks was relatively new, having become common only around the middle of the seventeenth century. Until the end of the Baroque, many works or movements lacked them entirely, and musicians relied on their understanding of convention and style to judge the proper tempo. Even where tempo marks are present, they require careful interpretation. In the *allemanda*, Corelli's marking *largo* today might be taken to indicate a very slow tempo. But the Italian words used to indicate tempo were then understood literally, in this case to mean "broadly." Contrary to modern usage, then, the word *largo* here may imply quick, full bow strokes but not necessarily a slow tempo.

The Sonata in C, op. 5, no. 3

Corelli's twelve solo sonatas, published in 1700, consist of six *sonate da chiesa* and six *sonate da camera* (distinguished only as "Part 1" and "Part 2" in the original). Most of the latter resemble Corelli's trio sonatas *da camera* in consisting

---

[11]The original edition includes an indication that the entire gavotte is to be repeated—perhaps more than once.

of a *preludio* followed by dances. Only the last sonata differs; it comprises a single movement, a set of variations on *La Folia*, a traditional ground bass.[12] Unlike the works of Marini and Biber considered above, these are true duo sonatas in which the figured bass part frequently contains essential melodic material, especially in the six "church" sonatas.

These first six sonatas resemble the trio sonatas *da chiesa* in that they lack designated dance movements. Nevertheless, many movements in these works contain readily identifiable dance characteristics. A more significant element of these sonatas is the presence of fugues, usually as the second movement and sometimes as the last movement as well. Music history texts often describe the church sonata as comprising a four-movement sequence, slow-fast-slow-fast. The first six sonatas of Opus 5, however, each contain five movements. These are

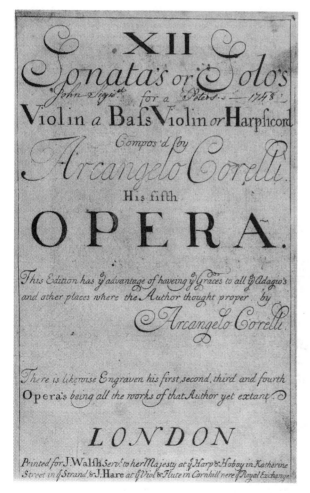

Figure 12.8 Title page of Corelli's Opus 5 as printed about 1711 by the London publisher John Walsh. Marcellene and Walter Mayhall Collection. Copyright laws were virtually nonexistent in the eighteenth century, and Walsh pirated many of his editions from ones published on the Continent. This edition is a copy of that of the Amsterdam publisher Etienne Roger of 1710, but Walsh translated the title for the benefit of his English market. An early owner of the volume has signed his name just below the title.

---

[12]Corelli's Opus 2 had similarly concluded with a *ciacona*, a chaconne in the form of variations on an ostinato bass line.

arranged in varying orders, but the sonatas always open with a slow prelude followed by a fugue and conclude with a quick movement.

In one of the many eighteenth-century reprints of Opus 5 (Amsterdam, 1710), the Dutch publisher added an embellished version of the violin part. This, according to him, contained "the ornaments for the adagios . . . composed by Corelli as he plays them." It seems improbable that the publisher had truly obtained Corelli's embellished versions of these movements, which he might never have written down. Nevertheless, this edition illustrates the type of embellishments that a virtuoso of the time might have improvised in the slow movements of the "church" sonatas. Modern editiions of Opus 5 often reproduce these embellishments on a separate staff above the original violin part.

The opening adagio of the Sonata in C, op. 5, no. 3 (anthology, Selection 36) serves as prelude to the second movement, the fugue. One might expect a fugue for violin and continuo to contain only two voices, but the violin's double-stopping capabilities permit it to provide both soprano and alto parts. There are three- and even four-part chords as well, but the extra notes provide additional sonority rather than real contrapuntal voices.

Although this movement is a genuine three-voice fugue, it is not a *strict* fugue. As Table 12.1 shows, after the initial two entries of the subject, the latter never appears in its complete form again, and there are no subsequent en-

Figure 12.9 Corelli, opening of the Sonata in C, op. 5, no. 3, from Walsh's edition. Marcellene and Walter Mayhall Collection. The lower two staves of each system show Corelli's original score as previously published at Rome and elsewhere; the top staff gives embellishments which, as the title page advertises, were claimed to be also by Corelli. Unlike the typeset music shown in Figure 6.1, this page was printed from an engraved plate and thus presents a more elegant appearance, with unbroken staff lines, beams, and slurs.

TABLE 12.1
Corelli: Sonata in C, op. 5, no. 3, second movement

	Exposition	Episode	Exposition	Episode	Exposition	Coda
Soprano	C—+'		(a)—		(C) + (C) —+	
Alto	G—				+	
Basso continuo	+ (C)		+		+ (C) —(G) — + (C) —	
Measure	1	9	14b	21b 30b	31 35	42 50
Cadence		C	a	C e	G	C:V → I

letters = keys of normal fugal entries (real answers)

+ = countersubject

(symbols in parentheses) = incomplete or substantially altered entries

' (prime) = varied (embellished) version of entry

— (dash) = bridge (free continuation of an entry)

tries at all in the alto. There is a countersubject, but it consists of nothing more distinctive than a short chain of suspensions; it is more a single motive than a complete subject. Much of the movement is taken up not by fugal expositions but by two long episodes. The first of these (mm. 9–14a) initially employs a motive from the subject but soon moves on to unrelated material. The second episode (mm. 21b–30) is composed entirely of virtuoso figuration of the type that would soon become especially characteristic of the solo concerto.

This free sort of construction illustrates how Baroque composers used fugal texture as a way of opening a movement that then moves to different types of writing. After beginning fugally, the movement reaches its climax in the virtuoso figuration of the middle. It then returns to fugal texture (mm. 31–41), only to conclude with a coda that is again composed of virtuoso figuration (mm. 42–50). Similar fugues occur in the other "church" sonatas of Corelli's Opus 5. They provided models for the dazzling virtuoso fugues in Bach's three sonatas for unaccompanied violin, as well as some of his fugues for organ, harpsichord, and lute.

Corelli did not write out the figuration for the final five measures. Instead, the word *arpeggio* indicates that the player is to invent a way of arpeggiating the chords in some idiomatic pattern. Similar markings appear occasionally in keyboard and lute music as well.

Like the fugue, the remaining movements represent types that recur in other sonatas. The second adagio is in a contrasting key, the relative minor, a practice adopted in the slow movements of many sonatas and concertos of the later Baroque. Its true ending is on the downbeat of measure 50. This is followed, however, by a short passage ending with a so-called Phrygian cadence to the dominant chord (E major). The passage serves as a bridge to the next movement—even though the latter is in C, not the expected A minor. Many Baroque works contain bridges of this sort, which depends on the close relationship between a major key (C) and its relative minor (a).

The fourth movement, an allegro, is virtually an étude (study piece or exercise) consisting almost entirely of virtuoso figuration for the violin. All the church sonatas of Corelli's Opus 5 contain such movements, but they are rare in sonatas by other composers. As in the episodes of the fugue, the figuration consists of arpeggiation such as would soon become typical of the solo sections of a concerto. Although such figuration may appear mechanical on the page, the precise pattern of the arpeggiation changes constantly, and it falls into phrases of varying lengths. A good performer can bring out this variety through subtle inflections of tempo, dynamics, and articulation.

The closing movement is a *giga* (jig) although not marked as such, in keeping with the conventions of the church sonata. Much longer than the dances of Corelli's Opus 2, it retains their binary form. It ends with a touch of *bizzarria*, for the final phrase shifts without preparation to the minor mode (m. 35b). Moreover, the phrase is repeated *piano*. This type of **echo** effect can be found in works composed throughout the seventeenth and eighteenth centuries, even in vocal music.[13] Not every repeated phrase was meant to be played softly;

---

[13]It was once thought, incorrectly, that sudden contrasts of *forte* and *piano* were the only type of dynamics used in Baroque music; some modern writers refer to them as "terraced dynamics."

Corelli and other composers reserved it for special effects, in this case perhaps a humorous one. Here the echo serves to exaggerate the surprise created by ending in the minor mode. In this manner Corelli anticipates the ending of the sonata K. 182 of Domenico Scarlatti—who undoubtedly knew this piece and might have been influenced by it (see Chapter 11).

CHAPTER 13

THE BAROQUE INSTRUMENTAL CONCERTO

The instrumental concertos of the late Baroque by Bach, Handel, and Vivaldi are probably the best-known products of the entire period and among the few that are familiar to virtually all mainstream musicians and audiences today. The term *concerto*, like *sonata*, has meant different things at different times. In the early Baroque it referred to works combining voices and instruments, sometimes in relatively large numbers (see Chapter 7). In later music it describes works for one or more instrumental soloists and orchestra. The element common to the two meanings is the idea of a virtuoso ensemble work, usually one of relatively ambitious dimensions. This was probably the basic sense of the term when, in the late seventeenth century, it began to be applied to certain types of instrumental music that might otherwise have been considered special types of sonatas.

Early Concertos

Certain instrumental works of the late seventeenth century have many of the features of the eighteenth-century concerto, although most do not yet bear that title. Among them are sonatas for one or two trumpets with strings and continuo composed especially at Bologna and a few other Italian cities. In these works, the trumpets have special prominence, and in some passages they play as soloists, accompanied only by the continuo. Trumpet sonatas of this type were written by Purcell and Biber, in addition to many Italian composers. Similar soloistic writing for violins or trumpets occurs occasionally in the overtures and other instrumental numbers (called *sinfonias*) of Italian operas and oratorios from the same period; Handel even included a "sonata" for solo organ and orchestra as a movement in his first Italian oratorio, *Il trionfo del Tempo e del Disinganno* (The triumph of time and truth, ca. 1707).

The first important composer to write works of this type that were actually designated as concertos was Giuseppe Torelli (1658–1709). A violinist, he spent much of his career at the church of St. Petronius in Bologna, a major center of instrumental music. Torelli's works include a number of pieces for trumpet and strings, variously titled *sonata* and *sinfonia*, as well as some of the earliest examples of what we now recognize as the solo concerto, scored for solo violin and larger ensemble.

Hundreds of concertos were composed during the first few decades of the eighteenth century. As with the sonata, the first generation of concerto composers were mostly Italians, but the genre was soon taken up in Germany, England, and even France. Apart from Torelli himself, important composers included Corelli and the Venetian composers Tomaso Albinoni (1671–1750) and Antonio Vivaldi (1678–1741). Albinoni is known in particular for his oboe concertos—works for one and for two oboes, with strings and continuo—some of the first significant solo works for that instrument. Vivaldi was a particularly prolific and influential concerto composer; his works were widely published and imitated in Germany, France, and England, as well as in Italy. Among the German composers influenced by Vivaldi were Georg Philipp Telemann (1681–1767) and J. S. Bach, as well as the latter's sons, whose numerous concertos for keyboard instruments transformed the genre, providing models for the Classical piano concerto of Haydn, Mozart, and Beethoven.

Types of Concerto

Modern writers often distinguish between a concerto in which a single solo part is pitted against a larger ensemble, described as a "solo" concerto, and a work involving multiple soloists, referred to as a *concerto grosso*. But eighteenth-century musicians did not always use the terms in this way. An early eighteenth-century concerto might have multiple solo parts in one movement and only one soloist, or none at all, in another. Although patterns of scoring and structure were becoming standardized by the 1720s, earlier works show a wide variety of formal designs and instrumentation. Emblematic of this variety are the twelve concertos of Vivaldi's *L'estro armonico* (published in 1711) or the six of Bach's Brandenburg Concertos, all composed by 1721, which lack the predictable patterns of scoring and structure typical of the next generation. For example, in the Fourth Brandenburg Concerto a solo violin and two recorders are joined by four additional string parts and continuo. It is fruitless to agonize over whether this work is a solo violin concerto or a "concerto grosso" in which the recorders are also soloists; Bach, clearly, was satisfied with the designation *concerto* alone.

ARCANGELO CORELLI AND THE CONCERTO GROSSO

The twelve works of Corelli's Opus 6, published a year after his death in 1714, were indeed designated concerti grossi, an indication that they are actually not concertos at all in the sense that the word later acquired. Like many vocal concertos of the seventeenth century, they are in principle small-scale chamber works with optional extra parts. The latter are referred to as the **ripieno**: literally, the filling-out of the basic texture. Thus each concerto in Corelli's Opus 6 is for a basic texture of two violins and continuo—that is, a trio sonata ensemble. To this a ripieno of two violins, viola, and a second continuo part may be added. Indeed, an early account of Corelli's performance practice, by the German composer Georg Muffat, showed how a work in trio sonata scoring could

ARCANGELUS CORELLIUS de FUSIGNANO dictus BONONIENSIS

Liquisse Infernas Jam Credimus Orphea Sedes | Divinus patet Ipse Orpheus, dum numine digna
Et terras habitare, hujus sub imagine forma. | Arte modos fingit, vel chordas mulcet utramque
Agnoscit Laudem, meritosque BRITANNUS honores

Figure 13.1 Arcangelo Corelli, engraving by William Sherwin after a portrait by Hugh Howard (ca. 1698), published as the frontispiece to Walsh's edition of Opus 5 (London, ca. 1711). Marcellene and Walter Mayhall Collection. As in many Baroque portraits, the composer holds a page of music as a symbol of his occupation and learning. The lines of Latin poetry beneath the portrait liken Corelli to Orpheus.

be augmented by the addition of ripieno players.[1] Following a tradition that seems to have arisen in the 1660s at Rome, passages for the small ensemble alone alternate with ones in which they are joined by the ripieno. In later concertos, the ripieno is not usually optional; indeed, its presence is an essential el-

---

[1] For Muffat's account, published in 1701, see the translation in Strunk, *Source Readings*, listed in the bibliography under "Collections of Readings."

ement in the solo concerto. Even Corelli's concerti grossi, although playable without the ripieno parts, contain four-part fugues and other textures distinct from those of his trio sonatas and must have been conceived primarily for orchestral performance.

Corelli's Concerto Grosso in G Minor, op. 6, no. 8

This work (anthology, Selection 37) is a church concerto (*concerto da chiesa*), composed for performance on Christmas Eve. It is therefore often referred to as Corelli's "Christmas" Concerto. Specific liturgical designations such as this were rare for instrumental works, although there is a similarly entitled concerto by Torelli.

In modern scores of Corelli's concerti grossi, the basic trio sonata group is notated on the three upper staves and is designated the *concertino* (literally, the "small ensemble"). The ripieno appears on the lower four staves, which are labeled, somewhat confusingly, as the *concerto grosso* (the "big ensemble"). The concertino plays throughout; the two ripieno violins and the ripieno continuo part enter now and then to double the concertino in select passages. The viola has an independent part, but although it augments the sonority it adds nothing essential to it; in works by other composers, the viola often just doubles the bass line.

The work opens with a brief introductory passage followed by a fugal movement. The latter alludes to vocal polyphony of the sixteenth century through its use of *stile antico*, as is shown by its archaic notation in whole and half notes. In addition, Corelli specifies a departure from normal practice by adding, after the tempo mark: "Use sustained bows and [play] as is." An unusual indication, this is evidently a request that the players not add embellishments, such as they would normally have done in a slow movement. The reason, presumably, is to create an effect of heightened solemnity and mystery appropriate to the Midnight Mass at which this music was meant to be performed.

The remaining movements, however, consist largely of dances, although only one is labeled as such. The first Allegro is close in style to the *allemanda* of the D Major Trio Sonata, op. 2, no. 1 (anthology, Selection 35). The Vivace (mvt. 4) and the second Allegro (mvt. 5) constitute a *menuetto* (minuet) and a *gavotta*, respectively. Only the third movement lacks a dance character; it is a free da capo form, with an *adagio* A section and an *allegro* B section.

The final movement is designated a *pastorale ad libitum*. A **pastorale** is a slow version of the *giga*, using the same duple meter $\left(\begin{smallmatrix}12\\8\end{smallmatrix}\right)$ and skipping rhythm (quarter, eighth). The dance was associated with shepherds, as its name implies (Latin *pastor* = "shepherd"). Its use here is a reference to the shepherds mentioned in the New Testament as tending their flocks on the night of Jesus' birth. A more up-to-date reference, however, would have been to a Roman practice in which peasants from the surrounding countryside made a Christmas pilgrimage into the city's churches.[2] The movement contains a programmatic detail unique in

---

[2]The march of the shepherds in Charpentier's Christmas oratorio (anthology, Selection 17) may reflect a similar tradition.

Corelli's works, although it is encountered in other "pastoral" music of the period: much of the movement is built over pedal points, such as the repeated G's of the first continuo part in measures 1–2. These pedal points represent the *zampogne*, a type of bagpipe played by the Italian peasants. The **bagpipe**, a traditional wind instrument, is characterized by a **drone**, an unchanging bass note that is held out underneath the melody. This drone was imitated in works by later composers, including Bach in the musette movement of his Third English Suite and Handel in the *pifa* movement of his *Messiah*.[3]

THE SOLO CONCERTO

A number of composers, notably Handel, published imitations of Corelli's concerti grossi. By the time of the latter's publication in 1714, however, other types of concertos were becoming more fashionable. These concertos provided greater opportunities for virtuoso display by the soloists and frequently by the ensemble as a whole as well. The increasing emphasis on soloistic expression and display paralleled developments in opera, where the aria had long been established as the principal element, at least in Italy. In concertos with a single soloist, the latter thus played a role somewhat analogous to that of the virtuoso singer in opera, and composers found various ways of emulating the drama of the operatic aria in their concertos. Hence it is not surprising that the newer types of concerto borrowed elements from the aria, especially the use of ritornello form in the quick movements (and increasingly in the slow ones as well).

Ritornello Form

As employed in the concerto, ritornello form involved an alternation between passages scored for the entire ensemble, called the **tutti** (Italian for "all"), and more lightly scored passages usually involving one or more soloists accompanied by continuo. Like aria, a concerto movement of this type opens with a ritornello, followed by what we will refer to as the first of several **solo passages** or **solos**. These alternate with restatements of the ritornello, which may be abbreviated; the movement always concludes with another restatement of the ritornello, in whole or part.

Ritornello form involves more than just an alternation between tutti and soloist. Equally crucial is the presence of modulations, so that successive ritornellos are usually in different keys, the first and last in the tonic. Most of the modulations take place during the solos, so that the opening of each ritornello serves as a point of arrival. In other words, the ritornellos are the main guideposts of the movement, each one confirming any modulation that has taken place during the preceding solo section.

This type of ritornello form differs in several crucial ways from that typically found in contemporary opera arias. First, the number and length of the ritor-

---

[3]The **musette** is a French type of bagpipe; the *pifa* is a Mediterranean folk instrument.

nellos are generally greater than in an aria. Indeed, in many early concertos the passages for the tutti make up the bulk of each movement, the solo passages being relatively brief. In addition, there may be any number of ritornellos alternating with solo sections, although the number of solo sections tended to diminish in the course of the eighteenth century as the individual sections grew longer.

Unlike the singer in an aria, the soloist or soloists in a Baroque concerto normally play as part of the tutti. Thus the soloists are present in the ritornellos as well as the solo passages. Moreover, many concerto movements blur the distinction between ripieno and solo parts, and thus between ritornello and solo sections. This is particularly true in the early eighteenth century, when ritornello form had not yet become standardized, nor was it established as the principal form in concerto movements. Composers such as Vivaldi and J. S. Bach and their audiences were apparently less interested in the regular alternation of rigidly defined sections than in the free, fluid development of motivic material within a type of movement characterized by continually varied scoring. Particularly with Bach, a movement may open with well-defined ritornello and solo passages, but as the music progresses the two types of passage may exchange motivic material or otherwise become assimilated to each another, to the point that it is arbitrary to define one passage as a ritornello and another as a solo.

Vivaldi

Antonio Vivaldi (1678–1741) was born in Venice. He probably learned music from his father, a violinist (possibly also a composer) who held a position at St. Mark's Basilica. By Vivaldi's time, Venice's economic and political importance had declined in relation to that of France, Austria, and other European states. Nevertheless, it remained one of the busiest and most influential artistic centers on the continent, its thriving musical institutions including not only opera theaters and churches but several institutions known as *ospedali*, which resembled orphanages. At several of these, the women residents—who might spend their whole lives there—received advanced musical training and gave public concerts that were famous throughout Europe.

In 1703 Vivaldi became violin teacher at one of these institutions, the Pio Ospedale della Pietà. He continued to work there (with interruptions) for most of his life, and many of his concertos were composed for performance at the Pietà. At various times he also worked for a number of noble patrons as well as at several opera theaters, and he undertook journeys to Rome, Mantua, Amsterdam, and elsewhere in connection with performances of his operas and in search of further patronage. He died in Vienna while on one of these trips. Although ordained a priest in 1703, this did not prevent him from maintaining a long association with the contralto Anna Giraud, an opera singer at Venice and elsewhere from 1724 to 1747.

In addition to his students at the Pietà, Vivaldi taught, or at least was visited by and deeply influenced, such German composers as Johann David Heinichen (1683–1729), the violinist Johann Georg Pisendel (1687–1755), and the flutist Johann Joachim Quantz (1697–1773). All three were based at the

Figure 13.2 Antonio Vivaldi, from an engraving by J. Caldwall. This posthumous portrait appeared in *A General History of the Science and Practice of Music* by Sir John Hawkins (5 vols., London, 1776), one of the first serious attempts to write a comprehensive history of Western music.

Saxon court in Dresden, although Quantz later worked for the Prussian king Frederick the Great in Berlin. From Dresden they helped disseminate Vivaldi's works and style throughout northern Europe, not only through copies of his music that they brought back with them but through their own instrumental works closely modeled on his. Vivaldi found imitators in France as well; the violinist-composer Jean-Marie Leclair (1697–1764) made a particularly original adaptation of the Vivaldi style in his solo and trio sonatas and concertos.

Vivaldi's music includes some fifty operas and other theatrical works, forty or so cantatas, and over fifty sacred vocal works. He is best known for his enormous output of sonatas and concertos: some ninety solo and trio sonatas, and about five hundred concertos, including over two hundred solo violin concertos. Only a small portion of his output was published during his lifetime, but among this were some of his most important and influential instrumental works. Of especial significance were three publications, each containing twelve concertos. Opus 3, entitled *L'estro armonico*, appeared in 1711; it is discussed below. Opus 4, entitled *La stravaganza* (ca. 1714), was a set of solo violin concertos; Opus 8, *Il cimento dell'armonia e dell'inventione* (The contest of harmony and invention, 1725), includes the four solo violin concertos known as *The Four Seasons*. The latter are descriptive or programmatic works, like the last movement of Corelli's "Christmas" Concerto and a number of other Baroque concertos. *The Four Seasons* goes beyond other such works in the richness and ingenuity of its musical depictions, which represent various seasonal images described in four accompanying poems.

Like several other highly prolific Baroque composers, Vivaldi is often disparaged; one may hear, for example, that "he wrote the same concerto five hundred times." Yet Vivaldi's best works are characterized by inventive writing for individual instruments as well as clever and varied use of the ensemble as a whole. Many works also contain harmonic and rhythmic surprises that may be both witty and dramatic at the same time. The frequent repetitions and sequences in the music can make it seem simple, yet, as with Corelli, the impression of simplicity is actually an indication of its sophistication. From Vivaldi's music, Bach and other composers learned how to produce vivid, dramatic effects without indulging in the complex counterpoint or chromatic harmony of earlier Baroque composers. In this the music of Vivaldi and his contemporaries represents an important change in style—the beginning of the development toward the *galant* and Classical styles of the mid- and late eighteenth century, respectively.

Several catalogues or lists of Vivaldi's works exist, each referred to by a letter abbreviation. The most complete and up-to-date is that of the Danish scholar Peter Ryom, and his "R" (or "RV") numbers are now the preferred ones, used alongside opus numbers for Vivaldi's published works.

Vivaldi's Concerto in E, op. 3, no. 12, R. 265

The title of Vivaldi's Opus 3, *L'estro armonico* (Amsterdam, 1711), means something like "Harmonic inspiration"; it might have referred to the twelve concertos' brilliantly varied scoring. As is true of virtually all of the sonatas and concertos we have been examining, a purchaser acquiring a copy of the work—whether printed or in manuscript—would have gotten not a score but a set of separate parts. Opus 3 was published in eight partbooks: one each for four violins, two violas, cello, and continuo. The continuo part might have been shared by the keyboard player with either a second cellist or perhaps a double-bass player. The other parts would most likely have been used by single players, who would have quickly discovered that their roles varied from one work to another within the set.

Eight of the concertos are examples of what today are often termed, somewhat misleadingly, concerti grossi, since two or, in some cases, all four violin parts have solo roles, at least in certain movements. The first cello and even the violas have occasional solo roles as well. In the four remaining concertos, however, only the first of the violin parts takes a solo role. These concertos therefore constitute solo concertos; among them is the one in E major, the last in the set (anthology, Selection 38).

It is primarily from Vivaldi's solo concertos that the modern understanding of Baroque ritornello form has been derived. Like the great majority of solo concertos by Vivaldi and later composers, our work is in three movements, in the order fast-slow-fast. The outer movements, both marked *allegro*, employ ritornello form; the design of the third movement, the simpler of the two, is summarized in Table 13.1. As the chart shows, this movement has a nicely symmetrical form in which five ritornellos alternate with four solo passages. The most remote modulation—to the relative minor—is marked by the third ritornello, which occupies the center of the movement (mm. 31b–44). Similar designs can be found in many of Vivaldi's concerto movements.

Yet this symmetrical picture is not entirely accurate. For one thing, no two ritornellos are exactly the same. The opening ritornello of the third movement is never restated in full, and only a portion of it returns at the end. Whereas the opening and closing ritornellos remain in the tonic, the central ritornello (mm. 42–64) reaches the relative minor only after modulating from the dominant. Two short tutti passages in the later stages of the movement (at mm. 81 and 99) repeat motivic material from the opening ritornello but use it in new ways.[4]

Each solo section in the third movement is constructed in a logical way out of a relatively small number of motives. No material is ever literally restated, but subtle motivic relationships insure the integration of the movement as a whole. For example, the first solo section (mm. 22–41) opens with lively figuration in sixteenths, built out of two motives: a turning motive on beat 1 (with a slur on notes 1–3) and a repeated leaping figure on beats 2–3. These motives are repeated in sequence (mm. 23–26), to be replaced by a further series of sixteenth-note motives, one of which is similar to the original turning figure (compare beat 1 in m. 22 and m. 30). The second solo section (mm. 64–80) seems

TABLE 13.1
Antonio Vivaldi: Concerto in E, op. 3, no. 12 (R. 265), third movement

Section	R	S	R	S	r	S	r	S	R
Key	E	E →	B →	c# →	E:V	E	E	E	E
Measure	1	22	42	64	81	85	99	103	112

R = ritornello
S = solo section
lowercase letters = shorter sections

---

[4]The first of these abbreviated ritornellos, at m. 81, appears to be in the dominant, B major. But this key is only weakly tonicized, and the tonality immediately returns to E; for this reason Table 13.1 shows the passage as being "on" the dominant, symbolized as E:V.

unrelated; the solo violin part is notated in three-part chords, which probably were meant to be broken as rapid arpeggios. Accompanying this, however, the ripieno violins play a motive consisting of a chord broken in eighth notes. The same motive appears in the accompaniment to the first solo (mm. 22–35), thus connecting the two sections; the motive, moreover, derives from the ritornello (cf. m. 1, violins 1–2, last three notes).

The first movement is somewhat longer and more complex than the third, with a greater number of distinct ritornellos and solos. Moreover, it is unusual for the tonal instability of its ritornellos; even the opening one (mm. 1–8) modulates from tonic to dominant. Nevertheless, the fundamental design of this movement is similar to that of the last, with a move to the relative minor (m. 31) and a lengthy modulating ritornello (mm. 32–45) occurring in the inner sections.

As in most concertos, the second movement is simpler in form and in its technical demands on the players, although the soloist was presumably expected to supply improvised melodic embellishment. The movement differs from the slow movements of most later eighteenth-century concertos in being in the tonic; in other concertos an inner slow movement is usually in a contrasting key, most often the relative minor. Also notable here is the four-part fugal texture of the ritornello; even the violas enter with a statement of the short four-note subject (m. 2). This is unexpected although by no means unheard-of in eighteenth-century Italian instrumental music, which is predominantly homophonic.

J. S. Bach and the Concerto

In a sense, J. S. Bach was one of Vivaldi's best students. Though he never traveled to Italy or met Vivaldi, Bach studied the latter's Opera 3 and 4, arranging a number of works from each set as solos for harpsichord or organ around 1713.[5] At the time, Vivaldi's music represented an exciting avant-garde, and Bach, like other German composers, must have eagerly acquired copies of it for study, performance, and imitation. A number of Bach's harpsichord and organ works—the preludes of the English Suites and several *praeludia* whose first movements resemble ritornello forms—might have been among his first original compositions based on Vivaldi's models. Real ensemble concertos for violin and other instruments followed, most of them probably composed during his last few years at Weimar (1714–17) and at Cöthen (1717–23).

The Brandenburg Concertos

Bach's most famous concertos are the set of six works that he copied out in 1721 into a manuscript dedicated to Christian Ludwig, the margrave of Branden-

---

[5]Bach's arrangement of Vivaldi's Concerto op. 3, no. 12, is the fifth in the series of such transcriptions for harpsichord (BWV 976). Bach later arranged one of the multiple-soloist works from Opus 3 (Concerto no. 10 in B minor, R. 580) as a concerto in A minor with four solo harpsichord parts, BWV 1065.

burg. Eighteenth-century works were often referred to by the name of their dedicatee—hence the nickname Brandenburg Concertos. Brandenburg was ruled from Berlin, where Bach had played several years earlier for the margrave. The latter did not, however, acknowledge Bach's dedication or even have the works performed, so far as is known. Bach, however, must have played all six of the concertos with the Weimar or Cöthen court ensembles, and at Leipzig he arranged several movements for use in his cantatas.

Reflecting Bach's study of Vivaldi's ingenious and varied instrumentation, the set is remarkable for its diversity. No two of the works have the same scoring or form. They include such novelties as a work for three violins, three violas, and three cellos with continuo (Concerto no. 3) and a work with a solo harpsichord part (Concerto no. 5), in which Bach himself must have served as soloist. Modern impressions of the Brandenburg Concertos have been distorted by performances in which parts intended for single players have been given to entire orchestral sections. In fact, like many Baroque concertos, these were probably composed as chamber works in the modern sense, with a single player on each part (both solo and ripieno).

Brandenburg Concerto no. 2 in F, BWV 1047

As with all six concertos, the date of composition for Concerto No. 2 (anthology, Selection 39) is unknown, although details in its instrumentation suggest it originated at Weimar, that is, by 1717. It contains solo parts for trumpet, recorder, oboe, and violin, as well as a continuo part for cello and harpsichord and ripieno parts for two violins, viola, and "violone."[6] The trumpet part is for a natural (valveless) instrument in F, higher than the usual trumpet in C or D and thus presenting particular difficulties to players of modern instruments.[7]

Despite its colorful instrumentation, in its scoring the work comes closer than any of the others in the set to Corelli's concerti grossi. This work, too, is a genuine concerto grosso, performable by soloists and continuo alone, that is, without the four ripieno string parts. Indeed, Bach may have originally written it in this form, although no such version survives. Nevertheless, the first movement is in ritornello form, never used by Corelli. In addition, its three movements fall in what would soon become the standard fast-slow-fast sequence.

The first movement, although opening with the usual passage for the tutti (mm. 1–8), soon begins to blur the lines between ritornello and solo sections. Passages for soloists and for the tutti alternate in rapid succession, and the ritornello never returns in its original form. For this reason, no analysis along the lines of a simple alternation of ritornello and solo sections is entirely satisfactory, and the diagram in Table 13.2 employs a number of special symbols intended to reflect the unique elements of this movement.

---

[6]The *violone di ripieno* called for in Bach's score of this work was perhaps not a double-bass instrument but a French bass violin or a large viola da gamba playing at written pitch.

[7]Bach's performances might have used the normal D trumpet if the other players tuned to what is known as *tief Kammerton*, the lowest of several different pitch standards used in Bach's day.

TABLE 13.2
J. S. Bach (1685–1750): Brandenburg Concerto No. 2 in F (BWV 1047), first movement

Section	R	S*	r	s	R*	seq	BACH	r	S*	R*	seq	R*	r	BACH	r
Key	F	F→	C	→	d	d→	→	B♭	B♭→	g	g→	a	F	→	F
Measure	1	9	23	29	31	40	50	56	60	75	84	94	103	107	115

S* = begins as a solo, but includes tutti passages

R* = a tutti passage combining portions of R with a new sequential phrase

seq = a long sequence derived from mm. 1–2 of the ritornello

BACH = a sequence with the "BACH" motive in the bass line

The texture throughout is highly contrapuntal, as one might expect of Bach. As in Cantata 127, the opening ritornello combines three distinct motivic ideas in invertible counterpoint (played by trumpet, the other soloists, and continuo, respectively). The first few solo passages then introduce a contrasting theme, played by each of the soloists in a series of imitative entries (mm. 9, 13, 17, 21), beginning with the violin.

One later passage in the movement, labeled "BACH" in Table 13.2, is of special interest. In the first appearance of the passage, in measures 50–55, the bass line begins with the notes e♭–d–f–e♮. This may seem unremarkable, but when the passage is restated later in the movement the notes are transposed to spell out B♭–A–c–B♮ (mm. 109–11). In German, the note B♭ is designated simply B, whereas B♮ is called H; thus the bass line spells out Bach's name (B–A–c–H). This was no accident, as is clear from the recurrence of this BACH motive in other works by Bach and his sons.[8]

The restatement of this passage points to an important aspect of Bach's compositional process. Unlike Vivaldi, who composed in a seemingly improvisatory manner, rarely repeating anything exactly, Bach often restates substantial portions of a movement, frequently in transposed or otherwise varied form. This procedure helps establish the "architectural" quality for which his music is sometimes noted—that is, the impression that each movement resembles a monumental, solidly constructed edifice. The recurrence of the BACH passage is particularly striking, for it stands out against the surrounding music by virtue of its relatively homophonic texture, its *piano* dynamic marking, and its somewhat surprising harmonies. Clearly, Bach gave the passage in which he "signed" his name a crucial role in the movement's formal design.

The trumpet and the ripieno instruments drop out in the second movement, an Andante in D minor. The natural trumpet could have played only a very limited part here, and its military associations would have been inappropriate to the quiet tone of the movement. Similarly reduced scoring characterizes the slow movements of most of the other works in the set and is common throughout the eighteenth-century concerto repertory. Here, the three remaining soloists and continuo are enough to provide complex four-part counterpoint. The texture stays constant throughout the movement: sustained lines for the three upper parts are written in imitative counterpoint, while the continuo moves in steady eighth notes, except at cadences.

The use of a single, unvarying texture is typical of many late Baroque works; we have seen an earlier example in the fourth movement of Corelli's Sonata in C, op. 5, no. 3, with its steady arpeggiation in sixteenths for the violin. Some contrast arises out of the modulations through a series of different keys, and the imitative technique used in the three upper voices produces a kaleidoscopic effect as the main theme passes from one part to another, creating a constant variation of sonority.

Two aspects of the movement are particularly characteristic of Bach. First, it is extremely dissonant. The chord on the downbeat of measure 6, for example,

---

[8]The most famous instance of the BACH motive is in the incomplete *Fuga con 3 soggetti* from Bach's *Art of Fugue*.

TABLE 13.3
J. S. Bach (1685–1750): Brandenburg Concerto No. 2 in F (BWV 1047), third movement

	1st Exposition	Episode	2nd Exposition	Episode	3rd Exposition	Episode & Coda
Trumpet	F * x C	1	*	4 3	(x) * *	2 (F)
Recorder	C—*	2	(x) * x	1 5	F x	3
Oboe	C—*x +	3	d	5 1	Bb x	4
Violin	F* x	4	C—	2 2		1
Basso Continuo	(x x + +)	5	(*) + A/d—	3 4	(*) C/F—	5 (*)
Cadence	C		C d:V	g	Bb F:V	F'
Measure	1	41	57 72	80 85 97	107 119	126 139

letters = keys of fugal entries
numbers = melodic lines of invertible-counterpoint passage
X/Y (slash between letters) = entry on note X but in key Y
*, x, + = countersubjects; (symbol in parentheses) = incomplete or highly altered entry
— (dash) = bridge (free continuation of an entry)

The "cadence" line lists major arrivals, not all cadences.

is a IV^7, with the dissonant seventh (f″) appearing in the oboe. When the oboe resolves the dissonance, moving downward by step (to e″), it creates another dissonance, forming a tritone with the bass and the recorder. (The sonority as a whole is a diminished seventh chord). Similar progressions occur in almost every measure of the piece, giving it an anguished character shared with many of Bach's works.

The same passage illustrates a second aspect of the movement, its high frequency of so-called **sigh motives**. A sigh motive is a two-note slurred figure consisting of a dissonant appoggiatura (accented passing tone) and its resolution, such as the oboe's two-note motive on the downbeat of measure 6. The slur implies a decrescendo from the accented appoggiatura to its unaccented resolution, producing an expressive effect. Sigh motives are particularly prominent in the passage beginning at measure 16 (recorder: c‴–b♭″, b♭″–a″, etc.).

Sigh figures are extremely common in sonatas, concertos, and arias written in the so-called *galant* style of Bach's younger Italian and German contemporaries (see Chapter 14). His use of such a figure here and in other works is one of many signs that he was happy to incorporate up-to-date, fashionable gestures into his music. But few of his contemporaries would have used such motives within such a densely contrapuntal texture, preferring a simpler and more direct style. Movements like this one eventually gave Bach the not entirely undeserved reputation of a composer of complex, difficult music—which might explain why the margrave of Brandenburg apparently ignored him.

Bach's penchant for complexity comes to the fore in the last movement, a five-voice fugue. The trumpet returns, stating the subject at the opening. It is joined by the other soloists, entering in turn with the subject. After the completion of the first exposition, the *ripieno* instruments return as well in a sort of episode (mm. 47–57; see Table 13.3).

Like many episodes in other Bach fugues, this one is restated several times in different keys, varied each time through invertible counterpoint (at mm. 79, 97, and 126). An essential element in strict fugues and other contrapuntal genres, invertible counterpoint always involves the exchange of two or more melodic lines between different parts. In **double counterpoint**, two parts exchange two melodic lines; **triple counterpoint** involves three lines and three parts. This episode, exceptionally, employs **quintuple counterpoint**—invertible counterpoint in which no fewer than five distinct melodic ideas are shuffled between the four soloists and continuo, as shown by the numbered entries in Table 13.3.

Most listeners will not consciously follow such a device. Nor need they do so in order to enjoy this movement, which, despite its fugal complexity, is as energetic and accessible as any work of Vivaldi's. This might have been Bach's point: the same music could satisfy both a learned composer such as himself and a prince who was, at best, a musical amateur. The composition of such music was an intellectual and creative feat of the highest magnitude. It was the type of achievement toward which most Baroque musicians probably aspired, even if few approached or even attempted it.

CHAPTER 14

A MID-EIGHTEENTH-CENTURY EPILOGUE
The *Galant* Style

As noted at the outset of this exploration of Baroque music, the periods into which we divide music history are in many respects arbitrary. It has become customary to see a dividing line at the mid-eighteenth century, partly because 1750 is a conveniently round figure, partly because a number of important composers, especially Bach and Handel, died in or about that year. Nevertheless, as in the period around 1600, few people at the time could have guessed that they were living through what would later be regarded as a transition period. The most prestigious and influential genre of the eighteenth century, opera seria, continued in an unbroken tradition right through the century.

Nevertheless, by 1750 the late Baroque style exemplified by the concertos of Vivaldi and Bach was a thing of the past. Rameau and Handel were still alive and composing, but many younger composers, including Gluck, the sons of Bach, and even Haydn, had already begun their careers. An old-fashioned work such as J. S. Bach's *Art of Fugue* had yet to be published. But Bach's son Carl Philipp Emanuel was already writing keyboard sonatas and concertos that have many points in common with those of Haydn and even Beethoven. Opera composers such as Hasse and Jommelli were creating a style that in some respects anticipated the so-called reform operas of Gluck and those of Mozart. And G. B. Sammartini, Monn, and Wagenseil were writing symphonies and chamber music that are at times virtually indistinguishable from early works of Haydn. Although we think of 1750 as the end of the Baroque, by that date Monn and some other short-lived pre-Classical composers, notably Giovanni Battista Pergolesi (1710–36), had already passed away.

THE *GALANT* STYLE

The French expression *style galant* is one of several terms that have been applied to the music of Telemann, C. P. E. Bach, and other composers active in the decades before and after 1750.[1] The term is sometimes translated literally

---

[1] Other terms in use are *pre-Classical* and *rococo*, the latter particularly with respect to French music (and art) of the period.

as "gallant style," but the English adjective *gallant* hardly conveys an accurate idea of what the expression signifies in music history. The French word *galant* originally meant fashionable or up-to-date; eighteenth-century writers applied it to everything from clothes to conversation. A *galant* musical work was, essentially, one that avoided strict counterpoint and chromatic harmony or modulation, which were increasingly seen as archaic. Instead such a work employed simple homophonic textures, with diatonic harmony and singable melodies. By this standard, most Italian opera arias and French dances were *galant*. So too were solo sonatas and concertos, at least as long as they avoided fugues. Today, however, the term is used more specifically to refer to mid-eighteenth century works whose melody, harmony, and texture represent a simplification of those of the preceding late Baroque period.

The term *galant* is particularly appropriate for various types of Italian vocal and instrumental music that have been viewed as direct predecessors of the Viennese Classical style. Among these are the operatic works of Pergolesi, including his famous comic intermezzo *La serva padrona* (Naples, 1733). In such works, even fully scored orchestral passages tend to consist of simple textures in which a single melodic line—often played by first and second violins in unison—is accompanied by a simple continuo part (doubled by the viola, whose part may not even be written out). If two upper lines are present, they often move in parallel thirds or sixths (Ex. 14.1). One rarely finds independent inner voices, and harmony in four or more real parts is rare. This trend was already evident in Italian instrumental and vocal music of the late seventeenth century. But in the *galant* style it extends to a point where even the bass line loses much of its former melodic and rhythmic independence, often being reduced to repeated notes (so-called **drum basses**), as in measures 2 and 9 of Example 14.1. Also typical of the style are the so-called Lombardic rhythm seen in measure 1 of the example, the appoggiaturas (written as small notes) in measures 2 and 9, and the slow **harmonic rhythm** or rate of harmonic change. In the example, the harmony rarely changes more than twice in each measure, and is moreover restricted to little more than an alternation of tonic and dominant. An earlier Baroque composer would have been embarrassed to write such music, but the aim here was a directness and simple elegance that could not be achieved in the older style.

This style proved popular throughout Europe, particularly in its operatic manifestation, although a distinct style descended from that of Lully remained recognizable in French music through the time of Mozart. In Germany, Italian opera dominated theaters at Dresden, Berlin (after 1741), and other capitals and courts, where the *galant* style served as a vehicle for such virtuoso singers as the castrati Farinelli and Senesino and the (female) sopranos Faustina Bordoni and Francesca Cuzzoni. Germans such as Handel were among the leading composers of eighteenth-century Italian opera; among them were Johann Adolph Hasse (1699–1783), who became the chief opera composer at Dresden (and who married Bordoni), and Carl Heinrich Graun (1704–57), his counterpart at Berlin. Their works exerted considerable influence on instrumental as well as vocal music by their contemporaries. Solo and trio sonatas adopted the styles of melody

Example 14.1 Pergolesi, duet "Per te ho nel core" from the opera *Flaminio* (1735), used as a replacement for the final duet of *La serva padrona* in some posthumous productions (violins and viola omitted)

Serpina, Uberto	Serpina, Uberto
E vero il sento già,	It's true, I hear it {heartbeats},
Ma questo ch'esser può,	But what it might be
Io nol so, nol so io.	I don't know.
Caro sposo/cara sposa! Oh Dio!	Dear spouse—Oh, God!—
Ben te lo puoi pensar.	You may well think yourself such.

and accompaniment employed in operatic arias and duets, and concertos increasingly took on the dramatic style and ritornello form of the aria.

One result of the spread of *galant* writing was a weakening of the sharp division between French and Italian styles that had marked seventeenth- and early eighteenth-century music. Another was the abandonment of what were seen—rightly or wrongly—as overly complicated, inexpressive or incomprehensible types of outmoded music, including the contrapuntal choral and instrumental works of J. S. Bach, whose style was seen by many as awkward and "unnatural" by the middle of the century.[2]

Older traditions were not entirely abandoned. In England, some composers continued to write in a simplified version of Handel's style until the end of the century. In Italy and Austria, many composers continued to cultivate the contrapuntal *stile antico* in church music; Haydn and Mozart still used it in some of their masses and other choral works. In Germany, the wide circle of musicians who had studied with J. S. Bach (or with his students) preserved the legacy of contrapuntal keyboard music. It is often thought that Bach's music was forgotten after his death, only to be revived in the nineteenth century, but this applies chiefly to his vocal music and works for instrumental ensemble. His organ and "clavier" works enjoyed ever widening circulation and were eagerly studied by such musicians as Mozart and Beethoven.

Modern writers have sometimes found *galant* music to be stylistically impoverished by comparison with the more complex music of J. S. Bach, Handel, and others. But eighteenth-century musicians and their audiences, including Bach and Handel, clearly found positive values in it. The relatively simple textures and harmony of galant music focused attention squarely on what was viewed as expressive and "natural" melody. Moreover, the changes in bass-line writing and instrumentation made possible new types of orchestral scoring, paving the way for the wide variety of orchestral textures used in later Classical and Romantic music. Solo keyboard music was equally transformed as the new focus on melody led to the invention of new types of idiomatic accompaniment. Among the latter was the so-called **Alberti bass,** a type of accompaniment consisting chiefly of broken chords. Named for one of its early users, the Venetian composer Domenico Alberti (ca. 1710–1740), it found widespread use as a keyboard equivalent for some of the new types of orchestral accompaniment. The broken chords of the left hand (lower staff) in Example 14.2 were an idiomatic keyboard adaptation of such orchestral textures as the repeated notes of the upper strings in Example 14.3, from *Cleofide*, a famous example of opera seria by Hasse. Bach is thought to have attended the Dresden premiere of the latter work in 1731, and he evidently encouraged his sons and students to imitate such music.

Example 14.2 Domenico Alberti, Sonata in E♭, second movement, mm. 1–4

---

[2]The most famous document for this view is the attack on Bach's vocal music published in 1737 by Johann Adolph Scheibe, a critic and composer who favored the *galant* style; see *The New Bach Reader*, 337–38.

Example 14.3 Johann Adolph Hasse, *Cleofide* (1731), Act 3, aria "Dov'è? si affretti," mm. 1–3

To be sure, the *galant* style does seem to have made it possible for mediocre composers to produce vast quantities of bland, forgettable vocal and instrumental music, much of it for the amateur market. Such music uses major keys almost exclusively and avoids surprises and intensely expressive or dramatic effects. Yet even Bach admired and imitated the *galant* works of some of his contemporaries, such as Telemann and Hasse, and his students were among the most important proponents of the style. In short, the musical developments of the later eighteenth century, including the emergence of the Viennese Classical style, cannot be fully understood without considering the *galant* music that preceded it.

GEORG PHILIPP TELEMANN

Although we tend to focus on Bach and Handel when considering music history in the first half of the eighteenth century, at the time the most respected and possibly the most influential composer in the German-speaking parts of Europe was Georg Philipp Telemann (1681–1767). He was capable of writing both contrapuntal church music in the manner of Bach and expressive oratorio and opera seria such as Handel's. But unlike those composers, Telemann was not a virtuoso performer, and much of his enormous output consists of relatively undemanding, accessible music. Born in Magdeburg, in eastern Germany, in 1701 he began university studies in nearby Leipzig. By the following year had founded the Leipzig Collegium Musicum—later directed by Bach—and was also directing the Leipzig Opera.[3] After holding a series of musical positions in Poland and Germany—including that of kapellmeister in Bach's hometown of Eisenach—Telemann was appointed cantor and music director at Hamburg in 1723, a prestigious position that he held until his death. Telemann knew both Handel, with whom he carried on a lifelong correspondence, and J. S. Bach, whose son Carl Philipp Emanuel was his godson and who succeeded him in his Hamburg position.

Like Vivaldi, Telemann's reputation has suffered because of the enormous quantity of his works. In the case of Telemann the judgment is particularly un-

---

[3]The Leipzig Opera had ceased operation by the time Bach came to town in 1723.

fair because relatively few of his major works have been published. Among his best-known compositions today are certain charming but relatively insignificant solo and trio sonatas for recorder, violin, and other instruments. Virtually unknown are many more substantial instrumental pieces—including sonatas for three and even four soloists, concertos, and overtures—as well as over a thousand cantatas and larger church works. Telemann also wrote some three dozen operas, such as his comical *Der geduldige Socrates* (The patient Socrates, 1721), as well as many other large and small secular vocal works. His instrumental music includes over one hundred orchestral suites, a hundred or more concertos, and numerous smaller works.[4]

Telemann's "Paris" Quartets

In 1737 Telemann visited Paris. There, as he proclaimed in his autobiography of 1739, a number of his quartets were played with great success by an ensemble comprising several of the most famous French musicians of the day. Among them were the flutist Michel Blavet (1700–1768), composer of flute sonatas and other works, and the viola da gambist Jean-Baptiste Antoine Forqueray (1699–1782), son of the composer Antoine Forqueray. The works in question were no doubt the six *Nouveaux quatuors* (New quartets) that were published at Paris in 1738 during Telemann's stay here. This set was a continuation of six similarly scored works that had been first published in 1730. Both sets became widely known and are now often referred to as Telemann's "Paris" Quartets; among the subscribers whose names appear printed in the 1738 volume was "Bach of Leipzig."

A "quartet" in the early eighteenth century was a sonata for three melody instruments and continuo—that is, one more instrument than in a trio sonata; the present works are for the unusual combination of violin, flute, and viola da gamba. By including an independent part for the viol, Telemann continued the long tradition of chamber music for that instrument in France (there were also still a few famous viol players in Germany). Nevertheless, to facilitate performance for ensembles without a gambist, Telemann included an alternate part for cello. A harpsichord furnishes the continuo, to which might be joined a second cello, although this option is not made explicit.

Nouveau quatuor no. 6 in E Minor, TWV 43:e4

The "new" quartets can be described as suites. Particularly impressive is the concluding work in E minor (anthology, Selection 40), which consists of a French overture followed by five dancelike movements designated by the tempo indications *Gay, Vite, Gracieusement, Distrait,* and *Modéré*. The presence of an overture and dances signifies that the style is French, yet the music throughout contains substantial elements of the Italian style, as in the frequent use of

---

[4]A multivolume thematic catalogue of Telemann's works is being published gradually; it assigns a TWV number to each work.

Figure 14.1 Telemann, *Nouveau quatuor* no. 6 in E minor, TWV 43:e4, opening page of the flute part, from its first edition (Paris, 1738). Note the clean lines of the stems and beams and the precise placement of slurs and ornament signs (in the form of crosses or plus signs), typical of French music engraving in the eighteenth century.

arpeggiated figuration. To be sure, by this date Italian style had thoroughly permeated French music, as in the operas of Rameau.

The opening movement reveals some of the ways in which the old ceremonial genre of the Lullian overture could be transformed in the hands of an inventive *galant* composer such as Telemann. In the opening section the dotted rhythms are maintained less consistently than in the pure Lully style; indeed, they are interrupted by some Italianate arpeggiation for the violin (mm. 9–11). The tempo marking *à discrétion* (with freedom) probably applies in particular to this violin solo, which might therefore be played rhapsodically, like an improvisation—a far cry from the rhythmic precision of the Lullian opera orchestra.

The following section, marked *très vite* (very quick), opens without the fugal exposition frequently encountered at this point in the traditional French overture. Moreover, the main theme contains some catchy hemiolas, a witty surprise in such a movement (mm. 15–16, 17–18, etc.). All three upper parts, especially the violin, have virtuoso passagework also characteristic not of the traditional French style but of Vivaldi and other Italians. Yet the texture remains predominantly contrapuntal, including some passages in invertible counterpoint, and the movement closes with the conventional recapitulation of the opening section.

Of the four short movements that follow, two are clearly dances: the second movement, marked *Gay*, is a gavotte, as is evident from its half-measure upbeat, whereas the fourth, designated *Gracieusement* (gracefully—not in the anthology), is probably a *loure*, a type of slow French gigue resembling the Italian pastorale (Ex. 14.4). The fifth movement, headed *Distrait*, does not belong to any of the traditional categories; rather, it is a sort of character piece that reflects the expressive implications of its title, which means something like "distraught" or "crazy." This explains the syncopations that dominate the flute and violin in the first section (mm. 1–24) and the gamba in the second (mm. 25–56). But in keeping with the polite tone of the *galant* style, the music does not attempt a dramatic representaiton of true madness, such as occurs in the second act of Handel's *Orlando* (composed just a few years earlier), or even of feigned madness as in Purcell's *From Rosy Bowers*. *Galant* audiences evidently preferred music that cleverly suggested the idea of distress without portraying it too vividly, and Telemann's witty music accomplishes this admirably.

Example 14.4 Telemann, *Nouveau quatuor* no. 6, fourth movement, mm. 1–5

The form of this movement is the same used in the paired dances that formed the Baroque antecedent of the Classical minuet and trio. Couperin, Bach, Telemann, and other contemporaries frequently grouped two short binary-form movements together, repeating the second one at the end to produce an ABA design.[5] The *Gay* movement has the same form; like the B section of many such movments, its second section is in a contrasting mode (major) and uses altered instrumentation—exceptionally, without continuo.

The last movement is a chaconne over a six-bar ostinato bass. A passacaglia for solo harpsichord by the German composer Johann Philipp Krieger

---

[5]It is uncertain whether both halves of the A section were repeated the second time around, as has been argued for the Classical minuet and trio.

(1649–1725)—an uncle of Haudel—has the same unusual bass line, and it is possible that Telemann borrowed this as well as a few melodic ideas from the older composer. But instead of the rhythmic energy of the traditional Lullian or Ramellian dance, this movement has a languishing, elegiac character. This comes from such details as the sustained notes of the bass line, the drooping motive of the flute and violin at the opening, and the slurred chromatic lines that come a bit later (mm. 13–15). The movement creates a profoundly moving effect in performance, belying the notion that Telemann's music lacks depth or seriousness.

CARL PHILIPP EMANUEL BACH

C. P. E. Bach extended to the *galant* style the expressive harmony and rhythmic complexity found in earlier music, especially that of his father. Emanuel Bach's lifespan almost exactly straddled the middle of the century, overlapping what we consider the late Baroque and early Classical periods. We can recognize elements of both styles in his music, but his works are best understood as an intensely personal development of the same *galant* style seen in the works of Telemann, Hasse, and other older contemporaries.

The Bach Sons

J. S. Bach (1685–1750) had altogether five sons who became professional musicians. Four were also composers, and of these three were of considerable importance. All tended to avoid the contrapuntal aspects of their father's music in favor of the *galant* style. This may well have been at J. S. Bach's insistence, for only by adopting the more fashionable and up-to-date style could they hope for successful careers of their own. Both Wilhelm Friedemann (1710–84) and Carl Philipp Emanuel (1714–88) were keyboard virtuosos whose instrumental works, especially keyboard sonatas and concertos, are of special significance. On the other hand, Johann Christian (1735–87), the youngest son, became a composer of Italian opera and Italianate symphonies and chamber music. He settled in London, where his music was a major influence on the young Mozart, whose early works closely resemble Christian Bach's.

In the music of Friedemann and Emanuel Bach, the conventional *galant* style is deepened by chromatic harmony and expressive, often improvisatory, melodic fragmentation and surprise. Their style and that of a few contemporaries in northern Germany is often described today as the *empfindsamer Stil* ("sensitive" or "expressive style"). This is a reference to its frequent use of pathetic or dramatic expressive effects, although the music of both composers is also marked by touches of witty humor, like that of Telemann.

Emanuel Bach was probably the most prolific and original of the Bach sons. He was widely admired for his keyboard playing as well as his compositions, which, like those of his father, include all of the major genres of the time except for opera. He was born at Weimar and grew up in Cöthen and Leipzig, where, according to his autobiography of 1773, his sole teacher was his father.

In 1740 he became court keyboard player to the Prussian king Frederick II (the Great) at Berlin. There he regularly accompanied the flute-playing king in private concerts alongside Quantz, the king's teacher, the opera composer C. H. Graun (who played violin), and other distinguished musicians.[6] In 1768, after the death of Telemann, Bach left Berlin to take over his godfather's position as cantor and church music director at Hamburg, where he spent his remaining twenty years.

Emanuel's career roughly paralleled his father's, culminating in a position as music director in a major city after a period as a court musician. But both Emanuel's style and the musical genres in which he composed were substantially different. Although he wrote a substantial quantity of cantatas and other sacred vocal works at Hamburg, his most important works are his 150 keyboard sonatas and 52 keyboard concertos.[7] In addition to old-fashioned solo and trio sonatas (mostly before 1750), he also composed German songs (lieder), piano trios (for keyboard, violin, and cello), and a number of fantasias, rondos, and other keyboard pieces. Like his Berlin colleague Quantz, he also wrote an influential performance treatise: *The True Manner of Playing Keyboard Instruments*, which provides important material on keyboard playing in the *galant* and earlier styles. The book was published in two volumes; volume 1 (Berlin, 1753) is a treatise on keyboard playing in general, with special focus on the clavichord, whereas volume 2 (Berlin, 1762) is concerned with figured bass realization and improvisation. Much in the book, particularly in the second volume, probably derives from the teaching of J. S. Bach. But its immediate concern is the performance of *galant* music, naturally including Emanuel's own.

A thematic catalog of Emanuel's works was prepared early in the twentieth century by Alfred Wotquenne. A later catalog by E. Eugene Helm is far more complete but already in need of revision in the light of recent research. Both "W" and "H" numbers are in use.

The Keyboard Sonatas

The keyboard sonatas constitute the earliest important repertory of multi-movement sonatas for solo keyboard instruments. Written throughout Bach's career, they reveal the composer's stylistic evolution from a post-Baroque manner, containing occasional echoes of Sebastian Bach's inventions and suites, to a style that is often described as Classical or even pre-Romantic. The keyboard sonata hardly existed as a genre when Emanuel began writing such works, in the early 1730s, while still a student at Leipzig. Since his father wrote no keyboard sonatas of this type, Emanuel must have modeled them on solo sonatas for flute or violin and continuo by such *galant* composers as Telemann and Hasse. But even Emanuel's earliest sonatas reveal an original, idiomatic adaptation of the genre to the keyboard.

---

[6]Among the violinists was Graun's brother Johann Gottlieb (1702/3–71), an imaginative composer of trio sonatas and other chamber music.

[7]A few of the concertos also exist in versions for flute or cello. Much of Emanuel Bach's sacred music, until recently thought lost during World War II, appears to have survived in a large collection of manuscripts recently located in Kiev, Ukraine.

During his first few years at Berlin, Emanuel Bach published two influential sets of six sonatas each, the "Prussian" Sonatas of 1742 and the "Württemberg" Sonatas of 1744. Further sets appeared after 1750, including a famous series of six volumes published at Hamburg under the subtitle *für Kenner und Liebhaber* ("for connoisseurs and amateurs," 1779–87); the first volume comprised six sonatas, whereas the next five included distinctive types of rondos and fantasias as well. Following eighteenth-century tradition, Emanuel did not usually specify the medium of his keyboard works, and they can be played on the harpsichord as well as the fortepiano. In his own playing, however, he is known to have favored the clavichord. Eighteenth-century German instrument makers expanded the clavichord's keyboard compass and dynamic capabilities, and contemporary accounts of Emanuel's playing, such as that published in 1773 by the English writer Charles Burney (1726–1814), describe his brilliant performances and impassioned improvisations on such instruments.

The Concertos

Like the sonatas, the concertos are a genre that Emanuel Bach essentially invented, insofar as works for keyboard are concerned. His father's harpsichord concertos, thought to have been written at Leipzig in the 1730s, are arrangements of earlier works in which the solo parts were for violin or perhaps other instruments. Thus the first three harpsichord concertos that Emanuel composed at Leipzig in the early 1730s are among the earliest original works of this type for a stringed keyboard instrument. During the 1740s Emanuel devoted particularly intensive efforts to the genre, composing twenty such works as well as one concerto for two harpsichords, all with string accompaniment. He continued to write harpsichord concertos into his Hamburg years, when he probably played many of them at public concerts under his direction. His last concerto, written in 1788, is a double concerto for harpsichord, fortepiano, and orchestra.

The Concerto in D Minor for Harpsichord and Strings, W. 23 (H. 427)

This work (anthology, Selection 41) was composed at Potsdam, outside Berlin, in 1748. It is one of a half-dozen unusually dramatic concertos in minor keys—thus bucking *galant* trends—that C. P. E. Bach wrote during the 1740s. Like the others, it was most likely composed for performance not at the royal court, where Bach's music appears to have fallen out of favor at an unknown date, but for private or semipublic gatherings elsewhere. Among these were the regular Saturday concerts given at the home of Johann Friedrich Agricola (1720–74), a student of J. S. Bach and C. H. Graun's eventual successor as royal opera composer.[8]

---

[8]Agricola, like Quantz and C. P. E. Bach, was also an important writer on music; he was responsible for the German translation of Tosi's singing treatise as well as an annotated version of an encyclopedic work on organs and other keyboard instruments by Jacob Adlung, *Musica mechanica organoedi* (Berlin, 1768), which provides valuable information about the performance of J. S. Bach's music.

Wherever the concertos were performed, C. P. E. Bach must have had at his disposal many of the same virtuosos who accompanied the king, for the string parts in his concertos are as challenging and as expressive as those of the soloist. The latter plays in both the solo passages and those for the tutti, directing the ensemble and providing a continuo realization in the latter. This had been the practice in the keyboard concertos of J. S. Bach, and it remained so for later eighteenth-century composers (including Mozart and Beethoven).

Although Emanuel composed no operas as such, there can be little doubt that much of the inspiration for his dramatic harpsichord concertos of the 1740s came from opera, especially after King Frederick's Berlin opera house had opened its doors in 1742. The ritornello form employed in each movement recalls that of the contemporary opera aria. The two genres share the same basic orchestral texture as well, as a glance at the opening ritornello reveals. The latter rarely employs more than three real parts—the violins often play in unison—and the continuo part consists largely of drum basses (compare Ex. 14.3).

Despite its conventionally *galant* texture, the ritornello is decidedly un-*galant* in its melody, harmony, and rhythm. The violin parts are filled with dramatic leaps (m. 2), fragmented rhythms (signified by the rests in mm. 3, 5, etc.), sharp dynamic contrasts (*pianissimo* alternating with *forte* in mm. 8–11), and striking chromaticism, such as the dissonant appoggiatura on the downbeat of measure 9. This appoggiatura, although played softly, is emphasized by being held out as a half note, resolving only on the third beat. There are also some departures from the typically homophonic *galant* texture, notably in measures 33–36. Here the entire ensemble plays in octaves before coming to rest on a nondiatonic scale degree (E♭, the Neapolitan).

Most of these individual gestures could be found in operatic works by *galant* composers such as Hasse and C. H. Graun. The octave passage, for example, is reminiscent of the unison writing for strings typically heard in the ritornello of a so-called rage aria.[9] Nevertheless, the close juxtaposition of so many striking passages is uniquely characteristic of C. P. E. Bach's music. This style may seem as far from that of J. S. Bach as it does from, say, that of Telemann. Yet the chromatic harmony and sudden modulations reveal the inspiration of J. S. Bach, as does Emanuel's precise notation of ornaments and written-out embellishments.

The length and complexity of this opening ritornello exceed those of a typical concerto movement by Vivaldi or even J. S. Bach, but they are characteristic of concertos by C. P. E. Bach and other midcentury composers. On the other hand, the number of ritornellos in the movement as a whole is smaller, and there are only three main solo sections (see Table 14.1). Yet, as in earlier concertos, the solo sections still consist in large part of modulating passage-work, composed mainly of arpeggiation (see, e.g., mm. 61–78).

Much of the solo material is accompanied by the strings, which also punctuate the solo sections with brief passages taken from the ritornello (as in mm.

---

[9]Although not exactly a "rage" aria, Jephtha's aria "Open thy marble jaws" (anthology, Selection 20a) is comparable in its use of octave or *unisono* passages (it actually dates from two or three years *after* C. P. E. Bach's concerto).

TABLE 14.1
Carl Philipp Emanuel Bach (1714–88): Concerto in D Minor, W. 23
(H. 427), first movement

Section	R	S	R	S	R	srt	r*	S	R
Key	d	d →	g	g →	a	a →	d	d	d
Measure	1	44	98	126	202	221	253	262	313

R = ritornello
S = solo section
srt = solo retransition
r* = return, played by tutti
→ = modulation toward the key of the following section

54 and 58). J. S. Bach and other Baroque composers had previously employed ritornello ideas within solo sections. But Sebastian Bach often used the ritornello material contrapuntally, combining it simultaneously with melodic material stated by the soloists. Emanuel's procedure more closely resembles a dialogue with rapid exchanges between the two speakers. His concertos demonstrate how the homophonic texture of the *galant* style encouraged a more dramatic type of interplay between soloist and tutti, anticipating that found in the concertos of Mozart and later composers.

The second and third movements of the concerto are similar in form to the first, although the second is very different in expressive character—more singing and less harshly fragmented. It opens with a harmonic surprise: a dominant seventh chord in first inversion, such as one might find at the beginning of a recitative (Ex. 14.5). The tonality—F major—is not clearly defined until later in the ritornello. Hence, the tonally unstable ritornello serves as a sort of bridge between the end of the first movement and the first solo passage in the second. This device, which was not unusual for C. P. E. Bach, illustrates the care with which the movements of a midcentury sonata or concerto might be integrated with one another, even though each is a formally closed, self-contained unit.[10]

Formal Structure

All three movements of the concerto follow a version of the type of ritornello form shown in Table 14.1 for the first movement. Although the individual sections are longer and more complex than in earlier concertos, the concerto as a whole is more regular in design. There are no fugues or other departures from ritornello form, and despite the frequent punctuation of solo passages by the tutti, the basic alternation between ritornello and solo sections remains clear. This would remain typical of C. P. E. Bach's concertos to the end of his career, save for a few exceptional pieces, such as the C Minor Concerto, W. 43/4

[10]Several flute concertos by Quantz may have furnished models for C. P. E. Bach's use of this device.

Example 14.5 C. P. E. Bach, Concerto in D minor, W. 23, second mvt., mm. 1–8

(H. 474) of 1771, composed as a single quick movement interrupted by a Poco adagio and a Tempo di menuetto.

It was characteristic of the midcentury concerto that, despite the great length of the ritornellos, in each movement it is the solo sections that constitute the main body of the music, as they do in an aria. Indeed, by removing the ritornellos one could reduce each quick movement to something close to a typical midcentury sonata movement for solo keyboard. That is to say that the three main solos of the outer movements correspond to the three main sections of a typical midcentury sonata-allegro.[11]

The first movement contains one important exception to this principle. At measure 253 the strings enter with an abbreviated statement of the ritornello. Although greatly shortened, this ritornello serves the crucial purpose of restating the main theme of the movement in the tonic. Such an event is called the **return**; it marks the moment at which the movement's cycle of modulations is closed.[12] The return is prepared by a modulating passage called the **retransition**.

---

[11]The three sections of a *galant* sonata-allegro movement correspond with what came to be known as the exposition, development, and recapitulation in Classical and nineteenth-century sonata forms. That eighteenth-century musicians understood concerto form in the way described here is clear from several early keyboard concertos by Mozart, who inserted ritornellos into existing pieces by other composers (including C. P. E. and J. C. Bach) to create typical concerto movements.

[12]Because of the dual restatement of tonic key and main theme, this type of return is sometimes referred to as the **double return**.

By 1748, when this concerto was written, the threefold basic design described above (including retransition and return) had become a feature of most concerto and sonata movements, at least in Germany. That Emanuel Bach should have adopted this formal convention reveals a paradox fundamental to his so-called *empfindsamer Stil*. Despite the highly individualized, irregular thematic material, each movement follows essentially the same formal pattern, one also used by his more conventional contemporaries. Hence, for all their expressive unconventionality, most of C. P. E. Bach's works are more regular and predictable in their formal designs than are the works of Vivaldi or J. S. Bach. Exceptions occur chiefly in his fantasias and other improvisatory works for solo keyboard.

Some such regular patterning was typical of music at midcentury. It was probably necessary in order to produce movements of the length and complexity found in this concerto. An intense musical drama lasting over eight minutes, as in the first movement, could not have been achieved with the more irregular or episodic forms employed in most Baroque works, including the fugues and choruses of J. S. Bach or Handel. Paradoxically, some standardization of musical form was necessary in order to make individual musical compositions more dramatic. This idea would be central to the symphonies, sonatas, and string quartets of the Classical and Romantic styles.

BIBLIOGRAPHY

This is less a comprehensive bibliography of Baroque music than a guide to further reading. It is restricted largely to books in English; a few journal articles, dissertations, and foreign-language works are included where appropriate. The existence of scholarly collected editions and, in some cases, facsimiles and other special resources is noted, but editions of specific compositions must be sought in library and thematic catalogs. The burgeoning number of World-Wide Web (WWW) sites includes several worthy of inclusion, but the ephemeral nature and inconsistent quality of many others militates against their being listed.

Items are listed by type and subject under the following categories: (1) reference works, collections of readings, and other general works; (2) writings about repertories, genres, and music theory; (3) performance practice and organology (instruments); and (4) writings about specific composers and their music (including information about musical editions).

REFERENCE WORKS, COLLECTIONS OF READINGS, AND OTHER GENERAL WORKS

Background: General European History

Recent historical writing has tended to focus on cultural, sociological, and economic approaches, which can be useful for understanding the contexts in which artistic production has taken place. But such writings are frustrating if one seeks information about specific rulers, historical events, or political structures as they affected individual composers, compositions, and musical performance. Moreover, important musicians, such as J. S. Bach, often worked in regions of Europe that were relatively unimportant politically and consequently have been neglected in current English-language historiography.

For general historical background, one may turn to such works as Helmut Georg Koenigsberger, *Early Modern Europe, 1500–1789* (London: Longman, 1987), and John M. Merriman, *A History of Modern Europe: From the Renaissance to the Present* (New York: Norton, 1996). For information about specific events, rulers, and places, particularly in more "peripheral" regions such as Italy and Saxony during our period, one may need to turn to older reference works such as *The New Cambridge Modern History*, vols. 4–6 (Cambridge: Cambridge University Press, 1970, 1961, 1970); vol. 14 includes a good historical atlas.

Reference Books on Music

Music dictionaries and encyclopedias. The standard English-language music reference is *The New Grove Dictionary of Music and Musicians*, edited by Stanley Sadie, 20 vols. (London: Macmillan, 1980). A revision is currently in progress. Particularly valuable are the detailed work lists and bibliographies attached to the articles on major composers. Updated and expanded articles from this work, including revised work lists and bibliographies, have been published in two series, the Grove Musical Instrument Series and the Composer Biography Series, as well as in two separate encyclopedias: *The New Grove Dictionary of Musical Instruments*, edited by Stanley Sadie, 3 vols. (London: Macmillan, 1984), and *The New Grove Dictionary of Opera*, edited by Stanley Sadie, 4 vols. (London: Macmillan, 1992). The latter includes entries for individual operas by title, summarizing synopses and listing parts.

Good one-volume music dictionaries include *The New Harvard Dictionary of Music*, ed. Don Michael Randel (Cambridge, Mass.: Harvard University Press, 1986), and *The Oxford Dictionary of Music*, edited by Michael Kennedy (Oxford: Oxford University Press, 1994), each of which exists in a smaller "concise" version as well.

Special-topic reference works. Of special relevance to our topic is the dictionary-style *Companion to Baroque Music*, edited by Julie Anne Sadie (Berkeley and Los Angeles: University of California Press, 1998). Useful dictionaries on special subjects include the Grove dictionaries on instruments and opera, mentioned above, and *The Norton/Grove Dictionary of Women Composers*, edited by Julie Anne Sadie and Rhian Samuel (New York: Norton, 1994). Valuable for understanding Baroque librettos and ballet scenarios is *The Oxford Guide to Classical Mythology in the Arts, 1300–1990*, edited by Jane Davidson Reid with the assistance of Chris Rohmann (New York: Oxford University Press, 1993).

Historical music dictionaries. Encyclopedic works produced during the Baroque remain valuable today. Among these are Michael Praetorius, *Syntagma musicum*, 3 vols. (Wolfenbüttel, 1613–20; facs., Kassel: Bärenreiter, 1958–59), portions translated by David Z. Crookes as *Syntagma Musicum II: De organographia: Parts I and II* (Oxford: Clarendon Press, 1986); Marin Mersenne, *Harmonie universelle* (Paris, 1636; facs., Paris: Centre National de la Recherche Scientifique, 1963), portions translated by Roger E. Chapman as *Harmonie universelle: The Books on Instruments* (The Hague: Nijhoff, 1957); and Athanasius Kircher, *Musurgia universalis* (Rome, 1650; facs., Hildesheim: Olms, 1970).

Usable for both French and Italian terminology around 1700 is Sébastien de Brossard, *Dictionnaire de musique* (Paris, 1703), translated by Albion Gruber (Henryville, Pa.: Institute of Mediaeval Music, 1982); for an eighteenth-century English adaptation, see James Grassineau, *A Musical Dictionary* (London, 1740; facs., New York: Broude, 1966). From the circle of J. S. Bach comes Johann Gottfried Walther, *Musicalisches Lexicon* (Leipzig, 1732; facs., Kassel: Bärenreiter, 1953).

Music Bibliography and Writing about Music

For general bibliography on our subject one might consult John H. Baron, *Baroque Music: A Research and Information Guide* (New York: Garland, 1993). More specialized is Diane Parr Walker and Paul Walker, *German Sacred Polyphonic Vocal Music between Schütz and Bach: Sources and Critical Editions* (Warren, Mich.: Harmonie Park Press, 1992). A guide to scholarly editions of music, which are especially numerous for our subject, is George R. Hill and Norris L. Stephens, *Collected Editions, Historical Series and Sets, and Monuments of Music: A Bibliography* (Berkeley, Calif.: Fallen Leaf Press, 1997).

For proper style and formatting in writing about music, the standard guide is Kate L. Turabian, *A Manual for Writers of Term Papers, Theses, and Dissertations*, 6th ed., revised by John Grossman and Alice Bennett (Chicago: University of Chicago Press, 1996).

Collections of Readings

A widely used anthology of readings has recently appeared in a new edition: *Source Readings in Music History*, ed. Oliver Strunk, rev. ed., edited by Leo Treitler (New York: Norton, 1998). Another collection is *Music in the Western World: A History in Documents*, edited by

Piero Weiss and Richard Taruskin (New York: Schirmer Books, 1984). Both include sections on Baroque music. See also the Lippman work under "Baroque Music Theory and Compositional Practice," below.

Surveys and Collections of Essays

An older textbook valuable for its keen critical insights is Manfred F. Bukofzer, *Music in the Baroque Era from Monteverdi to Bach* (New York: Norton, 1947). More recent and highly influential is Claude V. Palisca, *Baroque Music*, 3d ed. (Englewood Cliffs, N.J.: Prentice-Hall, 1991). For somewhat broader coverage consult the *New Oxford History of Music* (London: Oxford University Press, 1994), vols. 4–7. Strong on sociological aspects, though limited to the earlier Baroque, is Lorenzo Bianconi, *Music in the Seventeenth Century*, translated by David Bryant (Cambridge: Cambridge University Press, 1987). For special emphasis on cultural context, see two volumes in the series Music and Society: *The Early Baroque Era: From the Late 16th Century to the 1660s*, edited by Curtis Price (Englewood Cliffs, N.J.: Prentice-Hall, 1994); and *The Late Baroque Era: From the 1680s to 1740*, edited by George J. Buelow (Englewood Cliffs, N.J.: Prentice-Hall, 1994).

Of the numerous collections of essays on special topics, only a few can be mentioned here. Valuable for insights into the origins of Baroque style is Nino Pirrotta, *Music and Theatre from Poliziano to Monteverdi* (Cambridge: Cambridge University Press, 1982). An excellent survey of women in music, including several chapters on the Baroque, is Jane Bowers and Judith Tick, *Women Making Music: The Western Art Tradition, 1150–1950* (Urbana: University of Illinois Press, 1986). More specialized collections are listed below.

REPERTORIES, GENRES, AND MUSIC THEORY

Baroque Repertories

On music in specific regions of Europe, see the Music and Society series (under "Surveys and Collections of Essays" above) as well as James R. Anthony, *French Baroque Music from Beaujoyeulx to Rameau*, rev. ed. (Portland, Ore.: Amadeus Press, 1997); Eleanor Selfridge-Field, *Venetian Instrumental Music*, 3d ed. (New York: Dover, 1994); and *Church, Stage, and Studio: Music and Its Contexts in Seventeenth-Century Germany*, edited by Paul Walker (Ann Arbor: UMI Research Press, 1989).

On polychoral music, with copious musical examples, see Anthony F. Carver, *Cori spezzati: The Development of Sacred Polychoral Music to the Time of Schütz*, 2 vols. (Cambridge: Cambridge University Press, 1988).

For early Baroque string music: Willi Apel, *Italian Violin Music of the Seventeenth Century*, ed. Thomas Binkley (Bloomington: Indiana University Press, 1990).

There are many works on keyboard music. For the period before 1700, a useful reference work, if somewhat dated, is Willi Apel, *The History of Keyboard Music to 1700*, translated by Hans Tischler (Bloomington: Indiana University Press, 1972). More up-to-date essays on individual regions and composers can be found in *Keyboard Music before 1700*, edited by Alexander Silbiger (New York: Schirmer Books, 1995), and *Eighteenth-Century Keyboard Music*, edited by Robert L. Marshall (New York: Schirmer Books, 1994). Special aspects of French music are subjects of David Ledbetter, *Harpsichord and Lute Music in 17th-Century France* (Bloomington: Indiana University Press, 1988), and *The Art of the Unmeasured Prelude for Harpsichord, France, 1660–1720*, 3 vols., edited by Colin Tilney (London: Schott, 1991).

Baroque Genres

The madrigal. A general survey: Jerome Roche, *The Madrigal*, 2d ed. (Oxford: Oxford University Press, 1990). A detailed study of an important pre-Baroque repertory, with a volume of musical examples: Anthony Newcomb, *The Madrigal at Ferrara, 1579–1597*, 2 vols. (Princeton, N.J.: Princeton University Press, 1980).

Opera, cantata, and oratorio. Strong on Baroque opera is this older survey: Donald J. Grout, *A Short History of Opera*, 2d ed. (New York: Columbia University Press, 1965). A more recent study of early opera in one of its first major centers, with many substantial examples from otherwise unavailable works, is Ellen Rosand, *Opera in Seventeenth-Century Venice: The Creation of a Genre* (Berkeley and Los Angeles: University of California Press, 1991). On later opera see Reinhard Strohm, *Dramma per musica: Italian Opera Seria of the Eighteenth Century* (New Haven, Conn.: Yale University Press, 1997), as well as the works on Handel and Rameau under "Composers and Their Works," below.

On the vast Italian cantata repertory one must consult works on individual composers (see below). For France there is David Tunley, *The Eighteenth-Century French Cantata*, 2d ed. (Oxford: Clarendon Press, 1997).

Oratorios are surveyed in Howard E. Smither, *A History of the Oratorio*, vol. 2, *The Oratorio in the Baroque Era: Protestant Germany and England* (Chapel Hill: University of North Carolina Press, 1977).

Sonata and concerto. Although somewhat dated, useful information can be found in the following surveys: William S. Newman, *The Sonata in the Baroque Era*, 4th ed. (New York: Norton, 1983), and Arthur Hutchings, *The Baroque Concerto*, rev. ed. (New York: Scribner's, 1979). See also Selfridge-Field, *Venetian Instrumental Music* (above, under "Baroque Repertories").

Baroque Music Theory and Compositional Practice

History of theory and composition. On sixteenth-century modality, see Bernhard Meier, *The Modes of Classical Vocal Polyphony: Described According to the Sources*, translated by Ellen S. Beebe (New York: Broude, 1988). A classic study of the emergence of tonality is Carl Dahlhaus, *Studies on the Origin of Harmonic Tonality*, translated by Robert O. Gjerdingen (Princeton, N.J.: Princeton University Press, 1990). Also valuable on this topic is Stein, "Between Key and Mode" (see below, "Composers and Their Works," under Carissimi).

On later theory, centering on the role of Rameau, see Joel Lester, *Compositional Theory in the Eighteenth Century* (Cambridge, Mass.: Harvard University Press, 1992), Thomas Street Christensen, *Rameau and Musical Thought in the Enlightenment* (Cambridge: Cambridge University Press, 1993) and chapters 1 and 3 in David Kopp, *Common-Tone Tonality in Nineteenth-Century Music* (Cambridge: Cambridge University Press, 2001). For Rameau's own writings, see under his name in "Composers and Their Music," below.

For case studies of compositional teaching and practice, see Alfred Mann, *The Great Composer as Teacher and Student: Theory and Practice of Composition: Bach, Handel, Haydn, Mozart, Beethoven, Schubert* (New York: Dover, 1994), as well as individual items on Bach and Handel under "Composers and Their Music," below.

Fugue. The theory and practice of fugue have a large modern literature, centering on the works of J. S. Bach. Three representative works are Alfred Mann, *The Study of Fugue* (New Brunswick, N.J.: Rutgers University Press, 1958), William Renwick, *Analyzing Fugue: A Schenkerian Approach* (Stuyvesant, N.Y.: Pendragon Press, 1995), and Paul Mark Walker, *Theories of Fugue from the Age of Josquin to the Age of Bach* (Rochester, N.Y.: University of Rochester Press, 2000).

Expression, meaning, and aesthetics. The vast literature on the philosophy of music can be divided between historical writings and those presenting contemporary views. Among historical treatments, Edward Lippman, *A History of Western Musical Aesthetics* (Lincoln: University of Nebraska Press, 1992), includes two chapters on our period. Relevant writings from the period can be found in works by Mattheson (see below) and by C. P. E. Bach and Quantz (under "Voices and Instruments," below) and in extracts in Strunk, *Source Readings* (under "Collections of Readings," above).

A modern work that draws particularly on the Baroque writer Johann Mattheson is Peter Kivy, *Sound Sentiment: An Essay on the Musical Emotions, Including the Complete Text of "The Corded Shell"* (Philadelphia: Temple University Press, 1989). An older classic article is Manfred Bukofzer, "Allegory in Baroque Music," *Journal of the Warburg and Courtauld Institutes* 3 (1939–40): 1–21. On musical rhetoric, a useful handbook is Dietrich Bartel, *Musica poetica: Musical-Rhetorical Figures in German Baroque Music* (Lincoln: University of Nebraska Press, 1997), but see the cautionary article by Peter Williams, "The Snares and Delusions of Musical Rhetoric: Some Examples from Recent Writings on J. S. Bach," in *Alte Musik: Praxis und Reflexion,* ed. Peter Reidmeister and Veronika Gutmann (Winterthur: Amadeus, 1983), 230–40.

Baroque theoretical treatises. Numerous works from the period, ranging from elementary pedagogic manuals to sophisticated technical treatises, appear in modern facsimiles and editions. A selection follows.

For translations of three manuscript treatises on performance practice and composition by a student of Heinrich Schütz, see Walter Hilse "The Treatises of Christoph Bernhard," *The Music Forum* 3 (1973): 31–79. The classic eighteenth-century work on counterpoint is Johann Joseph Fux, *Gradus ad Parnassum* (Vienna, 1725; facs., New York: Broude, 1966), whose German translation by Bach's friend and student Lorenz Christoph Mizler appeared as *Anführung zur regelmässigen musikalischen Composition* (Leipzig, 1742; facs., Hildesheim: Olms, 1974). Portions appear in English in Alfred Mann, *The Study of Counterpoint from Johann Joseph Fux's "Gradus ad parnassum,"* rev. ed. (New York: Norton, 1965).

See also the writings listed in "Composers and Their Works," below, by the composers C. P. E. Bach, Rameau, and Schütz.

PERFORMANCE PRACTICE AND ORGANOLOGY

Reference, Bibliography, and Readings

Useful for performance practice in general (as well as organology) is *The New Grove Dictionary of Musical Instruments* (see above under "Reference Books on Music"). Revised and expanded articles from this work include *The New Grove Early Keyboard Instruments* (New York: Norton, 1989), *The New Grove Organ* (New York: Norton, 1988), and *The New Grove Violin Family* (New York: Norton, 1989). See also the historical music dictionaries listed under the same heading, especially the translations from works by Praetorius and Mersenne.

For bibliography, see Roland Jackson, *Performance Practice, Medieval to Contemporary: A Bibliographic Guide* (New York : Garland, 1988). Updates to this work appeared in the journal *Performance Practice Review*; a website continuing the series at ⟨http://www.performancepractice.com⟩ is to become a *Performance Practice Encyclopedia.*

For extracts from Baroque treatises, see *Readings in the History of Music in Performance,* selected, translated, and edited by Carol MacClintock (Bloomington: Indiana University Press, 1979); there is also some matter in Strunk, *Source Readings* (above, under "Collections of Readings"). An encyclopedic work valuable for its documentation of contemporary practice is Johann Mattheson, *Der vollkommene Capellmeister* (Hamburg, 1739; facs. ed. Margarete Reimann, Kassel: Bärenreiter, 1954); some portions relevant to performance practice appear in Ernest C. Harris, *Johann Mattheson's "Der vollkommene Capellmeister": A Revised Translation with Critical Commentary* (Ann Arbor, Mich.: UMI Research Press, 1981).

General Works on Historical Performance

For general essays, see *Performance Practice: Music after 1600,* edited by Howard Mayer Brown and Stanley Sadie (New York: Norton, 1990). On the history of the discipline, which has focused to a considerable degree on Baroque music, see Harry Haskell, *The Early Music Revival: A History* (Mineola, N.Y.: Dover, 1996), and *Authenticity and Early Music,* edited by

Nicholas Kenyon (Oxford: Oxford University Press, 1988), which also contains essays on philosophical issues.

An influential if increasingly dated introduction to the topic, still immensely valuable for its numerous extracts from historical treatises, is Robert Donington, *The Interpretation of Early Music*, new rev. ed. (New York: Norton, 1989). More specifically on our subject is Mary Cyr, *Performing Baroque Music* (Portland, Ore.: Amadeus Press, 1992). Essays on special topics appear in Stewart Carter, *A Performer's Guide to Seventeenth-Century Music* (New York: Schirmer Books, 1997). For very valuable in-depth examinations of specific performance issues in works by Bach, Corelli, Couperin, and Handel, see Peter Le Huray, *Authenticity in Performance: Eighteenth-Century Case Studies* (Cambridge: Cambridge University Press, 1990).

Special Topics

A survey of rhythmic conventions: Stephen E. Hefling, *Rhythmic Alteration in Seventeenth- and Eighteenth-Century Music: Notes Inégales and Overdotting* (New York: Schirmer Books, 1993).

Indispensible as a comprehensive reference on ornaments, despite the author's tendentious interpretations, is Frederick Neumann, *Ornamentation in Baroque and Post-Baroque Music: With Special Emphasis on J. S. Bach* (Princeton, N.J.: Princeton University Press, 1978).

Figured bass realization and continuo playing have been subjects of numerous works. For extracts from historical treatises, with commentary, see Frank T. Arnold, *The Art of Accompaniment from a Through-Bass*, 2 vols. (Oxford: Oxford University Press, 1932; reprint, New York: Dover, 1965), and Peter Williams, *Figured Bass Accompaniment*, 2 vols. (Edinburgh: Edinburgh University Press, 1970). Some representative treatises in translation: *Accompaniment on Theorbo and Harpsichord: Denis Delair's Treatise of 1690*, translated by Charlotte Mattax (Bloomington: Indiana University Press, 1991); and the relevant chapters of the works by C. P. E. Bach (listed in the next section) and Rameau (under his name in "Composers and Their Works," below).

On other issues of performance practice, see also Tilney, *Art of the Unmeasured Prelude*, above under "Baroque Repertories," and the works on the music of specific composers listed below under Bach, Handel, and Purcell.

Voices and Instruments

Baroque vocal technique has been unduly neglected; for a recent modern study including "sound bites," see Sally Sanford, "A Comparison of French and Italian Singing in the Seventeenth Century," *Journal of Seventeenth-Century Music* 1.1 (1995) ⟨http://www.sscm.harvard.edu/jscm/v1/no1/sanford.html⟩. On the castrati, see Angus Heriot, *The Castrati in Opera* (London: Secker and Warburg, 1956). Early recordings of actual castrato singers from the early twentieth century are collected in *Alessandro Moreschi: The Complete Recordings* (New York: Opal [no. 823], 1987). For examples of period embellishment, see Franz Häbock, *Die Gesangskunst der Kastraten* (Vienna: Universal, 1923) and Dean, *Three Ornamented Arias* (under Handel in "Composers and Their works," below).

Two important treatises that present the mature French and Italian Baroque styles respectively are available in translation: Bénigne de Bacilly, *Remarques curieuses sur l'art de bien chanter* (Paris, 1668), translated by Austin B. Caswell as *A Commentary upon the Art of Proper Singing* (Brooklyn: Institute of Mediaeval Music, 1968); and Pier Francesco Tosi, *Opinioni de' cantori antichi e moderni*, translation of the German version by Johann Friedrich Agricola (*Anleitung zur Singkunst*, Berlin, 1757) by Julianne C. Baird as *Introduction to the Art of Singing* (Cambridge: Cambridge University Press, 1995). An eighteenth-century English translation of Tosi's original also exists: John Ernest Galliard, *Observations on the Florid Song* (London, 1743; facs., New York: Lang, 1968).

On earlier Italian vocal technique, see under Caccini, below, and Christoph Bernhard (above, "Baroque Music Theory and Compositional Practice").

Instruments and instrumental practice are often discussed together in the encyclopedic works listed above, many of which contain entries on individual instruments.

On performance on bowed string instruments, see David Dodge Boyden, *The History of Violin Playing from Its Origins to 1761 and Its Relationship to the Violin and Violin Music*, 2d ed. (London: Oxford University Press, 1990). Among the most important Baroque sources are Georg Muffat's prefaces to his published music, issued in modern edition in German, Latin, French, and Italian in *Denkmäler deutscher Tonkunst*, vols. 1/2 (Vienna, 1894), 2/2 (Vienna, 1895), and 11/2 (Vienna, 1904). For translation with commentary see Kenneth Cooper and Julius Zsako, "Georg Muffat's Observations on the Lully Style of Performance," *Musical Quarterly* 53 (1967): 220–45; extracts also in Strunk, *Source Readings* (see above, under "Collections of Readings"). A later treatise on string playing, valuable for early eighteenth-century practice in the Italian style, is Leopold Mozart, *A Treatise on the Fundamental Principles of Violin Playing*, trans. Editha Knocker, 2d ed. (Oxford: Oxford University Press, 1985).

Of woodwinds, the flute and recorder have received the most attention. For an introduction to historical flutes, see John Solum, *The Early Flute* (Oxford: Oxford University Press, 1992). The two major Baroque treatises are Jacques Hotteterre, *Principles of the Flute, Recorder, and Oboe*, translated by Paul Marshall Douglas (New York: Dover, 1983); and Johann Joachim Quantz, *Versuch einer Anweisung die Flöte traversiere zu spielen* (Berlin, 1752), translated by Edward R. Reilly as *On Playing the Flute*, 3d ed. (New York: Schirmer Books, 1985). For a study of the latter in relation to music and surviving instruments by Quantz, see Mary Oleskiewicz, "The Flutes of Quantz: Their Construction and Performing Practice," *Galpin Society Journal* 52 (2000): 201–20.

Brass: Anthony Baines, *Brass Instruments: Their History and Development* (New York: Scribner, 1978); Don L. Smithers, *The Music and History of the Baroque Trumpet before 1721*, 2d ed. (Carbondale: Southern Illinois University Press, 1988).

Two often overlooked Baroque instruments are the subjects of Albert R. Rice, *The Baroque Clarinet* (Oxford: Oxford University Press, 1992), and James Tyler, *The Early Guitar: A History and Handbook* (London: Oxford University Press, 1980).

Stringed keyboard instruments have a large literature. A thorough guide to Baroque keyboard organology can be obtained from the earlier entries in John Koster, *Keyboard Musical Instruments in the Museum of Fine Arts, Boston* (Boston: Museum of Fine Arts, 1994). Two major eighteenth-century performance treatises are Carl Philipp Emanuel Bach, *Versuch über die wahre Art das Clavier zu spielen* (Berlin, 1753–62), translated by William J. Mitchell as *The True Art of Playing Keyboard Instruments* (New York: North, 1949); and François Couperin, *L'Art de toucher le clavecin/The Art of Playing the Harpsichord*, simultaneous edition of the original French with English translation by Mevanwy Roberts (Leipzig: Breitkopf und Härtel, 1933).

Modern studies especially relevant to the organ but useful for all keyboard players are Quentin Faulkner, *J. S. Bach's Keyboard Technique: A Historical Introduction* (St. Louis: Concordia, 1984), and George Ritchie and George Stauffer, *Organ Technique: Modern and Early* (Englewood Cliffs, N.J.: Prentice Hall, 1992).

Dance

For bibliography: Judith L. Schwartz and Christena L. Schlundt, *French Court Dance and Dance Music: A Guide to Primary Source Writings, 1643–1789* (Stuyvesant, N.Y.: Pendragon Press, 1987). For a catalog of dances preserved in Baroque choreographies: Meredith Little, *La danse noble: An Inventory of Dances and Sources* (Williamstown, Mass.: Broude, 1992).

The classic survey of French Baroque dance is included in *Dance and Music of Court and Theater: Selected Writings of Wendy Hilton* (Stuyvesant, N.Y.: Pendragon Press, 1997), including her pathbreaking work on French Baroque choreography, *Dance of Court and Theater: The French Noble Style, 1690–1725*. A unique study and edition of a seventeenth-century French ballet is Rebecca Harris-Warrick and Carol G. Marsh, *Musical Theatre at the Court of Louis XIV: Le mariage de la Grosse Cathos* (Cambridge: Cambridge University Press, 1994).

COMPOSERS AND THEIR WORKS

J. S. Bach

Bach's complete works were issued in the nineteenth century by the German Bach-Gesellschaft (Bach Society) as *J. S. Bach's Werke* (Leipzig, 1851–99); known as the "BG," this edition has been the source of many subsequent reprints, including volumes of cantatas, keyboard music, and concertos issued in recent years by Dover. Usually more accurate and complete is the so-called NBA (Neue Bach-Ausgabe) published as the *Neue Ausgabe sämtlicher Werke* (Kassel: Bärenreiter, 1954–). Several volumes in this series have already been superseded, however, notably that of the B Minor Mass; for that work, see *Messe in h-moll*, edited by Christoph Wolff (Frankfurt: Peters, 1997), or the forthcoming edition by Joshua Rifkin (Wiesbaden: Breitkopf und Härtel). For an excellent edition, with analytical commentary, of the *Well-Tempered Clavier*, see Johann Sebastian Bach, *The Well-Tempered Clavier, Part I: BWV 846–869 {and} Part II: BWV 870–893*, edited by Richard Jones with commentaries by Donald Francis Tovey (London: Associated Board of the Royal Schools of Music, 1994). Numerous facsimiles of Bach's manuscripts and original editions are also available in several series.

Editions of individual works within the BG or NBA are most quickly located through the work list in the *New Grove Dictionary* or *Bach* Composer Companion (see below). More complete bibliographic information is available in the thematic catalogue by Wolfgang Schmieder, *Thematisch-Systematisches Verzeichnis der musikalischen Werke von Johann Sebastian Bach: Bach-Werke-Verzeichnis (BWV)*, 2d ed. (Wiesbaden, Breitkopf und Härtel, 1990). For even more detailed listings, see Hans-Joachim Schulze and Christoph Wolff, *Bach Compendium: Analytisch-Bibliographisches Repertorium der Werke Johann Sebastian Bachs (BC)* (Frankfurt: Peters, 1986–).

A good point from which to begin a survey of the vast literature on Bach and his music is Daniel R. Melamed and Michael Marissen, *An Introduction to Bach Studies* (New York: Oxford University Press, 1998). Work is in progress toward an indexed Bach bibliography in CD-ROM format by Walter Mayhall and Marcellene Hawke. There is also a searchable website, Yo Tomita's *Bach Bibliography*, at ⟨http://www.music.qub.ac.uk/″tomita/bachbib⟩, mirrored at ⟨http://www.npj.com/bach/⟩.

Available in the Oxford Composer Companions series is *Bach*, edited by Malcolm Boyd (Oxford: Oxford University Press, 1999), a dictionary-style reference book that includes entries for most of Bach's individual works, including each cantata. Essays on more general topics are found in *The Cambridge Companion to Bach*, edited by John Butt (New York: Cambridge University Press, 1997).

A German annual containing scholarly articles and reviews is the *Bach-Jahrbuch* (Berlin: Evangelische Verlagsanstalt, 1904–). Two American serials featuring writings in English are *Bach Perspectives* (Lincoln: University of Nebraska Press, 1992–) and *BACH: The Quarterly Journal of the Riemenschneider Institute*.

The New Bach Reader: A Life of Johann Sebastian Bach in Letters and Documents, edited by Hans T. David and Arthur Mendel, revised by Christoph Wolff (New York: Norton, 1998), includes translations of numerous fascinating documents, among them the complete text, in translation, of the first biography of Bach, by Johann Nicolaus Forkel (1802).

Recent biographies of Bach include Christoph Wolff, *Johann Sebastian Bach: The Learned Musician* (New York: Norton, 2000), and Malcolm Boyd, *Bach*, 3d ed. (New York: Oxford

University Press, 2000). A comprehensive study of Bach's practice as a composer, including an edition of his sketches, is Robert L. Marshall, *The Compositional Process of J. S. Bach*, 2 vols. (Princeton: N.J.: Princeton University Press, 1972).

On the cantatas, in addition to the Oxford Bach Companion (see above), see *The World of the Bach Cantatas*, ed. Christoph Wolff (New York: Norton, 1997). An older work still of great value on the cantata texts is James Day, *The Literary Background to Bach's Cantatas* (London: Dobson, 1961). Analyses of the text and music of individual cantatas can be found in Alfred Dürr, *Johann Sebastian Bach: Die Kantaten*, 7th ed. (Kassel: Bärenreiter, 1999), English translation by Richard D. P. Jones forthcoming (Oxford: Oxford University Press). A valuable study of one of Bach's greatest vocal works is George B. Stauffer, *Bach: The Mass in B Minor* (New York: Schirmer Books, 1997). On the controversial subject of the size of the vocal forces in Bach's sacred works, see Andrew Parrott, *The Essential Bach Choir* (Rochester, N.Y.: Boydell and Brewer, 2000).

On individual instrumental works one might consult Malcolm Boyd, *Bach: The Brandenburg Concertos* (Cambridge: Cambridge University Press, 1993); Michael Marissen, *The Social and Religious Designs of J. S. Bach's Brandenburg Concertos* (Princeton, N.J.: Princeton University Press, 1995); David Schulenberg, *The Keyboard Music of J. S. Bach* (New York: Schirmer Books, 1992); Peter F. Williams, *The Organ Music of J. S. Bach*, 3 vols. (Cambridge: Cambridge University Press, 1980–84); Russell Stinson, *Bach: The Orgelbüchlein* (New York: Oxford University Press, 1999); and Joel Lester, *Bach's Works for Solo Violin: Style, Structure, Performance* (New York: Oxford University Press, 1999).

C. P. E. Bach

A modern edition of C. P. E. Bach's collected works was suspended after issuing just four volumes, but a new project is now underway. For editions of individual works one can consult the Helm catalog (below). Particularly useful is a facsimile edition of the solo keyboard works, by Darrell Berg (New York: Garland, 1985), who has also edited selected keyboard sonatas in 3 vols. (Munich: Henle, 1986–89).

In addition to the old thematic catalog by Alfred Wotquenne (Leipzig: Breitkopf und Härtel, 1905) there is E. Eugene Helm, *Thematic Catalogue of the Works of Carl Philipp Emanuel Bach* (New Haven, Conn.: Yale University Press, 1989).

A recent biography is Hans-Günter Ottenberg, *C. P. E. Bach*, trans. Philip J. Whitmore (Oxford: Oxford University Press, 1987). On individual works, see David Schulenberg, *The Instrumental Music of Carl Philipp Emanuel Bach* (Ann Arbor, Mich.: UMI Research Press, 1984). A collection of essays, *C. P. E. Bach Studies*, edited by Stephen L. Clark (Oxford: Oxford University Press, 1988), includes a comprehensive bibliography.

Bach's indispensible *Essay* on keyboard performance is listed above under "Voices and Instruments."

Biber

Most of Biber's music has now appeared in modern edition in various volumes of the *Denkmäler der Tonkunst in Österreich*; the "Mystery" Sonatas appear in vol. 25. The only English-language monograph is Eric Thomas Chafe, *The Church Music of Heinrich Biber* (Ann Arbor, Mich.: UMI Research Press, 1987), which discusses many instrumental as well as vocal works, including the "Mystery" Sonatas.

Buxtehude

An unfinished collected edition, *Dietrich Buxtehudes Werke* (Klecken: Ugrino, 1925–37), has recently been revived (New York: Broude Trust, 1977–) and thus far includes vocal works and works for instrumental ensemble. There are several editions of the keyboard works, most recently that of Klaus Beckmann (Leipzig: Breitkopf und Härtel, 1971–72).

Thematic catalog: Georg Karstädt, *Thematisch-Systematisches Verzeichnis der musikalischen Werke von Dietrich Buxtehude: Buxtehude-Werke-Verz (BuxWV)* (Wiesbaden: Breitkopf und Härtel, 1974).

The exemplary biography is Kerala J. Snyder, *Dieterich Buxtehude, Organist in Lübeck* (New York: Schirmer Books, 1987). On context, see Geoffrey Webber, *North German Church Music in the Age of Buxtehude* (Oxford: Oxford University Press, 1996).

Giulio Caccini and Francesca Caccini

Giulio Caccini's *Le nuove musiche* (Florence, 1601) is available in facsimile (New York: Broude, 1973) and in a modern edition by H. Wiley Hitchcock (Madison, Wis.: A-R, 1970), which includes a translation of Caccini's important preface. Excerpts from the latter also appear in Strunk, *Source Readings* (see above, under "Collections of Readings").

The vocal chamber music of Francesca Caccini is available in facsimile in *Florence, Italian Secular Song, 1606–1636*, vol. 1, ed. Gary Tomlinson (New York: Garland, 1986).

Carissimi

For "Urtext" editions of Carissimi's oratorios one must turn to the rare edition (using "old" clefs) by Friedrich Chrysander, *Oratorien*, vol. 2 of *Denkmäler der Tonkunst* (Bergedorf: Weissenborn, 1861). Most of the more recent editions add stylistically inappropriate "expression" markings or basso continuo realizations; an exception is *Jephte*, ed. Gottfried Wolters (Wolfenbüttel: Möseler, 1969).

On Carissimi and his works, see Graham Dixon, *Carissimi* (Oxford: Oxford University Press, 1986); Andrew V. Jones, *The Motets of Carissimi* (Ann Arbor, Mich.: UMI Research Press, 1982); and Beverly Ann Stein, "Between Key and Mode: Tonal Practice in the Music of Giacomo Carissimi" (Ph.D. diss., Brandeis University, 1994).

Cavalieri

The music by Cavalieri and others for the *intermedi* to *La pellegrina* appears in *Les fêtes du mariage de Ferdinand de Médicis et de Christine de Lorraine, Florence, 1589* (Paris: Editions du Centre National de la Recherche Scientifique, 1963).

Cavalli

The prologue and Act 1 of *Giasone* appear in *Publikationen älterer praktischer und theoretischer Musikwerke*, edited by Robert Eitner, vol. 12 (Leipzig: Breitkopf und Härtel, 1883; reprint, New York: Broude, 1966). Further selections appear in Rosand, *Opera in Seventeenth-Century Venice* (see under "Baroque Genres," above).

For biography, see Jane Glover, *Cavalli* (London: Batsford, 1978), and the revised *New Grove* article and work list by Thomas Walker in *The New Grove Italian Baroque Masters* (New York: Norton, 1984).

Charpentier

There exists a rare modern *Oeuvres* (Paris, 1948–53); fortunately, Charpentier's autograph manuscripts survive for virtually everything he wrote, and these are being published in facsimile as his *Oeuvres complètes* (Paris: Minkoff, 1990–).

Thematic catalog: Hugh Wiley Hitchcock, *Les oeuvres de Marc-Antoine Charpentier: Catalogue raisonné* (Paris: Picard, 1982).

Biographies: Catherine Cessac, *Marc-Antoine Charpentier*, translated by E. Thomas Glasow (Portland, Ore.: Amadeus Press, 1995); revised *New Grove* biography and work list by H. Wiley Hitchcock in *The New Grove French Baroque Masters* (New York: Norton, 1986).

Corelli

The old collected *Oeuvres*, edited by Joseph Joachim and Friedrich Chrysander (London: Augener, 1888–91; numerous reprints), remains serviceable; it has, however, been superseded by a more accurate modern edition, *Historisch-kritisch Gesamtausgabe der musikalischen Werke* (Cologne: Arno Volk, 1976–). Numerous "practical" editions of the solo violin sonatas and concerti grossi containing unstylistic slurs, dynamics, and continuo realizations are to be avoided.

There is a new biography: Peter Allsop, *Arcangelo Corelli: New Orpheus of Our Times* (Oxford: Oxford University Press, 1998).

Couperin

An existing collected edition, *Oeuvres complètes* (Paris: l'Oiseau Lyre, 1932–33), is in process of revision. The four books of harpsichord pieces have been issued in facsimile (New York: Broude, 1973) and in a good modern edition, *Pièces de clavecin*, 4 vols., edited by Kenneth Gilbert (Paris: Heugel, 1969–72).

The standard biography is Wilfrid Howard Mellers, *François Couperin and the French Classical Tradition*, rev. ed. (London: Faber, 1987); see also the revised *New Grove* biography and work list by Edward Higgenbottom in *The New Grove French Baroque Masters* (New York: Norton, 1986).

Frescobaldi

A collected edition has issued only a few volumes: *Opere complete* (Milan: Suvini Zerboni, 1976–). Many of the keyboard works must be consulted in an older edition by Pierre Pidoux (Kassel: Bärenreiter, 1949–54); additional, recently identified works appear in facsimile in vols. 1, 2, and 15/1–3 of *17th-Century Keyboard Music: Sources Central to the Keyboard Art of the Baroque*, with valuable prefaces by Alexander Silbiger (New York: Garland, 1987–89). Some of the latter are edited (not always entirely accurately) in the *Corpus of Early Keyboard Music*, vols. 30/1–3 and 32 (American Institute of Musicology, 1968). The works for instrumental ensemble appear in *The Ensemble Canzonas of Frescobaldi* (London: London Pro Musica Edition, 1970).

Bibliography: Frederick Hammond, *Girolamo Frescobaldi: A Guide to Research* (New York: Garland, 1988).

Biography: Frederick Hammond, *Girolamo Frescobaldi* (Cambridge, Mass.: Harvard University Press, 1983).

Froberger

The old edition of the keyboard works in *Denkmäler der Tonkunst in Österreich*, vols. 8, 13, and 21, has been superseded by the edition of Howard Schott, 2 vols. in 4 "tomes" (Paris: Heugel, 1979–92). Facsimiles of Froberger's autograph manuscripts, with informative prefaces by Robert Hill, appear in volumes 3/1–3 of *17th-Century Keyboard Music: Sources Central to the Keyboard Art of the Baroque* (New York: Garland, 1988). A new edition by Siegbert Rampe reflecting the latter's idiosyncratic views is in progress (Kassel: Bärenreiter, 1993–). Two articles containing valuable biographical information are Alexander Silbiger, "Tracing the Contents of Froberger's Lost Autographs," *Current Musicology* 54 (1993): 5–23, and Claudio Annibaldi, "Froberger in Rome: From Frescobaldi's Craftsmanship to Kircher's Compositional Secrets," *Current Musicology* 58 (1995): 5–27. On performance, see Howard Schott, "Parameters of Interpretation in the Music of Froberger," in *J. J. Froberger, musicien européen* (N.p.: Klincksieck, 1998), 99–120.

Giovanni Gabrieli

A modern edition of Gabrieli's ensemble works (vocal and instrumental), *Opera omnia*, Corpus mensurabilis musicae 12/1–11 (American Institute of Musicology, 1956–) is now complete; several older volumes in the series have recently appeared in revised versions. The popular works for instrumental ensemble are in vols. 10–11. What little survives of Gabrieli's keyboard music is in *Composizioni per organo*, ed. Sandro Della Libera (Milan: Ricordi, 1957–59).

Thematic catalog: Richard Charteris, *Giovanni Gabrieli (ca. 1555–1612): A Thematic Catalogue of His Music with a Guide to the Source Materials and Translations of his Vocal Texts* (Stuyvesant, N.Y.: Pendragon Press, 1996).

Biography: Denis Arnold, *Giovanni Gabrieli and the Music of the Venetian High Renaissance* (London: Oxford University Press, 1979).

Gesualdo

Gesualdo's madrigals appear in his *Sämtliche Werke*, edited by Wilhelm Weisman and Glenn E. Watkins (Hamburg: Ugrino, 1957–67). The standard biography, recently updated, and with a foreword by Igor Stravinsky, is Glenn Watkins, *Gesualdo: The Man and His Music*, 2d ed. (Oxford: Oxford University Press, 1991).

Handel

Handel's music was edited in the nineteenth century by Friedrich Chrysander in *Werke* (Leipzig: Breitkopf und Härtel, 1858–1903). Numerous volumes have been issued in unaltered reprints, notably the opera *Giulio Cesare* by Dover. A twentieth-century successor in progress is the *Hallische Händel-Ausgabe* (Kassel: Bärenreiter, 1955–).

Thematic catalog: *Händel-Handbuch*, ed. Kuratorium der Georg-Friedrich-Händel-Stiftung, 4 vols. (Kassel: Bärenreiter, 1978–).

Bibliography: Mary Ann Parker-Hale, *G. F. Handel: A Guide to Research* (New York: Garland, 1988).

Two German periodicals, both containing occasional English-language articles, are the *Händel-Jahrbuch* (Leipzig, 1928–33 and 1955–) and *Göttinger Händel-Beiträge* (Kassel: Bärenreiter, 1984–).

The most up-to-date biographical work is Donald Burrows, *Handel* (New York: Schirmer Books, 1994). The Handel tercentenary year 1985 also produced two valuable biographies: Christopher Hogwood, *Handel* (New York: Thames and Hudson, 1985), and Jonathan Keates, *Handel: The Man and His Music* (London: Gollancz, 1985). Older but still valuable for its keen critical observations on the music is Paul Henry Lang, *George Frideric Handel* (New York: Norton, 1966). See also the updated *New Grove* biography by Winton Dean, with work list by Anthony Hicks, in *The New Grove Handel* (New York: Norton, 1983).

For essays on special topics, see *The Cambridge Companion to Handel*, edited by Donald Burrows (Cambridge: Cambridge University Press, 1997).

On the theatrical works, see Winton Dean, *Handel's Dramatic Oratorios and Masques* (London: Oxford University Press, 1959), and Winton Dean, *Handel and the Opera Seria* (Berkeley and Los Angeles: University of California Press, 1969). For a detailed chronicle, full of useful information, see Winton Dean and John Merrill Knapp, *Handel's Operas, 1704–1726* (Oxford: Oxford University Press, 1995). On Handel's borrowings in *Jephtha*, see William D. Gudger, "Handel's Last Compositions and His Borrowings from Habermann (Part 2)," *Current Musicology* 23 (1977): 28–45.

Instrumental music: Alfred Mann, *Handel: The Orchestral Music* (New York: Schirmer Books, 1996).

Handel's written-out vocal embellishment for the opera *Ottone* is in *Three Ornamented Arias*, edited by Winton Dean (London: Oxford University Press, 1976). His teaching of composition and figured bass is the subject of David Ledbetter, *Continuo Playing According to Handel* (Oxford: Oxford University Press, 1990); see also Mann, *The Great Composer*, under "Baroque Music Theory and Compositional Practice," above.

Hasse

The only English-language monograph is Fredrick L. Millner, *The Operas of Johann Adolf Hasse* (Ann Arbor, Mich.: UMI Research Press, 1979).

Jacquet de La Guerre

Jacquet de La Guerre's keyboard works (including the long-lost first book) have been edited by Carol Henry Bates (Paris: Heugel, 1986). The only monographic biography is Catherine Cessac, *Elisabeth Jacquet de La Guerre: Une femme compositeur sous le régne de Louis XIV* (Paris: Actes Sud, 1995). For a recently identified portrait, see Florence Gétreau, "The Fashion for Flemish Harpsichords in France: A New Appreciation," in *Kielinstrumente aus der Werkstatt Ruckers*, edited by Christiane Rieche (Halle: Händel-Haus, 1998), 114–29.

Lassus

A complete modern edition of Lassus's motets using modern clefs is being edited by Peter Bergquist (Recent Researches in Music of the Renaissance, various vol. nos., beginning with 102; Ann Arbor: A-R, 1995–). For motets and madrigals not yet issued in that series, one must consult the *Sämmtliche Werke* (Leipzig: Breitkopf und Härtel, 1894–1927); the masses and magnificats have been published in the more modern *Sämtliche Werke, neue Reihe* (Kassel: Bärenreiter, 1956–).

Bibliography: James Erb, *Orlando di Lasso: A Guide to Research* (New York: Garland, 1990). For biography, see the updated *New Grove* biography and work list by James Haar in *The New Grove High Renaissance Masters* (New York: Norton, 1984); also Jerome Roche, *Lassus* (London: Oxford University Press, 1982).

Lully

A modern edition of Lully's works has only recently commenced. Ten volumes, including several ballets and operas, appeared in the incomplete collected edition by Henri Prunières (Paris, 1930–39). For *Armide* (prologue and Acts 1–2 only) one must turn to *Publikationen älterer praktischer und theoretischer Musikwerke*, edited by Robert Eitner, vol. 14 (Leipzig: Breitkopf und Härtel, 1885; reprint, New York: Broude, 1966), or a facsimile of the eighteenth-century vocal score (Paris, 1713) published by the Société de Musicologie de Languedoc (Beziers, ca. 1980). This and the remaining works can also be consulted in vocal scores in the nineteenth-century series *Les chefs d'oeuvres classiques de l'opéra français* (reprint, New York: Broude, 1972).

Thematic catalog: Herbert Schneider, *Chronologisch-Thematisches Verzeichnis sämtlicher Werke von Jean-Baptiste Lully (LWV)* (Tutzing: Schneider, 1981).

Bibliography: Caroline Wood, *Music and Drama in the Tragédie en Musique, 1673–1715: Jean-Baptiste Lully and His Successors* (New York: Garland, 1996).

In the absence of an English-language biography, one must consult the revised *New Grove* biography and work list by James R. Anthony in *The New Grove French Baroque Masters* (New York: Norton, 1986). Entertaining but not entirely dependable is Henry Prunières, *La vie illustre et libertine de Jean-Baptiste Lully* (reprint, New York: AMS Press, 1978).

Collections of essays on aspects of Lully's life and work (many of them in English): *Jean-Baptiste Lully: Actes du colloque Saint-Germain-en-Laye, Heidelberg 1987*, ed. Jérôme de La Gorce and Herbert Schneider (Laaber: Laaber, 1990), and *Jean-Baptiste Lully and the Music of the French Baroque: Essays in Honor of James R. Anthony*, ed. John Hajdu Heyer (Cambridge: Cambridge University Press, 1989).

Luzzaschi

Luzzaschi's solo madrigals for the *concerto delle donne* are in *Madrigali*, edited by Adriano Cavicchi (Brescia: L'Organo, and Kassel: Bärenreiter, 1965); additional vocal works are in Newcomb, *The Madrigal at Ferrara* (see above under "Baroque Genres"), which also contains biographical matter.

Monteverdi

An unreliable but reasonably complete edition of Monteverdi's works is *Tutte le opere*, ed. G. F. Malipiero (Asolo: Malipiero, 1926–42; reprint, with minor revisions, Vienna: Universal, 1926–42, 1968). The fourth, fifth, and eighth books of madrigals have been reprinted from this edition with translations of texts by Stanley Appelbaum (New York: Dover, 1986–91). More reliable is a new edition in progress: *Opera omnia*, Instituta et monumenta, vols. I/5/1– (Cremona: Athenaeum Cremonense, 1970–). The best available editions of *Orfeo* and *Poppea* are those of Clifford Bartlett (Huntingdon: King's Music, 1993) and Alan Curtis (London: Novello, 1989), respectively.

Bibliography: K. Gary Adams and Dyke Kiel, *Claudio Monteverdi: A Guide to Research* (New York: Garland, 1989).

Biographical works: Paolo Fabbri, *Monteverdi*, translated by Tim Carter (Cambridge: Cambridge University Press, 1994); Denis Arnold, *Monteverdi*, 3d ed., revised by Tim Carter (London: Dent, 1990); Silke Leopold, *Monteverdi: Music in Transition*, a translation by Anne Smith of *Claudio Monteverdi und seine Zeit* (Oxford: Oxford University Press, 1991).

Also valuable are *The New Monteverdi Companion*, edited by Denis Arnold and Nigel Fortune (London: Faber and Faber, 1985), and *The Letters of Claudio Monteverdi*, translated by Denis Stevens, rev. ed. (Oxford: Oxford University Press, 1995).

On specific works, see Gary Tomlinson, *Monteverdi and the End of the Renaissance* (Berkeley and Los Angeles: University of California Press, 1987); *Claudio Monteverdi: Orfeo*, edited by John Whenham (Cambridge: Cambridge University Press, 1986); and Iain Fenlon and Peter N. Miller, *The Song of the Soul: Understanding "Poppea"* (London: Royal Musical Association, 1992).

Palestrina

The more recent of the two collected editions of Palestrina's works is that of Raffaeli Casimiri (Rome: Fratelli Scalera, 1939–65), most of which has been reprinted in a different format by Kalmus. A useful (and necessary) concordance is Alison Hall, *An Index to the Casimiri, Kalmus, and Haberl Editions* (Philadelphia: Music Library Association, 1980).

Biographical works: Updated *New Grove* biography by Lewis Lockwood and work list by Jessie Ann Owens in *The New Grove High Renaissance Masters* (New York: Norton, 1984); Jerome Roche, *Palestrina* (London: Oxford University Press, 1971).

Purcell

A new, much improved version of the undependable collected edition organized by the Purcell Society (London: Novello, 1878–) has been underway since 1957. For Purcell's songs, the best sources are often the original printings in his *Orpheus Britannicus* (reprint, New York: Broude, 1965).

Bibliography: Franklin B. Zimmerman, *Henry Purcell: A Guide to Research* (New York: Garland, 1989).

The Purcell tercentenary year, 1995, elicited a large number of works, including *The Purcell Companion*, edited by Michael Burden (Portland, Ore.: Amadeus Press, 1995). Biographies include that of the conductor Robert King, *Henry Purcell* (New York: Thames and Hudson, 1994), as well as Jonathan Keates, *Purcell: A Biography* (Boston: Northeastern University Press, 1996), and Peter Holman, *Henry Purcell* (Oxford: Oxford University Press, 1994).

Essays on performance are in Michael Burden, ed., *Performing the Music of Henry Purcell* (Oxford: Oxford University Press, 1996). Very useful for understanding the songs and dramatic works is Curtis Alexander Price, *Henry Purcell and the London Stage* (Cambridge: Cambridge University Press, 1984). For a study of Purcell's most famous work, including a complete score, see Ellen T. Harris, *Henry Purcell's "Dido and Aeneas"* (Oxford: Oxford University Press, 1987).

Quantz

For editions of Quantz's music, see the thematic catalog by Horst Augsbach, *Johann Joachim Quantz: Thematisch-Systematisches Werkverzeichnis (QV)* (Stuttgart: Carus, 1997). For Quantz's important essay on flute playing, as well as a study thereof, see above under "Voices and Instruments."

Rameau

The old collected edition, *Oeuvres complètes* (Paris: Durand, 1895–1924), was in fact never completed, and many of its volumes are rendered useless by inaccuracies and the addition of fabricated wind and string parts. A new edition has only just begun to issue volumes; for most of the operas, one must therefore consult vocal scores in the nineteenth-century series *Les chefs d'oeuvres classiques de l'opéra français* (reprint, New York: Broude, 1972). The two sets of keyboard suites originally published in the 1720s are available in facsimile (New York: Broude, 1967) and in a modern edition by Kenneth Gilbert (Paris: Heugel, 1979).

Bibliography: Donald H. Foster, *Jean-Philippe Rameau: A Guide to Research* (New York: Garland, 1989.

The only English-language biography remains Cuthbert Morton Girdlestone, *Jean-Philippe Rameau: His Life and Work* (New York: Dover, 1969). Essential is the revised *New Grove* biography and work list by Graham Sadler and Albert Cohen in *The New Grove French Baroque Masters* (New York: Norton, 1986).

A new study of his stage works is Charles William Dill, *Monstrous Opera: Rameau and the Tragic Tradition* (Princeton, N.J.: Princeton University Press, 1998).

Rameau's first and most important treatise, the *Traité de l'harmonie* (Paris, 1722), is available in facsimile (New York: Broude, 1965), edited as part of *The Complete Theoretical Writings of Jean-Philippe Rameau*, edited by Erwin R. Jacobi (n.p.: American Institute of Musicology, 1967–72), and translated by Philip Gossett as *Treatise on Harmony* (New York: Dover, 1971).

See also Christensen, *Rameau and Musical Thought*, under "Baroque Music Theory and Compositional Practice," above.

Salamone Rossi

A collected edition of Rossi's works by Don Harràn is near completion as volume 100 of the *Corpus Mensurabilis Musicae* (Stuttgart: Hänssler, 1995–). Published thus far are his madrigals and the sonatas and dances for instrumental ensemble. For the quasi-liturgical Hebrew settings (*Hashirim ashir liSh'lomo*) one can consult the edition by Fritz Rikko, 3 vols. (New York: Jewish Theological Seminary of America, 1967).

A new biography is Don Harràn, *Salamone Rossi, Jewish Musician in Late Renaissance Mantua* (Oxford: Oxford University Press, 1998).

Alessandro Scarlatti and Domenico Scarlatti

There is no collected edition of the works of either composer. Several of Alessandro's operas appear in *The Operas of Alessandro Scarlatti* (Cambridge, Mass.: Harvard University Press, 1974–83), but virtually none of his cantatas is available in a dependable modern edition; one must consult instead the selections given in facsimile in his *Cantatas*, edited by Malcolm Boyd (New York: Garland, 1986). Domenico's keyboard sonatas have been published in facsimile, edited by Ralph Kirkpatrick (New York: Johnson Reprint, 1972), and in a good modern edition by Kenneth Gilbert (Paris: Heugel, 1971–); the edition by Alessandro Longo (Milan: Ricordi, 1906–8), although available in cheap reprints, is inaccurate and groups the sonatas arbitrarily into suites.

Bibliography: Carole Franklin Vidali, *Alessandro and Domenico Scarlatti: A Guide to Research* (New York: Garland, 1993).

The only English-language biography of Alessandro remains Edward Joseph Dent, *Alessandro Scarlatti: His Life and Works*, revised by Frank Walker (London: Arnold, 1960). Thus the revised *New Grove* biography by Donald J. Grout and Edwin Hanely and work list by Malcolm Boyd in *The New Grove Italian Baroque Masters* (New York: Norton, 1984) are essential. On his operas one can consult Donald Jay Grout, *Alessandro Scarlatti: An Introduction to His Operas* (Berkeley and Los Angeles: University of California Press, 1979), and Strohm, *Essays on Handel and Italian Opera* (see above under Handel).

The standard biography of Domenico, colorful if at times idiosyncratic, is Ralph Kirkpatrick, *Domenico Scarlatti*, 2d ed. (Princeton, N.J.: Princeton University Press, 1983); the German translation, under the same title (Munich: Ellermann, 1972), includes a thematic catalog. More recent are Malcolm Boyd, *Domenico Scarlatti: Master of Music* (New York: Schirmer Books, 1987), and Frederick Hammond, "Domenico Scarlatti," in *Eighteenth-Century Keyboard Music*, edited by Robert L. Marshall (New York: Schirmer Books, 1994), 154–90.

Schütz

Two collected editions of Schütz's works exist: the *Sämmtliche Werke*, edited by Philipp Spitta and Arnold Schering (Leipzig: Breitkopf und Härtel, 1885–1927), and the *Neue Ausgabe sämtlicher Werke* (Kassel: Bärenreiter, 1955–). In some cases the latter transposes the music, making the earlier edition preferable, despite its "old" clefs.

Bibliography: Allen B. Skei, *Heinrich Schütz: A Guide to Research* (New York: Garland, 1981).

The best English-language biography, with a comprehensive list of works (including SWV numbers), is the updated *New Grove* biography by Joshua Rifkin in *The New Grove North European Baroque Masters* (New York: Norton, 1985). Schütz's own numerous writings appear in Gina Spagnoli, *Letters and Documents of Heinrich Schütz, 1656–1672: An Annotated Translation* (Ann Arbor, Mich.: UMI Research Press, 1990). An annual publication of scholarly articles (occasionally in English) is the *Schütz-Jahrbuch* (Kassel: Bärenreiter, 1979–).

Strozzi

Most of Barbara Strozzi's music has yet to appear in a modern collected edition, but facsimiles of most of her original publications are available; for a selection, including an informative introduction, see her *Cantatas*, edited by Ellen Rosand (New York: Garland, 1986). An important biographical article is Ellen Rosand, "The Voice of Barbara Strozzi," in Bowers and Tick, *Women Making Music* (see above under "Surveys and Collections of Essays"); for recent biographical discoveries, see Beth Glixon, "More on the Life and Death of Barbara Strozzi," *Musical Quarterly* 83 (1999): 134–41.

Sweelinck

A good introduction is Frits Noske, *Sweelinck* (Oxford: Oxford University Press, 1988). A more specialized study is Pieter Dirksen, *The Keyboard Music of Jan Pieterszoon Sweelinck: Its Style, Significance and Influence* (Utrecht: Koninklijke Vereniging voor Nederlandse Muziekgeschiedenis, 1997).

Telemann

Selections from Telemann's vast output have been appearing in his *Musikalische Werke* (Kassel: Bärenreiter, 1950–), including the 1725–26 set of cantatas *Der harmonische Gottesdienst* (in vols. 2–5) and numerous instrumental works.

The vocal works have been cataloged by Werner Menke, *Thematisches Verzeichnis der Vokalwerke* (Frankfurt: Klostermann, 1982–), instrumental ones by Martin Ruhnke, *Georg Philipp Telemann: Thematisch-Systematisches Verzeichnis seiner Werke: Telemann-Werkverzeichnis (TWV)* (Kassel: Bärenreiter, 1984–)

The chief English-language discussion, including a complete work list, is by Martin Ruhnke in *The New Grove North European Baroque Masters* (New York: Norton, 1985). See also Richard Petzoldt, *Georg Philipp Telemann*, translated by Horace Fitzpatrick (New York: Oxford University Press, 1974). Books on the instrumental music are forthcoming from Jeanne Swack and Steven David Zohn.

Vivaldi

Virtually all of Vivaldi's instrumental works are available in the edition of Gian Francesco Malipiero (Milan: Ricordi, 1948–72), which, unfortunately, often adds inappropriate expression markings and distorts the original scoring of many works. The quickest way to locate works in this edition is to search for "M" numbers in the work list in the *New Grove Dictionary* (for the *New Grove Italian Baroque Masters*), which correspond to volumes in this series. Few of Vivaldi's many vocal works are published, although the cantatas and sacred works have begun to appear in the new *Edizione critica* (Milan: Ricordi, 1982–).

There exist several catalogs and numbering systems for the instrumental works; the one now in use is Peter Ryom, *Répertoire des oeuvres d'Antonio Vivaldi* (Copenhagen: Engstrom & Søndering, 1986). For bibliography, consult Michael Talbot, *Antonio Vivaldi: A Guide to Research* (New York: Garland, 1988).

The most authoritative biography is Michael Talbot, *Vivaldi* (New York: Schirmer Books, 1993); see also Karl Heller, *Antonio Vivaldi: The Red Priest of Venice*, translated by David Marinelli (Portland, Ore.: Amadeus Press, 1997). For material on the operas, see Strohm, *Essays on Handel and Italian Opera* (listed above under Handel).

INDEX

Page numbers in **boldface** indicate a term's definition or principal discussion (for a few terms this occurs more than once); *italics* indicate that the term is illustrated in a figure or example. Asterisks designate works whose scores are included in the anthology.